D1329369

FORERUNNERS OF SAINT FRANCIS
And Other Studies

Ellen Scott Davison

FORERUNNERS OF SAINT FRANCIS

And Other Studies

BY

ELLEN SCOTT DAVISON

EDITED BY

GERTRUDE R. B. RICHARDS

WITH A FOREWORD BY

JAMES T. SHOTWELL

BOSTON AND NEW YORK

HOUGHTON MIFFLIN COMPANY

The Riverside Press Cambridge

1927

The Riverside Press

CAMBRIDGE . MASSACHUSETTS

PRINTED IN THE U.S.A.

EDITORIAL PREFACE

At the time of her death, Miss Davison was devoting herself to historical research, the results of which were to appear in a series of studies on the social and economic aspects of the life of the common people in France during the twelfth and thirteenth centuries, a period and phase of history whose importance she thought was not generally appreciated. From the material she had collected, it seemed to her friends that a most fitting memorial might be shaped — one which would reveal the wide scope of her interests and the unique integrity of her scholarship.

Her intellectual achievements, covering many years, included a variety of experiences, in each of which she found new opportunity for delving into the life of bye-gone ages and of presenting whatever she found from a new angle in order to meet the needs of those with whom she chanced to be associated at the time — whether college students, or those of less mature minds in whom she was endeavouring to awaken a deeper love for the past.

The material she has left falls into two general groups: the one centering about the forerunners of Saint Francis of Assisi (the theme of her doctoral dissertation, which she planned to expand into a more comprehensive work) and the other centering about thirteenth-century France. In its original form the first study included an introductory chapter, one on the sects allied to the Cathari, one on Arnold of Brescia, and one on the Humiliati. These have all been rewritten and given larger scope, and the chapters on the Monastic Reformers and the Waldensians added in accordance with her own plan. Her ideas as to the development of these seemed quite definite from her notes, so it is hoped that they follow more or less closely her own conception.

The second group, about which her interest centered in later years, the interpretation of the civilization of mediæval France, was scarcely begun. The tragedy of her untimely death lies in the fact that she could not herself complete what would have been so distinctly a contribution to historical literature. With her rare ability to think behind the barriers of time and place, she would have been able to reconstruct pictures of groups as well as of individuals that would have been of great value to historian and layman alike. But a vision so peculiarly her own could not be glimpsed by another.

A tentative list of subjects for these studies was found among her papers. They include: 'A Merchant Prince of Long Ago'; 'Street Cries of Old Paris'; 'Notes of a Notary Public'; 'Roads and Bridges'; 'Eustace the Monk'; 'The Bishop's Workshop'; and 'Financing a Crusade.' None of the group was far enough advanced to enable one to infer her plan of development, for, unlike the other pre-Franciscan studies, this was not to be simple narrative, but rather interpretation through presentation of personalities. From the rough notes on the siege of Bellême, it was possible to derive an idea of how to finish it, and give it a shape somewhat in harmony with her conception.

The study of the merchant princes of the commercial cities in southern France was to have included much more than their adventures at the fairs, but it has been impossible to connect the various fragments of details without departing absolutely from the plan suggested in the small part that was drafted. Even less could be done with the others, as, except for the studies on Paris and Eude, they were not even begun.

In addition, Miss Davison had done some work on the *fabliaux* and troubadour lays, collecting interesting bits of information as to social life and classes of people. These are so very fragmentary and so lacking in unity that it has not seemed feasible to attempt any combination of them into a separate study. They do not add greatly to our knowledge of the period, but they do furnish interesting confirmation of well-known facts.

It is with a keen sense of its shortcomings that this collection of studies is presented. To have followed for four years the trail blazed by one so instinctively a pioneer has been no small privilege, but it has been a privilege fraught with great responsibility. So often the way has been confused or lost entirely. While it seems incredible that one who had every expectation of herself finishing her task should have left it in so systematic a state, it is inevitable that there should be places where no one else could know her intentions; omissions which only she could supply; apparent contradictions which only she could reconcile.

There has always been the problem of deciding what to use and what to reject; what clues to follow and what ones to disregard. Likewise difficult has it been to give to what has been retained the significance and interpretation she would have given. One ever-recurring problem has been tracing the sources of her material. While most of her notes were accurately documented, others were not, doubtless because she knew exactly whence they had come. Her intellectual honesty would have scorned the appropriation of any idea, however commonplace, and if there seems to be lack of recognition of sources, it is not intentional.

In giving this work to the public, every effort has been made to keep it distinctly her own in thought and in expression. It is hoped that those who knew her may see in it something of her spirit and personality, and that those who had not that privilege may glimpse the versatility of her mind and the rare quality of her scholarship.

Deep and sincere thanks are due to those who have aided in the completion of this work, particularly to the librarians of the Vatican, of the Biblioteca Casanatense and the Biblioteca Vittorio Emanuele at Rome, of the Biblioteca Comunale at Assisi, of the Biblioteca Nazionale and the Biblioteca Laurenziana at Florence, of the Ambrosiana at Milan, of the Biblioteca Reale and the Biblioteca dell'Università at Turin, of the Biblioteca Comunale at Pinerola, of the Theological Seminary at Torre Pellice, as well as to the members of the faculty of the Bibliothèque Nationale of Paris, of Cambridge University and Trinity College, Dublin, of the British Museum and the Bodleian at Oxford, and to the many custodians of archives who so generously offered their treasures for consultation.

Especial thanks are due Professor Rostagno, of the Waldensian College in Rome; to Signorina Luisa Socci, who aided in the reading of Waldensian literature; to the librarians of Harvard College, particularly Mr. Walter B. Briggs for special privileges and assistance, and to Professor C. H. Haskins, of Harvard, who read part of the manuscript.

To Professor James T. Shotwell and to Miss Davison's sister, Mrs. William R. Belknap of Louisville, Kentucky, no words can adequately express my appreciation of their patient understanding and never-failing coöperation in this arduous but inspiring task.

Gertrude Randolph Bramlette Richards

The Lee School
107 Marlborough Street
Boston

CONTENTS

NOTES ON SOURCE MATERIAL

FOREWORD

By James T. Shotwell

The pages which follow contain almost all the work of one who, had she lived the full measure of years, could have won recognition among those historians who have made of history, not merely an interpretation of events, but of life itself. It is difficult for a friend to appraise the value of what is at best the fragment of an achievement; but the fragment presented here is one of those in which the outlines of the whole are already discernible, and is so touched with the historic imagination and so informed with sympathetic understanding that one hardly needs the missing sections to catch the meaning of its message. The clue of events lies less in a mere accumulation of data than in an understanding of the characters of those responsible for them. In these studies, this clue has been given time and again for actors in the drama of medieval history, even when the drama itself has been left for others to describe. When the synthesis lies in broad human sympathies, the completed chronicle of happenings is of minor importance. It is fortunate indeed that this should have been the almost unconscious technique of the writer of these pages; for it may be that, as we have them now, they bring back to us with greater charm and clarity the picture of medieval society than if the author's rounded life had permitted that constant retouching and rebuilding of phrase and thought which is the scholar's ideal.

These sketches of medieval history bear witness to such creative qualities. They were written by one whose supreme happiness it was to recover from such records as this itself the incomplete but ever-appealing picture of those long dead. From chronicles and poems, customary laws and letters, from those primary sources which vanished generations leave us as a basis for our conception of them and their times, the historian traces again the blurred outlines of events. But only here and there is it possible to follow the originals with sufficient distinctness to convey an impression of reality. It may be that this collection of studies will similarly convey to others only a partial notion of the mind that worked upon them to remake this section of the past for us. But, just as the sources of history suggest their open message to those at least who are already somewhat aware of their meaning, so we feel sure that the reader who turns these pages over for the story of Saint Francis and his forerunners will find as well a living contact with the American scholar whose own ideal of life they so largely embody.

Most of the studies in this volume grew out of the stimulus supplied, years ago now, in the historical seminar of Professor James Harvey Robinson, in Columbia University. Subsequent researches led to European libraries — where the careful and competent reviser, Miss Richards, has checked up their results, verifying notes and texts, fastening the loose threads of sections where the author had not written down final conclusions or had been unable to finish the task in hand. It has been a work of years, and even now the printed pages do not contain more than a fraction of the intended survey. Fortunately, that survey of medieval life had been so planned that most of the separate sketches stand by themselves, dealing as they do with individuals or local scenes, with descriptions that are typical and characterizations that hold.

The greater part of this volume is devoted to a theme that has a never-failing human interest, the story of those who kept alive ideals of intellectual or spiritual freedom in a world which never quite knew whether to burn its emancipators as heretics or hail them as saints. The forerunners of Saint Francis often met the former fate. It was a real sympathy with their brave adventure, not the lure of mere academic research, which led the author to devote the last margin of her frail strength to a subject so appealing. Her heroes were not the outstanding figures of history, soldiers, princes, or ecclesiastics; they were rather the obscure, or those who sought obscurity and poverty instead of wealth and power. Peter Waldo, merchant of Lyons at the end of the twelfth century, who gave his goods to the poor in order to live up to the call to apostolic poverty of the New Testament, was something more than the founder of an heretical sect. He was a poet of the common life, with a message of kindly comfort for the humble, — that is, for most people, — a message so plain and so transparent in its honesty of purpose as to call out a following that all the terrors of the inquisition could not suppress. The 'Poor Men of Lyons,' like those of Milan or elsewhere, only protested against the Church of their day because it lacked the insight to sympathize with them in a vision which justified their own lives. It was not necessary, as Saint Francis was later to show, that such beliefs as theirs, or rather such moral conviction, even when carried out in action, should make them rebels. Puritanism is not the monopoly of Protestantism; monasticism is but one aspect of its Catholic counterpart. For that matter, it is wider than Christianity itself, being inherent in the very nature of religion — as much a part of it as the pomp and ceremony against which it lodges its protest. The proper conception of Catholicism is one which embraces this antithesis. Not a little of the significance of the Franciscan movement was the emphasis upon this ultimate compromise. The compromise is no surrender of the ideal, but a recognition of the conditions under which it must find realization. Unworldliness was seen to be not denial of the validity of the world — as in the Cathar heresy — but the recognition of its own power of spiritual stimuli. Thus for Saint Francis all the world was a sacrament; flowers, birds, sun and rain, being but the outward sign of the invisible grace of God. At last the poetry of the realistic mysticism of the common life found fitting utterance.

That such a saga of the obscure should have attracted much historical research in recent years was only to be expected. But few, if any, of Miss Davison's predecessors have followed the spiritual trail so carefully or understandingly as she. It must be remembered that what is offered here is only in part worked over into final form: the rest is more like a traveller's notebook. But because the traveller, in this instance, knew and loved the scenes through which she journeyed, the notes suggest more to the mind than a fuller account might offer if the writer had not been stirred by a vital interest in the subject.

There are other roads to Assisi than that which was built in the 'Franciscan year' 1926 to commemorate the seven hundredth anniversary of the death of Saint Francis. The automobile road from Rome across the Apennines may call the dilettante and the tourist to the grey and amber-toned city on the Tiber hillside and the church among the peach orchards below which is sacred to his memory. But no creations of modern engineering can reach the real home city of the Poverello, for it is more a spiritual city than a hill town of Italy. It lies in the heart of the thirteenth century still as definitely as it rests in its corner of the Apennines, and only those can reach it who are pilgrims in the spirit, who travel with that understanding and sympathy which the historical imagination alone supplies. The reader of these pages will find that the traveller's notes which it contains will reach the true Assisi of Saint Francis' day.

The sketches of social life in France in the thirteenth century are part of an unfinished survey of one of the most vital periods of European history, that in which the anarchy of the feudal era broke down before the rising tide of nationality, symbolized in the royal power, and actually more embodied in the rapidly growing towns and cities with their newly developed bourgeoisie, their cathedrals and market halls. Miss Davison's studies in this field of history are especially graphic and interesting. Here the reader has the full benefit of the strictly scientific method, which always based its detail upon original sources and not upon the secondary texts of other historians. Had this section of the book been finished, we should have had a contribution to the social history of Europe which would have been a fitting parallel to the studies in what might be called the pre-history of the Franciscan movement. But the secular phase had been worked up more for actual use in class rooms than for the printed text. Accordingly only a few chapters are included here.

Such is the volume before us, a singularly genuine piece of research which will offer many a suggestion to the student, and to the general reader will open fields of unexpected interest and unfailing charm. The secret of this charm is to be found, not so much in the research, however, as in the author's breadth of culture and wide experience of life which gave the sense of reality to whatever she touched. When her imagination drew from the crabbed texts over which she loved to puzzle the living figures of the past, it was to invest them with the universal interest of men and women facing the problems still confronting us in religion, art, or literature. They were remote in time, but near in spirit. Their problems were hers as well; and so these chapters in medieval history give back the picture of the author herself, but they give little hint of the quiet courage with which she met the chief of all problems in a long and losing fight with death, of the brave spirit who shared the fellowship of those whose lives she chronicled.

PART I

THE FORERUNNERS OF SAINT FRANCIS OF ASSISI

THE FORERUNNERS OF SAINT FRANCIS OF ASSISI

• •
•

PART I
THE FORERUNNERS OF SAINT FRANCIS OF ASSISI

CHAPTER I
INTRODUCTORY

EARLY in the thirteenth century there appeared almost simultaneously in different parts of southern Europe two men destined to influence the lives of multitudes for all time to come, Dominic in Spain and Francis in Italy. They were widely different in ancestry and in environment, but singularly alike in aims and in ideals. Dominic, of the noble Guzman family, received his education in royal Palencia; Francis, the son of a merchant of Assisi, was all but destitute of the learning of the schools: Dominic was born to share the best that his age could offer; the little that Francis might have claimed by right of heritage, he rejected. If it be true that the canons of San Giorgio[1] taught Francis what he knew of reading and writing, of Latin and theology, they had as little reason to feel pride in their pupil as he had to claim inspiration from their teaching. All

[1] Bib. Cas., MS. B, III, f. 25; Fiamma, *Cron. Ord. Præd.*; *AA. SS.*, I Aug., p. 388: '*missus Palentiam, ubi tunc temporis studium generale florebat, post-quam liberalibus artibus diligenter insudans sufficienter edoctus est, ne in eis diutus tempus, debitum salubrioribus disciplinis, expenderet, ad theologiam se transtulit cujus studiis per quattuor annos ardenter invigilans, de thesauris ejus hausit avide, quæ postæ effudit abunde*'; Quétif et Echard, vol. I, col. 26.

Palencia at this time was not a university, but an episcopal school in charge of the *Magister Scholarum* of the Cathedral.

his life he remained indifferent to formal learning,[1] accepting only what was necessary to make the ritual intelligible, although he and his followers did their share toward turning the vernacular into a literary language, for the rhythmic prose of the Minores constitutes one of the earliest examples of religious literature in the Italian dialect.

To Dominic the vision of the salvation of the world came in the scholarly quiet of the melancholy windswept plains of Castile: Francis glimpsed it in the smiling fields of his fair Umbrian valley: Dominic expressed the yearnings of his soul in meticulous sermons: Francis poured his forth in joyous troubadour songs, learned perhaps at his mother's knee,[2] perhaps caught from some wandering minstrel in the lanes of Assisi or brought by his father from his journeyings in southern France. But wherever he heard them, it was the troubadours rather than the churchmen who quickened in him a desire to enter the lists as champion of Lady Poverty, and their rondels rather than the hymns of the Church which, transmuted into a spiritual minstrelsy, filled his life with lyric sweetness and saved him from the coarseness and vulgarity of the times.

To scholar and troubadour alike came the vision of salvation through service. Both felt, as disciples of Christ, the necessity of literal obedience to the commands of their Master, of living as he had taught his Apostles to do, in utter poverty, humility, and contempt of the world; of following not only his precepts but his example of self-denial, of self-renunciation, of service to those sick in body, mind, or in faith; of doing for their fellow men what the monks were doing for themselves; of finding the pathway

[1] *Vita*, auct. S. Bonaventura, *AA. SS.*, II Oct., col. 744; *Legenda Prima*, auct. Thoma de Celano, cc. II, III (ed. Rome, 1906); *Legenda Secunda*, *ibid.*, cc. III, XCIX, CX; *Legenda Trium Sociorum*, c. I (ed. Rome, 1899); Bernard de Besse, *De Laudibus*, MS. J, VI, 33, f. 96r, Biblioteca Reale, Turin.

[2] The legend that Pica, the mother of Saint Francis, was a Provençal of noble birth, is as yet unproven as is also the one saying she was a Waldensian.

to Heaven through their ministrations to the unfortunate and the despairing. Because they answered so fully the needs of countless other souls in seeking to satisfy their own, they attracted to themselves throngs of followers eager to spend their lives in the practice of evangelical poverty.

As we look backward, these friars seem to stand forth as great social reformers spiritually akin to those of our own day, but in reality they were in no way emancipated from the religious and ethical ideals of their own age, with its continual warfare and its shifting social orders. Rather they expressed the faith of the century as definitely as did cathedral or crusade. They came into the critical discontent and restlessness, resultant upon the crumbling of feudal institutions and the growth of commercialism, teaching to the new controllers of wealth the responsibilities of large possessions, and to the lower strata, who had lost their protectors in the upheaval and were as yet unable to fend for themselves, the blessings of poverty nobly borne. They combated unbelief; they removed the barriers between layman and cleric, so that religion was no longer the especial prerogative of priest, monk, or nun; they alleviated spiritual suffering by their example of gentleness and boundless patience; they lessened material hardships by undermining the principles from which these originated. Themselves austere but without the gloom of asceticism, they conceived and practised a poverty dominated by an element of joy rather than by starving or undue torturing of the flesh, presenting a far more potent example of their ideals than did those equally earnest souls who spent their days in solitude apart from their fellow men.

Dominic's aim was primarily to refute heresy, to bring men back to the subjection of the Church. Unusually astute in reading the signs of the times, he not only realized the danger which threatened civilization from a widespread spiritual revolt, but also, as a result of his labours in that part of southern France where the Albigensians were most numerous, he saw how unfavourably the ignorance and sloth of the lower clergy and the worldly splendour of the higher, contrasted with the simple, ascetic lives of the heretics and with their diligence and zeal. What he learned through experience, Francis gained by intuition: that the salvation of the Church and the renewal of the human spirit could be accomplished only in the practice of that poverty which was not so much a lack of property or of money as a poverty of the spirit, a renunciation of the world without morbidness, a kindly and sympathetic sharing with the unfortunate of the worst of their lot. Dominic, striving for the restoration of the purity of the Catholic religion, and Francis, endeavouring to renew the faith of the individual in the goodness of God, alike saw the need of setting up new ideals, of stirring the impotent religion of their times into a more vigorous life. The former undertook to restore the institution by an appeal to reason and intelligence; the latter, to restore the individual soul by lifting men from the mire of the commonplace to the mountain-top from whence they might see the vision of their own potentialities. A troubadour in the age of troubadours, Francis appealed through the charm of poetic mysticism to the imagination of his hearers, who, not unfamiliar with the songs of the minstrels, whose themes of love and war he made his own, were able to visualize his teachings and translate them into action.[1]

Both Francis and Dominic were born leaders of men, but in no age can any man lead the masses save along the paths toward which that age is tending. Despite the turbulent infidelity of the times, religion, debased though it

[1] I Cel., I, 7; III Soc., III; *Speculum perfectionis S. Francisci*, Mazarin Library, MS. 8531.

was, and shackled by the meticulousness of the Schoolmen and by the formalism and triviality of dogma, was never more vitally a part of life; yet, on the other hand, never did people feel more conscious of the inadequacy of its expression, of the need for some manifestation of faith that would give substance to the new dreams, the new idealism, the new generosity, the new daring. It was this almost unintelligible aspiration that Francis and his followers sought to answer in their enthusiasm for freedom of the spirit born of poverty.

The movement quickened by the friars into a world force was not new, neither in its underlying principles nor in its details. From the earliest times the history of Christianity presents a series of protests against the conformity of the Church with universal social and economic laws, and since the opening of the eleventh century, apostles of evangelical poverty, aiming to restore primitive Christianity, had been especially numerous. Almost without exception, their efforts had been directed toward clearing away the dust of the centuries that a simpler system might be revealed. Though seldom impugning the Faith itself, they often subjected the doctrinal fabric of the Church to severe attacks. Yet until we approach the very borderline of modern history, such efforts were almost invariably futile. Rarely did they exert even a momentary influence beyond the narrow circle of their inception, and although nobly conceived and heroically sustained, they failed because they seldom embodied principles broad enough to justify their continuance. After troubling the world a few years, they faded into oblivion.

Considering the rapid growth of the Church by the admission of half-converted Gentiles, it is not strange that there was much disagreement throughout the Middle Ages as to matters based on the interpretation of the Scriptures or as to practices growing up in later times. The great mass of the Germans had been forced into the Church in the beginning for the political convenience of their chiefs, and had accepted the ministrations of her clergy and attended her services while knowing but little of her doctrines until the popular faith, stained by the still dimly remembered paganism, became an agglomeration of the old and the new. Deviation from the original organization was inevitable, although each alteration brought protest and withdrawal on the part of the dissenting minorities and many outcries that the Church was departing from its pristine dignity and defiling its ceremonials by the superstitions of the heathen.

Early Christianity was an enthusiasm for an ideal, an attempt to regulate the individual life according to the precepts and commands of Christ, among which were several which if followed literally would have effectually barred the development of any institution based on Christianity and have made of those vowed to spend their lives in his service a company of penniless wanderers. When the young man who had great possessions asked Jesus what he should do to inherit eternal life, the answer was: 'Sell that thou hast and give to the poor.' When Christ sent the Twelve forth to preach, he said to them: 'Provide neither gold nor silver in your purses nor yet staves.' While no institution has ever existed in a society based on property without itself acquiring property, and while every individual that holds possessions must manage and defend them, the Apostles were told to 'Resist not evil; but whosoever shall smite thee on thy right cheek, turn to him also the left. And if any man shall sue thee at law and take away thy coat, let him have thy cloke also.'

To these oft-repeated precepts enjoining indifference to wealth and property were added others which could not but result in organization and centralization of power, such as the obligation to take constant care of the weaker brethren, to teach and baptize all nations, to establish and maintain the cult of Christ throughout the world. The claim of the Church to a hierarchy established by Jesus is strengthened by the fact that, while he was on earth, his followers were undertaking tasks which could not be performed by them as individuals. As soon as they were left to face the future alone, they had elders who were organized into boards or councils, administrators who enacted ordinances, discussed questions with the Twelve and assisted them to enforce discipline, who settled disputes between Christians, prayed for the sick and anointed the dying.

The process by which the Church became an organized, property-holding institution is obscure and difficult to trace. As the Apostles neared the end of their labours on earth, they designated their successors who were to continue what they had undertaken, teaching and ordaining, establishing churches and acting as heads of congregations. These first Christians, who were awaiting the almost immediate second coming of Christ, did not as yet feel the need of an elaborate constitution and had no fixed and final form of government. It was not long before the persecutions, the increase of members and the decrease of fervour and spirit, due in part to the rapid conversion of pagans, made closer organization necessary, as in these chaotic times an efficient government was the only check on the erring and the only protection to the faithful, as well as the one force potent enough to expel those whose conduct disgraced the congregation. As a result, the leaders found themselves controlling ever wider interests. At Jerusalem, under the direction of the Apostles, seven men had been selected 'to minister to the unfortunate and to wait on the table in love feasts.' Since they were to act as teachers as well as ministers, it was stipulated that they be 'of honest report, worthy of the Lord, meek, not lovers of money, truthful and approved in wisdom.'

In order to expedite business, a chairman, usually distinguished for some marked ability, was chosen from this group. By the second century, he had become primate of the presbyters and soon afterward he was professing to occupy the place of the Apostles, representing Christian unity of doctrine and of discipline, and, as he took unto himself more and more power and influence, becoming the ruler of a recognized territory, church and province.

The advantages of the episcopacy were so immediately obvious that its universal adoption was inevitable. By the time of Tertullian no church of any importance was without this prelate whose duties were both spiritual and administrative. The majority of the earlier bishops united in themselves the qualities of saintly martyr and the ability of the energetic statesman, and consequently their power and influence steadily increased until the people were charged to look upon them 'as we would upon the Lord himself.'[1] At the same time the minor officials, lectors, acolytes, etc., came into existence with varying duties at first, the gradations of rank and office becoming definitely fixed as the hierarchy of the Church supplanted that of the Empire.

In the first and second centuries, when the Church was obscure and unpopular, its officials depended on individual labour or secular profits for a living. Landed property was undesired by the Apostles and their immediate successors, and before the close of the third century, its possession was illegal. Before the age of the persecutions was over, however, the Church suddenly found herself invested with honours, wealth, and privileges. As a result, a feeling arose that it was unwise to combine the spiritual and secular functions, not because of any feeling as to the unworthiness

[1] I Tim., III, IV; *Didache*, c. 15; Jerome, *Ep.* 146, Migne, *Pat. Lat.*, vol. XXII, col. 1194; Ignat., *ad Philadelphenses*, c. 3; *ad Trallianos*, c. 2; *ad Smyrnæos*, c. 8, Migne, *Pat. Græc.*, vol. V, col. 699, col. 675, col. 714; Cyprian, *Ep.* 65, 66, Migne, *Pat. Lat.*, vol. IV, col. 303, etc.

of the latter, but rather because of a conviction that the ecclesiastical duties should occupy all the time; therefore provision was made for the support of the clergy from the common treasury.

The edicts of Galerius and of Constantine [1] bear witness to the fact that the Church had become quite definitely organized before it was given legal existence. The recognition of its corporate rights antedates the Edict of Milan, while the property rights of the individual congregations were recognized as early as the third century. The development of the institution along lines already indicated was stimulated by the Constantinian policy, which combined with the weakening of the civil power to create, as time went on, the most powerful moral, social, and political agent the world has seen. The Christians were no longer a separate people, grouped in small independent republics, characterized by definite peculiarities of habit and manners. Indeed, their officials, exempt from economic obligations to the state, were possessed of corporate privileges so extensive as to necessitate erelong, restrictive measures, for, as the expansion of membership had continued, the number of clergy over whose choice the emperor exercised no control, was also increased, and the state was deprived of the services of a large privileged class whose immunities tended to become hereditary. So many curiales sought refuge from economic burdens by entering the priesthood, that as early as the year 320, Constantine forbade that class to enroll in the services of the Church unless they submitted their property to taxation,[2] and Valentinian I required them to resume their obligations to the state, forbidding all rich plebeians to take orders.[3]

[1] Edict of Galerius (311), Lactantius, *De Moribus Persecutorum*, c. 34; Edict of Constantine (Milan, 313), *ibid.*, c. 48; *Codex Theodosianus*, lib. XVI (ed. Haenel); Boyd, *The Ecclesiastical Edicts in the Theodosian Code, passim.*

[2] *Cod. Theod.*, lib. XVI, II, 3; IV, VII, I; Euseb., *Hist. Eccles.*, lib. X, c. VII, Migne, *Pat. Græc.*, vol. XX, col. 894.

[3] *Cod. Theod.*, lib. XVI, II, 23.

Despite this the early emperors superadded to the spiritual authority of the bishops an ever-increasing temporal power, giving them a large part in the administration of civil affairs, particularly of those interests most closely connected with the welfare of the people and with public order, an example followed by the new states during the succeeding centuries.[1] Gradually the clergy, as members of the councils of kings and of political assemblies, assigned to posts of high honour and influence in all departments of civil government, presiding over the election of princes, became as completely identified with the state as they were with the Church.[2]

By the fourth century, the church of the poor had become the church of the rich and powerful, for although the wealth belonged to the institution rather than to the individual and was to be used for the maintenance of the fabric, for charity and for the relief of the poor, still the administration of it gave those in charge a power and prestige quite as definite as if it had been held by them individually.

The desire to command possessions stole imperceptibly into so intimate a connection with religion that it appeared to be a vital part thereof. Christianity vied with paganism in the magnificence of the edifices it erected for the worship of God as well as in the ceremonial it adopted, in its lamps and altar vessels of gold and silver, in its veils and hangings and in its priestly robes. While this adoption of an elaborate ceremonial was in a way necessitated by the demands of those whose pagan or Jewish background made mystery the handmaid of worship and whose devotion could not be maintained otherwise, it was nevertheless willingly enough developed by the early Fathers.

[1] Milman, *Latin Christianity*, vol. I, pp. 95, etc.; pp. 162, etc.; Allard, *Le Christianisme et l'empire romain*, pp. 159, etc.

[2] Milman, *l.c.*, pp. 399, etc.; Montalembert, *The Monks of the West*, vol. II, pp. 123, etc.

The law of Constantine which empowered the clergy to receive testamentary gifts was a truly regal provision. Erelong it became almost a sin to die without bestowing something on the Church, and Saint Jerome charged the whole Roman priesthood with the pagan vice of legacy hunting. Before the end of the fourth century the mass of ecclesiastical property was so enormous that the most pious of emperors had to issue a restrictive law and the most pious of Fathers could make no protest.

As soon as the democracy of apostolic days began to yield to the hierarchy, communism was abolished. By the seventh century the Church had become quite definitely feudalized and was gradually acquiring inalienable fiefs. Bishops and abbots alike aspired to the dignity and power of lay barons and began to contest sullenly and refuse haughtily the payments of vassalage, an attitude toward the civil powers in which they were encouraged by the pontiffs. In the eighth century Pepin asserted no claim to the lands which at the call of Pope Gregory III he had freed from the Lombards; and Charlemagne, drawing the southern boundary of his Italian possessions somewhat north of Rome, made the ancient capital of the world the capital of the Church and of the surrounding territory, and the occupant of the chair of Peter the Fisherman became the administrator of an enormous patrimony.

Under the Carolingians a new and convenient method for acquiring still greater wealth arose, by whose instigation is not known. This was the buying-off punishment for sin by elaborate donations to Church, saint, or priest. It soon became prevalent, the rich loading the institution with gifts to avoid penance. Christ's Apostles, commanded by him to have neither gold nor silver, to wander from city to city teaching and baptizing and having no settled homes, were succeeded by those who held and administered property as if they were secular potentates.

The bishops now had two functions: they were shepherds of men as Christ had commanded them to be; they were also temporal princes, vicariously if not actually, an office forced into their hands by the inevitable logic of events and full of arduous duties and grave responsibilities. As the legislative authority of the congregations was superseded by that of the councils, the power of the prelates became more exacting, more arbitrary. United by a common interest, they were able to attack with vigour the original rights of the lower clergy and of their congregations, and victorious, exalted the unity of the institution as a whole. By promulgating at the same time a claim to divine origin, they paved the way for demanding implicit obedience from those within their jurisdiction, which was not obtained without strong effort on one side and equally strong resistance on the other. The lower clergy and the people struggled to retain the democratic constitution of the primitive Church, but lacking the influence that comes from temporal power, their efforts were generally fruitless.

Then came preëminence of rank among the bishops followed by superiority of jurisdiction. Metropolitans and their primates began to dictate to their less important neighbours. The next step was emulation among the metropolitans due to the temporal honours and advantages of their respective cities, to the size and wealth of the parishes, to the saints and martyrs each claimed, and to the purity of faith each maintained, a movement culminating in the supremacy of the Roman Church in the west.

Constantine, actuated by motives both political and religious, and the first representative of that theory which made the Church and state two sides of God's government on earth, had enabled Christianity to become the moulding spirit of western civilization, by endowing it with that unity which alone could withstand the disintegrating elements of heresy and paganism. As the Petrine claim fell into harmony with the imperial policy, the union of the state and Church became not only natural but inevitable.

After the seventh century the secular obligations of the clergy grew constantly heavier, a natural result of many factors. Devout landowners, often in unprotected border lands, made over their possessions to the Church and retired to monasteries, leaving their successors to meet as best they could the onslaughts of tax collector and barbarian. Before the time of Constantine, the strength of the empire had been taxed to keep the invaders beyond the frontiers. Later, as province after province fell into the hands of Germanic chiefs and the civil organization was shattered, the bishops, as the sole representatives of law and order in many districts were able to make their influence felt by creating in the midst of chaos and anarchy a new bond of union between nations distinct and opposed in interests and character. The Church became a common center and rallying-point for all, as well as a supreme tribunal which decided without appeal the controversies of king and baron.

The civic functions possessed by the bishops while the Rhine and Danube still separated the Roman world from the barbarian were expanded as the need for them grew greater. Each new century brought to the Church greater wealth and greater responsibilities. Barbarian kings, used to offering gifts to their gods, just as they sent presents to chieftains whose friendship they sought, gave as freely after their conversion to the God who now gave them the victory. Huge tracts and accompanying powers, administrative and fiscal, came into the hands of the Church through the workings of this naïve faith, as well as through even more complex motives and forces. Alongside of this growth in wealth came another source of power as the Franks and Lombards came to share with the Romans the great hierarchical dignities, replacing the old aristocracy of superior civilization with one based on ambition and power.

Men who ruled vast lands had to become princes rather than shepherds if they were to keep their possessions.[1] In times of political disorder all owners of property must protect it by means more drastic than interdict or excommunication. At all times when a foreign foe harried the land, prelates as well as counts and dukes had to arm themselves against the invaders. Not only was defence necessary on the battlefield, but often in the courts. While some laymen gave generously to the Church to secure rest for their souls, others were ever ready to seize such property on any plausible pretext or on no pretext whatsoever.[2] At times, it is true, prelates were able to protect themselves by such ecclesiastical penalties as came within their jurisdiction, but quite as often the lay barons countered this by thrusting their own nominees, generally relatives, into the most lucrative offices of the Church, or else by keeping the benefices vacant and appropriating the revenues. Naturally, as the bishops became more and more involved in secular affairs, they more and more lost their sacerdotal character; embroiled in politics, they neglected their episcopal duties; while the iron fiscal system necessary to the administration of such great holdings was fast extinguishing all sense of moral obligation to the people. Bishops who sought preferment in the Church for the sake of wealth and power were almost of necessity engrossed with the

[1] At the time of Charles Martel, a great proportion of the best cultivated land of western Europe was in the hands of the monks and secular clergy, while over half the nobility were bishops and abbots.

[2] See Suger, *Gesta Ludovici regis cognomento grossi*, cc. 2, 23 (ed. Molinier, in *Collection de textes*), for accounts of attacks on ecclesiastical property in France in the early twelfth century.

Seher, Abbot of Chamonzey in the diocese of Toul, tells of his struggle to keep his property, in Seherus, *Primordia Calmosiacensia*, *M.G.H. SS.*, vol. XII, pp. 324–47.

The canons of Lucca had to build a castle for defence against the aggressions of Count Guido. Muratori, *Antiq.*, vol. IV, p. 733.

material cares which wealth and power brought with them.[1]

Side by side with this secularization and feudalization of the Church came the institutionalism of monasticism, whose beginnings were coincident with the recognition of Christianity and whose greatest extension was contemporary with the triumph of the Church as a secular power. Every period marked by a growth of the Church as an institution has been also a period characterized by a reaction toward asceticism. The age of the early councils was the age of Jerome, the prophet of monasticism; the rule of Benedict of Nursia found numerous and enthusiastic adherents during the pontificate of Gregory I; under Gregory VII, or during the fifty years following his death, were founded the Order of Grammont, most rigid in discipline, the Carthusian brotherhood, the Præmonstratensian Order, and by the great Bernard, the monastery of Clairvaux, while the age of Innocent III is the age of Francis of Assisi and of Dominic.

Although monasticism was, it is true, based on most complex human motives, yet in the origin of the many rapidly growing communities there was one ever-present, all-compelling factor, that is, a protest against the non-apostolic character of the Church and the over-centralization of power in the hands of the higher clergy. There was little room for the development of the individual within the Catholic Church, where a powerful hierarchy blocked the approaches to self-expression. Freedom of thought and inquiry were at first discouraged and later quite forbidden. It was impossible to seek for new truths or for

[1] Cæsarius of Heisterbach says that the episcopacy leads to hell and the Church has the bishops it deserves. *Dial. Mir.*, lib. II, dis. 28.

See also Hugo, *Destructio Farfense, M.G.H. SS.*, vol. XI, pp. 532, etc.; Ekkehard, *Cas. S. Galli.*, *M.G.H. SS.*, vol. II, pp. 105–07; Desiderius, Abbatis Casinensi, *Dial.*, Migne, *l.c.*, vol. CXLIX; *Bibl. Max. Vet. Pat.*, vol. XVIII; Peter Damian, *De Fuga Dignitatum Eccles.*, Migne, *Pat. Lat.*, vol. CLXV, col. 455; Ratherius, *De Contemptu Canonum*, Migne, *l.c.*, vol. CXXXVI, col. 417.

new expression of accepted truth in the face of a tenet that all doctrine had been given in a fixed and final form by the Apostles. So the rising spirit of individualism in the later Middle Ages was driven into strange and devious ways for the utterance and unfolding of the deeper impulses of the human soul. Protest, of which the three vows were the external symbol, was the only way out. While not originally a Christian instinct, and the heritage rather than the product of Christianity, monasticism not only furnished opportunity for uninterrupted enjoyment of the soul, but it served also as a mould in which the individual spirit might be recast when seeking possible escape from the tyranny of conventional religion or worldly indifference to spiritual realities. Not that those whose devotion to the apostolic life furnished centers for these movements were all of them led to do so by a conscious dissatisfaction with the worldliness of the Church. Francis apparently was influenced but slightly by this motive, although doubtless the rapid growth of his followers was due to the fact that many of his contemporaries felt the need of a life given to strict obedience to the teachings of Christ, and to the difficulty of following such a life in the Church. Certainly it was this need which caused, in close succession, the growth of the various sects of heretical Christians, the Arnoldisti, the Humiliati, the Waldensians.

Monasticism, beginning as a protest against the institutional side of Christianity, became itself an institution, and so transformed, reversed its earlier policies and ideals. Indifferent in the beginning to the extension of the visible Church, it became the chief missionary agent in the west; originating with the desire to renounce the world, the monks attracted to themselves such crowds of admirers and dependents that small towns sprang up wherever they established a convent; rejecting all natural laws at first, they became the foremost nature-lovers in the modern world; starting with the conception that the body was evil and at war with the soul, they came to recognize the divinity of the human form and were definite forerunners of the artists of the Renaissance. Their contempt for the reasoning processes was replaced by a delight in philosophical studies, expressed in the intricacies of scholasticism; their indifference to the political order and their lack of loyalty were forgotten as they rallied their forces to support the pontiff in his struggle for world dominion; forgotten, too, was their insistence on poverty as they became the owners of great territories: in many ways was the intensely spiritual purpose of the earlier monks lost sight of in their efforts to preserve and develop the material civilization of the Middle Ages. The noble works done by them when their faith was young, saving Europe from famine, developing the germs of those institutions which kept alive some traces of antique culture, revolutionizing agriculture, and conserving learning, are too familiar to need repetition.[1] We can go with the early missionaries into Germany and Gaul, with Sturmi into the forest hard by the 'fell Saxons,' with Columban into Frisia or Gall into Suabia, all fugitives from the world, seeking a life of poverty, simplicity, and self-denial, combating paganism and the wilderness. The rigours of the conflict forced upon these men and their devoted followers close and efficient organization. Their very virtues led to their undoing. Gifts to God brought salvation to the givers and gifts to the monks were gifts to God. So secular responsibility increased and with it the power to command luxury. The growing institution of monasticism was already departing from the spirit of its first enthusiasts as early as the sixth century when the genius of Benedict of Nursia gave it definite shape

[1] Montalembert, *l.c.*, vol. I, pp. 30–47; vol. II, pp. 185, etc.
On the services of the monks to civilization see also Sommerlad, *Die Wirtschaftliche Thätigkeit der Kirche im Mittelalter, passim.*

in the rule which seeks, while organizing the institution, to maintain for the individual something of literal obedience to Christ's command, 'Be ye poor.' But Benedict undertook what was impossible; he tried to combat by formal laws the inevitable sequence of events. Monastic communities became rich, powerful, luxurious and pleasure-loving. As time went on, the monks, losing the hermit temper of earlier days, often degenerated into motley crews composed of victims of parental greed or of their own illusions, visionaries of inferior character, idle weaklings, only rarely leavened by some truly high-minded religious who craved an absorption of self in God.[1] Yet so potent had the institution become that even when a strong superior was lacking, all these vitiated, marred, and diseased elements became amalgamated. As wealth and luxury crept into even the more ascetic communities, irony and skepticism came to replace devotion, and unrest and incredulity emanated from the cloisters in the place of the now forgotten fervent ecstasy of penance and virtue.

Voices were never lacking to demand that the monks be true to their original aims, and, despite the many instances of degeneracy, in the eleventh century monasticism alone among Christian institutions kept alive even the tradition of evangelical poverty. Through personal influence the monks were at times enabled to quicken into life whatever zeal and faith lingered on to redeem the omnipresent corruption of the late Middle Ages.

Like the hierarchy, monasticism became also a feudal institution and as such enjoyed the dignity, wealth, and power accompanying great possessions. Heads of families and scions of illustrious lines founded, as penance for their sins, the monasteries which they themselves ofttimes entered and transformed into fortresses, ruling the surrounding country with even greater prestige than they had en-

[1] Dresdner, *Kultur und Sittengeschichte*, *passim.*

joyed in the world.[1] Charlemagne gave much land to the monks as did his successors, so, although they had been well enough supplied before, after the ninth century the abbots were among the greatest feudal chieftains.

So did the institution evolved from the teachings of Christ come to be at variance with the commands of Christ, and the contradiction of the ideal by the realities did not escape the notice of the more thoughtful, who from the beginning of the Church's triumph united in protest against its growing institutionalism, and in constant attempts to return to the asceticism of the Master, a continual, tangible manifestation of the conflict which has characterized its history since the earliest times and in which may be seen the evidence of its combined human and divine origin.

As the Church became organized and centralized, with one supreme head and a complete gradation of officials, a comprehensive system of law courts, penalties and prisons, the clergy proved themselves to be far more efficient administrators than the laymen. Ecclesiastical offices were sought by those who coveted their revenues, but paid all too little attention to the duties involved. There was scarcely a preferment which a bishop could not and did not sell.[2] The supreme qualification for priesthood came to be the ability to pay for the benefice. Simony was rife, especially after the eighth century.[3] In some cities, Milan for example, scarcely a priest was free from this sin. Coun-

[1] E.g., the Counts of Andech, Arnstein, Cappenberg, etc.

[2] Gerohus Reicherspergensis, *De Investigatione Antichristi*, lib. I, c. 42 (ed. Scheibelberger, p. 88); De Wette, *Geschichte der Christlichen Sittenlehre, passim;* Delarc, *Saint Grégoire et la réform de l'église, passim; Gesta Archiepiscoporum Salisburgensium, M.G.H. SS.*, vol. XI, p. 38.

[3] Joachim of Flora called the Roman Church the house of a courtesan where all practise simony. *In Apoc.*, p. 190, Peter Damian, *Ep.* XIII, Migne, *l.c.*, vol. CXLV; Mansi, vol. XIX, col. 899; *Vita Benedicti Abb. Clunensis, M.G.H. SS.*, vol. XII, p. 198; *Chron. Novaliciense*, app. 9, *M.G.H. SS.*, vol. VII, p. 125; Mabillon, *Annales Benedic.*, vol. VI, p. 287.

cil after council promulgated decrees against it, all of which were conveniently disregarded, and as a result, a great part of the clerical order became submissive to the will and to the interests of a temporal master, lay or cleric. Also, the revenues and benefices of the Church were increased in questionable ways, each order of the clergy having its own artifices for fleecing the people and for profiting by their ignorance. Where bishops used indulgences, abbots and monks had processions of relics, until finally the popes were forced to interfere and to take plenary remission into their own hands.

Bishops and abbots alike saw in the adoration of relics a means by which the wealth and prestige of their churches might be increased, and they were not always scrupulous as to the way in which these were obtained. Sometimes prelates invented and circulated histories of the saints whose relics they possessed, exalting their merits and the miracle-working power of their bones. The most difficult doctrine that the Christian faith imposed on the converted pagan was the belief in one invisible God, who, compared with their old deities, was remote and inaccessible. The Son, though gentler than the Father and more human, the Virgin, ever tender to the poor, and the greater saints, could not be expected to interest themselves in the doings of the common people, who craved those of their own kind to live among them and to give them some tangible reassurance against the terrors of day and night. Therefore, local saints, theologically mere men and women, sprang up everywhere, beatified by popular reverence and adopted as protectors against the awful powers of nature.[1]

The early Fathers had encouraged the worship of relics, Saint Ambrose refusing to consecrate a church not possess-

[1] August., *De Civit. Dei*, lib. XXII, c. 22, Migne, *l.c.*, vol. XLI, col. 784; Gregory of Tours, *De Gloria Martyrum*, lib. I, c. 84. See also Guib. Nov., *De Pignoribus Sanct.*, in which he deplores extravagances of such faith among the people.

ing them, and from the early Carolingian times the traffic in holy objects grew ever more widespread. There was no violence but was justified in the effort to secure them. At the same time the number of saints increased until by the end of the thirteenth century there were no less than ten thousand recognized by the Church each attracting numbers of pilgrims. Besides these there were the miraculous images which drew an equally great number of the devout. New objects for veneration were constantly discovered by ambitious prelates whose visions, guiding them to the resting-places of what was holy and venerable, always coincided with some especial need which an influx of pilgrims could supply.

It is hardly to be wondered at that the prelates had little time left for their dioceses, which they frequently did not attempt to organize nor to place in the care of active and competent priests. Consequently the lower clergy suffered from lack of supervision. It is impossible to speak of the inferior orders as a class in the period immediately preceding the reform movements of the eleventh and twelfth centuries. Although the literature of that time abounds in drastic criticism of the evil lives of the priests and of their neglect of their duties, this might quite as easily indicate an awakening of conscience in all classes as a lowering of standards. There is no denying, however, that conditions were bad enough even at the best. From the seventh century on, Europe was full of tramp priests, drunken and licentious, and from the coming of the Carolingians, the minutes of the synods are full of censures and punishment for the secular clergy, who are condemned for betting, gambling, hawking, intemperance, avarice, fornication, and for other offences even more serious.[1] The wealthy

[1] Gregory of Tours, *Historia Francorum*, lib. VII, col. 392; Bib. Vat., MS. Vat. Lat. 3378, n. 2, p. 10.

Of the eighty councils held in France in the eleventh century, all denounced the lawlessness of the laity and the unchastity of the clergy.

prelates squandered their patrimonies on luxury, leaving their underlings deprived of legal income and degraded almost to the rank of agricultural labourers,[1] trying to eke out a bare sustenance by the sale of masses and absolutions, and counting themselves fortunate if they were not forced into open crime. There is abundant evidence of the corruption of all classes of the hierarchy during the later Middle Ages.[2] Apparently exemption from the civil courts led the clerks to fancy themselves at liberty to follow unchecked any impulse whatsoever. The spiritual penalties which the Church courts could inflict were of little or no significance and the holy orders became a cloak for great enormities.

The church buildings were used for secular purposes; their vessels were neglected or stolen; indeed, the picture given by Desiderius, Abbot of Monte Cassino, later Pope Victor III, might well be taken as universally true. 'The Italian priesthood,' he says, 'and among them most conspicuous, the Roman pontiff, are in the habit of defying all law and all authority, thus utterly confounding together things sacred and things profane. . . . The people sold their suffrages for money to the highest bidder; the clergy, moved and seduced by avarice and ambition, bought and sold the sacred rites of ordination, and carried on a traffic with the gifts of the Holy Spirit. Few prelates remained untainted with the vile pollution of simony; few, very few, kept the commandments of God or served him with upright hearts; following their chiefs to do evil, the great sacerdotal herd rushed headlong down the precipice into the quagmire of licentiousness and profligacy; priests and deacons, whose

[1] Stutz, *Geschichte der Kirch. Benefizialwesens, passim.*

[2] Cæsar. Heisterbac., *l.c.*, lib. III, dis. 35, 40; IV, 41, 42, 44; Salimbene, *Chron.*, pp. 274–75 (ed. 1857); Luc. Tudens., *De Altera Vita*, *Bibl. Max. Vet. Pat.*, vol. XXV; Ughelli, *Italia Sacra*, vol. II, p. 14; Lamius, *Memorabilia Ecclesiæ Florentiniæ*, vol. II, p. 1313; *Annales Camaldulenses*, vol. I, app. 221 (ed. Ven., 1755); Hugo, *Destruct. Farf.*, II, *l.c.* p. 537.

duty it was to serve God with clean hands and with chaste bodies to administer the sacrament of the Lord, took to themselves wives after the manner of the laity; they left families behind them and bequeathed their ill-gotten wealth to their children; yea, even bishops, in contempt of all shame and decency, dwelt with their wives under the same roof, a nefarious and execrable custom, prevailing, alas! most commonly in that city where the laws, thus shamelessly set at naught, first issued from the sacred lips of the Prince of the Apostles and his holy successors.'

Over a century later, Innocent III's vigorous epistle to the Archbishop of Narbonne gives definite evidence that conditions had changed but little. 'Blind, dumb dogs that cannot bark,' he calls the priesthood. 'Simoniacs who sell justice, absolve the rich and condemn the poor. They do not keep the laws of the Church, much less of the state. They accumulate benefices for themselves and entrust the priesthood and the ecclesiastical dignities to unworthy priests and illegitimate children. Hence the insolence of the heretics. Hence the contempt of the nobles and people for God and his Church. In this region, the prelates are the laughing stock of the laity. And the cause of this evil is the archbishop himself. He knows no god other than money. His heart is a bank. During the ten years he has been in office, he has never once visited his province, not even his own diocese. He took five hundred golden pennies for consecrating the Bishop of Maguelonne, and when we asked him to raise subsidies for the Christians in the east, he refused. When a church falls vacant, he refrains from nominating an incumbent and appropriates the income. For the same reason, he has reduced by half the number of canons and kept the arch-deaconries vacant. In his diocese, monks and canons regular have renounced their order and married wives; they have become money-lenders, lawyers, jugglers, and doctors.' [1]

[1] Migne, *l.c.*, vol. ccxv, col. 355.

In the ninth century, Alfred the Great said hardly a priest in England could translate the services, and Eudes of Rigaud, Archbishop of Rouen, found the same situation in France four centuries later. In a report of a visitation he made, he says the services meant but little to either priest or laic. The duty of the one was to be present and say prayers; the ministration of the other seemed to be merely to conduct the routine of the mass. The Host was fly-blown, the churches filthy or in ruins, and the priests sold every sacrament and abused the confessional.[1] The whole situation as he found it could hardly have been more demoralizing. One of the gravest consequences of such corruption was the natural alienation of the common people, who, far from being saints themselves, yet refused to respect such idle and shameless leaders.

Nevertheless, there were doubtless God-fearing priests labouring in obscurity, sincerely fulfilling their duty to their parishes so far as their ability and education allowed. Inconspicuously good men seldom attract attention, be they priests or laymen. Although an eloquent preacher occasionally came into notice, or some reformer or ascetic attracted a large following, yet for the most part the more worthy members of the priesthood lived and died leaving no record.[2] Such noteworthy examples of purity as Aribert of Milan (1036), Ratherius of Verona (b. 890), Agobard of Lyons (d. 840), and Claude of Turin (d. cir. 830), whose virtues would have adorned any age, go far to prove the existence of an energy of renovation at the heart of the Church strong enough to redeem its more glaring shortcomings, as do also the continuous efforts put forth under even the most passive or reprehensible of the pontiffs to

[1] *Regestrum Visitationum Archiepiscopi Rothomagensis*, 1248–1269. (Rouen, 1852.)

[2] Saint Bernard says there were only two vicious priests in his neighbourhood, yet no heretic was more scathing than he in his denunciation of clerical disorders.

abolish corruption and to promote the more spiritual aims of the institution.[1]

However, there is ample justification for the abuse heaped upon the priests. Indeed, it could not well be otherwise. Little effort was made to secure proper preparation for the ministrants of the holy office, or to limit ordination and installation to those of blameless life; nor was episcopal supervision directed to securing faithfulness to duty. The bishop who had paid a high price for his preferment exacted in his turn payment for the humbler offices in his gift as a matter of business. All too often a priest was chosen because he could pay for his benefice, not because he was fit to have the cure of souls; all too many of the simoniacal incumbents were ignorant, neglectful, and sinful. Churches fell into ruins while their priests took the tithes, sold the altar vessels, and evaded all semblance of pastoral duties.[2]

It is true that to secure trained priests was not easy; indeed, at times, it was all but impossible. Educational facilities were scanty in the eleventh and twelfth centuries, but, on the other hand, most bishops were too busy with the cares of state even to make the effort. Cathedral schools had never disappeared even in the most confused periods,[3] although their standards varied in different ages and different localities. University men generally sought their careers in teaching or in administrative work. Rarely did they undertake charge of a parish, and when they did so, it was because they were forced to, rather than because they saw in it an opportunity for service. The literary revival of the twelfth century had not been without its effect on the inferior orders, but save for a few favoured localities conditions improved slowly.[4] The Church required the

[1] Landulf. Sen., *Hist. Med., M.G.H. SS.*, vol. VIII, p. 57; Ratherius, *De Contemptu Canonum, l.c.*, col. 499.

[2] S. Bernard., *De Consid.*, lib. IV, col. 771, Migne, *l.c.*, vol. CLXXXII.

[3] Landulf., *l.c.*, p. 76; Peter Damian, *l.c.*, col. 352.

[4] Ratherius, *l.c.*

priests to know the Psalms and the order of service, but very often it was impossible for the bishops to insist on even so small a qualification. By decreeing that 'since the Church of God, like an affectionate mother, is bound to provide for the poor as well in matters which redound to the profit of the soul as in those which concern the body, therefore, lest the opportunity of reading and improving be denied to a poor person who cannot be assisted from the resources of his parents, we command that in every Catholic parish some competent benefice be assigned to a master who may gratuitously teach as well the clerks of the same church as the indigent scholars,'[1] the Church tried to meet the situation, but wise as this provision was, the difficulty of enforcing the reservation of such a benefice made it practically a dead letter.

Within the Church itself, the source of the prevailing evils was usually declared to be the possession of wealth by the institution as well as by the individual clerics. The Church had always praised poverty; but generally the eulogies refer to individual poverty, which did not preclude communistic possession on the one hand, nor individual enjoyment on the other. The inconsistency between the actual wealth of the priesthood and their theoretical renunciation of temporal goods was not lost upon thoughtful and conscientious churchmen.[2]

'We seek,' says Abælard, 'to be richer as monks than we were in the world.'[3] Gerohus of Reichersperg laments: 'The bishops claim that evangelical perfection in which Peter gloried, saying to the Lord, "Behold, we leave all and follow thee," and of which the Lord said, "Unless a man has given up all that he possesses, he cannot be my disciple," and this perfection belongs to monks alone and not to the

[1] Mansi, vol. XXII, col. 999.

[2] *Sermo: In Solemnitate Omnium Sanctorum*, Guerrici Abbatis Igniacensis discipuli S. Bernardi, in *Opera*, S. Bernard., Migne, *l.c.*, vol. CLXXXV.

[3] *De Sancto Joanne Baptista Sermo.*, *Op.* (ed. Cousin), vol. I, p. 572.

secular clergy.'[1] Fleuffroy, abbot of Epternach, tells his monks: 'It matters not that our churches rise to the heavens, that the capitals of their pillars are sculptured and gilded, and that our parchment is tinted purple, that gold is melted to form the letters of our books and that their bindings are set with precious stones, if we have little or no care for the members of Christ, and if Christ himself lies naked and dying before our doors.' Moneta of Cremona argued that prelates are not possessors but dispensers of the wealth of the Church, and of those using it for their own purposes, he says: '*non excuso eos*.'[2] To him as to many earnest churchmen, money became a source of evil only when it was hoarded or used for purposes not strictly charitable.[3]

Of all the condemnations heaped on the wealth of the Church and on the sordid greed of prelates and monks, none was more biting in its satire than was that of a Henrican priest who wrote in the eleventh century. Taking as a theme the zeal of Pope Urban II for temporal possessions, he derides the pontiff for a trip into France undertaken to secure the relics of Saints Rufinus and Albinus (that is, gold and silver), and on the festival held in Rome to celebrate the arrival of the 'saints.' The ceremonies are described as taking place before His Holiness enthroned on a marble seat, clad in purple and surrounded by the fattest of cardinals all holding gilt cups filled with choicest wine. All who approached confessing these holy saints might enter freely even though they were guilty of adultery, of homicide, of envy, or of perjury; the sacrilegious detractors, the inebriates, the traitors, the malevolent, infamous, or avaricious ones, all were absolved once they came bearing the holy relics. 'Come, come, simoniacs, archbishops, abbots, deacons, friars!' he cries. 'Offer these two martyrs

[1] Geroh. Reicherspergensis, *De Investigatione*, *l.c.*, c. xx, p. 43. Cf. the practical protest against the wealth of the clergy by Arialdo of Milan, Norbert of Magdeburg, Bruno, founder of the Carthusian Order, etc.

[2] *Adversus Catharos*, p. 449.

[3] Ratherius, *l.c.*

to the Roman Church. . . . Behold there stands the host with open hands, calling all, exhorting all, inviting all and repelling none who confess Albinus. Ask for Albinus and you will be received; seek Rufinus and you shall find favour; for whoever asks for Rufinus, receives, who seeks for Albinus, finds; . . . who denies when Rufinus commands? These martyrs take king and emperor, duke and prince, and indeed all the powers of the earth by force. They subdue triumphantly bishops, cardinals, archbishops, abbots, deacons, priors, priests, and even the Roman pontiff himself. They are most powerful in council; they are heard most plainly in the synagogue. They finished Pope Guibert; [1] they subdued the Emperor Henry IV; they curbed the Roman Senate; these are the precious martyrs for whom the Roman pontiff destroyed the home of the 'Crescenzi', [2] opened the seat of Tarpeia, and ascended the capitol. These are the saints who close so that none can open and open that none can close.' [3]

Most of these criticisms were passed on members of the clergy because they as individuals possessed property. Reformers protesting against the individual possession of wealth and the misuse of property held in common were arising everywhere [4] and at the same time there was being developed a more radical conception of evangelical poverty which excluded even communism on the part of the clergy and in some instances, by the laity as well. The Church, rapidly approaching the height of her power and outwardly united, was inwardly torn by bitter dissensions over this question. The proletariat as it became more powerful was in a condition of rebellious agitation, attacking the wealth

[1] Anti-Pope Clement III. [2] In 1097.

[3] In Pflugk-Harttung, *Iter Italicum*, pp. 439, etc.

[4] Note the many passages in the sermons of Berthold von Regensberg; in Guib. Nov., *l.c.*; in Jacques de Vitry, *Exempla* and *Historia Occidentalis;* in Desiderius, *Dial. de Miraculis S. Benedicti*, *l.c.*; also in John of Salisbury, *Polycraticus*, lib. IV, cc. 2–5.

and sordid greed of all orders of the hierarchy, and flocking to the standards of heretic leaders who were bitterly attacking clerical avarice, scorning those who, ministering at the altar of Christ, did no other duty in his service. Everywhere and in all things there was arising a desire for a more austere moral life, a more absolute poverty as means to an immediate union with God.

We cannot know to what degree this tendency to emphasize poverty as an integral part of Christianity was due to a realization that wealth was corrupting the Church, to the contrast between the simple life and the privations of Christ and the Apostles and the magnificence and luxury which surrounded the clergy. That it had a profound effect on many is indubitable.

While the efforts to restore primitive Christianity by following literally the commands of Christ and the teachings of the Apostles in daily life as in religious observance, were very numerous in the eleventh and twelfth centuries, yet the conceptions men formed of the essence of apostolic Christianity varied widely. The fundamental motive was always the same, however: they would live as Christ taught men to live; they would conform their worship to that of the little group of believers who first followed him in far-off Palestine. Arialdo and Waldo, Arnold and Francis agreed in basing the apostolic life on evangelical poverty. But Waldo wished to sweep away all doctrines, all religious observances which were not found in the Church of the apostolic age; Arnold believed that the Vicar of Christ should not be a secular prince and assailed the vast fabric of the temporal power of the Church; Arialdo tried to purge the Church of simony, to teach the priests to lead pure lives; the monastic reformers sought salvation through the renunciation of temporal goods; Francis saw clearly his own duty to be poor as Christ had commanded, to help suffering humanity and at the same time to uphold the Church as an institution. Nowhere did he directly oppose the Church or place a distinct counterplan against its policy.

These two centuries witnessed a great religious awakening in all parts of western Europe. The eleventh century was the age of the Cluniac reform, of the foundation of the Cistercian and Carthusian Orders, of the first great crusade. The twelfth century brought to light many new enthusiasts, most of whom the Church counted as heretics. These men were in most cases reformers as truly as were Norbert and Bernard. The leaders among them spoke in Christ's name and voiced Christ's commands, but the multitude following found itself outside the Church which claimed to be the fold of Christ. They did not plan heretics; in many instances they thought themselves champions of the Faith. Waldo, like Francis, asked the Pope to sanction his work, to authorize him to help the Church in teaching the people to follow Christ. Orthodox and heretical reformers were alike products of the religious enthusiasm of the age and all found a following. Wherever an enthusiast appeared proclaiming his message as an appeal to return to evangelical poverty, he was sure of a hearing. When he preached obedience to the commands of Christ, some were always ready to obey.

The Church finally awoke to the facts. The Papal Curia was convinced that if the dangerous growth of heresy were to be checked, it must of necessity be through a popular appeal to the enthusiasm for evangelical poverty which was carrying thousands into the ranks of heretics. Then began a consistent effort to enlist under the banner of the Church apostles of primitive Christianity and of these apostles, the chief in beauty of life, in power over the masses, in influence upon the age, is Francis of Assisi. Of that age he is the true child and a study of the primitive Christians who preceded him may throw some light upon the movement he sponsored.

CHAPTER II

MONASTIC REFORMERS OF THE ELEVENTH AND TWELFTH CENTURIES

1. *The Carthusians*

The eleventh century had reached its prime ere western Europe began to shake off the lethargy which since the time of Charlemagne had stifled her intellectually and politically, resulting in a degeneration of all manifestations of the creative spirit. Then a variety of forces, working simultaneously in different strata of the social order, combined to bring about an awakening as gradual as it was universal. The reform of the papacy, the reorganization of the empire, the influence in Church and state of such dominant personalities as Gregory VII, William the Norman, and Conrad the Salic, furnished a measure of security quite lacking in the disturbed decades of the preceding century. The serfs were beginning their struggle for freedom; industry was asserting her independence of feudalism; the organization of guilds, the opening of new markets, fairs and trade routes, were contributing in no small degree to the quickening of energy and self-confidence. Occasional monastic reforms were to some extent clearing the atmosphere of moral turpitude and providing more favourable conditions for intellectual pursuits, the embryonic cravings for which were then being stimulated by a series of notable teachers.

In art, realism, whose very uncouthness was full of promise, was replacing the rigid imitation of pseudo-classic models. Here and there a noble Romanesque cathedral was arising,[1] an unmistakable forerunner of the majestic

[1] The eleventh century may claim as hers such Romanesque edifices as the cathedrals of Pisa, Cremona, Modena, Parma, Como and Genoa, and the

Gothic edifices of the coming centuries. Everywhere, amid the chaotic crudeness, were apparent the stirrings of new desires, new forces, new appreciations, new life, which were to bear abundant fruit in the twelfth and thirteenth centuries.

Although ignorance was still widely prevalent, and was accompanied by childish savagery and impetuous passions, yet Christendom was slowly yielding to forces making for an increased sensibility, a more cultured wisdom, greater self-restraint, and a more intelligent piety. In this striving for ampler life may be found one cause of the monastic revival of the eleventh and twelfth centuries. Earnest souls, awakening to a consciousness of their own possibilities and seeking spiritual perfection on earth, rallied to the standards of a Robert, a Norbert, and a Bruno in a spirit of knightly quest and high adventure. The age of troubadours was dawning: the age of Crusades was approaching: the spirit of romance and adventure which gave them being was finding expression also in the vocation of the religious as he girded on the armour of the Most High to fight the invisible hosts of Satan.

Gradually in Italy, France, and Germany men were being taught by the logic of facts, reiterated and forced upon their notice, that the temporal possessions and secular power of the Church had led her far from the apostolic ideal. Unwilling to admit the defeat or the inefficiency of the theory of monasticism, however lacking it might be in practice, these restless, strenuous spirits never doubted but that the only adequate protest against the general moral laxity lay in a rigorous observance of monastic vows, particularly that of poverty. Since the existing Orders, despite recent attempts at reform, were too obviously

churches of San Miniato at Florence, San Zeno at Verona, San Michele and San Pietro in Cielo d'Oro at Pavia, San Marco at Venice, Santi Pietro e Paolo at Bologna, San Sepolcro at Milan and Santa Maria at Cologne. Many of them, however, have been altered or rebuilt in later years.

ignoring the discrepancies between their rule and their practices to respond to the needs and aspirations of the times, the restoration of faith in the ideals they embodied could be achieved only by the establishment of new orders. The age-long desire to seek in solitude the opportunity for meditation and to escape complicity in the evil it seemed hopeless to combat, plus the imposition of celibacy on the priesthood, combined, in the latter part of the eleventh century, to bring about a revival of the ideals of monasticism. The question of a married clergy was by no means new,[1] but the rather intermittent legislation aimed to enforce celibacy had been quite generally ignored, and by the tenth century clerical marriage was general enough to pass with little comment save from the most ardent reformers, and it was becoming increasingly evident that unless the Church wished to abolish the practice altogether, steps must be taken to enforce it. For economic reasons if for no other, a married priesthood would be detrimental to the extension of papal power. In the first place, as soon as clergy began to provide for their offspring by gifts of ecclesiastical property, the temporal possessions of the Church were in danger of becoming completely alienated; and in the second place, a married priesthood would naturally tend to become a hereditary caste little inclined, as its local power increased, to subject itself to the supreme pontifical authority.[2]

[1] Even those most earnest in their efforts to secure the enforcement of celibacy admitted that it was not an apostolic requirement. The legislation of the early Church on the subject may be found in Burchard., *Decret.*, Migne, *Pat. Lat.*, vol. CXL, col. 555, etc. See also I Tim., III, 2; Titus, I., 6; *Apostolical canons*, 17, 18, 19, 21, 26; Tertullian, *De Monogamia*, c. 2, Migne, *l.c.*, vol. II; *Constitut. Apostol.*, lib. VI, c. 17, p. 144; Gratian., *Decret.*, col. 150, 159, 290, Migne, *l.c.*, vol. CLXXXVII; S. Thom. Aquit., *Summa Theol.*, II, Quæst. 186, Art. 4, par. 3, p. 493, vol. X, *Opera Omnia* (ed. Rome, 1899).

[2] Desiderius, *Dial.*, *l.c.*, pp. 953, etc.; Johannis, *Vita S. Pet. Dam.*, c. 16, Migne, *l.c.*, vol. CXLIV, col. 133. Throughout Italy clergy of all orders, from the bishop down, were publicly married and were providing for their children from their prebends, even willing church property to them.

In the middle of the tenth century, the incipient reform instigated by the Emperor Otto I had lifted the papacy from the depths into which it had fallen, while the Cluniac movement, complementing his labours, bade fair to lighten the darkness everywhere enveloping the Church. The succeeding decades were too inert to push either effort to full fruition, and there followed a century of actual degradation when the pontiffs were mere creatures of the Counts of Tusculum and the Roman barons. Such shameful conditions could not last, particularly in an age of awakening religious consciousness. The opening of a new era was marked by a series of vigorous pontificates, those of Leo IX (1048–1054), Nicholas II (1059–1061), and Alexander II (1061–1073), in which the papal efforts to eliminate irregularities in the priesthood were aided and abetted by the denunciations of such ascetics as Peter Damian, Giovanni Gualberto (founder of the Vallombrosan Order) and Hildebrand, each fiery enough to stimulate in the most acquiescent a desire for reform. Even before their coming, a series of synods and councils [1] had passed new laws against clerical marriage, but these canons, admirable in themselves and supported by the King of France and by the emperor, had not been enforced.

In 1059 the Council of Rome, probably at the instigation of Hildebrand, had decreed that any priest who had either a wife or a concubine must dismiss her or resign his sacred calling, together with whatever ecclesiastical revenue he might be enjoying.[2] Although Pope Nicholas followed up the decree most vigorously in Italy and in France,[3] the lower grades of the clergy were apparently those most affected.[4] However, the war was on, and when, in 1073,

[1] 1022, Concil. Ticin., cc. 1, 2, 3, 4, Mansi, vol. XIX, col. 351; 1031, Concil. Bituricens., cc. 5, 6, 7, 8, 10, 16, *ibid.*, col. 501; 1056, Concil. Tolosan., c. 7, *ibid.*, col. 847.

[2] 1059, Concil. Rom., c. 3, *ibid.*, col. 907.

[3] *Decret.* Nicol. PP., cc. 3, 4 (1060), *ibid.*, col. 875–76.

[4] Peter Damian, *Opusc.*, XVII, *De Cœlibatu Sacerdot.*, Migne, *l.c.*, vol. CLXV, col. 379.

Hildebrand became Pope Gregory VII, there could be little doubt as to the outcome.

What in the early days of the Church had been a more or less voluntary ideal, slowly developing into a custom, was now to become a rigid law. Possibly Gregory was the first to realize just how important the enforcement of celibacy would be to the power of the papacy. Whether his predecessors had seen the situation as clearly as he did or not, it can never be argued that they, any of them, were prompted solely by the desire to extend the monastic ideal. Gregory aimed above all else to free the Church from the secular state and to give it power to act independently of worldly authority. It seemed to him that any reform must of necessity be along the line of increased asceticism and that the churchman could meet the discipline of arms imposed on the warrior only by the stern training of the cloister. Early in 1074, his first synod adopted a canon prohibiting sacerdotal marriage, refusing orders to all but celibates and ordaining that priests put away their wives and concubines.[1] Although this was no more severe in tone than had been the legislation of his predecessors,[2] he was determined that it should not remain, as had theirs, a mere protest, but that it should be enforced wherever the power of the Church extended. The measure was predestined to succeed, but it was also predestined to arouse bitter opposition especially in Germany.[3]

Doubtless some of the bishops wished to avoid responsibility for the suffering such a separation of families would mean; some were prompted by loyalty to the Emperor, then at bitter odds with the Pope; others refused to

[1] Concil. Rom., 1074, c. 3, Mansi, *l.c.*, col. 403.

[2] Leo IX, for instance, had ordered that the wives of clerics be given as slaves to Saint John Lateran. Peter Damian, *Opusc.*, XVIII, Dis. II, c. 7, col. 410, Migne, *l.c.*

[3] Only two German prelates out of forty-one published the canon. These two were the Archbishop of Mainz and the Bishop of Passau.

accept the imposition of monastic ideals on the secular clergy; while others, and these not a few, hesitated lest they arouse a civil war.[1]

Secure in the support of powerful lay barons,[2] Gregory then took the unprecedented step of authorizing them and their vassals to withdraw obedience from priests and prelates who disregarded the decree,[3] thus not only allowing the parish to sit in judgement on the pastor, but also indirectly denying the doctrine that the priest derived virtue from his office. In his desire to purify the Church, to restore civilization along ecclesiastical lines, and to render supreme the papal power, little went untried. The secular clergy having failed in their allegiance for the most part, he transferred the powers usually assigned to them to the more loyal monks.[4] These, conscious of the significance of the imposition of their vow of chastity on their age-long adversaries, now took occasion to reap the harvest so clearly their own, and to add new converts to their orders.

Among the agents of this religious revival in the hands of the monks was the Carthusian Order, in its inception a protest against simony, against the magnificence of the prelates and against the ignorance and indifference of the clergy.[5] Its founder, Bruno, a German of noble parentage,[6] was born at Cologne in the first half of the eleventh century.[7] He studied first in the cathedral school there and

[1] *Vita S. Altman*, Gretser, *Opera Omnia*, vol. VI, p. 445; *Regesta*, Greg. VII, vol. I, *Ep.* XX, p. 321. There was at this time open warfare in Lombardy over this question.

[2] E.g., Erlembaldo of Milan, Leopold of Austria, Frederick of Montbéliard, Rodolph of Suabia, Robert of Flanders, Berthold of Carinthia, and the great Matilda of Tuscany.

[3] *Regesta*, Greg. VII, vol. I, *Ep.* LV, p. 246; *Ep.* XLV, p. 234; *Ep.* XI, p. 311; Mansi, vol. XX, col. 217.

[4] Such as Desiderius of Monte Cassino; Gerald, Grand Prior of Cluny; Odo, Prior of Cluny; Bernard of Saint Victor of Marseilles: Bernard of Hirschau and Peter Damian. Giovanni Gualberto never saw Gregory, but he was unswerving in his loyalty to the Hildebrandine ideal.

[5] Guib. Nov., *De Vita Sua*, c. 7.

[6] *Ibid.*, c. 11.

[7] The exact date of Bruno's birth is not known, but it was probably between

then at Rheims and possibly at Tours [1] under Berengar. Returning to his native city, he was made canon of Saint Cunibert's, although it is uncertain if he took orders.[2] From there he went again to Rheims where he was chancellor of the cathedral, head of the cathedral school and master in theology,[3] winning no little renown for his scholarship and probity of life.

In 1070,[4] while he was at Rheims, a certain Manasses, a conspicuous example of the worst type of prelate of his day, became archbishop. Having bought the See outright, he aimed to make it as profitable to himself as possible, which he did by leaving benefices vacant that he might enjoy their income, by openly robbing rich monasteries, and by selling costly vessels from the treasury. Taken all in all, the See was proving an excellent investment and Manasses was fairly content, remarking on one occasion that 'it would be good to be Archbishop of Rheims if one did not have to say masses.' Opinion, however, became rather general that it was not so good to have Manasses as Archbishop of Rheims.[5] As early as 1073 he had received a well-merited papal rebuke for neglecting his responsibilities toward certain monasteries,[6] and four years later his abuses had become so flagrant that his own clergy complained to the Holy See,[7] whereupon he was summoned to the Council of Autun to answer to a charge of simony.[8] He failed to appear and was declared suspended from his office.[9]

As Bruno was among those preferring charges against

1030 and 1042. Löbbel, p. 57, n., *Der Stifter des Carthäuser-Ord.*; *Annales Ord. Cart.*, vol. I, p. xxxi.

[1] Schnitzer, *Berengar von Tours*, p. 336.

[2] *Apologia Manassæ*, *l.c.*, p. 121.

[3] *Vita Antiq.*, *AA. SS.*, III Oct., p. 704.

[4] Marlot, *Hist. de Reims*, vol. III, p. 175.

[5] Guib. Nov., *l.c.*; Marlot, *l.c.*, p. 178; Gförer, *Pabst Gregorius VII*, vol. VII, pp. 175, etc.; *Hist. Litt.*, vol. VII, pp. 648, etc.

[6] *Regesta*, Greg. VII, vol. I, pp. 114, 158.

[7] *Chron.*, Hugo Flav., *M.G.H. SS.*, vol. VIII, p. 415.

[8] *Regesta*, Greg. VII, *l.c.*, p. 416.

[9] *Ibid.*, p. 425.

him,[1] he probably felt the prelate's vengeance when he tore down the houses, seized the property, and sold the prebends of his accusers.[2] Manasses, however, did not dare defy the Pope of whom he stood in awe and with whom he tried to make peace.[3] But Gregory was obdurate. The Archbishop was one of the most flagrant simoniacs of that time and toward him and his kind the Pontiff was merciless. In 1080 he was summoned to the Council of Lyons. The prelate feared the wrath of Gregory should he refuse a second time to answer for his offences; he feared equally a public trial. So he offered heavy bribes to Hugo, the papal legate, trying to induce him to substitute for the trial purgation by the testimony of six bishops, suffragans of the See of Rheims whom Manasses was to select and whose good word he doubtless intended to buy. But Hugo proved incorruptible,[4] and Manasses, fully aware that his case was already lost, chose to exile himself at the court of the Emperor Henry IV,[5] then under the papal ban, rather than face a trial and the subsequent inevitable disgrace. The Council declared him deposed,[6] and Gregory, confirming the sentence, went still further and excommunicated him.[7]

Apparently Manasses considered Bruno leader of the opposition against him at Rheims, for after the Council of Autun the latter was not allowed to return to his duties at the cathedral. Manasses gone, he ventured back, but the aftermath of the bitter conflict was evidently intolerable, for when the following December he was chosen archbishop,[8] he not only refused to accept the dignity, but resigned his benefices and left the city.[9] The motives prompt-

[1] *Apologia Manassæ*, *l.c.*, p. 117. [2] *Annales Ord. Cart.*, vol. I, XVIII.
[3] Manass., *Ep. ad. Greg.*, *Regesta*, Greg. VII, vol. II, p. 110.
[4] *Regesta*, Greg. VII, vol. I, p. 425, *Ep.* XX; *Chron.*, Hugo Flav., *l.c.*, p. 422.
[5] *Vita Antiq.*, p. 703; Benzo, *M.G.H. SS.*, vol. XI, p. 657.
[6] Mansi, vol. XX, col. 551. [7] Jaffe, *Regesta*, vol. I, nos. 3915, 3916, 3917.
[8] *Ibid.*, no. 3915.
[9] Guib. Nov., *l.c.*, c. XI; Löbbel, *l.c.*, p. 98, n. 1. See the *Vita Antiq.*, p. 703, for an incredible legend regarding Bruno's departure into solitude, and the *Vita*

ing this action can only be surmised. Possibly he was unwilling to assume the charge of clergy who, having forgotten their apostolic office and model, were so absorbed in an unseemly struggle to gain for themselves the wealth of the Church that any effort at reform would only serve to arouse their hostility; possibly, too, he doubted his own ability to resist the dangers and temptations accompanying archiepiscopal power. It seems fairly certain, however, that he had already determined to devote himself to a life of poverty, when accompanied by two of his pupils, Peter of Bethune and Lambert of Burgundy,[1] he set out in search of some remote solitude wherein he might find peace. The pilgrims made their first stop at Molesme,[2] where the saintly Robert was endeavouring to secure implicit obedience to the Benedictine rule, but evidently such strict adherence to a superimposed discipline was not to their liking, even though the community was, in a way, realizing the ideals they themselves were seeking. Pushing on to Sêche-Fontaine,[3] between Molesme and Bar-sur-Seine, they halted again for some months. They were joined here by more of Bruno's pupils also eager to share their master's quest:[4] Landwin, later his successor at the Grande-Chartreuse, Stephen of Bruges, Stephen of Dijon, who was canon of Saint Ruffin's at Avignon, Hugo, a priest, and two laymen, André and Guèrin.

Despite his friendship with Robert, Bruno felt the proximity of Molesme to be a hindrance, and Sêche-Fontaine not coming up to his expectations, he with six of his disciples wandered southward, arriving at Grenoble early in 1084.[5] The little band obtained permission from Bishop Hugo to settle in the diocese and they chose a rocky wilder-

Altera and *Vita Tertia*, *AA. SS.*, III Oct., pp. 708–14 and 724–26, for an augmented version of the legend.

[1] Mabillon, *Annales Benedic.*, vol. v, lib. XVI, p. 192.

[2] *Ibid.* [3] *Ibid.* [4] *Ibid.*; *Vita Hugonis Grat.*, *AA. SS.*, I Apr., col. 40.

[5] Mabillon, *l.c.*

ness not far from the city, but difficult of access and stern and forbidding in appearance.[1] Here on Saint John's Day, they took possession of a small hut, the cradle of the Carthusian Order.[2]

The keynote of their life in this secluded spot was rigid simplicity.[3] Each of the brethren lived alone in a little cell in which he slept, worked and ate in silence,[4] passing the days in prayer and contemplation, for like the Camaldosi, the Carthusians tried to unite western ideas of monasticism with the practices of eastern hermits. The food consisted for the most part of bread and vegetables which each cooked for himself,[5] with cheese and fish on Sunday, 'if these were given them,' Sunday being the only day in the week in which they ate together.[6] Water was brought to the cells by means of a conduit. 'They drank but little wine and that was not good nor strong.' For clothing there was nothing besides coarse sackcloth.[7] Their only riches were the books which they copied,[8] a labour forming the chief industry of the order until the invention of printing, and the results of which undoubtedly helped keep learning alive among the priesthood.[9]

From the beginning they were ardent in their devotion to Lady Poverty, desiring absolute freedom from earthly possessions and temporal cares. Even after the first days of enforced privation were over and their holiness of life began to attract offerings, they remained faithful to their ideals. For the altar-service only one silver cup was allowed, nothing more.

[1] *Gallia Christiana*, vol. IX, p. 275; Guib. Nov., *l.c.*

[2] Labbé, *Nov. Bib.*, vol. I, p. 639; *Vita Tertia*, *l.c.*, p. 728.

[3] Bruno gave his followers no written rule. The *Practice of the Order* was first formulated by Guido, the fifth prior, in 1130.

[4] *Vita Alt.*, p. 175. [5] *Ibid.* [6] *Ibid.*, p. 716. [7] *Ibid.*, p. 715.

[8] Later, when Bruno went to Italy, he wrote Raoul, provost of the Cathedral at Rheims, '*Vitam S. Remigii nobis transmittas oro quia nusquam in partibus nostris referitur.*'

[9] Poole, *Mediæval Thought*, p. 75.

'Once the Comte de Nevers visited them,' says the author of *Vita Antiquior*. 'He was a good man, and admonished them about greed for secular things and bade them beware of it. When he went home, however, he remembered their indigence and forgot the advice he had given them. He sent them I know not what of silver plate and platters of great price. He did not find them unmindful of what he said, for they refused his gifts.'

The Order grew rapidly.[1] Its severity appealed to those who like Bruno craved holiness through renunciation of the world. While it is true that in later years this severity was somewhat relaxed, yet of all the great orders, this one best maintained the ideals of the founder,[2] despite the many noble buildings later erected for them by their patrons.

Bruno was not long content with this wilderness. The increase of followers necessitated organization, and organization was abhorrent to him. It bound him to earth when his soul was set toward those things which are above. He had no desire to found an order. He wished rather to institute a mode of life wherein any one who cared to join him might serve God and free himself from the slavery of temporal things. In 1089, therefore, he left the Chartreuse and went to Rome,[3] possibly in response to a summons from Pope Urban II,[4] who had studied under him at Rheims.[5] Whatever the occasion of his going, however, he did not tarry long, but turned his steps toward Calabria, home of visionaries, where in 1090 he began living among the

[1] In 1137 there were three daughter houses; in 1131, fourteen. Lefèvre, *Saint Brunon et l'ordre des Chartreux*, p. 25.

[2] This order was never subjected to a general reform. During the period of the French Revolution it was suppressed, but in 1819 it was reorganized.

[3] Labbé, *Nov. Bib.*, vol. I, p. 639; Guib. Nov., *l.c.*, '*nescio occasione*'; *Vita Antiq.*, p. 705, '*Cum igitur præfatus magister Bruno jam sex annis heremum Cartusiæ inhabitasset, et vocatus ad curiam Romanam, oporteret eum summo Pontifici obedire.*'

[4] *Vita Antiq.*, *l.c.*

[5] Mann, *Lives of the Popes*, vol. VII, p. 252.

hermits who inhabited the caverns about Della Torre.[1] Here he found the freedom and the solitude that his soul desired, and here he died in 1101.[2] In 1094, Bruno had been offered the See of Reggio,[3] but he was too content among these hermits even to consider it. They were indeed men after his own heart. Having renounced whatever possessions and occupations had been theirs, they had retired to this rocky, mountainous desert of the most remote corner of Italy, passing their days in solitary worship, taking no thought of the morrow, and withstanding every effort of their admirers to force on them gifts in recognition of their virtue.[4]

From Della Torre, Bruno wrote Raoul, provost of the cathedral at Rheims, describing the beauty of his retreat: 'I dwell in a hermitage far enough removed on all sides from the haunts of men, in the territory of Calabria with brethren religious and somewhat lettered. Constant in vigils, they await the coming of their Lord, so that when he shall knock, they straightway open unto him. How can I do justice to the mildness and softness of the air, and to the plain, wide and pleasing, which extends far among the mountains where there are green fields and flower-strewn meadows? Or what words can adequately picture the more distant view of hills rising gently on all sides; of shaded valleys; of the numerous rivers, brooks and springs? And there is no lack of well-watered gardens nor of various fruitful trees.'

The body of this letter, however, is an exhortation to Raoul to fulfill a vow he had made when the two had talked together in a garden at Rheims — a vow, evidently, to become a monk. The reasoning Bruno employs is most interesting as it may well be that which had determined his own course.

[1] *Vita Antiq., l.c.*; *Vita Alt.*, p. 719.
[2] *Vita Antiq., l.c.*
[3] *Ibid.*
[4] *Vita Tertia*, p. 719.

'Be not held back by deceitful riches which do not avail to banish want,' he says; 'nor by the dignity of your office which cannot be administered without great danger to the soul. For to turn to your own use the property of which you are the manager and not the possessor, is as baneful as it is wicked. If desiring pomp and splendour, you should wish to keep a great retinue, so great that the resources which are justly yours do not suffice, will you not be forced to take away from some that you may bestow upon others? This is not benevolent nor liberal, for nothing is liberal which is not also just. What course is so wise as to choose goodness? And what is so good as God? Nay, what other good is there save God alone? So the holy soul, realizing in part the incomparable beauty and grace and splendour of God's goodness, on fire with love, said: "My soul thirsteth for God, for the living God; when shall I come and appear before God?" [1] What then, do you think you should do, dearest friend? What but yield to the divine counsels, to the divine truth which cannot err? "Come unto me all ye who labour and are heavy laden, and I will give you rest," and Wisdom further saith unto us, "Whoever he be of you that forsaketh not all he hath, cannot be my disciple."' [2]

It would be easy to read into the above much of Bruno's experience at Rheims. Did he learn there that power and probity of life are incompatible; that responsibility is accompanied by weakness before temptation rather than strength? One can only conjecture. An earlier letter from Della Torre is addressed to his followers at the Grande-Chartreuse, and is full of enthusiastic praise for the simple, vigorous life they were living, and for their constancy to their vows, closing with an earnest admonition that they continue as they had begun, avoiding 'sickly troops of vain laics,' lest they be contaminated.[3]

[1] Psalms, XLII, 2. [2] Migne, *l.c.*, vol. CLII, col. 420.
[3] Migne, *l.c.*, col. 418.

Absolute renunciation of the world, implicit reliance on the providence of God for the necessities of their life, and for the rest, prayer and contemplation — these were the ideals of Bruno and the early Carthusians. 'They left all riches, luxury and honour of this world to take up each one his cross and naked to follow the naked Christ along the narrow way.'

2. *The Cistercians*

Of the twelfth-century seekers after apostolic poverty the Cistercians are the foremost even as they are the most widely known of the reformed Benedictines. The Order was founded in 1098 by Robert of Molesme and his immediate successors in the abbacy,[1] Alberic and Stephen, who like him were ready to 'serve God in the fulness of their hearts, in hunger and thirst, in cold and nakedness.' Robert, a Champenois noble, was a restless soul, ever tormented by a desire for evangelical perfection and intent on a literal obedience to the rule of Saint Benedict. Early in life he entered a monastery at Moutiers-la-Celle of which he became prior as soon as he had completed his novitiate. While still a young man he was chosen Abbot of Saint-Michael-de-Tonnere.[2] The brethren there refused to accept his ideals of poverty and manual labour, while he for his part found their disregard of the rule intolerable and returned to Moutiers-la-Celle. He was then made Prior of Saint-Ayoul in Provins, but soon afterwards the hermits of Colan,[3] by virtue of an appeal to Pope Alexander II, succeeded in securing him as their superior.[4] In 1075, he removed them to Molesme in the diocese of Langres,[5] where

[1] *Annales Benedic.*, vol. v, pp. 87, 367; *Hist. Litt.*, *l.c.*, p. 2.
[2] *AA. SS.*, III Apr., pp. 669–71.
[3] Colan was in the forest between Tonnere and Chably.
[4] *Annales Benedic.*, *l.c.*, pp. 87, 204, 367. They had tried to persuade him to join them when he was at Saint-Michael-de-Tonnere.
[5] *Ann. Cist.*, vol. I, p. 7; *AA. SS.*, *l.c.*

he erected a rude oratory and a few scarcely habitable cabins on a hillside in the heart of a dark forest.[1]

Molesme was a barren place and although many of the monks were, like Robert, of noble birth and not inconsiderable learning, they were forced to toil beyond their strength for their daily bread,[2] and to suffer all the hardships that loneliness and destitution can afford. By a mere chance, when their need was greatest, the Bishop of Troyes, who had once visited them and was aware of their holy lives,[3] learned of their necessity and relieved their want.[4] After this, though just how is not told, they grew more prosperous and Robert's ideals were again rejected.[5] Twice at least during the succeeding years he withdrew as a protest against their laxity, but each time was prevailed on to return by promise of obedience. The last time the pope was appealed to, and ordered him to go back, thus making it impossible for him to leave again without permission.[6]

In 1098 there was another revolt against his rigorous asceticism, and this time Robert, with six of his monks, including both Alberic and Stephen, went to the papal legate Hugo, Bishop of Lyons, 'a veritable angel in mortal flesh,'[7] asking that they be allowed to establish a new monastery.[8] The request being granted, he returned to Molesme, resigned his office and set forth with twenty-one brothers [9] who shared his discontent. They took with them only a breviary which was to be copied and returned before Saint John's Day.[10]

[1] *Annales Benedic.*, *l.c.*, p. 378.

[2] *AA. SS.*, *l.c.*; *Annales Benedic.*, *l.c.*, p. 88. [3] *AA. SS.*, *l.c.*

[4] *Annales Benedic.*, *l.c.*, p. 204. [5] *AA. SS.*, *l.c.*; *Hist. Litt.*, *l.c.*, p. 2.

[6] *Annales Benedic.*, *l.c.*, pp. 17, 69; *Exord. Mag.*, lib. I, c. 10. Migne, *l.c.*, vol. CLXXXV, b., col. 993. On one of these occasions he was accompanied by Alberic and Stephen; on the other, these two withdrew later.

[7] *Ann. Cist.*, *l.c.*, p. 11.

[8] *Ibid.*, p. 7; *Exord. Mag.*, lib. I, c. 13; *AA. SS.*, *l.c.*

[9] *AA. SS.*, *l.c.*; *Exord. Parv.*, c. 2, Migne, *l.c.*, vol. CLXVI.

[10] *Ann. Cist.*. *l.c.*

Chance or design led the little band to a 'horrible and vast solitude' known as Citeaux or the place of cisterns, situated on the marshy banks of a stream called Sans-fond in the diocese of Châlons-sur-Saône, in Burgundy.[1] Renaud, Vicomte of Beaune, to whom the wilderness belonged, gave them permission to settle here, so they set themselves to clearing away the underbrush and erecting an oratory.[2] Odo, Duke of Burgundy, recently converted by Anselm of Bec and eager to 'bring forth fruits meet for repentance,' heard of the coming of the monks and sought them out. So troubled was he over the hardships they were facing and so fearful lest they be unable to withstand the inclement weather that he set some of his own servants to help them build a shelter.[3] On March 21st, the feast of Saint Benedict, and that year Palm Sunday as well, the 'Novum Monasterium,' as it was called, was dedicated to the Virgin,[4] and Robert, who had been chosen abbot, was given the pastoral staff by the Bishop of Châlons, who thus erected the monastery into an abbey,[5] while Odo and Renaud confirmed the community in possession of the land 'that they might undertake a life of evangelical poverty.'[6]

Robert remained at Citeaux but a year. The monks at Molesme, disgusted with the impotence of his successor and conscious of the disrepute into which they had fallen, sent again to Rome asking for his return.[7] Urban felt but little sympathy for them; moreover he was unwilling to

[1] *Exord. Parv.*, c. 3; *Annales Benedic.*, *l.c.*, p. 367.

[2] One account says they arrived at Citeaux because they had chosen the most rugged road from Molesme; another says the place had been decided on in advance.

[3] *Exord. Mag.*, lib. I, c. 13.

[4] All Cistercian monasteries, following this example, were dedicated to the Virgin. *Exord. Mag.*, lib. I, c. 13; Mansi, vol. xx, col. 890; *AA. SS.*, III Apr., p. 497; *Ann. Cist.*, *l.c.*, pp. 10, 11.

[5] Jaffé, *Regesta*, vol. I, p. 481, no. 4370; *Ann. Cist.*, *l.c.*, p. 7; *Exord. Mag.*, c. 15.

[6] *Ann. Cist.*, *l.c.*, pp. 7, 11; *Exord. Mag.*, lib. I, c. 10; *Gall. Christ.*, vol. IV.

[7] *Exord. Mag.*, lib. I, c. 14; *Annales Benedic.*, *l.c.*, pp. 205, 369, 377; *Ann. Cist.*, vol. I, p. 12.

overrule the decision of his legate, so he sent them away with evasive answers. But being troubled over the condition of the monastery and wishing to save it from utter degeneracy if possible, he wrote Hugo, suggesting that he lay the matter before Robert and see if he were willing to return; but he expressly stipulated that the 'Novum Monasterium' be not disturbed, and that the monks of Molesme make satisfactory promises of future obedience.[1] Hugo carried out these suggestions, and Robert, ever a lover of peace, resigned his office at Citeaux and returned to Molesme, where he died some years later.[2]

Alberic, his faithful companion and supporter during the troublesome days at Molesme,[3] who had been made prior of the new monastery at the time of its consecration, was now chosen abbot. Far too little is known of this able and vigorous administrator beyond the fact that he was probably French and that he was 'most learned, skilled in things human and divine, and a lover of the rule and of the brethren.'[4] He was abbot for nine years, and although his régime was too strict to attract novices, yet this drawback was more than compensated for by the ever-developing spiritual fervour of the community. He it was who secured from Paschal II a confirmation of their privileges;[5] who replaced the wooden buildings by more permanent though not less austere ones of stone;[6] and who adopted the white habit in place of the customary black one of the Benedictines, rejecting at the same time their soft warm garments of fine cloth, their full sleeves, their ample hoods and furred tunics,[7] and substituting for them the simple cowl and tunic modelled after the garb of the Roman

[1] *Exord. Mag.*, lib. I, c. 15; Mansi, cols. 666, 967; *Ann. Cist.*, *l.c.*, pp. 8, 12; Baron., *Ann.* 1099; Jaffé, *l.c.*, p. 476, no. 4336; Labbe, *Nov. Bib.*, vol. I, p. 641.

[2] Archives de la Côte d'Or, MS. no. 156.

[3] *Exord. Parv.*, c. 9.

[4] *Exord. Mag.*, lib. I, c. 18; *AA. SS.*, II Apr., p. 497.

[5] Mansi, col. 1182; *AA. SS.*, *l.c.*; *Exord. Mag.*, lib. I, cc. 19, 23.

[6] *Exord. Mag.*, lib. I, c. 24; *Ann. Cist.*, vol. I, p. 49.

[7] S. Bernard., *Ep.* I, Migne, *l.c.*, vol. CLXXXII.

peasant which Saint Benedict had prescribed for his followers.[1] When the Cluniacs, somewhat chagrined by the stern asceticism of their new neighbours, reproached them for having discarded the black robe of the penitent, they replied, like the troubadours they foreshadowed, that white was the colour of the dear Lady for whom they fought the powers of darkness, and whose service filled them with such unspeakable joy that they could wear naught else.[2]

Alberic died in 1109.[3] His successor, the ardent, lovable ascetic,[4] Stephen Harding, is generally regarded as the founder of the Cistercians, since he framed their constitution, formulated their rule of life, and adopted the name by which they have since been known.[5] His policy, however, shows no deviation from that of his predecessors. Like them he aimed at literal obedience to the Benedictine rule, which his longer administration enabled him to accomplish the more perfectly. His one distinctive achievement was the conversion of the monastery into an order by regulating the relation of affiliated houses to the mother convent when the increase of numbers made this necessary.

Of his life but little is known save that he was probably Saxon and said to be of noble birth;[6] that he was reared in the monastery of Sherborne in Dorsetshire;[7] that impelled by a love of learning, he journeyed first into Scot-

[1] Tradition says the Virgin appeared to him in a vision bearing the white habit which she told him was for the Order.

[2] *Dialogus inter Cluniacensem Monachum et Cisterciensem,* in Martène et Durand, *Thes. Nov.*, vol. v, col. 1644.

[3] *Exord. Mag.*, lib. I, c. 27; *Ann. Cist.*, *l.c.*; p. 50; *AA. SS.*, *l.c.*, p. 496.

[4] Wm. of Malmesbury, *De Gestis Regum,* lib. IV, par. 337. Rolls Series.

[5] *Exord. Mag.*, *l.c.*; *AA. SS.*, *l.c.*; *Annales Benedic.*, *l.c.*, p. 265.

[6] *Gall. Christ.*, vol. IV, col. 985. The *Vita* in the *Acta Sanctorum* says '*genere nobilis,*' but Wm. of Malmesbury differs, '*non ita reconditis natalibus procreatus,*' lib. IV, par. 334.

[7] Sherborne Monastery, still in existence, was founded early in the eighth century and was one of those reformed by Saint Dunstan. *Exord. Mag.*, lib. I, c. 24; *Annales Benedic.*, *l.c.*, pp. 403, 498; Wm. of Malmesbury, *l.c.*; *AA. SS.*, *l.c.*, p. 497.

land and then to Paris and Rome;[1] and that, stopping overnight at Molesme on his return from this pilgrimage to the tombs of the Apostles, was so delighted with the poverty and humility of the brethren that he asked and obtained permission to remain.

His generous and happy nature,[2] his radiant love and charity towards all mankind, his unswerving faith in the providence of God, and, above all, his yearning for a life of stern simplicity, make him in truth a worthy forerunner of Saint Francis. Like him, he was thoroughly imbued with a belief in the sanctity of poverty, in which both saw not only the literal fulfilment of the rule of Saint Benedict, but the realization of God's plan for the salvation of the world. Stephen's life was a strange mixture of repose and action. Although distinctly of the type known as the contemplative ascetic, he had the head to plan and the calm, unbending energy necessary to the execution of a great work.

During the years at Molesme he had served Robert with steadfast loyalty, accompanying him in 1098 to Citeaux, where, on the establishment of the 'Novum Monasterium,' he was appointed sub-prior. Under Alberic he held the priorship, and during those difficult first years, discharged with marked ability the arduous duties of minister to the abbot, whose logical successor he was. Somewhat overmodest as to his fitness for so responsible a position, he absented himself from the convent at the time of the elections,[3] although when the choice of the brethren fell upon him, he accepted the office with becoming dignity. The difficulties facing him were by no means inconsiderable. Thanks to his efforts, no less than to Alberic's, the convent was fairly well organized, while the Duke of Burgundy had

[1] Wm. of Malmesbury, *l.c.*; *AA. SS.*, *l.c.* He must have come to Molesme soon after its establishment.

[2] *AA. SS.*, *l.c.*, p. 496.

[3] Wm. of Malmesbury, *l.c.*, par. 337; *Exord. Mag.*, lib. I, c. 27; *Ann. Cist.*, *l.c.*, p. 50.

assisted in erecting new buildings more habitable than the original wooden huts. Pope Paschal's confirmation of their privileges had saved them to some extent from the depredations of unfriendly neighbours, but there was much yet to be done. Nine years had not sufficed to clear land enough to supply their needs; the brethren were growing old, and as yet there was a dearth of novices.[1] This was perhaps Stephen's most serious problem. His first act was one apparently designed to prevent its solution, although later events fully justified his course.

What he did was to forbid any princes to hold court at Citeaux, on the ground that the splendour of their retinues distracted the devotions of his monks, whom he wished to serve God in oblivion as well as in poverty, and that such visitors were all too apt to come heavily laden with gifts.[2] The prohibition was aimed particularly at the Dukes of Burgundy who had given Citeaux a great hall designed chiefly for their own use.[3] Odo, the first and ever-generous patron of the 'Novum Monasterium,' had died on a crusade, and by his own request was buried with the monks.[4] His successor, Hugo, who had followed his father's custom of visiting the monastery on all high feasts with his gaily caparisoned knights, was suggesting now that he decorate their chapel that it might be a worthy sepulchre of so illustrious a line of princes.[5] It was just this continued patronage that Stephen wished to prevent. He had seen Molesme turned from her high quest by rich gifts and benefices, and following the example of other contemporary Benedictine monasteries, sell her independence for the favour of princes; he knew far too many abbots who had

[1] All but eight monks had returned to Molesme with Robert. *Ann. Cist., l.c.*, p. 16; Guillelmus, *Vita*, c. III, par. 18, Migne, *l.c.*, vol. CLXXXV, col. 237.

[2] *Ann. Cist., l.c.*, p. 51; *Exord. Mag.*, lib. I, c. 27; *AA. SS., l.c.*, p. 497; *Annales Benedic., l.c.*, p. 498.

[3] *Ann. Cist., l.c.*; *Gall. Christ.*, vol. IV, p. 980.

[4] *Ann. Cist., l.c.*; Petit, *Histoire des Ducs de Bourgogne*, vol. I, p. 268.

[5] *Ann. Cist., l.c.*

become feudal lords, fighting for temporal possessions rather than seeking a more perfect life in Christ; and he did not intend that Citeaux or its abbot should follow their example. Then, too, he wanted his monks to feel that they were dependent on no earthly power in order that they might rely more absolutely on God.[1] So he discouraged even the casual visitors [2] whose alms filled the monastic coffers, and refused tithes, a recognized source of income.

One may well wonder how he hoped to attract novices by such austerity. What could Citeaux offer, for example, in comparison with Cluny, whose allowances and pittances made monastic life, if not luxurious, certainly far from abstemious? [3] Little, indeed, save desolate poverty, bleak self-denial, and exhausting manual labour. However, Stephen knew that this austerity was twice blessed since it would not only attract eventually the only type of novice he cared to receive, the one who would develop into a saint, but that it would just as certainly repel any who might desire to assume the cowl merely to escape the responsibilities of life. Such a policy was indeed heroic, but it well-nigh extinguished the little community.

Hugo was understandably indignant at what seemed to him base ingratitude and withdrew his support.[4] Others followed his example, and the monks were left without an earthly protector at a time when their own strength seemed insufficient for their needs. Then came a failure of crops and its consequent famine,[5] followed by pestilence, caused by the still undrained marshes.[6] Even Stephen might have questioned then the wisdom of his policy, but he was undaunted. Serene, even happy, he insisted that the routine of work and prayer continue without interruption.[7] He had

[1] Wm. of Malmesbury, *l.c.*, par. 337. [2] *Usus Cist.*, Migne, *l.c.*, vol. CLXVI.
[3] S. Bernard., *l.c.* [4] *Ann. Cist.*, *l.c.*, p. 53.
[5] *Ann. Cist.*, *l.c.*, p. 57; *Annales Benedic.*, *l.c.*, p. 513.
[6] *Ann. Cist.*, *l.c.*, p. 58.
[7] *AA. SS.*, *l.c.*, p. 497; *Exord. Mag.*, lib. I, c. 3; *Ann. Cist.*, *l.c.*

never desired that the life at Citeaux should be one of ease. Difficulties and hardships were to him but opportunities for increased service. Nowhere does he show himself more spiritually akin to Francis than in his acceptance of adversity. Indeed, it seemed to him that God's approval was lacking unless everything went against him. When the supply of food was exhausted, he went out with the brethren to the neighbouring towns to beg, but even in this extremity he would not allow them to accept the generous gift of a simoniacal priest.[1]

Once the countryside heard of the desperate need of the monks, gifts of food poured in,[2] and the immediate danger of starvation was past, although Stephen accepted only what was necessary to carry them over to harvest time.[3] As for the other danger, that of the extinction of the monastery, it was relieved by the advent in 1113 of a band of thirty noble Burgundians, men of all ages, under the leadership of Bernard,[4] who was to become in his time the greatest of all Cistercians. Their choice of Citeaux was a justification of Stephen's policy, for these who would have been a welcome addition to any community, had chosen this one as being the poorest and most isolated, and therefore the one above all others where the will of God rather than that of man prevailed.[5] So manifest a proof of divine favour did not go unnoticed. Hugo of Burgundy made his peace with Stephen. Other novices offered themselves for acceptance, and the tide set in their favour. Citeaux up to this time was not the seat of an order, but a poverty-stricken monastery with a most uncertain future. The first monks had all been Benedictines, familiar with the rule and desiring nothing better. When postulants began to

[1] *Ann. Cist.*, *l.c.*, p. 57; *Exord. Mag.*, c. 34; *AA. SS.*, *l.c.*, *Annales Benedic.*, *l.c.*
[2] *Exord. Mag.*, *l.c.*; *Annales Benedic.*, *l.c.*
[3] *Ann. Cist.*, *l.c.*, p. 54; *Annales Benedic.*, *l.c.*
[4] *Ann. Cist.*, *l.c.*, p. 56; *AA. SS.*, *l.c.*, p. 499.
[5] *Exord. Mag.*, lib. I, c. 27; *AA. SS.*, *l.c.*, p. 500; *Annales Benedic.*, *l.c.*, p. 513.

come in great numbers, a written rule was necessary for their instruction. Nor could Citeaux accommodate them all,[1] and when neighbouring barons offered tracts of woodland free for the clearing, the way seemed to open for the establishment of daughter houses. In the next two years four of these were founded: La Ferté in 1113, Pontigny in 1114, and Clairvaux and Morimond in 1115.[2]

The original Benedictine rule made no provision for anything like a congregation. Each monastery was independent and under the absolute jurisdiction of its own abbot, their common rule providing a sort of moral union. In the eighth century Benedict of Aniane had tried to organize the convents of western France into a congregation, but after his death in 821 the disorder was worse than it had been before.[3] Later the Cluniac movement worked a more permanent organization, but its defects were most decidedly evident at just this time when the abbot chanced to be both weak and worthless.[4] Anxious to avoid the possibility of such abuse of power on the part of a superior, Stephen devised a federal government, not only because it seemed more efficient, but because it was more apt to promote brotherly love among the different houses.[5] That it was successful is shown by its having been adopted later by the Franciscans and the Dominicans and even by the Benedictines themselves.

Stephen's constitution, the 'Carta Caritatis,' or Charter of Love, is 'a monument of constructive genius.' Apparently 'mindful of the various privileges recognized by the feudal system, it begins by renouncing on the part of the superior monastery, all claims to temporal emolument from the daughter foundations: "But for love's sake (*gratia charitatis*) we desire to retain the care of their souls;

[1] *Ann. Cist.*, *l.c.*, p. 69.
[2] *Ann. Cist.*, *l.c.*; *AA. SS.*, *l.c.*, p. 500. [3] *AA. SS.*, II Feb., p. 619.
[4] This was Pontus who soon afterwards gave up his office in disgust.
[5] *Cart. Carit.*, c. II, Migne, *l.c.*, vol. CLXVI.

so that should they swerve from the holy way and the observance of the Holy Rule, they may through our solicitude return to rectitude of life." Then follows the command that all Cistercian foundations obey implicitly the *regula* of Saint Benedict, as understood and practised at Citeaux, follow the customs of Citeaux . . . "so that without discordant actions we may live by one love, one rule and like practices (*una charitate, una regula similibusque vivamus moribus*).'"[1]

Uniformity of discipline was secured by making the strict observance of this rule obligatory on all monasteries and on the individual monks, and enforcement of this discipline was insured by the organization.[2] The Order is regarded as one family united by ties of blood and emerging from a common ancestor, Citeaux, whose abbot was the 'Pater Universale Ordinis,' and supreme over all the other abbots. He alone had the right of universal visitation, and during the time he was at any convent, was its acting head. He himself, however, was amenable to the general chapter, which consisted of the abbots of the four filiations, La Ferté, Pontigny, Clairvaux, and Morimond, and five abbots chosen from each group. This council could admonish him four times for such offences as disobedience to the rule, laxity, or lack of zeal, and could finally depose him if he still proved recalcitrant. In this way provision was made to guard against the weakness of any one official, as well as against worldliness, indolence, or general lack of zeal.[3] The first meeting of the council was in 1116,[4] which date may be considered the birthday of the Cistercian Order. The rule was adopted and was confirmed by Pope Calixtus II in 1119.[5]

Each convent chose its own head instead of having one

[1] Taylor, *Mediæval Mind*, vol. I, p. 377.
[2] *Cart. Carit.*, c. 3.
[3] *Ibid.*, c. 5.
[4] *Annales Benedic.*, *l.c.*, p. 581.
[5] Jaffé, *Regesta*, vol. I, p. 582, no. 4969.

appointed by the general superior; the abbots of the four filiations could visit the convents originating from theirs and were required to do so at least once a year. Controversies between abbots were settled by the general chapter at its annual meetings, where unruly abbots were corrected and deposed.[1] Thus every superior shared the power of enforcing the rule and of maintaining the organization. The government was on the whole aristocratic rather than monarchical.

The *regula* of Saint Benedict was far from easy, and Stephen, in his eagerness to make twelfth-century monasticism reflect the true spirit of the earlier age, intensified its austerity. The doctrine of asceticism was pushed as far as human endurance allowed. From the various constitutions dating from his administration may be gathered some idea of the extent to which he carried his insistence on absolute poverty:[2] on the altar a crucifix of painted wood, the simplest of silver chalices and earthenware cruets; in the church a single iron candlestick and censers of brass, vestments of coarse linen or fustian, and everywhere the simplest of furnishings. The stole could be of silk, but it must be without ornament; copes and dalmatics were forbidden.[3] Stephen's horror of outward ornamentation in sacred things led him to secure, in ritual as in vestment, the emphatic expression of a bare and unadorned simplicity. All Cistercian houses must be erected in secluded valleys;[4] the architecture must be most austere, neither high towers, pinnacles nor turrets, nor without rich ornaments, carvings, nor sculpture within.[5]

[1] *Usus Cist.*, c. 72, Migne, *l.c.*, vol. CLXVI.

[2] Besides the *Carta Caritatis* (1119), there are the *Usus Antiquiores Cisterciensis* (same period), the *Instituta Capituli Generalis* (1134), the *Exordium Magnum* and the *Exordium Parvum.*

[3] *Exord. Mag.*, lib. I, c. 27; Wm. of Malmesbury, *l.c.*, par. 336; *AA. SS.*, II Apr., p. 497; *Ann. Cist.*, *l.c.*, pp. 14, 28, 51.

[4] *Inst. Cap. Gen.*, c. 1, *Ann. Cist.*, vol. I, p. 272.

[5] *Inst. Cap. Gen.*, cc. 10, 19. That this insistence on simplicity did not preclude

In this barring of all signs of luxury from the churches they rejected the example set by their neighbours of Cluny, who were assembling painted glass, marble and alabaster statues, gold and jewelled vessels, silk and velvet vestments encrusted with precious stones, and a correspondingly ceremonious ritual on the ground that nothing was too good for the service of God.

The same austerity characterized the lives of the brethren. Saint Benedict had allowed the vegetables to be cooked in oil; Stephen forbade even that, although he allowed milk to be substituted for one of their cooked dishes in harvest time.[1] It is interesting to note that in this age, barely emerged from the darkness of the past centuries, he insisted on the observance of a certain nicety at table, forbidding the crudenesses that might naturally creep in as the accompaniment of poverty.[2]

The simple habit of undyed wool prescribed by Alberic was retained and worn day and night. They still slept on the bed of straw which they had in their little timber huts.[3] Certainly, these Cistercians may justly claim to have maintained an exact fidelity to both letter and spirit of the Benedictine rule longer than any other order that sprang from it. Such consistent asceticism, while it gained the admiration of laymen, was far from being appreciated by their Benedictine neighbours, who saw in it a censure of their own laxity. The rule provided for a scriptorium, but while the monks were diligent copyists, the ideals of the Order did not incline to learning. Stephen's insistence on the most accurate version of the Bible, to obtain which he even consulted Hebrew authorities,[4] and his efforts to

beauty of line is seen in the many ruins of Cistercian abbeys, notably Fountains and Heisterbach, and in the still existing churches of Fontenay and Pontigny which date from Stephen's time.

[1] *Exord. Mag.*, *l.c.*; *Usus Cist.*, c. 84; *Inst. Cap. Gen.*, cc. 14, 49.

[2] *Usus Cist.*, c. 76.

[3] *Ibid.*, c. 82; *Annales Benedic.*, vol. v, p. 498; *Inst. Cap. Gen.*, cc. 4, 15; Wm. of Malmesbury, *l.c.*, par. 336

[4] *Ann. Cist.*, *l.c.*

secure original Benedictine music, indicate an undoubtedly scholarly instinct. Later they had schools, but on the whole the Order produced but few great thinkers. Their manuscripts now extant lack the illuminations, elaborate capitals, jewelled covers, and golden clasps which make those of the Benedictines such priceless works of art.[1]

The Cistercians refused to avail themselves of such usual sources of monastic revenues as tithes, public masses, rich shrines, baptisms, the charge of parish churches,[2] etc., so they could do but little at first in the way of almsgiving, although Stephen's purse was ever the open treasury of the poor.[3] As the various tracts cleared by the monks became more productive, they gave away their annual surplus, stores to provide for lean years seeming a direct violation of their ideal of absolute dependence on God's bounty. They were primarily agriculturists, which may explain their ability to live on so meagre a diet, and may also explain their general contentment, as both of these virtues grew less pronounced after the care of the grange was given over to the *conversi* or lay brethren and the monks devoted themselves more particularly to the duties of church and cloister.

In Stephen's day all worked in the field. Like Saint Benedict, he insisted that all monastic labour be for necessity rather than for luxury, but he made the additional stipulation that when what was essential had been provided, the remainder of their time be used for meditation, and that whatever surplus there was be given away rather than sold.[4] He did not intend that the brethren should ever forget their high calling, nor that they should ever feel it was possible to relax their offices. Even in harvest time the regular round of service was preserved, although the

[1] *Inst. Cap. Gen.*, cc. 2, 3, 13, 82, 87.
[2] *Exord. Parv.*, c. 15.
[3] Wm. of Malmesbury, *l.c.*
[4] *Ann. Cist.*, *l.c.*, p. 29.

abbots themselves doffed the chasuble as soon as mass was said, and took up the rake.[1]

Stephen Harding was a truly notable man measured by the standards of any age, not only because he was the founder of a monastic order (an honour shared by not a few of his contemporaries), but because of rare administrative gifts manifested in his practical interpretation of a rule framed six centuries earlier, and the spirit of joy he infused into its observance. While most of the facts of his life have been lost, there has come down to us a sense of an ardent, generous humility and happy devotion to his task, which made him so beloved even beyond the walls of his monastery.[2]

The rapid increase of his Order [3] meant the sacrifice of that oblivion for which he longed. Like Bernard he felt that to the true religious the town should be prison and solitude be paradise; [4] but, although he kept his Order out of parish churches and away from the cities, he could not prevent its playing a most important part in the affairs of the world. The monks who came to Citeaux in those early years were men of ability, well able to act as leaders of the many outside the Order who joined them in insisting that the clergy renounce the wealth and luxury in which they lived; and during the twelfth century, at least, the Cistercians were at the bottom of every activity of the Church with their importunate poverty. 'Those frogs never ceased croaking from their marshes!' [5]

After 1119, Stephen was rather overshadowed by the

[1] *Hist. Litt.*, *l.c.*, p. 5.

[2] Wm. of Malmesbury, *l.c.*, par. 337; *Ann. Cist.*, *l.c.*, p. 55; *AA. SS.*, *l.c.*, p. 497; *Annales Benedic.*, *l.c.*, pp. 379, 513.

[3] By 1130 there were 30 houses; by 1168, 288; and by the fourteenth century, 738. *Gall. Christ.*, vol. IV, p. 985; *Ann. Cist.*, *l.c.*, p. 63.

[4] *Ep.* 365, *ad Henricum Moguntinum Archiepiscopum: 'quippe cui oppidum carcer esse debet, et solitudo paradisus. Hic vero a contrariis, et solitudinem pro carcere, et oppidum habet pro paradiso.'* Migne, *l.c.*, vol. CLXXXII.

[5] S. Bernard., *Ep.* 48, *ad Haimericum*, Migne, *l.c.*

magnetic and gifted Bernard de Fontaines, whose advent in 1113 had saved the life of the infant community. As Abbot of Clairvaux, he became not only the central figure of the Order, but the dominant personality and accepted evangelist of this century, whose close saw the coming of the friars. The account of his manifold achievements would fill volumes; [1] equally distinguished as a reformer, crusader, statesman, mystical philosopher, and man of letters, he still maintained the austere life of a simple Cistercian, propagating its ideals into every civilized country, filling its convents with novices from every walk in life, and ruling western Christendom in thought and action for more than twenty-five years. It is because the facts of his life are better known to us that he rather than Stephen has been somewhat erroneously regarded as the highest development of the Cistercian type. During the two years of his novitiate he went beyond all bounds of reason in his fervent asceticism, ignoring his physical senses and so torturing his body that at last it rebelled [2] and demanded thenceforth at least a modicum of consideration, which he never ceased to regard as weakness and a source of humiliation. His novitiate once over, he was sent, June 13, 1115,[3] with twelve disciples, most of them his kinsmen [4] and all of them his seniors, to establish a daughter house. The three other filiations of Citeaux, La Ferté, Pontigny, and Morimond, were founded on tracts granted them for that purpose by neighbouring barons, who recognized the value of the intelligent agricultural methods of these agents of a new

[1] An exhaustive bibliography of Bernardine literature would fill a large volume. The more important contemporary lives of him are to be found in Migne, *l.c.*, vol. CLXXXV b.

[2] *Vita Prima*, lib. I, Migne, *l.c.*,

[3] *Exord. Mag.*, lib. II, c. I; *Vita Prima, l.c.*; Bernard was then barely twenty-five years old.

[4] The company included four brothers, an uncle, and two cousins. Later the father and other brothers joined them, and the one sister entered a neighbouring convent. *Ann. Cist.*, *l.c.*, p. 60; *Vita Prima, l.c.*

civilization, and welcomed them as tenants, inasmuch as their clearing of forests and draining of marshes increased the value of adjoining property. Clairvaux was apparently a step in the dark. When the little band left Citeaux with their meagre appurtenances [1] they struck out toward the northeast, without knowing exactly where they were going. About four miles beyond La Ferté, they entered a deep valley enclosed by mountains, its gloom relieved only by the clear waters of the Aube.[2] The place was called Vallis Absinthialis,[3] either because of the loneliness or because of the dense growth of wormwood; but neither the portentous name nor the dreary solitude daunted these disciples of austere Citeaux,[4] who saw in the tranquillity of the forest a haven wherein they might undertake 'voluntary poverty, work and prayer, serving God in literal poorness of spirit, hunger and thirst, cold and nakedness, in many watches, undertaking the conquest of the wilderness for the welfare of their souls.'[5]

By autumn they had erected a rude shelter, with chapel, hall, and refectory all under the same roof, with earthen floors, windows barely a palm's width, and the crudest of furnishings. The loft formed the dormitory, where they slept in bare boxes made of wooden planks, strewn with chaff or leaves, and lacking even the single blanket allowed by the rule.[6] At first they subsisted entirely on nuts and soup made of beech leaves. With the coming of the winter this failed them, and their garments, mere fragments at the best, wore out.[7] Less heroic than the founders of Citeaux, probably because they had come through persua-

[1] They took a reliquary, sacred vessels, vestments, and liturgical books. *Vita Prima*, lib. I, cc. IV, V, VI, VII, IX.

[2] Guil. de Nangis; *Chron.*, Ann. 1115; *Vita Prima, l.c.*; *Ann. Cist., l.c.*, p. 80.

[3] *Ann. Cist., l.c.*

[4] *Vita Prima*, lib. I, cc. 5, 7; *Exord. Mag.*, lib. II, ch. 1.

[5] *Vita Prima, l.c.*

[6] Meglinger., *Iter*, cc. 66, 67, Migne, *Pat. Lat.*, vol. CLXXXV, b.

[7] *Vita Prima, l.c.*

sion as much as conviction, they became rebellious and threatened to return.[1] Bernard's eloquence was for once impotent. The hungry monks refused to listen to his exhortations. Finally, at his wits' end, we are told that he resorted to prayer, receiving an immediate response in the form of a gift of ten *livres*.[2] So Clairvaux's crisis was past, although the best of the succeeding days brought little beyond the barest necessities. The meagre diet Bernard prescribed for them naturally caused illness; then followed a period of anxious experimenting to learn to just what extent abstinence might be carried [3] and still make possible the manual labour enforced in all houses of the order. At length his system was regulated to their needs. The brethren lived on beans and cabbage while their work with hoe, scythe, and axe [4] by degrees transformed the Vale of Wormwood into the Valley of Light.

The austerity of the life at Clairvaux is shown with great exactness in the letters, sermons, and writings of Bernard and in the accounts of his contemporaries, sources which also reveal how conscious he himself was that its severity was a heroic test of faith and how intent he was on adhering to it as a means of attaining salvation by a life given to the practice of love and humility. In a letter written about 1119 to a young kinsman who had allowed himself to be persuaded to leave Clairvaux for the easier life at Cluny, he rebukes the youth for having abandoned a coarse habit for a costly robe, a diet of vegetables for dainties, and poverty for wealth; for having been betrayed into accepting new, fashionable, worldly garments for those of the peasant. Let him beware, however, for whatever indulgence he gives himself in food, dress, conversation, or pleasure is apostasy. He asks him if salvation is to be

[1] J. Eremita, *Vita Quarta,* lib. II, c. 5.
[2] J. Eremita, *l.c.* [3] *Ann. Cist., l.c.*, p. 84.
[4] *Vita Prima,* lib. I, c. 7; *Ep. Petri de Roya Novitii Claræ-Vallensis ad C. Præpositum Noviomensem,* Migne, *l.c.*, vol. CLXXXII.

furthered by these elegant garments and this fine living, rather than by frugality. 'Do soft and warm tunics, expensive cloths, large sleeves, an ample hood, a thick, soft coverlet and fine linen make a saint?' he asks. 'These are the comforts of the sick, not the weapons of the army. Wine and fine flavour and fat things fight for the body, not for the soul. Broiled meats fatten the flesh, not the spirit.' He reminds Robert that the hermits in Egypt served God many years without even fish. 'Pepper, ginger, and spices delight the palate, but salt with hunger is sufficient condiment to one who lives soberly and prudently: the food one spurns when indolent, one takes with a relish after a day's toil. Cabbage, beans, and coarse bread are unappetizing to an idle person, but are delicacies to the labourer, for idleness produces distaste, but exercise, hunger. Watchings, fastings, and manual labour are tiring, certainly, but compared with eternal burnings, are mere trifles; and solitude is far easier to bear than outer darkness. Nor is silence a trial when one considers the punishment meted throughout eternity to him who used vain words or dealt in lies. A couch of boards is as nothing when compared with weeping and gnashing of teeth; and he who keeps the night watch conscientiously knows not if his bed be hard or soft.' [1]

In this letter one sees not only an exposition of the ideals of the new monastery, but a condemnation of what seemed to Bernard the unpardonable laxity of the Cluniacs, then under the guidance of the worthless Pontus. Rich gifts from admiring laymen, privileges from grateful pontiffs, abolition of manual labour for the monks, had united to deprive the celebrated monastery of most of her pristine rigour. One can readily understand how the sight of a religious community living in such self-indulgence and luxury would rouse Bernard's ire. Even after Robert had been returned to Clairvaux and Pontus had been replaced

[1] S. Bernard., *Ep.* 1, Migne, *l.c.*

by Peter the Venerable, one of the most lovable men of his time, the censures continued. At last matters reached such a point that, about 1125, William, Abbot of Saint Thierry, near Rheims, himself a Cluniac and one of Bernard's closest friends,[1] urged him to present his charges that a defence might be made. In response to this request, Bernard wrote his *Apologia*, a vehement attack which rather exceeded the limits of prudence and of Christian charity, although the cause of his reproach was laxity inconsistent with their vows, rather than any gross immorality.

'I will not speak,' he said, 'of the immense height of their churches, nor their immoderate length, nor superfluous breadth. Is not this avarice rather than piety? By the sight of wonderful and costly vanities, men are prompted to give rather than to pray. In the churches are hung not mere *coronæ*, but wheels studded with gems and surrounded by lights scarcely brighter than the jewels with which the wheels are set. Instead of candlesticks, they have great trees of heavy brass, skilfully constructed and glittering with jewels. The very pavement is covered with images of the saints, which is irreverent, — often the mouth of an angel is spit upon, the face of a saint is battered by the heels of the passers-by. If we cannot spare sacred figures, can we not spare at least beautiful colours? Why should we decorate what must speedily be soiled? Is the object of such things to promote penitence of the contrite or the admiration of the beholder? The eyes of the pilgrim are gladdened by the sight of relics gleaming with gold. They show, indeed, far more admiration of what is beautiful than veneration for what is sacred. On the walls of the cloisters where the brethren read, what place have these absurd monsters, these odd and beautiful deformities, so

[1] William's unfinished life of Bernard is perhaps the best account of him that we have. It forms the first book of the *Vita Prima*, Migne, *Pat. Lat.*, vol. CLXXXV, b.

striking and varied that the brethren are attracted to gaze at them rather than read their books. The statues of stone are splendidly adorned but the poor are left naked and bare.[1] At dinner they have one course heaped upon another; large fish in place of meat and many dainties to tempt their appetite.'[2]

Peter defended his order vigorously, and for his part accused the Cistercians of a hypocritical poverty, so that the incident did little to lessen the existent antipathy. Some years later, when Innocent II, whose claims to the papacy Bernard championed with such marked success, visited Clairvaux, he was received with greatest courtesy by men in patched habits, carrying a roughly carved wooden cross. Not even the presence of so illustrious a guest altered the frugal repast, although Innocent was given a larger share of black bread and sour wine than they, and a fish caught in the river was served him and his court. In recognition of Bernard's services, Innocent granted all Cistercian houses freedom from tithes and taxes, but at his next visit to Burgundy, he stopped at Cluny.[3]

The wealth of the Church and the worldly-mindedness of the clergy were grievous sights to Bernard.[4] His denunciations of their lives and of their morals would, if collected, form a sizable volume. To him a monk with money was as great a sinner as Ananias and Sapphira, and a wealthy cleric was quite as bad. Of course 'he who serves the altar should live by the altar, but this does not mean that one should wallow in luxury, nor grow proud and avaricious. To live by the altar does not signify golden bridles, decorated saddles, silver spurs, purple and ermine.

[1] This is not a just accusation. In one year alone Cluny bestowed alms on at least 17,000 poor.

[2] *Apologia*, cc. 8, 9, 10, 12, Migne, *l.c.*, vol. CLXXXII.

[3] *Vita Prima*, lib. II; Jaffé, *Regesta*, vol. I, p. 568. The Cluniacs were so indignant at this exemption, especially as they owned large amounts of tithes payable from Cistercian land, that at Gigny they destroyed a Cistercian convent.

[4] *De Adventu Dom.*, *Sermo* 111, Migne, *l.c.*, vol. CLXXXIII.

Whatever is taken beyond bare necessity is robbery and sacrilege.'[1] For 'the faithful priest regards with the innocence of a dove all wealth, whether it be in the form of benefits bestowed by God on man, or offerings of men to God; he keeps nothing back for his own use, seeking never the gifts of the people, only their good.'[2]

Even the pontiffs themselves were fearlessly rebuked for their love of vanities, their indifference to the poor.[3] The ideal pope, he said, imitates him who had not where to lay his head;[4] who, although the Son of God, chose a life of privation as being his perfect example to men. The *castellum* he entered,[5] that is, voluntary poverty, is the only ark of safety remaining to his followers. As for the bishops, they were the worst sinners of all. Their golden ornaments and embroidered robes were signs of their depravity, witnesses of their downfall. 'If you, insensate sons of Adam, seek for luxury, to what is your desire? How can your preaching of blessed poverty be then convincing to men! To desire the pagans who live without God was the cause of the perfidy of Judas.'[6] In poverty, simplicity, and almsgiving alone will they find their salvation. Would there were more like the holy men at York[7] and at London[8] who chose to live lives of blessed self-denial for the sake of God's poor. But 'a good bishop is a rare bird.'[9]

[1] *Ep. 2, ad Fulconem.* '*Conceditur ergo tibi, ut si bene deservis, de altario vivas; non autem ut de altario luxurieris, ut de altario superbias, ut inde compares tibi frena aurea, sellas depictas, calcaria deargentata, varia griseaque pellicea a collo et manibus ornatu purpureo diversificata. Denique quidquid præter necessarium victum ac simplicem vestitum de altario retines tuum non est; rapina est; sacrilegium est.*' Migne, *l.c.*, vol. CLXXXII.

[2] *De Moribus et Officio Episc.*, cc. III, X, XI; Migne, *l.c.*

[3] Migne, *l.c.*

[4] *Super 'Missus Est,' Homilia* IV, *l.c.*, vol. CLXXXIII; *De Consid.*, lib. I, c. 8, *l.c.*, vol. CLXXXII.

[5] St. Luke, 10:38; *Sermones de Diverses*, 48.

[6] *In Festo Omnium Sanctorum, Sermo*, *l.c.*, col. 456.

[7] *Ep.* 95, 319, *ad Turstinum Archiep. Eboracensem*, *l.c.*, vol. CLXXXII.

[8] *Ep.* 24, *ad Gillebertum, Epis. Lond.*, *l.c.*

[9] '*Raris avis in terris,*' *Ep.* 372, *ad. P. Episc. Palenitum*, *l.c.* But even at

Poverty alone was not enough, however; there must be with it a love of poverty, a poverty of spirit. 'Blessed are the poor in spirit, the poor in intention, who desire only spiritual things. These alone are pleasing to God; these alone may hope for salvation.' It was this spirit which he praised in Pope Eugenius III, one of his own monks, who he said did not need to become the father of the poor to be poor in spirit.[1]

Bernard's influence over men was due to the intense love he bore them, and in this he is very like Francis of Assisi although the latter lacked the bigotry, intolerance, injustice, which at times characterized the noble Cistercian. A consuming passion for the welfare of his fellows dominates his letters, his sermons, his mysticism, and above all, his rule at Clairvaux. It made whoever heard him leave all to follow where he directed, to die on the Syrian sands or to live in the rigid austerity of the cloister. In spirit, Bernard was a true crusader. His father had followed Odo of Burgundy to Jerusalem. The departure and return of that great host must have made a great impression on his son, then a mere child. The failure of his own crusade was perhaps the great sorrow of his life. He never lost sight of the fact that his monks were poor soldiers for a poor Christ, and so long as he lived, they were unswerving in their allegiance to this ideal he held for them. Only when they turned from it did they become '*Lances Longinis, grex albus, Ordo nefandus.*'[2]

this time there were good prelates in Lyons, Rheims, Sens, Rouen, and Tours, all of whom he knew. *Gall. Christ.*, IV, 115, 117; IX, 83, 84.

[1] *Prologue to De Consid.*, bk. V, Migne, *l.c.*, vol. CLXXXII, col. 727.

[2] The austerity of the Order lasted until the thirteenth century. Jacques de Vitry, *Hist. Orient.*, c. 13.

CHAPTER III

THE MONASTIC REFORMERS (*continued*)

1. *The Good Men of Grammont*

Contemporary with the Carthusian Order was that of the Good Men of Grammont, founded about 1080 by Stephen, son of the Vicomte de Thiers, in Arvenne. Beyond the fact that he was born about 1048 and died in 1124,[1] there is, unhappily, little known of his life. Unlike Bruno, Stephen seems not to have been influenced by the condition of the Church, but like him, he was devoutly seeking apostolic poverty. The earliest life of him now extant was written by the seventh prior of Grammont about a century after the foundation of the Order and was based largely on tradition, aided by materials from an earlier biography no longer in existence.[2] According to this account, Stephen went to Italy when a mere child of twelve,[3] in company with his father. At Benevento he fell ill, and as his father was obliged to return to France, the boy was left in care of the good Archbishop Milo who was possibly a relative.[4] After his recovery he stopped on some years acting as assistant in the administration of the diocese. According to tradition, even at this time he was distinguished for his remarkable learning.

Benevento was not far from the mountain fastnesses of

[1] *Vita S. Stephani*, auctore Girardo, Martène et Durand, *Ampliss. Coll.*, vol. vi, col. 1043, etc. As this life contains the Bull of Stephen's canonization by Pope Clement, 1189, it was evidently written after that time. Jaffe, *Regesta*, *l.c.*, p. 877, no. 10141; *AA. SS.*, II Feb., p. 204.

[2] *S. Stephani, Dicta et Facta*, St. de Liciacus. See Introduction to *Vita* in Martène, *l.c.*; Migne, *l.c.*, vol. cc, col. 1163.

[3] The object of this journey is incorrectly given in the *Vita* as the translation of the body of Saint Nicholas of Bari. This event did not take place until 1087, some years after Stephen had left Italy.

[4] *Hist. Litt.*, vol. x, p. 410.

Calabria where dwelt those holy men who having renounced flocks, possessions, and all worldly occupations, were following the example of the Apostles, holding all things in common and distributing to every man according to his need. 'That the greater might obtain the place of the lesser, and the *præcessor* become *ministrator*, they had no servants, but themselves performed all tasks. They found favour with God and man and lacked not sufficient food and clothing. By their holy lives they incited clerks and laymen to loftier living. They avoided cupidity, the root of all evil.' [1]

Stephen was much impressed by the accounts Milo gave of these hermits whom he frequently visited and cited as patterns of holiness. It is not impossible that he himself went to their monastery. At all events, it was at this time apparently that he conceived the idea of following their example, although for some reason he did not consider joining them. After Milo's death in 1072 [2] he went to Rome, where he spent four years seeking permission, first from Pope Alexander II and then from his successor, Gregory VII, to form a community after the model of that in Calabria. Gregory's hesitation seems to have been due to fear lest Stephen's delicate frame prove unequal to so rigorous a discipline, but at length, in 1078, he yielded to the young enthusiast's solicitations [3] and granted his request. Stephen at once returned to France, bade farewell to family and friends, and set forth to find a place 'wherein he might most fitly serve God. He knew that to those who would seek and serve God, the presence of men and the abundance of temporal things are harmful, but poverty and solitude are useful. After a time he found what he sought.' [4]

He went first to Aureille in Aquitaine, a few leagues from

[1] *Vita*, c. 6, col. 1053. [2] *Ibid.*, cc. 8, 9, cols. 1053–54.
[3] *Ibid.* [4] *Ibid.*, c. 8.

Limoges where he placed himself under the direction of Saint-Gautier, founder of Saint-Jean d'Aureille, a monastery of canons. But Saint-Gautier had also erected a nunnery in the neighbourhood, and Stephen, disliking the proximity of women, soon left and, 'led by Christ, came to a wooded mountain hard by the city of Limoges, called Muret, where he found springs and rocks and a land desert and inaccessible, wooded, unfrequented by men, but frequented by wild beasts. The place offered to its new guests the coldest of drinks and a dwelling exposed to the winds, and by unmistakable signs, gave promise of hardship for the body and peace for the mind.' [1]

Here he built a small cabin, and then in a very special manner, vowed himself to Jesus Christ. He had retained but one thing belonging to his father — a ring, and this he placed on his finger with the words, 'I, Stephen, renounce the devil and all his pomps and offer myself to God.' Then, having written these words on a piece of parchment, he laid this on his head and added: 'O God Almighty, who livest eternally and reignest One in Three Persons, I promise to serve thee in this hermitage in the Catholic faith, in sign whereof I place this writing on my head and this ring on my finger, so that at the hour of my death this promise may serve as my defence against my enemies.' Next he addressed the Virgin Mary, saying, 'Holy Mary, Mother of God, I commend my body, soul and senses to thy Son and to thee,' [2] and so, by a literal forsaking of the world, he entered upon his life of service to an ideal.

Soon after he took this self-imposed vow, two cardinals, Gregory of Sant' Angelo and Peter Leone, who as Innocent II and Anacletus II, were later to contend for the papacy and well-nigh wreck the Church with schism, were sent to Limoges. While there they visited Stephen. Seeing the way he lived, alone on a frigid mountain, in a sterile land

[1] *Vita*, c. 13. [2] *Ibid.*, c. 15.

with no food in sight, they asked him if he were monk, hermit or canon. He replied that he was only a poor sinner who had been taught by Milo and that he had chosen the life of a hermit the better to avoid the tumult of the world and to devote himself to prayer.[1]

In this wild solitude, surrounded by rocks and trees, he passed forty-six years in the practice of almost unbelievable austerities. Disciples gathered about him by degrees to place themselves under his care, and he was ever most compassionate toward them, watching over them with a truly fatherly solicitude lest they suffer from the rigorous discipline he imposed upon himself. Life in the little community was ascetic in the extreme; their food was simple and scant, chosen 'for necessity, not for pleasure.'[2] Clothing was spare and neither increased nor diminished with the changing seasons,[3] although, as Girard says, it was almost always winter. Their couches were hard 'that they might not yield over much repose to the wearied flesh.'[4] At first they lived on wild herbs and roots until some shepherds saw their need, and brought them a little coarse bread each day. Stephen did not allow himself this regularly, as he often fasted all day, ministering to those who came to him for counsel, after the pattern of the Apostles 'who had not time to eat because of those going and coming.' More than this, he tortured his body by wearing always a coat of mail next his skin; while he was so constant in prayer, so frequent in his genuflexions, striking the earth each time with forehead and nose, that his knees grew callous as a camel's and his nose crooked.[5]

[1] *Vita*, cc. 32, 33, 34. [2] *Ibid.*, c. 16. [3] *Ibid.*, cc. 17, 18.

[4] *Ibid.*, c. 19: '*Erat enim ex tabulis ligneis instar sepulcri in terram consertis, omni stramento, omnique lecti stramine carens, præter illam turnicam ferream quam semper ad nudam gestabat carnem; et vilissimum dumtaxat habitum quo desuper manebat indutus.*'

[5] *Ibid.*, c. 21: '*Numerum autem genuflexionem ejus, quas terram deosculando et cum fronte nasoque percutiendo humiliter faciebat, scire non possumus, quem utique propter earum sæpissimam iterationem ipsum etiam credimus ignorasse. Scimus*

Poverty was the absolute fundamental idea that Stephen kept ever before himself. When he was dying, his disciples said to him: 'Holiest Father, when you were with us, God gave us necessaries because of your love, but after your death, how shall we live?'

'I leave you to God,' he replied. 'Adhere to poverty and love it, nor depart from the true way. If you go after temporal things you will lose much. We have lived in this desert well cared for, for fifty years. Others have gone to places more fertile, but the bounty of God has always surrounded us with abundance.' [1]

Further confirmation of Stephen's insistence on poverty is furnished by the rule,[2] the general tenor of which shows that he dreaded the effect of possession upon the spirit of the Order and tried to guard against accumulation of any form of wealth.[3] For example, Chapter IV, '*De terris non habendis,*' says: 'For every man when he is dead, land enough to make a grave. Verily the wonder would be great if a man should seek to rob of his grave another dead man who lay next to him. Brethren, ye ought to be dead to the world, as the Apostle saith: "We should be dead to sin that we may live to God." Doth it not suffice you to have land enough so that ye can build a cell wherein to dwell in seclusion? Men should wish to possess God with the Heaven and earth and whatsoever are his. As the Apostle saith: "All things are yours and ye are Christ's and Christ is God's."' There is danger in possessing any land beyond that on which the cell stands, danger due to the covetousness inherent in human nature, as 'all land is continuous, and if you should acquire any portion of it,

tamen quod manibus ac genibus in modum cameli earumdem assiduitate genuflexionum callos contraxerat et nasum curvarerat in obliquum.'

[1] *Vita,* cc. 39–40.

[2] Written in 1141 and confirmed by Pope Urban III in 1186. Jaffé, *Regesta,* vol. I, p. 858, no. 9831. Mabillon and Martène both claim that this was written by Stephen, but chapters 9, 10, 11, 12, 14, 15–33 seem to be of later origin.

[3] *Regula,* Migne, *Pat. Lat.,* vol. CCIV, col. 1140.

then you would wish to have that which adjoins it, and so your cupidity would never or scarce ever find an end. Thus you would incur that terrible curse which the Lord threatens through Isaiah the prophet. "Woe unto them that join house to house." Therefore, brethren, forego the earth that God may deign to draw you after him to Heaven.'[1]

For the same reason he disapproves of their having churches, 'without which they may more closely imitate the Apostle who says: "Forgetting those things which are behind, and reaching forth unto them which are before, I press toward the prize of the high calling of God in Christ Jesus."'[2] Moreover, if they have no churches, they will the more easily avoid another source of danger to monks, the coming of outsiders to ask spiritual solace which they should find in their own churches.

Stephen could not have been blind to the secularization of the older monasteries and their dependence on wealthy patrons which had paralyzed their activities, so it was only natural that he should desire to avert from his disciples the evil that followed in the train of those who sought to save their souls by gifts to holy men.[3]

Ownership of flocks was discouraged lest a great number be the occasion and ground of worldly pride. 'Nothing,' he said, 'is more apt to destroy religion than avarice and great wealth. Moreover, flocks need pasturage. If you have them, you must either possess land of your own or use other people's to furnish them food. Then there would arise great clamour among your neighbours who would say: "Would that these hermits had never come for their possessions do much inconvenience us."'[4]

Beasts were also forbidden, 'lest they be loved too well,

[1] *Regula*, c. IV, col. 1140–41. [2] *Ibid.*, c. V.

[3] See Jacques de Vitry's accounts of the deterioration of monastic orders from this cause.

[4] *Regula*, c. 6.

and interest in divine things be lost by over-interest in what is temporal. Your object is to ascend on high. Why, then, load yourself down with earthly things? Lay not up for yourselves treasures on earth.' [1]

Any just income (*redditus*) might be received if offered, but if the giver later repented of his generosity, or his heirs did not wish to continue it, the brethren were not to go to law to get it; [2] indeed, lawsuits were to be avoided always.[3] Alms, likewise, could be taken if offered, [4] and they might accept sites for dwellings, but they were not to improve these beyond what was necessary.[5] They were particularly enjoined to look upon God as their almsgiver. 'Your store shall never fail while you commit the keys to God.[6] Seek from him alone; if you beg of men, you may weary them.[7] In times of great need, when you have not provision even for one day, you may return to the world to beg,[8] but if you are true to poverty,' he added, 'this necessity will never or scarce ever arise. For if you make God your only treasure by loving poverty, while he has abundance you shall never want. Let poverty be your wealth and your riches for it leads to Heaven. In all things, so far as in you lies, seek to serve God. Be poor in this world, even as he was poor and so shalt thou be rich forever even as he is rich to all eternity.' [9]

After Stephen's death the brethren were driven from Muret by the canons of Saint-Augustin of Limoges, who, coveting the wilderness, laid claim to it and secured possession. The 'Good Men' then moved to Grammont.[10] They did not long maintain the rigid poverty which Stephen had enjoined upon them. Even before the rule was for-

[1] *Regula*, c. 8. [2] *Ibid.*, c. 23. [3] *Ibid.*, c. 31.
[4] *Ibid.*, c. 21. [5] *Ibid.*, c. 30. [6] *Ibid.*, c. 12.
[7] *Ibid.*, c. 10. [8] *Ibid.*, c. 13. [9] *Ibid.*, c. 14.
[10] *Vita*, c. 47. It may have been this experience which led to the insertion of the chapter in the rule (c. 33) which warns the brethren against building on the lands of monks.

mulated, murmurings had evidently begun, if the urgent appeal that they forsake not 'this life' be not misinterpreted; while the chapter concerning fugitives from religion,[1] as well as the significant provision that no men be received who had previously belonged to other orders lest they spread discontent, lends colour to the suspicion of lack of harmony. The simple cells, just sufficient for protection from the weather, which had been Stephen's provision for them, were replaced by substantial monastic buildings before a century had passed,[2] and the Order had begun to spread throughout western and northern France. Stephen had provided for no definite organization and the monks degenerated erelong into disorderly idealists,[3] for these brutal ages demanded iron-handed rulers to keep down the turbulent elements. Yet, although the heroic age of the 'Good Men' was short, while it lasted it furnished to devout souls a refuge from the sordidness of the times and, possibly more than any other twelfth-century order, opened the way for the mendicant friars.

2. *The Præmonstratensians*

On the west bank of the Rhine between Wesel and Nymwegen, the little old city of Xanten lies on the edge of the plain at the foot of Mount Fürstenberg. Here about the year 1080 [4] was born Norbert of Gennep, son of Count Heribert,[5] a wealthy and powerful nobleman of the Duchy of Cleves. A friend and contemporary of Bernard of Clair-

[1] *Vita.*, c. 53.

[2] Peter Bernard, the fifth prior of the Order, consecrated a second church and covered the refectory with a stone roof. *Thes. Nov.*, vol. I, col. 435, Petrus Bernardus Grandimontis, *Epistolæ*.

[3] See *Vita B. Hugonis de Lucerta*, Martène et Durand, *Ampliss. Coll.*, vol. VI, col. 1143. For the growth of the Order, see *Hist. Litt.*, vol. X, p. 410. It was suppressed in 1769.

[4] Cardinal Gasquet says 1080: *The English Præmonstratensians*, p. 1. Most of the biographers of Norbert give this date, but Wilmans, editor of *Vita A* in *M.G.H. SS.*, vol. XII, says he was born in 1085.

[5] *Vita A*, *l.c.*, p. 671.

vaux, Norbert shared the great Cistercian's eager quest for evangelical poverty, and in his career of wandering preacher and missionary, founder of the Order of Prémontré and Archbishop of Magdeburg, he united in himself the qualities of the mediæval mendicant and the modern statesman.

So far as can be conjectured he was educated in the collegiate church of Saint Victor in Xanten,[1] whose twin spires still mark the place of the martyrdom of the saints from whom the town is named;[2] possibly he went also to the cathedral school of Cologne[3] to which place he was called as canon[4] when he was about twenty years old. Distinguished for his eloquence, his erudition, and his great personal charm, and even at that early age the holder of several rich benefices,[5] this young sybarite found Cologne too limited a field for him and soon made his way to the court of his kinsman,[6] the young Emperor Henry V, where his unusual talents won for him the dual post of chaplain and almoner.[7] In the latter capacity, he was one of the more intimate counsellors of Henry and was often present at the imperial diets. In 1110, his address before the Diet of Ratisbon was so favourably received that he was one of those chosen to accompany the monarch to Rome for his coronation.[8]

[1] Vanden Elsen, G., *Het Leven van den H. Norbertus*, p. 6.

[2] Xanten, Santen. The town was named for Saint Victor and his seventeen companions martyred here during the reign of Diocletian. *AA. SS.*, V Oct., pp. 14–36.

[3] Madelaine, *Hist. de St. Norbert*, p. 33.

[4] *Vita A*, *l.c.*; Herm., *De Mirac. S. Mariæ Laud.*, *M.G.H. SS.*, *l.c.*, p. 655.

[5] Norbert was at this time a sub-deacon. *Vita A*, *l.c.*; *Gesta Arch. Magd.*, c. 26; *M.G.H. SS.*, vol. XIV, p. 412.

[6] Cardinal Gasquet says his mother, Hedwig, was a cousin of Henry IV, *l.c.*; Herm., *Hist. Rest. Abb. Tornac.*, *M.G.H. SS.*, vol. XII, p. 662.

[7] *Vita A*, *l.c.*; Herm., *Hist. Rest. Abb.*, *l.c.*

[8] Among the 'men of letters able to give reasons to all comers for the emperor's various undertakings' was the Welshman David, a teacher at Würtzburg, who was commanded by Henry to write an account of the excursion. This is now lost. *M.G.H. SS.*, vol. VI, p. 243; *Dict. Nat. Biog.*, vol. XIV, pp. 115–17.

The conflict over investitures was then at its height, and Henry's appearance at the papal court gave new zest to the struggle, so that Norbert was called upon to witness the quite unedifying spectacle of the greatest temporal power subjecting the highest spiritual power to indignities unusual even in that day — a spectacle which so disturbed him that, after a vain effort to secure a mitigation of the humiliation inflicted on the august prisoner, he went in person to him and begged absolution from whatever responsibility might rest on his head by virtue of his having been in the imperial train.[1] Moreover, on their return to Germany, when Henry, exercising his newly obtained powers, offered him the rich bishopric of Cambrai, he refused.[2]

Although evidently disapproving of the Emperor's part in the proceedings, he made no move to quit the gay and irresponsible life of the court until 1115, when a narrow escape from death by lightning on the road to Freden changed him from an affable, engaging courtier to the most ascetic of penitents.[3] Returning to Xanten, he retired to the little Benedictine abbey of Siberg, where for some time he shared the life of the monks without joining the order.[4] His next step was to present himself to his former superior, Archbishop Frederick of Cologne, with the rather unusual request that he be ordained as deacon and priest the same day.[5] Permission was given, though reluctantly, as the prelate could not at once forget the impression made by

[1] Hugo, *Vie de S. Norbert*, p. 8; Herm., *Hist. Rest. Abb.*, *l.c.*, p. 662.

[2] Herm., *l.c.*; Baronius, Ann. 1111. Cambrai was then conferred on Burchard, a friend of Norbert's.

[3] The fantastic account of Norbert's conversion, so manifestly borrowed from the scriptural account of Saint Paul's, is told in great detail by all of his biographers. *Vita A*, *l.c.*; *AA. SS.*, I Jun., p. 832; Hugo, *Vie*, pp. 10, 11, etc.

[4] Hugo, *Vie*, p. 13. The Abbey of Siberg was founded in 1057. At this time it was under the guidance of the able Conon, who in 1126 became Bishop of Ratisbon.

[5] *Vita A*, *l.c.*; *AA. SS.*, *l.c.*

the luxury-loving young canon who had graced his court a few years before, and was therefore inclined to distrust his sudden conversion.

The chroniclers have left so characteristic an account of his ordination that it bears repetition. On the appointed day the candidates presented themselves for the ceremony, but Norbert was not among them. After they had taken their places he came in alone, robed in silk and splendidly adorned with gold and jewels. Moving slowly down the aisle, he paused before the altar and while the curious onlookers who crowded the dim old church[1] watched in amazement, his servants came forward, removed his costly raiment and left him standing clad in a penitential robe of sheepskin, tied with a cord. Liturgical vestments were then handed him and he passed on with the rest.[2]

A few weeks more at Siberg, and he returned to Xanten where he attempted to reform the canons of Saint Victor, a thankless undertaking, for while the older priests were rather impressed by his exhortations, the younger ones, his contemporaries, were exasperated and resentful at the censures of one who had so recently outstripped them all in riotous living, and they made Xanten so uncomfortable for him that he was glad to withdraw to a deserted chapel high on Mount Fürstenberg. Here he spent three years, but returning at every possible opportunity in order to exhort the people to righteousness and to rebuke the canons for laxity. Little wonder is it that the latter organized themselves to prevent his ever setting foot in the place again.

He also visited other near-by villages, among them Rolduc,[3] with its adjoining monastery of Kloster-rath, where the Augustinian canons were devoting themselves

[1] Not the present cathedral, but the ninth-century edifice it replaced.
[2] *Vita A*, pp. 670, 672; *AA. SS.*, *l.c.*
[3] Now Herzogenrath. *Vita A*, p. 673.

to the practice of apostolic poverty, and where Norbert undoubtedly received the idea for some of the customs he later inaugurated at Prémontré.

During these years he was becoming more austere and rigorous in his self-discipline; his rude cabin provided a scarcely appreciable shelter from the elements; he went barefoot even in winter; his garb was a sheepskin tunic and a penitential cape, and he observed a strict Lenten fast for the entire year, all of which seemed to him a manner of life in accord with the teachings of the early Church and a fitting discipline for efficient service as a soldier of the Most High.[1] Like Bernard, Norbert grew up in the atmosphere of the Crusades; his mother was related to Godfrey of Bouillon and his father died in the Holy Land, although as his own active life lay in the lull between the First and Second Crusades, he manifested less definite interest in the movement than did his great contemporary.

The austerity of his life and teachings interested many who became converted by his eloquence, but his very success so increased the antipathy to him that when, in 1118, the papal legate, Cuno of Præneste, called a council at Fritzlar[2] in lower Hesse, the clergy of Xanten, led by the canons of Saint Victor, presented a formal complaint against him, accusing him of dangerous fanaticism, of preaching without proper sanction, of attacking the lives of the clergy and prelates, and of living like a monk when he was not a member of a religious order.[3] He was summoned to defend himself, which he did most ably, reminding his accusers that the power of preaching comes from above, that the chief requisite thereof is an immaculate

[1] *Vita A, l.c.*; *AA. SS., l.c.*

[2] *Vita A, l.c.*; Mansi, vol. XXI, col. 178; *Chron. S. Pet. Erphesfurdensis*, ann. 1118, *M.G.H. SS.*, vol. VI; *Vita Theogeri Epis. Mettensis, M.G.H. SS.*, vol. XII, p. 467. The Council of Fritzlar was called in order to establish Gelasius II's authority in Germany, against Henry V and his anti-pope.

[3] *Vita B*, c. 4; *Vita A*, p. 673.

life, and that true religion is to visit the poor and the widows and to keep one's self unspotted from the world. Not only Cuno, but the Archbishops of Mainz, Munich, and Cologne were convinced of the pettiness of the charges and he was absolved. However, because of the schism then existing in the papacy, he was advised not to engender further dissensions, but to present himself before the Pope to receive proper jurisdiction to preach in all countries, and for the present to substitute the conventional cassock for his penitential garb.[1]

By this time Norbert had many enemies among those who knew his early life, and who found him so intolerable after his conversion that to avoid '*nouvelles poursuites*' he resolved to leave his own country and try to get a hearing in France and the Netherlands.[2] Proceeding to Cologne, he renounced his benefices into the hands of the archbishop; then he sold his estates at Xanten distributing the money among the poor; the little chapel on Mount Fürstenberg he gave to his friend Conon of Siberg.[3] For himself, he reserved ten marks, a mule, and the vestments necessary for the celebration of the mass.[4] So at the end of the year 1115, he started forth barefoot, wearing the cassock and accompanied by two servants, one of whom had been the sole witness of his conversion.

As wildly uncouth in his appearance as was Peter the Hermit whose footsteps he now followed on this his first missionary journey, he turned southward to find the Pope of whose whereabouts he was quite ignorant. By the time he reached Huy on the Meuse, he decided the possession of

[1] *Vita A, l.c.*; *AA. SS., l.c.*; *Chron. Gratiæ Dei*, p. 327, *M.G.H. SS.*, vol. xx, p. 687.

[2] Bernhardi, *Lothar von Supplinburg*, p. 95.

[3] *Vita A*, p. 673. Rosenmund says this is an error, as the chapel belonged to Norbert's brother. The most he could do then was to relinquish any future claim he might have to it. *Die ältesten Biographien*, pp. 21–24. Hugo says it had been given Norbert by his friend, Henry d'Alpheim, a pious canon of Cologne.

[4] *Vita A*, p. 674.

a mule and money betokened a lack of faith in Providence, and, giving them away, began begging for his daily bread.

The winter was unusually severe and the strange land and strange language proved no slight obstacles, so that seven long weeks elapsed before Norbert and his companions finally reached Saint Gilles in Languedoc where Gelasius II was holding his court.[1]

Securing the coveted permission to go forth as a missionary apostolic,[2] he retraced his steps northward through the snow and ice, preaching continually, despite his unfamiliarity with the language. Palm Sunday, March 22d, he reached Valenciennes,[3] where his companions, exhausted by exposure and hardship, fell ill and died, and even he, unable to withstand the double strain of anxiety and overwork, was stricken with fever. While he was here, Burchard, Bishop of Cambrai, his former associate at the imperial court, visited the town. Norbert heard of his coming and went to see him. It was with difficulty that the Bishop recognized in the tattered, barefooted beggar the erstwhile courtier, but he welcomed him gladly, and cared for him most tenderly during his illness, while his secretary, Hugh of Fosses, impressed by the account of Norbert's renunciation of wealth for the sake of his soul's salvation, offered himself as his disciple.[4] In Rogation Week the two left Valenciennes and during the summer wandered through

[1] *Vita A*, *l.c.*; *Chron. de Mailros*, p. 164, ann. 1118, *SS. Rer. Angl. Vet.*, vol. I; Jaffe, *l.c.*, no. 4901; Muratori, *R.I.S.*, vol. III, pt. 1, p. 411. Paschal, whom Norbert knew in Rome, died in 1118. His successor, Gelasius II, had been unable to withstand the Roman barons and had fled to Languedoc.

[2] *Chron. de Mailros*, *l.c.*; *Dominus Norbertus papam Gelasium adiens officium ab eo prædicationis accepit. Vita A*, p. 674.

[3] Here occurred the 'miracle of tongues' which accredits Norbert with supernatural powers of making himself understood. Doubtless he was becoming more familiar with Gallic by this time, and was also aided by his gestures, as he was a fervent orator. *Vita A*, p. 674.

[4] The earlier accounts of Norbert's stay at Valenciennes and of his meeting with Burchard are careless and inaccurate. See Herm., *De Mirac.*, for a more authentic version. For the value of the contemporary lives of Norbert, see Rosenmund, *Die ältesten Biographien.*

castle, villa, and town, preaching, teaching, reconciling dissents, and healing the poor and lepers, relying on the charity of the people for food and shelter.[1] Everywhere they were accorded a most enthusiastic welcome: shepherds ran to the villages to announce their coming, and bells were rung as they entered city gates.

In the autumn, hearing that Gelasius was dead and that his successor, Calixtus II, was to hold a council at Rheims, Norbert decided to go there to secure a renewal of the favours received at Saint Gilles.[2] When he arrived in October, he presented so sorry a spectacle that he was unable to secure an audience with the pope. After three days of fruitless endeavour he left, sad and disheartened.[3] As he approached the Abbey of Saint-Thierry, some three leagues from the city gates, he stopped to rest by the roadside, when Bartholomew, Bishop of Laon and kinsman of Calixtus, passed by on his way to attend the council. Moved by curiosity, he paused and asked why they were there. Norbert eagerly told of his desire to evangelize people in all the world, and of his vain attempt to secure the papal sanction for his work, because of the great multitude about the court.[4] A more sympathetic listener than this good bishop could not easily have been found. Of noble birth, educated at Rheims where later he held a canonry, he had accepted the bishopric of Laon some six years before, chiefly because it was desolate enough to promise him hardship and poverty.[5] He had his attendants dismount, put

[1] *Vita B*, c. 6; *Vita A*, pp. 676–77; *Annales Cameracenses*, p. 513, *M.G.H. SS.*, vol. XVI; Madelaine, *l.c.*, p. 94; Hugo, *Vie*, pp. 42–48; Rosenmund, pp. 68–70.

[2] *Vita B*, c. 7.

[3] *Vita A*, pp. 677–78; Rob. Can. S. Mariani Autis., *Chron.*, ann. 1119, *M.G.H. SS.*, vol. XXVI, p. 230.

[4] Herm., *De Mirac.*, p. 655; Hugo, *Vie*, p. 51; Rosenmund, pp. 53–57. Herman says that as the bishop approached a voice from Heaven said, 'Behold Norbert and his companions,' and later, 'Behold Norbert and his companion,' and that Norbert was puzzled by this until later at Prémontré, the second disciple proved disloyal. Neither *Vita A* nor *Vita B* mentions the incident.

[5] Herm., *De Mirac.*, p. 654. De Florival, *Étude historique sur le XIIe siècle. Barthélemy de Vir, évêque de Laon*, p. 31.

Norbert and his friends on their horses, and, walking beside them back to Rheims, questioned them as to their work and ideals.[1]

Papal sanction was promptly secured, after which Norbert remained with Bartholomew until the council closed, preaching to the assembled clerics.[2] Then, accompanying the bishop to Laon, he agreed to pass the winter there, his relatives having urged the prelate to see that he did not utterly destroy himself by his austerities.[3]

At Laon, much against his will, Norbert was elected superior of the rich and corrupt Abbey of Saint Martin of Tours[4] which the Pope and Bishop longed to see reformed. 'Have I given up wealth and opulence at Cologne,' he asked, 'only to find it here at Laon? I am destined to preach the word of God; I have chosen the evangelical and apostolic life.'[5] However, he yielded to the persuasions of Calixtus and Bartholomew on condition that he receive absolute obedience,[6] and was duly installed. Trouble followed almost immediately. His rule proved too severe for the brethren, and they revolted against it, saying, '*Nolumus hunc super nos.*' After three months he withdrew,[7] planning to leave the diocese, but the Bishop, who was most unwilling to lose him, offered him every inducement to remain, and invited him to share the episcopal palace — the last thing Norbert would consider, and which he

[1] Herm., *l.c.*, p. 655; Hugo, *Vie*, p. 50. [2] Herm., *l.c.*; *Vita B*, c. 7.

[3] *Vita A*, p. 678; *Vita B*, *l.c.*; Rob. Autis., *Chron.*, *l.c.* '*Ubi ab episcopis et abbatibus qui convenerant cum gaudio susceptus est, admirantibus cunctis super excellentia verborum predicationis et responsis eius et super asperitate assumptæ penitenciæ et vite duricia; de qua cum vogaretur a plurimus sibi paulutum relaxari, nullatenus acquievit.*'

[4] Herm., *Hist. Rest. Abb.*, p. 662; *Vita A*, *l.c.*; Hugo, *Vie*, p. 76.

[5] Herm., *De Mirac.*, pp. 655–56. '*Non in urbibus volo remanere, sed potius in locis desertis et incultis.*'

[6] *Vita A*, p. 678; Herm., *l.c.* Bernhardi says Norbert was unwilling to stay here because he was ambitious and felt this place was not good enough, *l.c.*, p. 96.

[7] *AA. SS.*, *l.c.*, c. 6; Rosenmund, *l.c.*, p. 80, rejects the whole account. Herman does not mention it. Bernhardi says Norbert made things disagreeable on purpose because he did not wish to stay.

categorically refused to do.[1] Bartholomew, seeing that his heart was set on retiring to some wilderness where he might establish a missionary centre, set out to find something that would satisfy his rather exacting friend. Spring was at hand, and the two made many excursions in various parts of the diocese. Foigny was refused, charming as it was, also Thenaille, and several other places [2] before they at length chanced on a marshy valley called Prémontré, a wild, uncultivated swamp in the forest of Coucy. Hidden among the thorns was a little ruined chapel built by the Benedictines of Saint Vincent's at Laon, and abandoned because of their inability to wrest a living from so arid a spot. Undaunted by the desolation of the rain-soaked thicket, Norbert felt at once that this was the spot predestined for his labours,[3] and passed the night in prayer in the chapel. The good Bishop secured from its owners possession of the land in exchange for half a 'boisseau' of grain from the mill of Brancourt at harvest time, and the altar of Berry-au-Bac, and Prémontré was given free and in perpetuity to Norbert and his disciples, present and future, their only revenue being the income from the wood of the forest.[4] With his two companions, Norbert took possession of the solitude in the spring of 1120.[5] As soon as shelter, adequate for the moment, had been provided, he set out to collect disciples,[6] going first to the celebrated

[1] Herm., *Hist. Rest. Abb.*, p. 662; *Vita A*, *l.c.*; Hugo, *Vie*, p. 76.

[2] Herm., *De Mirac.*, *l.c.*; Hugo, *Vie*, p. 77; Madelaine, *l.c.*, pp. 130–41.

[3] According to tradition, Norbert had here a vision of the growth of his Order; he saw a multitude of white-robed men with silver crosses and candelabra, who pointed out the place where the monastery should be built. Herm., *De Mirac.*, *l.c.*; Sigebert, *Continuatio Præmont.*, ann. 1120; *M.G.H. SS.*, vol. VI, p. 447; Le Paige, *Bib.*, *Ord. Præm.*, p. 372.

[4] *Vita A*, p. 679; Herm., *l.c.*; Le Paige, *l.c.*, p. 373; Hugo, *Vie*, pp. 78–80; p. 135, for the deed to the land.

[5] *Vita A*, p. 679; *Gesta Arch. Magd.*, *M.G.H. SS.*, vol. XIV, p. 412; *AA. SS.*, I Jun., c. 7.

[6] Herm., *l.c.*, p. 656; *Vita A*, *l.c.* This was the generally accepted method of securing converts. Bernard of Clairvaux preached twice in the University of Paris

school of Ralph of Laon, where he himself is said to have studied.[1] Here he spoke so effectively of the vanity of worldly things and of the beauty of the religious life that seven youths from wealthy families of Lorraine followed him to Prémontré.[2] Then he journeyed to Cambrai, through Luxembourg, Westphalia, and Champagne, and to Utrecht and Verdun, where he secured not only converts but gifts of land and buildings for new monasteries.[3] In Antwerp the Abbey of Saint Michael's was made over to him as an expression of gratitude for his success in recalling to the faith the followers of Tauchelm.[4] Saint Martin of Tours, in Laon, which he had been unable to reform, was now transferred to him outright. Nothing that he desired was withheld.[5]

In 1122 he went to Cologne to secure relics for the new church he planned to build at Prémontré, which the rapid increase of numbers had rendered necessary. Here he discovered the relics of Saint Ursula and her virgins, and of Saint Gerson and his legion, parts of which he carried back to his monastery, and with the gifts he received from Cologne built the new church which was dedicated to these saints.[6]

in 1116 for this purpose and at the time he was preaching the Second Crusade quite filled his monasteries.

[1] *Vita A*, p. 678; Otto of Freising, *Gesta Frid.*, lib. I, sec. 47, *M.G.H.SS.*, vol. XX; Herm., *De Mirac.*, *l.c.* Ralph was the brother of Anselm, the master of Abælard.

[2] Herm., *De Mirac.*, *l.c.*, '*cum magna pecunia*'; *Vita A*, *l.c.*, says, '*cum parva substantia.*'

[3] Rosenmund, *l.c.*, p. 27; Le Paige, *l.c.*, pp. 372–73; Hugo, *Annales*, *l.c.*, pp. 50–51; *Diploma*, Alberos von Lüttich, 1124; *Vita B*, c. 8; *Vita A*, p. 683; Petrus Venerab., *Ep. ad. Matt. Alban. episc.*, Migne, *l.c.*, vol CLXXXIX, col. 66.

[4] Sigeberti, *Contin. Valcellensis*, ann. 1115, *M.G.H. SS.*, vol. VI, p. 459; *AA. SS.*, *l.c.*; *Annales Vetrocelles*, ann. 1112, *M.G.H. SS.*, vol. XVI.

[5] Herm., *De Mirac.*, *l.c.*

[6] *Vita A*, p. 680; *AA. SS.*, c. 10; Rodolphus *Epistola*, *AA. SS.*, V Oct., p. 58; Rosenmund, *l.c.*, p. 46; *Fundatio Gratiæ Dei*, *l.c.*, p. 687. The new monastery buildings were erected on the opposite side of the hill, on land claimed by Bernard of Clairvaux. Norbert wished to retain the original site, but yielded because of a vision beheld by one of the brethren which designated the second location. Certainly it was far more suitable for their purpose than was the original swamp.

The new foundation grew by leaps and bounds. At first there was no fixed rule. The brethren thought the word of Norbert sufficient, but he, anxious to insure evangelical poverty, and unwilling to remain constantly among them, saw the necessity of binding them to a definite form of life. He considered the Cistercian and Carthusian rules,[1] but rejected both, as he wished to establish a community of canons regular rather than of simple monks, as being better fitted to unite the active and contemplative life.

The rule best adapted to achieve what he had in mind was the so-called Augustinian,[2] and it was this which he finally chose,[3] altering it to meet conditions at Prémontré, and making it more rigid by providing for absolute poverty and by incorporating into it the Carta Caritatis of the Cistercians.[4] He aimed to reform the Church by reforming the priesthood, and to accomplish this, he must train his followers to explain articles of faith to the ignorant, to preach penance, to refute heretics, and to fulfill all pastoral duties. They were to live under the triple monastic vow, but they must always be attached to some particular church rather than live apart from the world. Whether at Prémontré or elsewhere, they were to observe

[1] *Vita A*, p. 683.

[2] About 750, Chrodegang, Bishop of Metz, framed a rule for his clergy based on the Benedictine. This was altered and supplemented by the Synod of Aix in 816. By its terms regular canons lived in a community without taking monastic vows; they were allowed to hold private property, but the Church revenues were to be used only for the maintenance of the establishment. On the whole, it did not prove satisfactory, and in the eleventh century various attempts were made to reform it, out of which grew the Augustinian rule; for as the reformers undertook a form of life essentially monastic, it was but natural they should look backward to a classical model for clerics living a community life. Their attention was directed to Saint Augustine's writings, especially his letter to some nuns, full of practical advice, as well as his account of the organization of his clerics at Hippo. From these and the spurious writings attributed to him were compiled two fragmentary rules and a third one, substantially complete, which were to be known henceforth as the Rule of Saint Augustine.

[3] It was adopted Christmas Day, 1121. *Vita A, l.c.*

[4] Herm., *De Mirac.*, p. 659.

all offices, to keep a strict Lenten fast throughout the year, and following the example of the primitive Christians, care for the sick and infirm of body and of soul and seek perfection of life through poverty.[1] All that came to them above what was absolutely necessary was to be used for hospitality and charity.[2] Nearly every house of the Order had the Xenodochium or almonry, not an original idea with Norbert, but given rather a greater importance by him than by other communities. He realized that nothing brought such rich returns as did charity. Alms to the poor meant gifts from the powerful; in other words, it paid to be benevolent. With all his insistence on poverty, Norbert could never bring himself to refuse donations to the Order,[3] although he justified himself for accepting them by decreeing that the income from them be used for relieving the needy and the unfortunate.[4] Even when their own store was all but depleted, he would not allow the brethren to refuse alms to those who came to the Xenodochium. On one occasion at least, they gave away all they had and fasted for three days before they could obtain more food. In times of famine the assistance they gave to the suffering was truly heroic, and their monasteries became asylums for the poor and hungry.[5]

Poverty of dress was required,[6] a single white woollen tunic [7] and a pair of sandals comprising their wardrobe; in the early days the brethren supported themselves by manual labour, by selling wood, and even by begging.[8]

[1] Le Paige, *l.c.*, pp. 390, 394–95. [2] *Vita A*, p. 684.

[3] Hugo, *Vie*, p. 274; Le Paige, *l.c.*, pp. 420–29; Jaffe, nos. 7244, 9650.

[4] Herm., *De Mirac.*, p. 658; *Vita God. Cap.*, p. 517, *M.G.H. SS.*, vol. XII.

[5] *Vita A*, p. 693; Hugo, *Vie*, p. 109; *Vita B*, c. 30. At times Norbert was given money to defray his expenses when he was sent on various embassies. This he usually sent to the monasteries and himself lived on alms.

[6] Hugo, *Vie*, pp. 100–03.

[7] Norbert claimed to have received instruction as to the tunic from the Virgin, who appeared to him in a vision. Le Paige, *l.c.*, p. 372.

[8] Le Paige, *l.c.*; *Chron. Magd.*, p. 374, *M.G.H. SS.*, vol. XIV; *Annal. Paled.*, ann. 1126, *ibid.*, vol. XVI.

Until the middle of the thirteenth century there was no mitigation of this asceticism, although often there were some among them who found it too severe, and deserting, published their grievances abroad.[1]

The earliest disciples, those from the school at Laon, were men of wealth and brought money with them to the monastery, which Norbert hid behind the altar unknown to any one, he thought. The companion who had joined him in the summer of 1119 [2] discovered it, however, and fled with it, leaving the brethren destitute.[3] While Norbert accepted this misfortune as a divine rebuke for his failure to rely absolutely on God's care, he did not relax his efforts among those whose gifts would keep his coffers full. One potent factor in the growth of the Order [4] was the interest manifested in his work by the wealthy nobles of the day. Chief among these was Godfrey of Cappenberg,[5] one of the most powerful princes of Westphalia, who in 1121 sought out Norbert, then on a missionary tour,[6] and offered himself as a disciple and his castles as monasteries. The transfer of the property was interrupted, however, by Godfrey's father-in-law, Frederick of Arnsberg, who, full of ire at the loss of his daughter's dowry, made private warfare on her behalf. Norbert, usually so successful as a peacemaker, tried to effect a compromise, but in vain. The old baron threatened to hang him from the castle wall if he did not leave at once.[7] Arnsberg's sudden death was readily interpreted as being a direct

[1] *Vita A*, p. 680; Madelaine, *l.c.*, pp. 416–17.

[2] He is spoken of as an Englishman. *AA. SS.*, I Jun., c. x.

[3] Herm., *De Mirac.*, p. 657; *Vita A*, p. 684.

[4] In 1141 there were a hundred convents; by 1160 the order had spread throughout western Europe, and was established in Palestine and Syria, everywhere holding valuable property. Herm., *l.c.*, p. 658; *Hist. Rest. Abb.*, p. 662; Potthast, *Regesta*, no. 11383; Hugo, *Annales*, vol. I, p. 517.

[5] 'Rich in castle, plunder and men,' *Vita God.*, *l.c.*, p. 512.

[6] *Vita God.*, p. 516; *Vita A*, p. 688; *AA. SS.*, *l.c.*, c. 13.

[7] *Vita God.*, p. 517; *AA. SS.*, II Jan., p. 130; *Vita A*, pp. 688–89.

evidence of God's displeasure with his opposition to Godfrey, and it was not long before the latter and his brother Otto became humble lay brethren at Prémontré, while the countess took the veil in a neighbouring convent.[1] The castles of Elofstat, Varlar, and Cappenberg all became monasteries, the last being open only to those with five quarterings of arms on both sides, and attaining great prestige because of its charity as well as for the austerity of life within its walls.[2]

The fame of Godfrey's conversion spread through France and Germany, influencing others to give their spare castles, if not themselves, to Norbert.[3] Theobald of Champagne was perhaps the most notable of these. The grandson of the Conqueror, he had been deeply impressed by the loss of his sister with the children of Henry I on the White Ship, and he now offered himself, his numerous castles and his large estates to the Præmonstratensians.[4] Possibly Norbert felt himself unable to cope with the disturbance such a change of ownership would make in the feudal hierarchy. At any rate, he declined to accept either Theobald or his possessions, urging him to continue his good work as a benefactor of the Church, and to marry and bring forth children who should follow his good example.[5] Theobald consented, but on condition that Norbert choose a wife for him, which he did, in the person of Matilda, daughter of the Marquis of Ratisbon,[6] himself concluding

[1] *Vita A*, p. 689; Rosenmund, *l.c.*, p. 50.

[2] *AA. SS.*, I Jun., p. 844; Anselm, *Cont. Sig.*, ann. 1124, *M.G.H. SS.*, vol. VI, p. 379; *AA. SS.*, II Jan., p. 130; Hugo, *Annales*, vol. I, p. 372.

[3] Hugo, *Vie*, pp. 183, 184; *Vita A*, p. 688.

[4] *Vita A*, p. 689; *AA. SS.*, I Jun., c. 12; *Gall. Christ.*, vol. X, p. 110. These early accounts are so confused as to be of questionable value. According to a charter of the foundation of Coincy, Theobald and Matilda were married two years prior to the date given here, 1125. The charter exists only in a third copy. H. D'Arbois de Jubainville, *L'Histoire des ducs et des comtes de Champagne*, vol. II, p. 263.

[5] *AA. SS.*, *l.c.*, c. 33; *Vita A*, p. 689; Rosenmund, p. 39.

[6] *Vita A. l.c.*; Albericus, *Chron.*, ann. 1126, *Recueil*, vol. XIII, p. 696; Bouquet, *Art de vérifier les dates*, vol. III, pp. 267, 581.

the negotiations. Through Theobald, he established in 1122 a third order, the *Frates et Sorores ad Succurrendum*, who should live in the world, but keep so far as possible certain canonical observances. In this he anticipated by a century the Franciscan Tertiaries.

In the same year an order of nuns was established, open at first only to women of noble birth; [1] lay brethren were also introduced in the monasteries to relieve the canons of manual labour. Thus he copied certain points from the older orders, while in other respects he launched out in new fields. For some reason, whether of organization or of membership, the Præmonstratensians seem to have been an unusually discontented body. On almost every occasion when he returned to the monastery, he had to quell some outbreak on their part.

June 28, 1124, the Order was confirmed by the papal legates at Noyon in Picardy; two years later, on the death of Pope Calixtus, Norbert decided to go to Rome to secure a renewal of this confirmation, which was granted, together with a recognition of their possessions.[2]

On the way home, in June, 1126, he stopped at the Diet of Speier,[3] then wrangling over the choice of an archbishop of Magdeburg; made a speech to clear up dissension; and was himself elected to the office,[4] which he accepted be-

[1] Herm., *De Mirac.*, pp. 657, 659; Jacques de Vitry, *Hist Occid.*, c. 22. Herman says there were more women than men in the Order at the time of Norbert's death. Some of the monasteries were double, that is, accommodated both sexes, although there was no intercourse between them.

[2] Jaffé, p. 553, nos. 5232, 5233; p. 572, no. 5472; Le Paige, *l.c.*, pp. 392, 662; Hugo, *Annales*, p. 369.

[3] The accounts in the earlier *vitæ* are confused and out of all chronological order. Some of the biographers say that it was at this time that Norbert was completing his negotiations of Theobald's marriage.

[4] Bernhardi, *l.c.*, says that the whole matter was arranged in Rome, and that this election before the Emperor Lothair and the papal legates was a mere formality. Herman, *l.c.*, says that Norbert told his friend, Godfrey of Chartres, in Rome, that he would be an archbishop, but that he did not know where. He claimed to have received his information from heavenly voices. Though confused as to chronology, *Vita A* is substantially correct in its facts, although it says there were three candidates, when there were only two.

cause he saw in it an opportunity to extend the Præmonstratensian ideals, and to develop more effectively his missionary work, far more important to him than the establishing of an order.[1] He left at once for Magdeburg,[2] barefoot, clad in a humble tunic, riding a donkey, from which he dismounted as he approached the city. He presented so poverty-stricken an appearance that when he arrived at the door of the palace, the porter refused him admission, thinking he was a beggar. On discovering his error, he was so chagrined that he would have fled, but that Norbert restrained him, saying, 'I fear you know me better than those who have forced me into this place.'[3]

The poor of the city welcomed him gladly as their friend, although later they proved themselves ready enough to give ear to whatever charges were made against him. So unconventional an entry to so great a dignity, however, antagonized many, who saw in him a fanatical reformer, and dreaded the changes the new régime would bring. Events soon proved that their fears were not without foundation. Norbert began by abolishing all signs of luxury from the palace,[4] that he might lead there a life of cloistered simplicity. Then he undertook to reform the canons and to put in order the finances of the See by recalling loans almost forgotten, and reclaiming diocesan lands taken over by relatives of the chapter.[5] Saint Mary's Abbey in the city he secured for his own canons,[6] with whom he took counsel rather than with the chapter, while others from

[1] *Gesta Arch. Magd.*, *l.c.*, ann. 1126.

[2] He was accompanied by Otto, Bishop of Halberstadt, and Ludolph, Bishop of Brandenburg, suffragans of Magdeburg. *Vita S. Ottonis*, c. 2, *AA. SS.*, I Jul.; Madelaine, *l.c.*, p. 343; Le Paige, *l.c.*, p. 395.

[3] *AA. SS.*, I Jun., c. 15. Also Winter, *Die Prämonstratenser*, p. 329.

[4] *Vita A*, p. 695; Rosenmund, pp. 97, 99, 100, n. 3.

[5] *Vita A*, *l.c.*; Hugo, *Vie*, p. 267; *Gesta Magd.*, *l.c.*, p. 414.

[6] Jaffé, *Regestas* no. 5303; Hugo, *Vie*, pp. 316–17, says Innocent II gave him permission to introduce his order in the cathedral, but there is no evidence to support this.

Prémontré were introduced into many of the parish churches.[1] Naturally this did not increase his popularity among the cathedral clergy, who busied themselves by influencing public opinion against him. On the vigil of Saint Peter-and-Paul, 1129, he was reconsecrating the cathedral, against the will of the chapter, who insisted on knowing how it had been defiled[2] and by whom, that they might punish the offender. Upon his refusal to comply, or to dismiss his own priests, his enemies spread the report that he and his Frenchmen were stealing relics from the altar and robbing the treasury,[3] and the opposition to him flared out in riot and rebellion.[4] He was able to calm them into a temporary reasonableness, but soon their suspicions were aroused again, and after more than one plot to kill him had all but succeeded,[5] he was forced to flee from the city by night.[6] The episcopal castle of Giebechenstein near Halle being closed against him,[7] he went on to the Augustinian monastery of Peterskloster,[8] from whence he sent dire excommunications on the offending city which at length repented and recalled him on his own terms.[9] The remaining years were spent in comparative peace at Magdeburg, carrying out reforms and sending missionaries to the Wends, whom Lothair wished him not only to Christianize but to Germanize.[10] He visited Prémontré occasionally, but took no part in the administration of the Order, Hugh having succeeded him as superior.[11] In 1131 he accompanied the Emperor to Rome as his chancellor, to

[1] Bernhardi, *l.c.*, pp. 153, *etc.*; Rosenmund, pp. 42–45.

[2] *Ann. Magd.*, p. 183, *M.G.H. SS.*, vol. XVI.

[3] Hugo, *Annales*, vol. II, CVIII; *AA. SS.*, I Jun., c. 17; Hugo, *Vie*, p. 277. Apparently hatred of 'the Frenchmen' whom Norbert had introduced into their midst was a not inconsiderable cause of this tumult.

[4] *Vita A*, p. 696; *Ann. Magd.*, *l.c.*

[5] *AA. SS.*, *l.c.*, c. 18.

[6] Rosenmund, *l.c.*, p. 71.

[7] *Vita A*, *l.c.*; Rosenmund, *l.c.*, pp. 42, 167.

[8] Bernhardi, *l.c.*, p. 228.

[9] *Gesta Magd.*, *l.c.*; Hugo, *Vie*, pp. 299–300.

[10] Bernhardi, p. 153.

[11] Herm., *De Mirac.*, p. 657; *Vita A*, p. 697; Norbert refused the title of abbot.

reinstate Innocent II, whom he, like Bernard, supported, and to negotiate terms for the imperial coronation. He was taken ill on his way home and died in Magdeburg in 1134.[1]

Norbert was dominated by his inconsistencies and by his ever-conflicting desires. The simplicity resulting from devotion to a single ideal, such as characterized Stephen Harding or the founder of the Carthusians, is lacking in him. Unquestionably sincere in his asceticism, the natural man never ceased to crave and to accept power and authority. His disciples were dedicated to work among the poor, whom he refused to admit to his first order. He preached the equality of all men under Christ and then set apart certain of his monasteries for those of highest rank. He possessed remarkable ability in reconciling feuds, yet he himself was almost constantly in conflict with those about him. He prescribed a life of rigorous self-denial for his followers, but so surrounded them with the responsibilities of great possessions that the permanence of evangelical poverty was impossible. That it was maintained as long as it was lay in the fact that after Norbert's death Bernard of Clairvaux became the protector of the Order into which he instilled some of his own ideals.

Despite his inconsistencies, Norbert was a memorable man, and a great preacher, as the numbers who flocked to hear him bear witness. Because of his culture, his keen insight and his persuasive powers, pope, emperor, and prince were guided by his counsels and sought his favour. His reputation for saintliness won for him the See of Magdeburg, although his restless energy caused those who had chosen him to repent of their bargain. A true child of the Age of Faith, he saw the hand of God in all the events of his life and was guided as much by voices and visions as by

[1] Herm., *l.c.*; *Vita A*, pp. 701–03; *Ann. Magd.*, *l.c.*, p. 184; *Annales Herbepolenses*, *M.G.H. SS.*, vol. XVI, p. 2.

the material conditions in the world about him. Many miracles were attributed to him and miraculous powers over wild beasts. Wolves became shepherds at his behest and restored what they had carried off. The greatest men of his age honoured him as a man sent from God and set apart by divine sanction. As Bernard typified love to his generation, so Norbert was the embodiment of faith.

It seems a far cry from the Carthusian huts to the palace of the Archbishop of Magdeburg, yet in Norbert, as in Bruno, in the Stephens, in Bernard of Clairvaux, may be seen the motive force of pure asceticism, the recognition of absolute poverty as the road to God marked out by Christ. The impulse to escape existing conditions, the desire for a life of poverty undertaken in the spirit of knightly adventure, was fundamentally characteristic of this group of monastic reformers. Each of them was seeking holiness and attracting countless followers by his righteousness. In the case of at least one of them, the obligation to embrace apostolic asceticism was the result of witnessing the degradation into which avarice had plunged the Church.

Not that these were all. New orders of more or less importance locally were springing up in France, England, Germany, and Italy through the eleventh and twelfth centuries; older communities were renewing their allegiance to Lady Poverty; and numerous individual reformers in cathedrals joined hands with mendicant preachers to give more abundant life to the newly awakened impulse to evangelical living. Earnest souls, sincere in purpose, ever facing forward, their work is not to be discredited because it does not fit our age. It fitted theirs, queer and perverted as it may seem to the unmystical eyes of this later day, and it was glorified by a spirit of self-abnegation not always found in the labours of the modern social reformer.

CHAPTER IV

ARNOLD OF BRESCIA AND HIS FORERUNNERS

Looked at in the large, the history of the Church in the eleventh century is dominated by two great conspicuous factors: the Investiture Struggle, an attempt to define the relations of the secular and spiritual powers, and the Cluniac Reform, an effort to bring the lives of the clergy into conformity with apostolic ideals. Calling attention as they did to the degenerate conditions of the institution, both movements influenced very decidedly the popular consciousness by producing spiritual unrest and confusion. Furthermore, they developed the political aspects of the ecclesiastical questions into party factions and thus brought into sharper relief the drastic need for reform.

These were years of bitter strife, civic, feudal, and religious. Men had become so accustomed to an atmosphere of turbulent dissatisfaction and of restless adventuring that inward peace and external tranquillity were alike beyond their ken. The long-drawn-out struggle between papacy and empire not only intensified all minor conflicts, but gave occasion for the waging of persistent warfare by the adherents of the two powers, whether factions, classes, or towns. In this struggle the victors were the communes of northern Italy, for whose favour each contestant had for half a century sought to outbid his rival. Privilege after privilege was offered and accepted until by the time the Investiture Struggle was at its height, the towns were well on the way toward emancipation from any external power, lay or temporal.

While the eleventh century witnessed the revival of communal independence throughout the west, a peculiar combination of circumstances gave the movement a marked impetus in Italy. Not only did the tradition of the municipal liberties of the Roman Empire linger on, but since the days of the early Church, each Italian town of any importance had been the seat of a bishop, who, as the temporal power declined, assumed the rôle of leader and protector of the people. The revival of the Empire and the transference of local administration to the hands of the imperial vicars submerged popular liberties for a time until the weakness of the central authority made it possible for the towns to revive the old freedom in local affairs, particularly those of Lombardy which were farthest removed from the seats of government, papal and imperial, and which were for the most part under weak feudal lords. The bishops were not blind to the fact that civic independence would of necessity bring them a renewal of the powers lost to the German barons and so realized that it was decidedly to their advantage to encourage municipal liberty if it could be developed under episcopal patronage.

The acquisition of political separation from the Empire was the first step, but before this was secured, the communes had entered on a period of great commercial and industrial prosperity which sought expression in the strengthening of the city walls, in the construction of roads, and in the building of churches and palaces. A consciousness of unity which a jealous hatred of neighbouring communes served to intensify, was developed by a tangible recognition of common interests. As the artisan class rose to prominence by the achievement of economic stability, the way opened for a revival of letters. Schools sprang up in the various municipalities, and scholars, no longer clerics, sought to give intellectual expression to the free and restless spirit dominating the times. Laymen became lawyers, political leaders of the people, and so did not a little to bridge the gulf between the new life of action and the old life of philosophic speculation. The natural result of this was a revolt against episcopal authority and the rise of consular government, while in the communes, parties developing into political factions arose over the question of temporal power of the priesthood.

Contemporary with this political and industrial progress and not wholly unrelated to it, came an excess of ecclesiastical evils such as might be found anywhere in western Europe, but which were especially flagrant in the Po Valley. Clergy and people alike tried to combat them, but as each group was actuated by a different motive, their efforts tended on the whole merely to increase the confusion. When in 1059 the Synod of Sutri enunciated new principles of reform, the Lombard bishops, assailed by their clergy as they tried to enforce the decrees, found support among the people. The alliance was not always, however, between bishops and commons. The Investiture Struggle often arrayed the commune against its spiritual overlord, since the burghers were striving for civic rights and political independence and the bishops, intent on retaining temporal power, were forced to ally themselves with the emperor and so became enemies of the commune. At such times the patriot leaders would join their forces with the papal legates against the prelates.

In the movement for civic freedom the part played by Milan was perhaps more important than that of other towns, despite her slowness in attaining her ends as the opposing parties were more evenly matched there than elsewhere. Abundantly conscious of the prestige she had enjoyed more or less intermittently since the days of the Roman Empire, she was little inclined to submit to any interference or surveillance, lay or ecclesiastical, local or foreign. At this time she was one of the strongest cities not only of Italy, but of western Europe. Her influence extended from Mantua to Turin, while her archbishops claimed jurisdiction over more than a score of dioceses.

During the period of the supremacy of the feudal nobles, the peasants had fled in great numbers to the city for protection against tyranny and injustice. There in the security of episcopal immunities, the dormant spirit of municipal liberty had been slowly awakened under the guidance of the able but arrogant archbishop Aribert (1018–45). Taking advantage of the popular favour bestowed on him at the time of his accession, of the constant hatred of the Latin industrial classes for their German oppressors, and of the rising spirit of popular independence, he formed a communal army, which he himself trained and commanded, and with which he successfully repulsed the encroachments of the barons, never notably strong in that region. During the middle decades of the eleventh century, while the conflict between papacy and empire was becoming chronic, the general tendency of the nobles had been to uphold imperial pretensions. The pontiffs were for the most part supported by the middle and lower orders, lay and cleric, under the leadership of the local prelates, notwithstanding the lavish grants of land and of privileges bestowed on the latter by emperor and baron. Under Aribert, the ecclesiastical power, based on popular support, had reached its apogee, but the archbishop belonged by birth to the upper nobility, and he found it difficult to maintain his determination to oppose the class whose interests he felt honour bound to uphold. He desired, above all else, to make the See of Saint Ambrose independent of the pope, and to organize a Lombard patriarchate, combining with ecclesiastical ascendancy, temporal power. To accomplish this, he needed the support of the popular elements, but, on the other hand, he could not dispense with the favour of the barons. The effort to reconcile the two classes whose interests were so fundamentally antagonistic led to long years of fruitless struggle, until he finally realized his inability to control the situation and withdrew from all participation in temporal affairs.

At his death in 1045, the commune was plunged into a civil war over the choice of his successor.[1] The struggle against the nobles at the same time resolved itself into a struggle for the reform advocated by the Roman Church, since the sale of the benefices had been one of the chief sources of income of the nobility. Also the main points at issue between the rich, luxury-loving prelates and the oppressed lower orders were the same as those between the great nobles and the common people.

Up to this time the Milanese Church, jealous of its Ambrosian ritual and of the prestige of its famous archbishops, had resisted the efforts put forth by the popes for uniformity of organization. The nobility and prelates were naturally the chief supporters of this independence which they now made an issue in the controversy, while their opponents, the popular party, composed chiefly of artisans, peasants, and merchants, and called Patarini from the district in which they lived,[2] united with the lower clergy in their insistence that the emperor possess no political rights in the city, upheld the counter pretensions of the pope to participate in the government, and advocated his reform measures as opening the way for municipal independence.

The Patarini were in the beginning but a local manifestation of that general reform movement sweeping over Europe in the late eleventh century, which sought to purify the Church of incontinence and simony and at the

[1] The meeting held to elect the new archbishop has well been called the first example of a general assembly of all classes of Milanese. Landulf. Sen., *Hist. Med.*, lib. III, c. 2: '*Aliquantis diebus post præclarissimi Heriberti decessum transactis civium universorum collectio adunata est.*'

[2] Edict of Fred. II, Cod. Vat. Lat. 1730, f. 125, says that they were called Patarini because they were exposed to suffering '*in exemplum martyrum qui pro fede catholica martria subierunt Patarenos se nominant veluti expositos passioni.*' Another etymology is that the term is derived from a Roman heretic called Paterinus. But the Patarini were so called before they became heretics. Still another theory holds that the term is a local form of Cathari, but the early Patarini were not dualists. For the later history of the movement see Cod. Vat. Lat. 3217, f. 123; Doat, vol. XXXVI, ff. 103, 108t, 111, 150–51t, etc.

same time strove to liberate it from the civil powers. They had first attracted attention early in the century as an association of faithful laymen, zealously opposed to the laxity of the priesthood [1] and bound by solemn oath to secure religious reform. 'I promise,' so ran their pledge, 'while I live, to make every effort, save to sacrifice money other than spontaneous alms, to destroy the two heresies of Nicolaitism and simony, and not to permit priest, deacon, or sub-deacon to hold wife and ecclesiastical office together, and I promise to prevent all venality in the confirmation of sacred things.' [2]

In Arialdo, an austere cleric of Cuzziago,[3] and in Landolfo and Erlembaldo, brothers of the noble family of Cotta,[4] they found able leaders. Arialdo was born of the class of lesser nobility and had travelled widely and studied much. He began his self-imposed mission about the year 1050 by fearlessly calling upon the clergy of Milan to renounce all their evil ways and to follow Christ as humbly as his first disciples had done. Throughout his ministry he held ever before his eyes the ideal of perfection of canonical life for the clergy and the reëstablishment of the evangelical Church.

Whether he had already met Hildebrand is not known, but at all events the two were equally desirous of reëstablishing the purity of the primitive Church; and to Arialdo the first step towards the accomplishment of this seemed to be to reform the ritual. Enthusiasts flocked to his sup-

[1] Bonizo, *Liber ad Amicum*, Migne, *l.c.*, vol. CL, lib. VI, col. 825.

[2] Peter Damian, *Opusc.* V, Migne, *l.c.*, vol. CXLV, col. 97. Two years after its organization in Milan, the association numbered over one thousand members.

[3] A little hamlet in the Brianza. '*Arialdus in loco Cuzago prope Canturium Mediolanensis Diocesis ortus fuit nobilibus parentibus De Alzati,*' Puricelli, *De SS. Martyribus Arialdo et Herlembaldo*, cc. 1, 10, Cod. Ambros. S 89 Sup.; Arnulf., *Hist. Med.*, *R.I.S.*, *l.c.*, p. 24; *AA. SS.*, V Jun., p. 281; Landulf. Sen., *l.c.*, p. 98.

[4] According to legend the Cotta family came to Milan with Saint Ambrose. At the coronation ceremony, two youths of this family had the right of inducting the emperor to the marble chair back of the altar. Puricelli, *l.c.*

port and in the revolt which followed, he and his party held the government in their own hands. Anselm of Baggio, at that time connected with the cathedral, was one of his supporters, and to him and to Landolfo Cotta [1] Arialdo gave over the task of carrying out the reform in the city proper, while he himself preached in the *contada* between Milan and Varese where he seems to have been already well known.[2]

Although an aristocrat by birth and education, Landolfo Cotta was possessed of a keen sympathy with the lower classes as well as a clear vision and a practical ability for dealing with the situation as it was. The majority followed him gladly, while the minority who feared him bore him a hatred which menaced his life.[3] His power over the masses was due to his eloquence and to his understanding of their needs and desires, qualities which won for the Patarini an ever-increasing number of adherents also among the middle classes and the lesser nobility.[4]

The successor of Aribert had been the mediocre Guido of Velato (1045–69) who obtained his high office through simony and imperial favour.[5] Now fearful of the effect of the reformers on his own power, he called the leaders to a conference and begged them to hide the sins of the clergy under the mantle of charity.[6] On their refusal to comply, he appealed to the Pope to remove Anselm by promoting him to the See of Lucca. The transfer was made and Guido

[1] Galvin. Flamina, *Manip. Flor.*, *R.I.S.*, vol. XI, col. 624, says all three of these men were candidates for the archbishopric, but he wrote two centuries after the events he described and is far from accurate. Landulf. Sen., hints at the same thing.

[2] *Vita Alex. II*, *R.I.S.*, vol. III, pt. 2, col. 356.

[3] Arnulf., *l.c.*, lib. III, c. 13, p. 103.

[4] Arnulf., *l.c.*, Damian calls him '*clerico et senatorii generis et peritiæ litteralis nitore conspicuo,*' *l.c.*, col. 667. Bonizo, *l.c.*, col. 825: '*Vir urbanus et facundissimus.*'

[5] Guido went to Rome in person to secure papal forgiveness of his sin and sanction for his office. Landulf., *l.c.*, lib. III, c. 2, p. 96.

[6] Mansi, vol. XIX, col. 772; Landulf., *l.c.*, cc. 6, 7.

felt he was rid of the chief instigator of the opposition, when as a matter of fact he had removed the least harmful member of the trio. Arialdo and Landolfo proved themselves quite able to carry on the reform alone. The former returned to Milan and was at once joined by such numbers of enthusiastic followers especially among the youth of the city, that the faint-hearted Guido was unable to combat their zeal and fled to Novara. From this retreat he held a synod at the rich monastery of Basilica Petri,[1] excommunicated the reformers, and summoned them to appear before him and defend themselves. Instead of complying, they appealed to the Pope to sanction their labours.[2] The latter at once dispatched to their aid their former colleague Anselm and with him Hildebrand, to act as his legates, but despite their warm championship they accomplished little beyond declaring Guido guilty of simony as he himself had already admitted.

All Milan was in tumult and in turmoil. Houses were sacked, families were dispersed, the clergy were persecuted, and nobles attempting to defend them by offering them protection were forced to flee to their castles beyond the city walls, while the priests themselves were allowed to remain in possession of their benefices only on condition that they signed a '*Pactacium de castitate servanda*,'[3] abandoning their wives. In other words Milan was witnessing a revival of morals and of justice in the hands of the people.

The authority of the Emperor in Milan was small, but he used what influence he had for the cause of the married priests, without, however, being able to check the fury of the people, who, now absolute in control, knew neither mode nor measure. In vain did Arialdo try to calm them

[1] *Novara Sacra*, lib. I. [2] Landulf., *l.c.*, c. 4.

[3] Baronius, Ann. 1067, vol. XVII, p. 294; Puricelli, *l.c.*, lib. IV, c. 26, n. 12, 19; B. Andrea, c. VII, *AA. SS.*, 27 June, p. 196; Arnulf., cc. 3, 10.

and to save from their vengeance such clerics as should promise to amend their lives. Rumours of the riot reached the Pontiff and so alarmed him that he sent Peter Damian to quell the disorder. He was received with open arms and given an ovation, until he tried to enforce the papal recommendation for a uniform ritual, when Patarini, as jealous of their ecclesiastical independence as were the nobles, at once adopted the position of their adversaries, that the Ambrosian Church was the equal of the Roman Church and never its subject, and rising against the envoy, all but expelled him from the city. After great difficulty he succeeded in convincing them of sympathy with their cause and withdrew.[1]

But scarcely had he passed through the gates than the tumult broke out anew, and this time it spread beyond the city walls. Landolfo was wounded when on the way to Rome and died soon afterward. His brother Erlembaldo, just returned from a pilgrimage to Jerusalem, was dissuaded by Arialdo from entering a monastery and induced to undertake his brother's unfinished work. Nicholas had died in 1061 and had been succeeded by Anselm of Baggio as Alexander II. He sent the reformers at Milan a message of encouragement, gave to Erlembaldo the title of Gonfaloniere or standard-bearer of the Church, and offered to make him ruler of Lombardy as papal vassal, an honour which Erlembaldo refused to consider.

The younger Cotta, more statesmanlike than his predecessors had been, reorganized the Patarini and created a league against married priests.[2] Then he turned his attention to the political situation, which the others had

[1] P. Damian, *Ep.* 7, lib. III, Migne, *l.c.*, vol. CXLIV, col. 295: *De Privilegio Romanæ Ecclesiæ*, Migne, *l.c.*, vol. CLXV, col. 90.

[2] A decree issued by him, probably at the instigation of the Pope, said that if priest or deacon supported by twelve witnesses could swear on the Gospel that he had not touched a woman since his ordination, he would not be molested, but that otherwise all his goods should be confiscated. Landulf., *l.c.*, c. 20; Mansi, col. 978.

recognized unwillingly. During his struggle for control of the government, municipal independence increased rapidly, and with it the opposition to Guido, until the latter, weary of the struggle, resigned the prelacy, proposing as his successor one Gervase, a bishop of noble birth. The people not only refused to accept him, but they failed to agree on any other candidate for the place so that the bloodshed continued until 1073, when Gregory VII appointed one Attone to fill the vacant See.

In the riots over the choice of a prelate, Arialdo was assassinated, probably at Isola Madre in Lago Maggiore. After his death Erlembaldo tried to continue the reform. He chose a council of thirty influential men, who were also Patarini, to preside over the government of the city. They undertook to impose their measures by force and in the civil war which ensued Erlembaldo was also killed. His followers soon disagreed among themselves and split into factions, so that the clerical party ultimately regained control of the government.

So long as the pontiffs were able to rely on the Patarini as allies in their efforts to enforce the Cluniac Reform and in their opposition to anti-pope and to emperor, the association flourished; but the opponents of the Holy See once humbled, the Curia left them to their own fate and their downfall was inevitable. The commune seems by this time to have been quite well established, and, under the guidance of the reformers, was fairly democratic, since this struggle for a reformed priesthood was but one phase of Milan's effort to attain communal liberty. The Patarin movement, a direct attack on the temporal power of the bishops, also contributed to the cause of political freedom which could not be secured unless the Church were to be loosed from ignominious services and compromising corruption. Fundamentally popular in organization as well as aiming for reform, the Patarini, under the strong guidance of a saint and a hero, had brought about the supremacy of the industrial class, and while the death of their leaders had resulted in disorganization, the principles they advocated had endured. In those Lombard cities where their ideals had spread most rapidly, there had spread also democratic institutions, so that feudalism was forced to choose between sharing its supremacy with the middle class or relinquishing it entirely. During the cataclysm following Hildebrand's attempt to unite the Christian world under a moral supremacy, the Patarini were his strongest advocates, but after his death, their aims were confused and, losing all significance, they were gradually merged into groups of other reformers, becoming for the most part either Cathari or Humiliati.

The history of the Lombard communes varied in details, but all attained political independence through strife with the ecclesiastical authorities and at the expense of the temporal power of the clergy. One of the most turbulent towns in this region was Brescia, which furnished a notable example of the unapostolic condition into which the Church had fallen. Despite the reform decrees the clergy remained almost without exception simoniacal. The evil effect of the possession of temporal power was nowhere more glaringly evident. Although the city was nominally governed by two consuls, the bishop controlled more than one fifth of the land which was infeudated to the Church.[1] Conflicts between the two powers were therefore inevitable and frequent.[2] In 1127 they came to some sort of a momentary agreement,[3] but almost immediately afterward the way opened for a renewal of the strife by the contested imperial and pontifical elections. The laity of Brescia, headed by the consuls, supported Lothair II and Innocent II against

[1] Odorici, *Storie Bresciano*, vol. IV, pp. 237, *etc.*
[2] Giesebrecht, *Geschichte der Deutschen Kaiserzeit*, vol. III, p. 129.
[3] Odorici, *l.c.*, vol. V, p. 92.

Conrad III and Anacletus II. The Bishop of Brescia, Villanus, was a follower of Anacletus and bitter strife existed between the clergy under his guidance and the popular party, until the autumn of 1132 when Innocent II visited the city, deposed Villanus, and replaced him by one Manfred, a creature of his own.[1]

It was during the confusion attendant on the schism of Anacletus that the man known to history as Arnold of Brescia first came into prominence. He was a native of the town,[2] of noble family,[3] born toward the close of the eleventh century.[4] Nothing is known of the events of his early life except that he had been ordained '*clericus ac lector*'[5] and had been a pupil of Abælard's. He probably spent his youth in Brescia and, since he was sent to France to complete his studies, it may be assumed that his parents were not destitute of means.[6] He seems to have been always a man of affairs rather than of theories. According to all accounts extant of his life and of the attacks made upon him by his enemies, he remained always a consistent figure, tracing the evils of the day to the wealth and temporal power of the Church and finding the remedy in a return to the conditions of the apostolic age. But there is no word of his own in existence to show how his opinions

[1] Odorici, *l.c.*, vol. IV, pp. 240, etc.; *Annales Brixiensis, M.G.H. SS.*, vol. XVIII, p. 812; '*Innocentius papa Brixiam venit et ejecit Villanum de episcopatu.*'

[2] Otto of Freising, *Gesta Frid.*, c. 19, *l.c.*; S. Bernard., *Ep.* 195, Migne, *l.c.*, vol. CLXXXII, col. 361.

[3] Faiono, *Brescia illustre nelle principale dignitá ecclesiastiche*, MS. in Libreria dei Padri dell' Oratorio di S. Filippo Neri di Brescia.

[4] The exact date of his birth is unknown. The conjectures are based on the fact that he died in Rome in 1155 and was not spoken of as being either young or old. The part he played at Brescia in the revolt of the citizens against Manfred in 1138 and in the Council of Sens two years later would indicate that he was then about forty years old.

[5] Giesebrecht, *l.c.*, p. 127, says he was abbot of an Augustinian convent in Brescia: *Hist. Pontif.*, p. 537, says: '*Erat his dignitate sacerdos habitu canonicus regularis.*'

[6] Gunther says: '*Arnoldus quem tenui nutrivit Gallia sumptu edocuitque diu,*' *Ligurinus, Veterum Script.*, vol. I.

were formed. Besides Arnold's Lombard environment, the only known influence in his early life is that of Abælard whose probable relation to the young Brescian's intellectual development can best be understood by recalling the former's position when the latter came under his influence.

Peter Abælard, one of the greatest scholars of mediæval times, had during his youth wandered from place to place, seeking instruction from the leading teachers of the day and by his unusual ability arousing jealousy and making enemies wherever he went.[1] About 1100, he studied under the great dialectician, William of Champeaux, chancellor of the cathedral at Paris and head of the cathedral school, whom he vanquished in argument and who thenceforth became one of his greatest enemies. After this, he taught in Paris for a time and then for a brief season in the cathedral school itself, where he stood forth as a herald of free thought by virtue of his bold assertions of the duty of private judgment as well as by his profound contempt of those who take everything on trust. While he himself ever started from the direct questionings of his own mind, he never doubted but that the roads of reason and of authority would ultimately converge.[2]

William's antagonism drove him from the cathedral. At the foot of Mont Sainte-Geneviève where the Latin Quarter was beginning to form, he gathered about him a community of pupils, many of whom had left the cathedral school for his sake. In 1113 he went to Laon to study theology and there he added Anselm, the master of the school, to the number of his opponents. Opinion grew so bitter towards him that some of his fellow pupils forced him to leave. About 1116, he returned to the cathedral

[1] The one authority for the life of Abælard down to his becoming abbot of Saint Gildas is his own *Historia Calamitatum*, Migne, *l.c.*, vol. CLXXVII.

[2] *Sic et Non*. Prol., p. 17. By doubting we are led to inquire; by inquiry we perceive the truth. Migne, *l.c.*, col. 1349.

school at Paris. William was no longer there and the opposition against Abælard was dying down. For about three years he lectured to thousands of students. This was the most successful period of his life, and it was at this time that he and Héloïse met and loved each other. Their idyllic bliss was ended by the persecution to which the uncle of Héloïse subjected the young scholar. Broken in health and in spirit, he entered the Abbey of Saint-Denis near Paris, probably about the year 1119. There the sight of the lax and indolent monks aroused him to something of his old energy and he attacked them so vigorously for their shortcomings that he was removed from the monastery and sent to one of its dependencies in Champagne. He resumed his teachings, drawing such great numbers of students to his lectures that his enemies became alarmed and renewed their attacks. Near at hand at the cathedral school of Rheims were two of Anselm's former pupils who had been among those instrumental in securing his banishment from Laon. They renewed their opposition, charging him with heresy and initiating a persecution which ended only at the grave. In thc beginning they secured the cooperation of Saint Bernard, as untiring in his efforts to uproot whatever he believed to be evil as he was in his desire to further whatever seemed to him to be right. From this time on he became the most relentless persecutor of Abælard. The '*Sic et Non,*' in which were set down one after another the opinions of the Church Fathers upon various questions that the reader might see their points of agreement and of contradiction, was already written at this time and the author had achieved that intellectual splendour which made him an inspiration to his students and a danger to conservative theologians. He idolized human reason and appealed to it as the highest authority. But as the tendency of his teaching was to loosen men from a sense of dependency on the sacraments, he was held to be a source of discord, 'a perfidious tongue.'[1]

His accusers at this time, however, did not cite the *Sic et Non*, but instead based the prosecution on his little treatise concerning the unity and trinity of God. The exact nature of his supposed heretical doctrine of the Trinity is indicated vaguely by the sources he used, which indeed contradict each other. Probably the fundamental difficulty lay in the plan of the book, for he tried to supply rational proof for mystical doctrine. He was summoned for a trial before the Council at Soissons. No one dared to meet him in public disputation and his opponents feared to let him speak at all before the clerics assembled, knowing he would inevitably carry his audience with him. In the end there was a travesty of a trial; Abælard's books were ordered burned and he himself was sent to a monastic prison for a short time, after which he was allowed to return to Saint-Denis, where he again aroused the fury of the monks, this time by casting doubts on the identity of their patron saint.[2] This new difficulty resulted, in 1122, in the exile of Abælard from all houses subject to the abbey and in his agreement to live according to their rules in a hermitage, a judgment he gladly accepted. Then followed one of the few tranquil periods in his stormy career.[3]

'I betook myself,' he wrote to his friend Philenthus, 'to a certain solitude in the neighbourhood of Troyes, with which I had been earlier acquainted. A piece of ground was bestowed upon me by certain persons and with the assent of the bishop of the diocese, I made me an oratory in the name of the Holy Trinity. I built it in the first instance of reeds and thatch. There I lay in hiding, to-

[1] Hilarius, *Elegia de recessiu Pietri Abælardo ex Paracleto*, Migne, *l.c.*, col. 1855.

[2] On the authority of Bede, he stated that their saint was not Dionysius the Areopagite of Athens, but the Bishop of Corinth, an opinion he later modified.

[3] *Hist. Calam.*, *l.c.*

gether with a certain one of our clerics, and there I could in very truth sing to the Lord as my song: "Lo I fled far away and dwelt in a solitude." When my pupils learned this, they began to flock together from all sides, and abandoning cities and châteaux, took up their residence in this solitude. In place of their spacious dwellings, they built for themselves tiny huts; instead of dainty dishes, they lived on the herbs of the field and on coarse bread; and instead of soft beds, they spread for themselves stalks and straws. . . . And these our disciples, building their cabins there above the Arbegon River, seemed hermits rather than pupils. But in proportion as a greater influx of students came there who endured all these discomforts of life for the sake of our instruction, so much the more did those who were jealous of me deem me vainglorious and without due consideration for them. When they had done all they could in my disfavour, they grieved because all things worked together for good in my case.

'Indeed, however, at that time, it was chiefly intolerable poverty which obliged me to take pupils since I could not dig and to beg I was ashamed; and so having recourse to the one industry in which I had been trained I was forced to support myself by my tongue.

'My pupils of their own accord, provided me with more than the absolute necessities of life; and whether in the way of food or of clothing or the tilling of the field or the expenses incident on building, they provided for me so that no domestic cause might withdraw me from my profession. When my modest oratory could no longer accommodate even a small part of the students, of necessity they enlarged it and improved it, too, building of stone and of wood. Though the foundations of the oratory had been laid and its dedication made in the name of the Holy Trinity, yet because I had fled hither a despairing fugitive and by the gift of divine mercy had won a breathing space, in memory of this goodness shown me, I named the place the Paraclete.'

When it is remembered to what extent Abælard exalted the province of human reason, it seems probable that the fearless independence of Arnold's later attitude was due in part to him. Abælard had, moreover, spent years in bitter conflict with ecclesiastical authorities, at whose hands he had received treatment severe if not unjust. He had protested against the disregard of monastic vows sadly prevalent at that time, so that Arnold's hostility to the clergy, natural enough in a citizen of Lombardy, may well have been stimulated by Abælard. Further, the beauty of the simple life at the Paraclete must have had its influence on a man of ascetic tendencies. That Arnold was devoted to Abælard, and therefore likely to feel his influence strongly, may be inferred from his return to his master some years later.

At this time the latter was teaching the necessity of clerical poverty and of freedom from the cupidity of earthly possessions, then contaminating the priesthood, as the only means of reviving the almost lifeless religious fervour characterizing the whole ecclesiastical institution. Monks, he said, were too wealthy to serve God well. The Church, seldom if ever contending against evil, could not hope to continue her existence unless she renounced her luxury and followed the teachings of Christ. While Abælard was not the only source of Arnold's ideas as to clerical poverty, it cannot be denied that what he heard at Mont Sainte-Geneviève must have strengthened his convictions.[1]

Of the further influences to which he was subjected, little can be said save that he was 'learned in the Scriptures'[2] and that he can hardly have failed to have heard

[1] *Joanne Baptista Sermo*, Migne, *l.c.*, col. 582, 'If you would be perfect you must devote yourself to almsgiving, frugality, and voluntary poverty.'

[2] *Hist. Pontif.*, *l.c.*, p. 537; Giesebrecht, *Arnold*, pp. 4, 124–26; Pauli, *Ueber*

some Patarin teaching. Moreover, the study of Roman law was becoming quite general in Lombardy and was tending to make men critical of the relation existing between the secular and ecclesiastical powers.[1]

Whether Arnold himself studied at Bologna under the great Irnerius or not can only be conjectured.[2] The remarkable knowledge he displayed of the Roman state lends colour to the theory, but it is not impossible that this information was acquired in Paris and later in Rome. He could not well have been ignorant, however, of the two great movements then attracting scholars, lay and ecclesiastical, to Bologna; the revival of civil law by the lectures of Irnerius, and the creation of a system of canon law through the *Concordantes discordantium* of Gratian.

The early years of the twelfth century were prosperous ones for the commune of Brescia which had grown strong and independent, economically and politically, enjoying under the consuls peace and wealth. A large and justly famed army had earned for it the respect of the neighbouring towns, and while it rendered dues to pope and emperor alike, it was in reality subject to neither.[3]

The population was a fusion of captains, vassals, and plebeians; each class intent on winning for itself utmost powers and privileges; each faction taking to itself every possible right and jurisdiction; and each need, social or political, finding its sustaining and defending apostle. During the years of schism between Anacletus and Innocent, the powers of the bishops had decreased until by 1135 they were merely nominal, notwithstanding the strenuous efforts put forth by various prelates to keep the *status quo*.

... *Johannes Sarisburiensis*, in *Zeitschrift für Kirchenrecht*, vol. xv, pp. 265, etc.

[1] Giesebrecht, *l.c.*, p. 120; Hausrath, *Arnold von Brescia*, p. 2, Breyer, *Die Arnaldisten*, p. 397. Note also the quotations from Justinian's *Institutes* in Wezel's letter in *B.R.G.*, vol. I, p. 539.

[2] Francke, *Arnold*, p. 15; Trithemius, *De Scriptoribus ecclesiasticis;* B. Nihusius, *Irnerius;* Fantuzzi, *Scrittori Bolognesi*, vol. IV.

[3] Odorici, *l.c.*, vol. IV, p. 230.

In 1132, when Innocent II came to Brescia, he attempted to restore the episcopal power, calling a synod to deal with the disorders, but Manfred, whom he left in charge of affairs, proved unable to cope with the situation and as soon as the Pontiff had departed, a revolt broke out on the part of those who were determined to prevent the restoration of the temporal power of the Church.

One can only conjecture how far the quarrel had advanced when Arnold returned from his sojourn at the Paraclete.[1] He seems, however, to have thrown himself heartily into the cause of those who were attempting to limit the power of the clergy. 'With absoluteness of conviction, with vigour of a manly eloquence, with the prestige of an immaculate life and with the enchantment of a moral ideality, this detractor of bishops and priests, this persecutor of monks who praised only the laity, came to espouse the cause of the commune.' The decree of the Lateran Council of 1139 confirms the conjecture that he advocated the tenets of the liberal party. 'He spread among the vulgar pernicious doctrines and filled their ears with impious words. The sacred laws, he said, did not sanction clerical possessions; the monks and priests had no right over the land; nor should the abbots relegate to themselves temporal power which belonged to the princes of the earth; government was the prerogative of the elected representatives of the people alone. Offerings and tithes should be tendered only for the needs of the body, not for their own pleasure. He condemned without restriction the luxurious lives of the priests, the delicacy of their viands, the splendour of their vestments, their lascivious joys and the relaxed manners of the monasteries.'[2]

[1] Otto of Freising, *l.c.*, p. 403; Sec. Arch. Vat., H.S. III, ix, 146. Gunther says he assumed the exterior of a sage and astounded the ignorant by his wise discourse; that he persecuted the clergy, denounced the monks and flattered the people, since he was avid of their favour.

[2] Gunther, *Ligur.*, III, col. 370.

Nothing in all this seems new. It was rather what the people had felt for years should be reformed. Innocent II himself had deplored the prevalent decadence of ecclesiastical discipline, but he had also insisted with all his eloquence that those who govern land must defend its interests, safeguard its peace and direct war when necessary, teachings which when applied to the clergy, Arnold felt were in direct contradiction to the precepts of Christ, although he approved of them for the laity. Moreover, he recognized the fact that the Gospel was not sufficient in itself to govern a commune. Even the saints of old had found such a task beyond their means. What, therefore, could a dissolute priesthood hope to accomplish?

It is uncertain what part he took in the government of Brescia. Undoubtedly he encouraged the citizens to follow the path chosen by the other Lombard communes, that is, political regeneration by a return to Roman institutions, and because he was supported by the people, he seems to have been the recognized head of the liberal reform party, although in all probability he held no office.

While the prelates were engaged in unseemly wrangles to gain or to retain power, he began to cry out that by possessing temporal goods the Church had departed from the way marked out by Christ and followed by the Apostles, and to teach that only by surrendering all property to the laity could the clergy hope to be saved.[1] With relentless logic, he called on the church of Brescia to renounce all temporal power.[2] A fresh schism arose. Manfred, Innocent's bishop, opposed Arnold, naturally, while the laity supported him. Popular feeling rose to new heights, and

[1] He is quoted as having said that as the clerics had the property, the monks the possessions, and the bishops the regalia, there was nothing left for the people but wisdom. '*Dicebat enim, clericas proprietatem, nec episcopus regalia, nec monachus possessiones habentes aliqua ratione salvari posse; cuncta hæc principis esse, ab ejusque beneficentia in usum laicorum cedere oportere.*' *Gesta Frid.*, *l.c.*

[2] Odorici, *l.c.*, vol. IV, p. 258.

when Manfred went to Rome, in 1137, the Brescians conspired to prevent his return. For a time, then, Arnold's party ruled the city, but in 1139, when Rome condemned him and his movement, his '*duo consules hæretici*' fell.[1] He had practiced so well what he preached that even his opponents were impressed,[2] but there is no proof that any of the doctrines he taught were heretical. Furthermore, the Council did not specifically condemn him, but merely silenced him.[3] Arnold was, however, a conspicuous influence in both the spiritual and the political life of the town. He shared Abælard's love of novelty and possibly his restless vanity and skeptical intellect. It seems probable that during these years he was busy writing, though the only basis for such conjecture is that later his books were ordered burned by Pope Innocent, which may have been only a precautionary measure.[4]

Exiled, Arnold joined Abælard,[5] who had returned from Saint Gildas in Brittany, where he had been abbot and where his attempt to reform the monastery had aroused a storm of protest. He was again teaching on Mont Sainte-Geneviève, still manifesting that critical spirit which had long made him obnoxious to such stout exponents of established ecclesiastical doctrine as Bernard of Clairvaux and Norbert of Prémontré. In 1140, the former declared that Abælard was teaching heresy, of which, he said, Arnold partook: 'that new form of belief which has been devised in France. Its standpoint toward virtue and vice is not moral, toward the sacraments is not faithful, toward the mystery of the Holy Trinity, something quite different from that simple sober one to which we have been trained.'[6]

[1] *Annales Brixiensis*, Ann. 1135, *l.c.*, p. 812. But this is not the year of Arnold's condemnation.

[2] Gunther, *Ligur.*, *l.c.*; *Gesta Frid.*, *l.c.*; S. Bernard., *Ep.* 195.

[3] Gregorovius, *Geschichte der Stadt Rom.*, vol. IV, p. 409.

[4] Mansi, vol. XXI, col. 565. After the Council of Sens.

[5] S. Bernard., *l.c.*

[6] S. Bernard., *Ep.* 330, Migne, *l.c.*, vol. CLXXXII, col. 535.

When Arnold returned to France, the strife between the ancient adversaries was flaming anew, and full of loyal zeal, he at once hastened to his master that he might defend him. Like Abælard, Arnold was lashed by Saint Bernard's denunciation: with him he went to the Council of Sens in 1141,[1] called at the Abbot's instigation.

Abælard hoped to make of the occasion an opportunity to disprove publicly the accusations against his teachings, as well as to confound Saint Bernard before the assembly of clerics. At first the Cistercian refused to attend the Council, saying that he was no match for Abælard, as, in comparison with one who had been accustomed to dialectics from earliest youth, he was a mere child. Furthermore, it was the duty of the bishops to judge the case, and quite outside the province of an abbot of a monastery.[2]

At this, the friends of Abælard were jubilant. The clergy, however, sensed the gravity of the situation, and, despite his renewed protests,[3] forced him to accept the rôle of defender of orthodoxy. Abælard, looking on the affair as an intellectual tourney, hoped for an easy victory.

The Council opened the first Sunday after Pentecost before a magnificent host of bishops, clerics, and laymen, splended in mitres and crowns, crosses and shields, embroidered vestments and emblazoned armour. The King of France was present, as were Henry the Boar, the Bishop of Chartres (a pupil of Abælard's and his defender at Soissons), Hugh of Auxerre (an intimate friend of Bernard's), the Archbishop of Rheims, the Bishops of Orleans, Troyes, and Meaux, besides a host of abbots, priors, deans, and scholars. Certainly it was a notable occasion, for Abælard and Bernard together represented not only the intellect of their age, but its two dominant movements,

[1] Deutsch, *Die Synode von Sens;* Mansi, *l.c.*
[2] S. Bernard., *Ep.* 337, 189, Migne, *l.c.*, vol. CLXXXII, col. 540, 354.
[3] *Ep.* 187, *l.c.*, col. 349.

the one conservative and orthodox, profound, subtle, and narrow; the other, the innovator, alert, ardent, equally inflexible, and as narrow in his tolerance as was his adversary in his intolerance.

The session was opened by a solemn exposition of relics after which Bernard recommended Abælard to the prayers of the faithful.[1] That same afternoon, the prelates held private conference with Bernard studying the Breton's works, noting his most daring propositions and comparing these with the Scripture and with the Fathers, especially with Saint Augustine, in an effort to discover and to prove his heresy.

The next day the public session was opened before the king, in the church of Saint Stephen, Saint Bernard occupying the place of honour among the prelates. After the prayers and introductory remarks, Abælard was introduced [2] and was asked to explain the seventeen propositions and extracts from the *Theologia Christiana*, the *Introductio ad Theologiam*, the *Scito Te Ipsum*, and the *Liber Sententiarum*, the last of which he disavowed.[3] These extracts from larger tracts of decided orthodoxy were dangerous when taken from the context. They were read and reread in public and Abælard was given the choice of denying them, correcting them, or justifying them. Despairing of justice from such a body, he appealed to the Pope,[4] a futile effort, as Innocent was even more the creature of Saint Bernard than were the bishops in the Council.

The next day Abælard composed a profession of faith in which, not content to defend step by step his theories and his errors, he accused Bernard of falsification, ignorance,

[1] Berengarius, *Apologia*, Migne, *l.c.*, vol. CLXXVIII, col. 1857.

[2] He is reported to have said ironically to Gilbert de la Poirret, '*Nam tua res agitur paries cum proximus ardet*,' *Vita S. Bernard.*, Migne, *l.c.*, vol. CLXXXV, col. 312.

[3] *Apologia*, p. 772.

[4] S. Bernard., *Ep.* 337, *l.c.*; *Gesta Frid.*, *l.c.*, p. 376.

and unjust fury,[1] and then attacked the vice and corruption of convents and the cupidity of bishops.[2] After this his condemnation was inevitable. Just what part Arnold took in the trial is not known. Bernard says: 'A Goliath has appeared armed for the conflict, preceded by his squire, Arnold of Brescia. Their scales are so closely united that a breath cannot penetrate them. The wasp of France has given a hissing to the wasp of Italy,[3] and both have attacked the Lord and his Church. Goliath has thrust his outcry on the phalanxes of Israel and insulted the army of the saints with an audacity greater than he felt when David was not there.'[4] A synodal letter, signed by the bishops of the province of Sens, exposed in details the motives of the condemnation. What Abælard taught was not in itself objectionable. It was his temerity, the spirit of criticism manifested in his writings, the influence of his works in the schools and in the streets, his insistence on reason as a preliminary to faith, which aroused antagonism.[5] With him reasoning was imperative, and while his doctrines were not in themselves alarming and his conclusions were generally orthodox, his methods aroused the fear and wrath of his contemporaries.

The acts of the Council no longer exist, but an interesting account of the proceedings (though manifestly inaccurate) has been given by Berengarius, in which he calls it an orgy presided over by Saint Bernard who could not 'distinguish oil from wine.'

'Already long has the rumour as if on wings, dragging the odour of your holiness through the world, announced your merit, spread your wonder. Happy prize we the new

[1] *Disputatio anonymo abbatis*, Migne, vol. CLXXX, col. 283. *Gesta Frid., l.c.*, gives the opening of the Apology, p. 378.

[2] He even accused Norbert of working fraudulent miracles. *Joanne Baptista Sermo, l.c.*; de Remusat, *Abœlard*, vol. I, p. 176.

[3] '*Sibilavit apis quæ erat in Francia api de Italia.*' See Isaiah, VII, 18.

[4] *Ep.* 190.

[5] *Ep.* 338.

time which is beautified by a glance from that countenance, and we believe that the corrupt world exists only through your service. From the might of your tongue hangs the mercy of Heaven, the fruitfulness of earth, the pledge of fruitfulness. Now you have done your worst, you have dealt your deadly stroke; you have declared Peter Abælard a heretic before the Synod; you have branded him as a bandit. You have burned his books. It is easy to see that this is not the work of Christ, but of Bacchus. The weaker became the one to be saluted. As the wine moistened the throat of the bishop, then when something high and godly sounded out of the writings of Abælard, the bishop's ears could not understand. So the teeth were gnashed against Abælard. . . . As the Jews they cry, "He destroys the temple of God." So judge the blind the word of light; so the drunk condemn the sober; so the dogs bite the saints and swine gnaw pearls. The sober bishop drinks too much wine or water and his heat presses all out of his brain. . . . While he reads his charges the hearers sleep, one on the elbow, one on a cushion; one has his head on his knee. When the bishop says: "Will you condemn him?" they catch the last syllable and with sleepy voices say: "Damnamus." Others just awakened cry: "Namus" (we swim). He swims indeed; you are merely soused.'[1]

Both Arnold and Abælard were condemned by the Council as fabricators of perverse dogma and aggressors of the Catholic Church and they were ordered imprisoned in separate convents,[2] although neither was branded as a heretic. Exhausted by the labours and contentions of a strenuous life, Abælard yielded to the persuasions of Peter the Venerable of Cluny, to make his peace with Saint Bernard and to submit to the Church.[3] Arnold was younger,

[1] Berengarius, *l.c.*

[2] Mansi, vol. XXI, cols. 564 etc.; S. Bernard., *Ep.* 189.

[3] S. Bernard., *Ep.* 195. Abælard died shortly after this.

more vigorous, and more uncompromising, and refused to yield.

Popular opinion in France did not support the sentence of the Council, and after Abælard's voluntary submission, no bishop was found to execute the harsh judgment against Arnold, so for the time being he was left unmolested.[1] He tarried awhile in Paris where he 'expounded sacred letters to the scholars. What he said agreed perfectly with the laws of the Christians, but differed as widely as possible from their practices. He did not even spare the bishops, because of their base and avaricious lives, and because they sought to build the church of God in blood.'

The substance of his teachings here, as in Brescia, was a poor Church based on liberty. There he had advocated popular liberty; here freedom of thought. In the chapel of Saint Hilary in Abælard's old school on the Mount, and later in his own school, he not only taught clerical poverty, but he practised it too strenuously to suit his listeners, who in their first enthusiasm for reform had flocked to his standard. The truth he proclaimed was intermixed with manifest error and his influence was also lessened by the almost vindictive satire which he directed against those in authority. Bernard he denounced as a seeker after vainglory, jealous of those who won fame in religion or learning,[2] while the Cistercian, for his part, called the Brescian an incorrigible schismatic, a sower of discord and a disturber of the peace.[3]

Bernard saw as clearly as did Arnold how the political influence and wealth of the Church were endangering its true mission and weakening its spiritual influence. In his *De Consideratione* he lamented the avarice of the ecclesias-

[1] S. Bernard., *l.c.*, Hyacinth, who was with Abælard and Arnold at Sens, and who later became a cardinal, declared that such judgment was beyond the power of a synod. He had been a pupil of Abælard's in Paris in 1136 with John of Salisbury. See S. Bernard., *Ep.* 338, for his annoyance with Hyacinth.

[2] *Hist. Pontif.*, c. 31.

[3] S. Bernard., *Ep.* 195.

tical overlords. 'Who will permit me to see before I die,' he wrote Eugenius, 'the Church of God so ordered as it was in the days when the Apostles cast their nets to fish for souls and not for gold and silver.' But he recognized in Arnold's teachings an attack on the essential strength of the institution, not merely an assault on worldly possessions and dignities.

It is strange how these adversaries shared the same standards in ideals and in life. Both were ascetic; both hated the pomp and show of priestly state; both wished to keep the Church apart from the world. Arnold represented the lay spirit; Bernard was the greatest pillar of sacerdotal autocracy despite his recognition of the dangers it held for the spiritual life. Their very similarities increased their antagonism.

While neither pope nor bishop disturbed Arnold in Paris, Saint Bernard was far from willing to lay down his arms. Unable to secure the enforcement of the articles of condemnation, he devoted himself most assiduously to driving Arnold out of Christendom. He hunted him from land to land, appealing to any one whom he could hope to influence, doing his utmost to make true his own words: 'Wherever he has once set foot, thither he never dares to return any more.' When he was chosen mediator between the Pope and King Louis VII in 1142, he seized the opportunity to secure from the monarch a decree expelling Arnold from Paris and from France.

For a time the latter found refuge in Zürich, where he may possibly have been before.[1] Here he taught and won many followers.[2]

Saint Bernard, always well served by his monks who acted as his police, discovered his retreat and wrote Her-

[1] *Gesta Frid.*, *l.c.*, c. 21.

[2] Possibly the way had been prepared for him here by Henry of Lausanne. Giesebrecht, *l.c.*, p. 133.

man, the Bishop of Constance, who had won his See by spending large sums in Rome the very year (1139) of Arnold's condemnation by Innocent II,[1] asking him to expel the schismatic. 'Expelled from Brescia, Italy, and France, Arnold of Brescia now works his iniquities in your diocese and devours your people like bread. . . . Would to God his teaching were as sane as his life is austere. He neither eats nor drinks, has neither hunger nor thirst (like a devil) save for the blood of souls. By his flattering discourse and his semblance of virtue he attracts rich and poor. Then when he has their good-will, he stirs them up against the bishops and clergy.'[2] He goes on to call Arnold a vagabond and fugitive on earth, like a roaring lion searching what he may devour, and, being rejected among his own, goes over to strangers. 'His mouth is full of malediction and bitterness; his feet are agile for shedding blood. Evil is in his words and he ignores the way of peace. The enemy of Christ, the disturber of peace, he changes unity into discord. His tongue is a sharp sword, his words are more sweet than oil, but in reality they are death and he seeks ever the favour of the rich and powerful.'

The effect of this letter may be judged by the fact that Arnold did not stay long in Zürich. While there, however, he seems to have preached the regeneration of the Church by a return to the conditions of apostolic days.[3]

He next went to Guido, the papal legate in Moravia and Bohemia.[4] To him also Bernard sent an emphatic letter of warning against Arnold as a man of 'ingratiating manner who never failed to make use of all the influence he could acquire, against the clergy.'[5] Although evidently very angry with the legate for his friendliness toward Arnold, he dissembled this as well as he could. 'Arnold of Brescia,'

[1] Hausrath, *l.c.*, p. 68. [2] *Ep.* 195. [3] *Gesta Frid.*, *l.c.*, p. 404.
[4] *Epistolæ Wibaldi*, Jaffe, *B.R.G.*, vol. I, p. 195; Gregorovius, *l.c.*, vol. IV, p. 458.
[5] S. Bernard., *Ep.* 196.

he writes, 'whose conversation is honey and whose doctrine poison, who has the head of a dove and the tail of a scorpion, whom Brescia has vomited, Rome held in horror, Germany abominated, and Italy will not receive, is with you. Have care, I beg you, that aided by your authority he does not prove more hurtful. For since he had the will and the ability to nourish, aided by your favour, he will have a triple tie that one breaks with difficulty. . . . There are two suppositions (if all is true and you have the man with you); either you do not know him or you have faith in his conversion. God grant you are not deceived. What could we not give to make this stone a son of Abraham? What agreeable present it would be for our mother Church to receive from your hands this vessel which has so long outraged her. It is permissible to attempt it.'[1] As Bernard does not give the history of Arnold in this letter, it is probable that Guido already knew something of him. The effect of his effort is not known. For two years (1143–45) there is no trace of Arnold, then at the end of that time he and Guido appear simultaneously in Italy.[2] He was evidently on his way to Rome, attracted, no doubt, by the rumours of the political revolution which, in its return to the institutions of classical antiquity, seemed to be so in accord with his own ideals.

The history of mediæval Rome will probably never be written, since the centuries of slaughter, pillage, and incendiarism combined to destroy most of the documents

[1] S. Bernard., *l.c.*, '*Arnoldus de Brixia, cujus conversatio mel, et doctrina venenum; cui caput columbæ, cauda scorpionis est; quem Brixia evomit, Roma exhorruit Francia repulit, Germania abominatur, Italia non vult recipere,*' etc. The date of this letter, according to Giesebrecht, is not before 1142, nor after 1143.

[2] Jaffé, *Regesta*, no. 6160, gives a document dated September 12, 1145, which shows that Guido was then in Italy. Tschudi, who does not give his sources, says Arnold spent five years in Switzerland. Francke (p. 133) says he was offered a public chair in Zürich and taught there. The city was at that time very liberal and the prelate was very weak, so that if Arnold had won popular favour, he probably would not have been expelled. At any rate, Saint Bernard seems to have stopped writing about him.

which might have thrown light on the growth of the commune. The few chroniclers whose works do remain were absorbed in the personalities of pope and emperor rather than in the development of a municipality.

The ancient organization, shattered by the impact of Teutonic invasion, was gradually replaced by a composite government, neither Roman nor feudal nor ecclesiastical, though bearing qualities of all three. The removal of the seat of the empire to Constantinople had left the local administration quite stable, and during the barbarian invasion, there remained at least the outward form of a commune. The Goths never penetrated the surface of the social order. Senate, curiæ, provincial, and municipal magistrates, prefects and judges, were allowed to continue as before. As early as the first century of the Christian era there had been a separation of civil and military powers. The maintenance of this principle by the Goths made no visible change in the constitution, save that now the military element was the conqueror, and the civil the conquered. The Byzantine rulers merely substituted one army for another. This was one fundamental difference between Rome and the provinces, where there was more fusion and consequently more conflict between the races.

Many of the republican institutions fell into decay during the Dark Ages, but their original features seem to have remained discernible, possibly because the Lombards who wrought such havoc elsewhere, abolishing ancient laws and robbing the people of whatever freedom their predecessors had left them, did not touch Rome. Almost simultaneously with the decay of the older institution, there had come into existence, as a third administrative element, the Church, which was to be a dominating factor in coming centuries. Long before the last representative of the empire had disappeared, the bishops were the real governors of the city. In 554, the Pragmatic Sanction conferred on them the superintendence of, and authority over, the provinces, thus increasing their already considerable powers. During the invasion of the barbarians, they had come forward as the defenders of the people. A definite and natural result of this service had been to increase their temporal and political importance until not only the superintendence of municipal affairs, but the nomination of public officials was in their hands.

The small council which Gregory the Great had created in order to administer the ever-increasing property of the institution, began to replace the municipal magistrates by taking over their judicial functions, by protecting and succouring the oppressed, by settling disputes, nominating judges, etc.[1] The members of this council, though papal officials, were not necessarily priests.[2] Changing conditions meant increasing judicial and civil powers, most of which fell into clerical hands as a matter of course, since the greater number were concerned in one way or another with papal interests, the ever-growing moral authority of the pope being enhanced by his great revenues. While the Republic did not acknowledge the head of the Church as the head of the city, it was quite willing to profit by his recognized influence and to overlook, for the most part, his usurpation of municipal powers.

The distinctive character of Rome's organization separated her from the communes of the north, which, with the possible exception of Venice, owed their existence to the perpetual conflict between the feudal or aristocratic elements on the one hand, and the popular or commercial elements on the other. In Rome no such grouping existed.

[1] It gave no criminal decisions, but it did exercise the powers of a double tribunal, civil and religious.

[2] There were seven of these who formed a sort of papal cabinet; the *Primicerius;* the *Secundarius;* the *Aracarius* or marshal; the *Sacellarius* or cashier; the *Protoscriniarius,* at the head of the chancery; the *Primus Defensor,* the advocate of the Church; and the *Adminiculator,* who pleaded the cause of widows, orphans, and paupers.

The deserted Campagna isolated the city from the rest of the peninsula quite as definitely as ocean or mountain range, checking any notable development of trade or industry, and preventing the establishment of guilds, elsewhere the supporting institution of the municipalities.

Imperial Rome had had its aristocracy which the barbarian invasions had disintegrated. The fragments existing after the fall of the empire in the west had been at the mercy of the pontiffs, who, eager to seize upon any opportunity, however slight, for the increase of their powers, had bestowed on those whose support they desired whatever lucrative posts, vast estates, and rich benefices the various cataclysms had given into their hands. In this way they added to the nobility a new class which in time completely altered its character. The new aristocracy, increased or modified by each succeeding Pontiff, became a most turbulent element, a permanent source of confusion, turmoil, and civil war, destructive rather than constructive and subversive not only of popular government, but of administrative efficiency of any sort.

This nobility was from the first divided into two groups; the *primates* or *optimates*, old families possessed of large estates and filling highest hereditary offices in state and army; and the *nobiles* or landed proprietors of moderate means, but high position. These controlled the army, which was often composed of their tenants, organized into *scholæ*.[1] The high clerics were the most important class of Romans, for though this was not an hereditary caste, the prestige acquired while in power generally remained in the family.

A double aristocracy, lay and cleric, a triple administration, municipal, papal, and imperial, caused the Roman commune to pursue a most erratic course of development. By degrees the old Roman institutions became more and more submerged under the new orders and are seldom men-

[1] Gregorovius, *l.c.*, vol. II, p. 494.

tioned. Only the innate reverence of the Roman for antiquity and for tradition kept them alive. The armed nobility, constituting the main fighting force, filled all high offices and met occasionally in council, calling themselves the Senate, but bearing not the slightest resemblance to that of either republican or imperial times. The exact position of the Senate in the pre-Carolingian period is difficult to establish. When mentioned at all, it seems to have been a class rather than an institution,[1] a sort of municipal council ornamented by a pompous name.[2]

Theodoric, prompted by policy no less than by his great respect for antiquity, tried to restore the importance of the institution, although he allowed it no share in the imperial administration, restricting the functions to criminal jurisdiction over municipal affairs and to some control of the finances. But whatever power he did bestow on it was lost in the cataclysm following his death. Justinian's effort, though no more permanent in itself, seems to have been remembered longer.[3]

The people as a whole, whether citizens or plebs, seem to have had no part in the government. In times of emergency, they may have met as a general parliament for consultation with the Senate, magistrates or clergy, but this might as easily be considered an ecclesiastical as a municipal assembly.

Naturally the magistracy was influenced by the constant shifting of the centre of administration and authority. The prefect, who as late as the time of Gregory the Great (590) seems to have kept his functions of supervision of police, public games, spectacles and monuments,

[1] Vedittini and Savigny say the Senate never ceased to function; Papencordt says it became a curia; Hegel, Giesebrecht, and Gregorovius say it had only a nominal existence after 579. It is not mentioned in documents or by chroniclers until the eighth century, when it seems to refer to some ceremonial.

[2] Rodocanachi, *Les Institutions de Rome*, p. 4.

[3] Procopius. *De Bello Gothico*, l. 26, *R.I.S.*, vol. I, pp. 248, 251.

streets and aqueducts,[1] became less and less independent. His powers were shared with the *magister militum*, and by the eighth century, his office had become subjected to so rigorous a supervision as to be a charge rather than an honour.[2]

As the prefect became less important, the dukes came into existence as heads of the Republic, appointed by the emperor[3] at first, and later by the pontiffs, who gradually assumed all powers and prerogatives ostensibly theirs. The duke himself lived on the Palatine in what remained of the palace of the Cæsars, commanding an army and presiding over the criminal court.[4]

The chief magistrate in the city was the pope himself, under whom there developed a complementary administrative system. In addition to his cabinet, there were his particular tribunal, the '*judices de clero*,' and also the '*judices de militia*,' leaders of the army, appointed first by the exarchs, but later by the pope.[5]

Under the Carolingians the constitution changed substantially. Dukes, prefect, and *magister militum* existed as before, it is true, and the social organization likewise changed but little, yet all were subordinate to the head of the Church, who was fast becoming a powerful temporal sovereign and who about this time began to consider himself the master of 'our Roman Republic.'[6]

While Charlemagne held supreme power nominally, and actively fulfilled his duties as patrician when in Rome, still he was there but occasionally, while the popes were ever

[1] Greg., *Ep.* 7, viii, Migne, *l.c.*, vol. LXXVII, col. 1071. '*Gloriosissimus filius noster Johannes, præfectus urbis.*'

[2] Rodocanachi, *l.c.*; Diehl, *Étude sur les admin. byz. dans l'exarchate de Ravenna*, p. 127; *Regesta di Farfa*, ed. Giorgi et Balgoni, no. 651.

[3] 716 A.D., Gregorovius, *l.c.*, p. 538.

[4] Diehl, *l.c.*, p. 132.

[5] Savigny, Gesch. des Röm. Rechts, vol. I, p. 291, etc.; Marini, *Papiri diplom.*, n. 102, Ann. 961; Galletti, *Del Primicerio*, p. 219.

[6] Halphen, *Études*, p. 2.

present and were able to contest the supremacy of the imperial officials and to make vigorous and effective protest when rebels fled to Charles or appealed to him for arbitration. Despite their ideals of the dignity of the imperial office, the Carolingians did no little to increase pontifical power by subjecting both duke and *magister militum* to the head of the Church.

The coronation of Charlemagne, without the slightest reference to Senate, army, or people, had aroused the resentment of the Romans, who refused to be placated by the formality of a later election. Important as was this event in the history of western Europe, its most marked change in the city seems to have been that the judges, formerly appointed by the pope, now became responsible to the emperor or his *missi*, and the imperial decree was the final decision in the courts.

The later Carolingians were in a way partners of the popes, who were as feeble as their imperial contemporaries. Under the impotence of the one and the corruption of the other, anarchy reached its climax. In the confusion the nobles, who still claimed power based on descent from the Roman patricians, seized the opportunity to wrest privilege after privilege from feeble pontifical hands and, calling themselves the Senate, ruled the commune under the shadow of ancient traditions. In all the succeeding confusion they continued to gain power, and aimed to restore the dignity and office of the patricians. Aside from the fact that they elected a chief as consul senator, or *princeps Romanorum*, who presided over the tribunals and was theoretically head of the city, nothing is known of their organization. This element was not feudal. Despite their claim to illustrious ancestry, many of them were related to the popes and had come into power through nepotism. A new pontificate naturally tended to lessen their power, so that while the nobility was powerful it was also divided and turbulent, continually plotting against pope or emperor, continually stirring up the *milites*, continually seeking popular support, so that orderly government was practically impossible.

Whatever the Senate had become, it seems to have been closely connected with the new baronage, and though permeated with non-Roman ideals, it did not entirely discard the ancient traditions. Possibly its chief was the same official who was nominally at the head of the commune.[1] Although the name of the Senate is often found during the succeeding centuries,[2] as has been said, it seems to belong to a class of citizens who numbered among their ancestors a Senator and who were given the old term by the chroniclers. That it really implies a social order is evidenced by the fact that it included women.[3]

As a class it wielded great influence. In the Campagna these nobles held grim castles which were easily turned into fortresses manned by troops composed of their numerous vassals and partisans; they claimed the right to elect the pope even after they had relinquished all deliberative prerogatives.[4]

Outside the city, feudalism did establish itself somewhat during this anarchy. In the Sabine hills the Crescenzi ruled as kings: Præneste and Tusculum were feudal strongholds, and as the barons of the Campagna increased in

[1] *Chron. Moissacense*, ann. 801, *M.G.H. SS.*, vol. I, p. 305. '*Leo papa cum consilio omnium episcoporum sive sacerdotum, seu senatu Francorum necnon et Romanorum.*'

[2] Letter of Pippin, 757: '*Omnis senatus atque universa populi generalitas a Deo servatæ Romanæ civitatis.*' When Pope Leo III crowned Charlemagne he confirmed his power, '*uno cum omni Senatu Romano.*' In 896, Arnulf of Carinthia was received at Rome by the Senate. See also Curtius, *De Senatu Romano*, p. 12; Peter Damian, lib. VIII, *Ep.* 4, 5, Migne, *l.c.*, vol. CXLIV; Ptolemæus Lucensis: *Hist. Eccl.*, Quétif et Echard, vol. I, p. 541. Udalricus Babenbergensis, *Chron.*, Eccard., *Corp. Hist. Med. Aevi*, vol. II, p. 226; *Cronaco Casinensa*, lib. IV, c. 54, *R.I.S.*, vol. IV, col. 530.

[3] Sigonius, *De Reg. Ital.*, lib. VI, p. 238; *Annalista Saxo.*, Eccard, *l.c.*, col. 515; *Liber Pontif.*, *R.I.S.*, vol. III, pp. 73, 179, 180, 192, 260, 313.

[4] *Annales Fuldenses, M.G.H. SS.*, vol. I.

power they were neither submissive to the pope nor faithful to the emperor whose claim to control of the city they resented. After the tenth century, however, it became the policy of the pontiffs to exclude this provincial nobility, formerly so powerful, from control of civic affairs, and they either fell into decadence or remained banished in their provincial towns, while newer families, such as the Frangipani and Pierleoni rose to the surface and from their castellated arches and porticoes governed the city.

The courts continued to function all through the Middle Ages, although just what their duties were is uncertain.[1] The *judices de clero* remained as ecclesiastical officials, ranking in the signatures of official acts after the imperial *missi* and the bishops, and before the consuls.[2] There were also *judices consulares* who had charge of the district courts.[3] The prefect was the criminal judge and in important affairs, bishops and cardinals were seated with him.[4]

The politico-religious unity established by Charles had disappeared by the tenth century, and the feudal system, slight as it was in Rome, was nevertheless converting imperial officers into independent princes there as elsewhere. Nor did the spirit of communal liberty, so potent in the north, fail to exert its influence. When Otto deposed John and set up Leo in his place, he was depriving the Romans of their valued privilege of choosing a pope, which arbitrary exercise of imperial power aroused long and obstinate resistance and did no little towards reviving the independence of earlier days. Under the plebeian prefect Peter, the discontented nobles joined with the commons under twelve *decarcone*,[5] against the Emperor. But the union of nobles and commons was transitory. In the confusion of the last

[1] Marini, *l.c.*
[2] Fantuzzi, *l.c.*, vol. I, pp. 218, 251, 253; 115, 27, 67, 70; 111, 12, 117; IV, 198.
[3] Savigny, *l.c.*, vol. I, p. 295.
[4] Rodacanachi, *l.c.*, p. 24.
[5] Probably heads of the regions. *Vita Joh. XII*, Cod. Vat. 2851, part II, f. 11.

years of the tenth century, the Crescenzi came into power and Giovanni of that name, backed by papal support, assumed the title of patrician. In 966 he was ousted by the emperor but the Romans rose in revolt against the German pope foisted on them and restored him.

After Otto III's attempt to reëstablish the ancient Republic the Senate and consuls are constantly mentioned. The office of patrician was also revived and given renewed honour, while the prefect was made imperial vicar. Germanic institutions also gained strength.

With the decline of population in the eleventh century, the nobles, divided into imperial and national groups, again predominated, enlarging their power by reserving to themselves the office of patrician and electing the popes from their own ranks. In the first half of the century (1033–45), the Church and the Roman state both assumed the aspects of hereditary possessions in the hands of the Counts of Tusculum, and in the efforts of other nobles to dispute this power, the city was given over to anarchy even worse than that of the preceding centuries. The streets thronged with thieves, cut-throats, and assassins; pilgrims were plundered, and rival popes were obliged to defend themselves by force until the situation was brought under control by the iron hand of Hildebrand.

The continual fluctuations of political power, the ravaging of the city and Campagna by imperial armies and the Norman wars, had all but ruined Rome. What had not been destroyed had been profoundly altered, so that the grandeur of the city had sunk into a desolation of ruins.

The lonely and deserted capital no longer commanded any great highway and maintained only a vague tradition of its former significance, emerging occasionally from its obscurity as a symbol which inspired some new outburst of civic liberty. Churches and chapels had replaced temples and basilicas; porticoes had become markets, and the citadel itself was the dwelling-place of monks who denied the dignity of man while tending cabbages amid the ruins of the palaces of the Cæsars.[1] From time to time since the fall of the Western Empire, the Capitol had been the centre of all purely civic affairs,[2] and had for a brief period regained its importance, but the Senators of the later day, in their tall mitres and mantles of gold brocade had but a dim idea of those earlier statesmen who had framed the laws of the civilized world and decided the fate of all nations.

On the neighbouring Palatine, gardens were planted within the walls and colonnades; goatherds clambered over the marble ruins; markets were held in the very heart of the imperial palace; the surrounding districts, especially the Forum, were deserted, as the populace retired to the Campus Martius; the Aventine and the Cœlian, once thickly populated, were becoming barren wastes, while the Colosseum was a fire-blackened ruin. A few imperial monuments arches and columns, still stood; most of the *termi* were more or less intact as were the theatres. The atrium of Saint Paul's was destroyed; so was the portico of the Vatican and the greater part of the Leonine city. Bridges and gates had been spared, however, and the palaces of Claudius at the Colosseum and of Constantine at the Lateran were to some extent still habitable.[3]

Many of these monuments were made into fortresses; for example, the Colosseum and Arch of Constantine were held by the Frangipani, while the Portico of Octaviana had

[1] The palace of Octavian was a convent. A bull of Anacletus II, ratifying the Abbot of Santa Maria in Aracœli in possession of the Capitoline, throws light on the labyrinth of grottoes, cells, courts, gardens, houses, and huts replacing the old temples, but it stirs the imagination more than it satisfies a desire for information. Mabillon, *Mus. Ital.*, II, 143, *Ordo Rom.*, XI.

[2] Under Otto III its ruins were reanimated by assemblies of nobles and people, and the city prefect took up residence there. See *Regesta Farfa*, n. 1098, for an act signed *Actum civitate Romana apud Capitolium.*

[3] Cod. Reg. Lat. 5912, ff. 125–27, Bib. Vat.

become the stronghold of the Pierleoni, a newly arisen Jewish family, lords of the district between the Tiber and the Capitol, known as the Ghetto. Tower-like houses, stretching from the Tiber to the Lateran, were the only evidence of power that the Middle Ages produced in the Eternal City.

When Paschal II became pope in 1099, then, he found himself entirely at the mercy of the nobles, who controlled not only Rome, but also the spiritual overlord. The only possible course open to him was to side with one faction in order to overcome the other. Aided by a nephew, Gualfredo, by the prefect Pierleone, and by the powerful Frangipani, he was able to hold down, or at least check, the Corsi and Colonna, the most disturbing elements in the city. In 1108, he felt secure enough of his position to turn the militia over to his nephew, the Campagna to the imperial margrave, Tolomeo of Tusculum, brother of the prefect and lord of all the land between the Sabine hills and the sea; and the government of Rome itself, to the prefect and consuls, Pierleone and Leone Frangipano, and go to Benevento. Events proved, however, that he had misjudged the situation, for as soon as he had departed the nobles seized control and he was allowed to return only by the aid of the Norman army.

The still unsettled Investiture Struggle just then took another turn which greatly complicated affairs in the city. Henry V started to Rome in 1110 to receive the imperial crown and to reëstablish the old rights of the Empire. Paschal, anticipating a struggle and realizing that neither Norman nor Roman would help him in a crisis, sent to Sutri, where Henry had stopped, to make terms. The Pope was not a statesman, nor was he distinguished for his moral courage, yet he merits credit for his effort to avert the calamity threatening both city and Church. While unwilling to relinquish freedom of elections or to allow lay investitures, he did propose that the bishops resign all property derived from the crown and depend solely on tithes and donations, while the Emperor should, for his part, resign the right of investiture. Apparently he was not prompted by any moral considerations as to the rectitude of the clergy holding temporal wealth, but rather by an earnest desire to promote harmony between the rival powers. It was a bold stroke, even a foolhardy one, this attempt to save the spiritual rights of the Church by abandoning its temporalities, lands, and jurisdictions.

At first Henry appeared willing to accept the offer, which would put the whole feudal and secular property of the Church at his disposal and reduce the clergy to reliance on their spiritual resources. He came on to Rome and began preparations for his coronation. At the ceremony in Saint Peter's, February, 1111, the compact was read before the services began, and the Pope renounced all intervention in secular affairs as incompatible with the spiritual character of the clergy. Naturally the bishops, German as well as Italian, protested vigorously at so casual a surrender of their property and their rights on the part of Paschal, who seemed to them to be quite carefully safeguarding his own prerogatives. A violent tumult arose. The congregation became a brawling mob and began to plunder the very church. Seeing that his coronation was impossible, Henry seized the Pope and the chief cardinals, while the mob outside retaliated by murdering any Germans they might meet. The turmoil lasted three days, when Henry left, taking his prisoners with him. Paschal secured his own liberty by renouncing the right of investiture 'for the peace and liberty of the Church' and the following April Henry was crowned. As soon as he left Rome, Paschal repudiated his renunciation as having been obtained by force and the old disorder broke out afresh.

In 1116, the prefect Peter died and the Pope appointed

to the office one of the Pierleoni. This family was especially hated by the people because of their wealth and their aristocratic sympathies. The prefect was at this time a most important and influential person, ranking next to the pope himself, by whose side he walked in processions, clad in a wide-sleeved dalmatic of red silk, a mantle sumptuously trimmed with gold, a mitre of purple velvet on his head, hose of gold on one leg and red on the other.[1]

For some time now he had been chosen by the pope and invested by him except in times of disorder when he had been occasionally named by the people.[2] It was customary even when nominated by the pontiff for him to show himself to the people from a pulpit and to swear before them to observe the laws of Rome, after which he was conducted in procession to the Lateran, where the pope formally ratified his appointment and where he was invested with the imperial eagle and a naked sword by the imperial plenipotentiary. However he was chosen, he was regarded by the emperor as his vicar in the city, but after the fall of the Frankish Empire the office had come to be regarded more and more as being dependent on the papacy.[3]

Paschal then was starting no precedent when he named a candidate for the office, but the contest with the emperor had so proven his inabilities that it was difficult for him to impose his will now on a reluctant populace and nobility. The two classes united in their support of the son of the late

[1] Mabillon, *l.c.*, p. 170, *Ordo Roman.*: '*Præfectus ab ecclesia sanctæ virginis Mariæ usque ad palatium indutus manto precioso, et calceatus zanca una aurea, id est una caliga, altera rubea — juxta dom. Papam collateraliter nullo medio equitando incedit.*' For the dress of the prefect see the effigy on the tomb of Peter de Vico in Viterbo, who wears a mitre that looks like a truncated pine cone. It was this Peter who had charge of the execution of Arnold.

[2] *Lib. Pontif.*, *l.c.*

[3] Geroh. Reichersperg., *l.c.*, '*Grandiora urbis et orbis negotia — spectant ad Rom. Pont. sive illius vicarios — itemque ad Rom. Imp. sive illius vicarium urbis Præfectum, qui de sua dignitate respicit utrumque, vid.* D. *Papam, cui facit hominium et Dom. Imp. a quo accipit suæ potestatis insigne, sc. exertum gladium.*' Baluze, *Misc.*, vol. IV.

prefect, who, although a mere youth, was important as being the nephew of Tolomeo of Tusculum.

Paschal rather unwisely tried to force the situation by taking possession of the insignia of the prefecture. Easter was near at hand, and while he was conducting services in the Lateran on Maundy Thursday, the mob broke into the church with young Peter in their midst, and, interrupting the sacred functions, noisily demanded his ratification. The Pontiff evaded the issue by promising to attend to the matter after Good Friday, and there was no alternative but to wait his pleasure. So they departed muttering threats. Barons and citizens divided into two parties and during the festivals the revolt waxed strong. Easter Monday, Paschal started for Saint Peter's. On the bridge of Sant' Angelo, he was met by a furious crowd, again presenting Peter and demanding his investiture. The papal retinue was attacked so violently that the procession was forced to return to the Lateran, where the youthful candidate was finally given the insignia of office. It is uncertain that Paschal ever recognized him, as he quitted Rome almost immediately for the Norman camp where he spent the summer.

During the remaining two years of his pontificate he lost control of the city to the nobles; and his successor, Gelasius II, a monk of Monte Cassino, was equally unable to cope with the revolt, fleeing to France, where he died shortly afterward.

The Burgundian Calixtus II (1119–24), a keen diplomat and wise statesman who numbered among his kinsmen half the sovereigns of Europe, was able to settle for all time the question of investitures and to inaugurate in the city of Rome a policy of peace and restoration,[1] but he died before he had completed his work and those who succeeded him in the pontificate were unable or unwilling to carry out his

[1] Cod. Vat. Lat. 1984.

plans. Henry V died soon after Calixtus, and for two decades rival candidates struggled for imperial crown and papal tiara. The Roman barons did not lose this opportunity for renewed civil war, and as neither faction was strong enough in itself to hold the city, the people were drawn into the struggle from which they emerged more on an equality with the populace of the Lombard communes than they had hitherto been.

By the middle of the twelfth century the movement for popular freedom had spread from Lombardy as far south as the Papal States. One of the first cities to adopt the new régime was Tivoli, which under the rule of bishops had already enjoyed many exemptions. Rome was uneasy at its growth and prosperity in the secluded gorges of the Anio. Moreover, she resented the loyalty it had shown to Anacletus during the recent schism and consequently, when in 1140, Tivoli for some unknown reason rebelled against Roman overlordship, the Roman troops marched up the valley to subdue it. They were repulsed and pursued even to their own gates. A second attack was made the next year which proved to be more successful and Tivoli was forced to surrender to save itself from the fury of the besieging army. It submitted to Rome in much the same way that, in Lombardy, Lodi and Como had accepted the overlordship of the emperor. Innocent made his own terms with them without consulting the people, a slight the soldiers were quick to resent. They felt the Pope had betrayed them and they demanded the submission of Tivoli, permission to demolish its walls and dwellings and to expel the population, terms which Innocent rejected as being inhuman; consequently the anger of the Romans was turned against the Pontiff.[1]

Smarting under defeat, they rushed to the Campidoglio and, declaring themselves free from papal domination, set

[1] Otto of Freising, *Chron.*, c. VII, *M.G.H. SS.*, vol. XX, p. 263.

up a new government under the name of Sacro Senato. Then they recommenced war with Tivoli.[1] Innocent tried in vain to arrest the tumult by menace and by prayer, but soon realizing the futility of his efforts, retired to the Lateran, where he died in 1143. Celestine II, in his six months' pontificate, was powerless to withstand the revolution which was gaining force every day. Lucius II (1144–45) allied himself to the nobles against the people, which both factions of the aristocracy were coming to fear, and then appealed to the Normans for aid, but in vain.[2] In the meantime a senate of twenty-six members had been established among the ruins of the Tabularium and this body, using the authority of the *Senatus Populusque Romanorum*, summoned the Pope to renounce all regalian rights and all money save tithes and free-will offerings. Next the people appealed to Conrad III for recognition of their republic. He received the ambassadors graciously enough, but took no definite steps to aid them. In the meantime Lucius tried to seize the Capitol by force, but being wounded in the head by a stone, he was carried to the monastery of San Gregorio, where he died a few days later.[3]

Although in its inception, the Roman revolution was the outcome of an historic necessity, of the renewed vigour of the people and their detestation of the aristocracy, from whom they attempted to wrest all power, it soon became essentially a popular uprising against the misrule of inefficient popes and the tyranny of their courtiers. In many respects similar to the revolutions in the Northern cities, it owed its later development to the lack of a commercial element in the city. The soldiers had acquired strength in the recent wars. Now they coveted a share in the government, and to secure this attempted to establish a demo-

[1] Otto of Freising, *l.c.*; Papencordt, *Gesch. der Stadt Rom.*, p. 254.
[2] Card. Aragon, *Vita Lucii Papæ II*, *R.I.S.*, vol. III.
[3] Godfrey of Viterbo, *R.I.S.*, vol. VII, cc. 460–61; Otto of Freising, *l.c.*, p. 107.

cratic republic. The nobles were to be excluded from all participation in governmental affairs; the temporal power of the papacy was to be abolished, and the popes themselves seemed destined to go the way of the bishops of Lombardy who, with the rise of the commercial class, had lost all civic power.

The new commune, Roman in little but name, was composed of one class, namely, burghers,[1] rude and ignorant, who called their plebeian leaders senators without having the slightest knowledge of Cicero, Cato, or Cæsar. Like the ancient plebs, they made war on the patricians, whose power they resented. Having excluded the aristocracy from the Senate, with a fine inconsistency they placed at the head of the city a noble, Giordano dei Pierleoni, brother of the anti-Pope Anacletus II, and conferred on him the judicial powers pertaining to the aristocratic and imperial office of prefect.[2] The number of Senators was increased to fifty-six,[3] and they were divided into two groups, the *senatores consiliarii* and the ordinary senators. The former formed a small council consulted on the more urgent or secret affairs of State. There was also a *Curia Senatus* composed of a few Senators and legal experts which had charge of judicial affairs.[4]

After the death of Lucius II, the timid cardinals had

[1] '*Et nos senatores; Joh. Berardi, Petro plangens, spatulam Uguicio gentis; Petr. Enrici; Romanus petri milluli; Astaldus David. Jordanus brutii Gregorius gaudentis. Nicol. philippi, Petr. Romani sperantis in Deo. Sebastianus gualtrade. Stephan. Falconis. Grisostus Cencii Gresus. Nicol. berezonis, Dompincus. Parentius. Petr. baffoini. Falco curozil. Rusticus nicolai rustici, Petr. rabic. Stephen. cezaronis Bonum tibi veniat h.e. bentivenga pictor. Joh. bonifilioli, Petrus demetri pro nobis et pro omnib. aliis consenatorib. nostris quor nomina non sunt his discripta.*' Galletti: *Del. Prim.*, p. 306. Some of these seem to have been nobles and some appear in the lists of earlier Senators.

[2] Martène et Durand, *Ampliss. Coll.*, vol. II, col. 398; Guibal, *l.c.*, p. 59; Romuald. Salernitan., *Chron.*, *R.I.S.*, vol. VII, p. 193.

[3] It may have been that these were chosen from the regions, although at this time there were probably only twelve of these. Halphen, *l.c.*, pp. 7–10; *Lib. Pontif.*, *l.c.*; Mabillon, *Mus. Ital.*, vol. II, p. 128.

[4] Gregorovius, *l.c.*, vol. IV, p. 469.

met at San Cesario and elected as pope the head of the Cistercian Abbey of Tre Fontane, who took the name of Eugenius III. A simple monk, unversed in statecraft, he was scarcely the right man for the place, and Saint Bernard, once his master, was dismayed that in so critical a time so incompetent a candidate should have been chosen. Despite the admonitions sent on from Clairvaux,[1] the new Pontiff, barred from Saint Peter's, met the demand for renunciation of all civil rights and recognition of the Republic by fleeing to Viterbo, where he undertook to raise an army.

During the eight months he was absent, the new government showed itself powerless to prevent rioting and the destruction of property belonging to the cardinals and other papalists. At the end of the year 1145, a compromise between Pope and revolutionists enabled the former to enter the city.[2] He agreed to recognize the Senate on condition that it hold its authority from him.[3] He was to pay the members a salary. The office of patrician was abolished, or rather was replaced by that of *gonfaloniere*, while the prefect, corresponding, in a way, to the *podestà* elsewhere, was revived, and the Senators were invested by the Pontiff.[4] The Senate as then constituted could not properly be called the commune, as it was not the fusion of orders of citizens. Nor was it exactly a victory of democracy over aristocracy, but rather it was the organization of one order in opposition to the other.

At this moment, Arnold of Brescia arrived in Rome. His ideas may have preceded him and it is not impossible that they may have inspired, or at least promoted, the revolution. Whether he now came to determine its method and direction is beyond conjecture. According to the *Historia*

[1] *De Consideratione, l.c.* [2] Otto of Freising, *l.c.* [3] *Ibid.*

[4] The prefect had been originally charged with police and justice. *Tabularium S. Prasidis*, ed. Fidele, no. 28, in *Arch. St. di Roma.*

Pontificalis, he 'promised satisfaction and obedience to the Roman See and was received by the Lord Eugenius at Viterbo. Penance was enjoined upon him, which he agreed to fulfil; fasting, vigils, and prayers about the sacred places in Rome.' The errors for which he made satisfaction are not stated; it is uncertain whether they were the heresies of Abælard or the direct attacks on the Church for possessing wealth and power which had caused his banishment from Brescia,[1] and which he had apparently continued to make in other lands. He owed satisfaction for both. When he was condemned for his teaching at Brescia in 1139, he had promised not to return to Italy; and the ban of Sens still hung over him.

If he did forswear at Viterbo his views on the wealth of the Church and on its secular power, the state of things he found at Rome forced him to resume his mission, although he lived quietly enough until Eugenius had left Viterbo and had gone to France to be near Saint Bernard.[2]

Even before his arrival, the aim of the revolutionists had included the abolition of the temporal power of the clergy from the highest to the lowest. The proposals of Paschal II, despite their rejection, had found a loud echo in Rome as they had in other parts of the peninsula. Enlightened public opinion in all parts of Europe had long recognized the evils dominating the institution, but neither councils nor monastic orders had been able to lessen them; more and more it was becoming evident that the only remedy lay in depriving the bishops of temporal power, a definite result of the Investiture Struggle. The immense progress of society during this period when the state was contesting the Gregorian hierarchy — the revival of industry, traffic,

[1] S. Bernard., *Ep.* 195. '*Adhæserat Petro Abælardo.*' But '*Videbitis hominem aperte insurgere in clerum,*' etc. Further he was cast out from Italy and from Rome '*pro simile causa.*'

[2] He was out of Rome from January, 1146, until November, 1149. Otto of Freising, *l.c.*; Jaffé, *Regesta,* no. 8850.

learning, the renewed interest in Roman law — brought the whole Christian world into bitter antagonism with the Church. Elsewhere the struggle was for communal liberty and for a reform of the institution with political autonomy as a side issue; here it was to a certain extent an effort to restore freedom through an intellectual awakening.

At Rome as at Brescia, Arnold saw the clergy engaged in unseemly strife to retain temporal power and leading the luxurious lives which he thought so inconsistent with their calling. Walter Map believed that it was the sight of the lasciviousness of the cardinals and their tables laden with gold and silver dishes that led Arnold once more to lift up his voice in protest. For the Prophet of Brescia could not keep silence. First, 'he censured the clergy temperately in letters to the Lord Pope; but they took it in bad faith and cast him forth. He then returned to the city and began to teach indefatigably. The people flocked about him and heard him eagerly.'[1] As Eugenius was in France, there was no power to prevent his speaking openly. 'He was heard frequently in the Capitol and in public disputations.' What were his subjects? Apparently he was busied more with discipline than with dogma. 'He was,' says Otto of Freising, 'a slanderer of the bishops and clergy, a persecutor of the monks, and a flatterer of the laity as well. For he said that the clergy who hold property, the bishops who enjoy regalia, and monks who have possessions cannot in any wise be saved. All these things pertain to secular rulers and should by their beneficence be given to the clergy to use.'[2] Arnold did not hold the ex-

[1] Until December, 1145, Giesebrecht, *l.c.*, p. 137.

[2] Otto of Freising, *Gesta Frid.*, *l.c.*, p. 404. Cf. Gerohus Reicherspergensis, *De Novitatibus hujus sæculi*, in Grisar, *Geroh über die Investitursfrage, Zeitschrift für Katholischen Theologie*, vol. IX, p. 549. '*Memini me, quum fuissem in urbe* (Roma), *contra quendam Arnoldinum valenter literatum in palatio disputasse.*' Breyer says this was not Arnold, but an Arnoldist, and considers it evidence of the existence of a sect founded by Arnold, a conclusion which seems hardly warranted. *Die Arnoldisten*, p. 397.

treme views of the Apostolics nor of Waldo, concerning evangelical poverty. He would allow the clergy to have the 'first fruits, and tithes and whatever the devotion of the people offered.'[1] They might then have an income without violating the commands of Christ and the customs of the apostolic age. Property they must not hold. The accounts extant of Arnold's teaching can hardly mean that he sanctioned even communistic possession or ownership of any kind by the Church as an institution. Specific charges were made against the clergy — simony, worldliness, evil living, and lack of charity. 'They love not God nor their neighbour,'[2] and all these vices were attributed to their wealth.

He then attacked the governing body of the Church, the Pope and the Cardinals, for their unapostolic position. The College of Cardinals, he claimed, 'was by reason of the pride and avarice of its members, their hypocrisy and manifold sins, not the Church of God, but the house of buying and selling and the den of thieves, who played the part of the scribes and pharisees toward the Christian people. He said the Pope was no pope because he was not an apostolic man and a shepherd of souls, but a man of blood[3] who maintained his authority by killing and burning; a tormentor of churches; an oppressor of the innocent, who did nothing in the world but feed on flesh and fill his coffers and empty those of others. Nor was he apostolic, because he did not imitate the doctrine nor the life of the Apostles, and therefore no reverence nor obedience was due him.[4] Further, 'nothing in the government of the city pertains to the supreme pontiff; ecclesiastical jurisdiction ought to

[1] Gunther, *l.c.*, p. 322.

[2] Cod. Ottob. Lat. 1463, Bib. Vat., *Gesta per imperatorem Federicum Barbam rubeam in partibus Lumbardiæ et italiæ*, vv. 780–99.

[3] Cf. Geroh. of Reichersperg, who regrets that Arnold was punished by death because the Church was thus guilty of bloodshed. (In *De Investigatione Antichristi*, *l.c.*, p. 89.)

[4] *Hist. Pontif.*, *l.c.*

be enough for him.'[1] Yet Arnold seems to have professed no anti-Catholic dogmas, only maintaining that when pope and prelate deviated from the gospel rule of poverty, they should not be obeyed, but fearlessly opposed. No tolerance should be shown to such as desired to reduce Rome, the seat of the Empire, to subjection.[2]

Thus he began to preach frequently in public parliaments to a people already up in arms against the corrupt rule of the clergy. His exhortations against the riches of the Church aroused their enthusiasm no less than did his classical reminiscences. His eloquence, inspired by a mysticism, by a love of liberty, and by a profound conviction that the Church could be purified only by a return to apostolic poverty, made him the man of the hour. The revolutionists were seeking to restore the mechanism of the Roman government to what it had been in the time of Constantine and Justinian, 'who held in their hands the whole earth, through the might of the Senate and the people of Rome.'[3] No one of their number could so ably lead them as this exiled Lombard, who saw in the overthrow of the temporal power and the establishment of the Republic the accomplishment of his ecclesiastical, social, and political ideals for a return to the democracy of the early, unpolitic Church.

The reorganized Senate, forced by necessity to recognize a German emperor, sent an envoy to him beseeching him to dwell in Rome and rule all Italy. It is not known whether this were Arnold's idea, or whether he preferred

[1] Otto of Freising, *l.c.*

[2] *Hist. Pontif.*, *l.c.* '*Preterea non esse homines admittendos, qui sedem imperii fontem libertatis Romam, mundi dominam, volebant subicere servituti.*'

[3] Cf. *Gesta Frid.* He formulates thus Arnold's doctrine: '*Proponens antiquorum Romanorum exempla, qui ex senatus maturitatis consulto et ex juvenilium animorum fortitudinis ordine et integritate totum orbem terræ suum fecerint. Quare reædificandum Capitolium, renovandam senatoriam dignitatem, reformandum equestrem ordinem docuit.*' Giesebrecht (*Arnold von Brescia*, p. 19, n.) does not credit this statement. Vacandard (*Arnauld de Brescia*, p. 73) does.

the imperial power to rest entirely in the hands of the people. He was not primarily a republican nor, on the other hand, was he an imperialist. He believed the Church was vitiated by the possession of wealth and of temporal power, and the Roman movement afforded an opportunity to purify the institution. With this object in view he made common cause with the revolutionists.

From this time our sources for the life of Arnold are very meagre. The *Historia Pontificalis* ends; Otto of Freising becomes unsatisfactory; there are only a few brief notices of Arnold in the chronicles of the progress and subsequent decline of the Roman revolution. Just here, however, may be placed two letters which are believed to have been inspired if not written by Arnold. These form part of a correspondence between the revolutionists and the Emperor. They are a letter from 'a certain friend of the Senate' to Conrad III,[1] and one from Wezel to Frederick.[2] Giesebrecht[3] believes that '*quidam fidelis senatus*' of the first letter may well be Arnold himself; for he had bound himself to the Senate by an oath of allegiance.[4] The friend of the Senate is at all events a thorough Arnoldist. Wezel is evidently an adherent of Arnold. His identity is unknown. It seems probable that he was a German. Possibly he and the group of men mentioned in his appeal to the Emperor, men who, like him, have German names, were followers won by Arnold during his sojourn in Constance.[5] It is also probable that in these documents we have reasoning after the characteristic Arnoldist method.

The letter of the man who describes himself as '*Quidam fidelis senatus*' is an earnest appeal to the Emperor to come quickly to Rome and reëstablish imperial control, thus

[1] *Epistolæ Wibaldi*, no. 216. Jaffé, *B.R.G.*, vol. I, p. 335.

[2] *Ibid.*, no. 404. [3] *Arnold.*, p. 142, n.

[4] Arnold of Brescia '*qui honori urbis et rei publice Romanorum se dicebatur obligasse prestito juramento.*' *Hist. Pontif.*, *l.c.*

[5] Clavel, *Arnauld de Brescia*, pp. 281–83; Giesebrecht, *l.c.*, p. 143.

limiting the ecclesiastical authority to its proper sphere. 'For,' he says, 'no wars should be waged nor murders committed in the world by priests, who are not permitted to bear the sword with the chalice. Their duty is to preach, and to support their preaching by good works.'[1] Wezel's letter was written after Conrad was dead, when Frederick had been chosen king, but before his coronation as emperor. He reproaches Frederick because he has failed to recognize the Roman people as the source of his power, but like his predecessors has obeyed the summons of his 'Julianists, heretics, apostate clergy, and false monks, who disregard their vows and wield authority despite the evangelical, apostolic and canon law, and in defiance of all other laws, both human and divine.' He then quotes Saint Peter himself to prove that the Pope is 'apostate'; that he is no true descendant of the Fisherman. 'Flee that which is of this world, add to your faith virtue, and to your virtue knowledge. How,' he says, 'could the members of the Curia say with Saint Peter: "Behold I leave all and follow thee"? And again, "Silver and gold have I none"?'

Wezel thus convicts the worldly See of Rome out of the mouth of the Apostle whom the mediæval world honoured as the founder of that See and the chief of the Apostles and proves that the papacy was unapostolic. He then turns to the foundation of all: — the commands of Christ, uttered when he sent his Apostles out into the world and, according to the belief of ecclesiastics, organized the Church. Referring again to the prelates, he says: 'How can such men hear from the Lord's lips, "You are the salt of the earth"? "Ye are the light of the world"? To Peter and the vicars (*vicariis*) of Peter the Lord said: "As my Father hath sent me, so send I you." But the manner of his sending by the Father he expressed, saying: "If I do not the works of my Father, believe me not."

[1] Jaffé, *B.R.G.*, vol. I, pp. 335–36.

If Christ, who did no sin, was not to be believed without works, how are those to be believed who do evil — nay, more, who do evil publicly?' 'How,' Wezel proceeds, 'can the clergy, given over to luxurious living, bear to hear the foremost of the commands of the Gospel: "Blessed are the poor in spirit," when they are not poor in fact or in aim?' He continues his argument, following up the quotations from the New Testament by passages from the early Fathers, showing how far the Church of his day has lapsed from the apostolic ideal of a ministry given to self-denial, humility, poverty, in obedience to the commands of Christ.[1] Wezel's letter, like that of '*quidam fidelis senatus*,' reflects Arnold's characteristic doctrine. The two documents go to show that, during the alliance with the Roman revolutionists, Arnold retained and championed the views which had led to his banishment from Brescia and from Italy in 1137.

In these letters of Wezel are found the attacks on the Donation of Constantine. The party of Arnold was one of the earliest to discredit the legend — led by their peculiar view of the power and privileges of the papacy. They contended that Constantine was already a Christian before he met Sylvester and that the Donation was a lying and heretical fable utterly beyond the possibility of defence, an attack which failed to alarm the Pope or to impress the Emperor.

During the turbulent years that Arnold remained in Rome, it is not certain just what part he took in the affairs of the commune nor can it be affirmed what was accomplished politically in this time. It is certain that the Republic was established before he entered Rome; it is equally certain that under his direction the constitution underwent certain modifications. He hoped to free Rome permanently from all priestly rule, to reduce the clergy to

[1] *Epistolæ Wibaldi*, no. 404.

a condition of apostolic poverty and limit them to purely spiritual functions. Rome was to be a free municipality subject only to the emperor who was to make the city a source of power as in the olden days. He then proposed to re-create the Campidoglio, to strengthen the senatorial dignity, and to reform the equestrian order. Nothing in the city was to belong to the pontiff beyond his ecclesiastical authority. In his desire to restore the ancient forms, he dreamed of patrician knights, plebs, and tribunes of the plebs. He wished to renew the old titles of the city, to recreate patricians and *quirites*. The patricians were to be the high nobles or captains which Arnold wanted to draw to himself. He had no desire to create a new nobility. It is not so easy to determine what he wanted for the equestrian order, whether he had in mind those of the early Republic or those of the later Empire, who had no power. Possibly he himself did not know just how this order would develop; possibly he did not know that there had been formerly two distinct orders of knights. Probably he had only the mediæval significance, a social order, in mind. As to the plebs, he seems to have thought not of those of the days of the Cæsars, but rather of those of his own day, free persons, landless and not noble, whose tribunes were the consuls of the *arti*, who had the double office of judge and general.

Despite his love for antiquity, apparently the most Arnold could do was to fuse the factions into a commune of the Lombard type, but since Rome to him was superior to these, he used for her a different terminology. What in another city would have been local here acquired a worldwide importance, for he intended that the governors of Rome should likewise rule the world. The *credenza*, therefore, must be a Senate; the captain a patrician, the vassals an equestrian order, and the consuls of the *arti*, the tribunes of the plebs. The blending of the idea of the mediæval commune and that of the mistress of the world prompted him to create a public opinion which should demand the return of Rome as the capital of the Roman Empire. The emperor was to be elected and was to owe his power to the recognition of the Roman people. While he was expected to make the city the centre of the government, yet the senatorial letters to Conrad offered to compromise on this point if he would help them against the pope and his allies. When Conrad failed to accede to their requests, Arnold collected two thousand followers, some of them minor nobles from whom he hoped to establish the nucleus of his state.

Arnold's Senate was a body somewhat similar to the communal councils of northern Italy. It sat in the palace of the Capitol and was the chief power in the city, exercising all legislative, executive, and judicial prerogatives, declaring war and making treaties. Civil justice belonged to the court of justice of the Capitol (*Curia Senatus*) composed of Senators and men learned in the law. The power of the Senate was exercised under the control of, and with the agreement of, the Council and Parliament, that is, an assembly of citizens called together by the sound of trumpets and bells and meeting in Santa Maria in Ara Cœli. It voted by acclamation without discussion.[1] The Council was a deliberate assembly chosen from the notables of the city. Measures were discussed by them before going to the communal Parliament, although its advice was not always taken.[2] Its number varied from twelve to forty-four; when small, it was always aristocratic; when larger, it included members from the middle class.

All of Arnold's suggestions were accepted by the citizens, who laboured strenuously on the fortification of the Capitol. It was not long before the revolt spread beyond the walls, and throughout the duchy, the cities proclaimed their inde-

[1] Halphen, *l.c.*, p. 62.
[2] Document of 1145; Halphen, *l.c.*, p. 65.

pendence, while the barons of the Campagna profited by the opportunity to establish themselves as independent sovereigns. The Senate, meanwhile, tried to force the provincial nobility to receive their investiture from its hands and to live in the city.[1]

The revolt of the nobles was destroying the patrimony of the Church,[2] and the petty despotisms that arose were hostile alike to pope and to Senate. Baronial rule was especially strong in Latium, a poor district where there were few wealthy communes to form a counterpoise such as existed in Tuscany or Umbria. The energy of the new republic was therefore dissipated in the struggle with towns.

Arnold's dream was from the first beyond his power of realization. While some of the barons supported him [3] the majority of them, unafraid for their power, saw no need of an alliance with the people and preferred to bide their time until the return of pope or emperor. But the greatest obstacle to his success lay in the absence of the class of free citizens who could have given strength to the movement.

The Senate recognized the consistent austerity of his life and the selflessness of his motives. By the term of his oath of allegiance, he had become counsellor of the commune in matters relating to the civil constitution. Unless he was also Senator, which seems doubtful, he held no office during the years he was in Rome. His desire to restore popular power and his reverence for classical antiquity were sufficiently strong to prevent any desire for dictatorship on his part.

While the democracies of northern Italy developed in accordance with local feudal conditions, the Romans, in their eagerness to restore ancient forms, lost themselves in a dream of world-wide supremacy, the presence of the

[1] Otto of Freising, *Chron.*, *l.c.*; Card. Aragon, *l.c.*, p. 439.

[2] Gregorovius, *l.c.*, vol. IV, 2, p. 501.

[3] *Ep. Eug. III*, '*Multi magnates Romanorum sequebantur eum*' (Martène et Durand, *l.c.*).

monuments and traditions of antiquity, combining with the revival of the study of the law of Justinian to hold them in the enchanted domain of memories which they mistook for hopes. Nor did the presence of notaries called to Rome to decide on cases called before the papal courts make for law and order in the distracted city. One of the strangest phenomena of the Middle Ages is this memory of a long-past glory becoming a political power and dominating three great expressions of government; pope, emperor, and republic all dreamed of universal sovereignty inherited from the Roman Empire of a thousand years before. In considering the Empire as the ultimate source of their power, the Romans had adopted an indestructible conception. Unable to conceive of the city as withstanding all powers, lay and temporal, they admitted the inferiority of the mediæval commune as compared with the ancient Republic, and accepted the Empire to insure their own existence. Their appeal to Conrad presumably expressing Arnold's theories is a medley of ancient and modern, sacred and profane ideas:

'To the illustrious ruler of the city and of the world, Conrad, by grace of God, King of Rome, always Augustus, from the Senate and people of Rome; health and a prosperous and glorious rule over the Roman Empire. We have already informed your royal nobility by frequent letters of that which has happened through our own means, have told you that we remain faithful to you and that your crown may increase in splendour, is our daily wish. We are, however, surprised that you have not vouchsafed us any answer. Our unanimous endeavour is that we may again restore the Empire of the Romans which God has entrusted to your guidance to the might that it possessed under Constantine and Justinian, who empowered by the Roman people and Senate, governed the world. We have, therefore, by the help of God, restored the Senate and defeated many enemies of your imperial rule, in order that what belonged to Cæsar should be yours. We have laid a solid foundation. We are security for your justice and peace to all such as shall desire them. We have conquered the fortresses of the civic nobility, who supported by Sicilians and Pope Eugenius hoped to defy you and have either held these towns for you or have destroyed them. We are therefore harried on every side by the Pope, the Frangipani, the sons of Pierleone (with the exception of Giordano, our standard bearer), by Tolommeo and by many others. They desire to prevent our crowning you emperor. Meanwhile we suffer much hardship out of love to you, since there is nothing too hard to those who love and you will give us the recompense due from a father and merited punishment to the enemies of the Empire. Shut your ears to the slanderers of the Senate; they will rejoice at our discord in order to ruin you and us. Remember how much harm the papal court and these our former fellow-citizens have caused your predecessors and how with Sicilian aid they have sought to do still further harm.'

Apparently to Conrad the whole matter seemed to have been merely another power demanding right to create the emperor. If an external power was to confer the imperial dignity, he preferred it should be the Pope rather than the Romans, yet he saw in the Roman movement a chance to force the Pope to yield to him as to a superior authority. As Eugenius had entered on an alliance with Roger of Sicily, however, the Romans based their hope on Conrad's being forced to listen to their proposals. The latter saw that since the time of Henry III no other emperor had been offered so favourable an opportunity of depriving the Pontiff of power.[1] But he was engaged in war with the Guelfs in Germany and was also intent on the Second Crusade, so, willingly or not, he let the opportunity slip.

[1] *Ep. Wibaldi*, no. 213.

In 1150 he addressed a letter to the prefect, making no mention of the Senate, and to the consuls, captains, and Roman people, a direct ignoring of the Republic. In polite but indefinite terms, he announced that he would accept their invitation and would come to tranquillise the cities, reward the faithful, and punish the rebels. The words promised ill to the revolution. Conrad had indeed made terms with the Pope, but he died before he could come to Rome.

In 1149 the Romans had been obliged to receive Eugenius again into the city,[1] and while the new peace formed between him and the Senate was as short-lived as the earlier ones, his return was significant. He was promised a restitution of all his pontifical rights, of the funds of all churches, and the possession of all fortresses outside the city. This was the first step in the overthrow of Arnold's influence. From this time on his government lost prestige and the opposition gained in definite purpose.

Conrad's successor was Frederick Barbarossa. Both Romans and Pontiff hastened to secure his support. He showed little inclination to recognize the Republic, ignoring the numerous letters urging him to come to Rome to receive the crown from those who alone had the right to confer it. Influenced by Wibald of Corvey, who worked continuously for the cause of Eugenius, he saw in the Roman revolution a rebellion against his power, and consequently he sent the Romans no notice of his election.

The papal envoys were received, however, and negotiations were begun which aroused the ire of the city. Eugenius represented the commune as being in rebellion against a German Emperor in order that they might select one of their own.[2] His quiet subtlety was gaining more for him,

[1] Mansi, vol. XXI, col. 684. Bull of Eugenius III given at the Lateran.

[2] *Ep. Eug.*, Martène et Durand, *l.c.*, col. 553. *Ad haec sanctitati tuæ quædam notificamus, quæ faciente A. hæretico rusticana quædam turba absque nobilium et majorum scientia nuper est in Urbe molita.*

both in Rome and at the imperial court, than a large army could have done. He laid the entire population of the city under great obligation to him by rich gifts; he reduced the power of the barons of the Campagna; in a short time he would have quite overcome the Senate. But just when he was succeeding most definitely, he died at Tivoli, July 8, 1153.

The immediate successor of Eugenius was short-lived. Then came the cultured, eloquent, strong-willed, and resolute Englishman, Adrian IV, who had no intention of recognizing either the Republic or the superior power of the Emperor, and least of all, of tolerating the presence of the Brescian trouble-maker in the city. His pontificate began inauspiciously enough with brawls and street fights, but although he himself was a prisoner in the Leonine city and unable to get to the Lateran, he lost no time in demanding the abolition of the Republic and the banishment of Arnold. Just before Easter a cardinal was stabbed in the Via Sacra. Adrian at once put the city under an interdict.[1]

The prospect of the financial loss resulting from the cessation of pilgrimages to the city was unpleasant, and after four days of the Easter festival had passed uncommemorated, the frightened people demanded that the Senate yield to the papal demands. Hoping to bury the Republic with the overthrow of Arnold, who was just then thundering with greater eloquence than ever before against the Papacy, Adrian refused to raise the ban unless the Lombard were expelled.

Frederick Barbarossa was on his way to Rome and the promise of his assistance stood Adrian in good stead. Now as an earnest of imperial good faith, the Pope asked that Arnold be arrested. Two months after the latter had left

[1] Card. Arag., *Vita Ad.*, *l.c.*, p. 442. '*Venerabilem namque virum magistrum D.... Presbyterum Cardinalem Titulo S. Potenianæ ad præsentiam ipsius Pontificis euntem quidam ex ipsis Hæreticis ausu nefario in via sacra invadere præsumpserunt et ad interitum vulneraverunt.*

Rome, Frederick reached Viterbo, where he was met by papal representatives demanding their adversary. For two years Frederick had been under promise to the Pope to subdue Rome. Independent as he was and flushed with his victories in Lombardy, the latter was still necessary to him and he dared not ignore his promise.

Arnold, abandoned by those with whom for the past nine years he had laboured for the cause of liberty, had wandered from castle to castle seeking some city independent enough to shield him from his enemies. He was arrested at Bricoli in the Val d'Orsia in Umbria, but had been rescued by one of the Visconti and taken to Campagnatio. Frederick seized one of the younger members of the family as hostage until Arnold was given over to him. As he was in orders, he was triable only by the Church, which, after condemning him and offering to free him if he would recant, handed him over to the secular arm. The prefect acting as his judge was Peter di Vico, a holder of large estates in Viterbo, who had for years made war against the commune and who was satisfying a private grudge in his condemnation of Arnold and gladly gave the order for his death.

Arnold refused to recant, asserting that his teaching was just and salutary and that he was ready to die. After a brief respite in which to confess, he was hanged, then burned, and his ashes scattered in the Tiber.[1] The significance of his death is unquestionable. The party which stood for evangelical poverty in the Church, which believed that the clergy should confine themselves to the duties enjoined upon the Apostles by Christ, had been crushingly defeated by the power of the Church as an institution. Rome, oppressed by the traditions of a magnificent past, and the prey of two powers contending for supremacy, could not permanently maintain either civic

[1] Cod. Ottob. Lat., *l.c.*

freedom or religious independence. The odds were too great.

The defeat of a party, however, by no means necessarily implies the conquest of the principles for which that party has contended. Did the triumph of the papacy and the death of Arnold mean the end of Arnold's influence? So Giesebrecht would have us believe.[1] The part Arnold played in the Roman revolution has, for the historian of the imperial age in Germany, obscured the fundamental doctrine which led him to cast in his lot with the revolutionists. That doctrine formed one of the great world currents in Arnold's time, and was destined to grow in strength during the two succeeding centuries, and Arnold had preached it untiringly with all the force of vivid, magnetic personality and overwhelming conviction. Politically the school of Arnoldists never died out and Arnold himself is the historical precedent for all forces which since his day have revolted against the secularization of the Church, and this is particularly true because his aims were not sullied by any sordid motives.

The extent of his personal influence in the great movement toward apostolic Christianity can never be determined, owing to dearth of evidence. His ideas were not spread by any writings of his own, so far as we know. There is in existence no written word which can be proved to be his. There is not even any certainty that he ever wrote books. As has been said, Innocent II, in condemning Arnold with Abælard after Sens, commanded 'that the books containing their errors' be burned, but Saint Bernard, in his account of the Council, speaks only of Abælard's books.[2] Moreover, Walter Map says: 'This Arnold was condemned by Pope Eugenius [3] undefended, in his

[1] Giesebrecht, *Arnold*, pp. 145, *etc.* See also *R.I.S.*, vol. III, p. 442, for a contradiction of this.

[2] S. Bernard., *Ep.* 189, *l.c.*

[3] A mistake, unless the reference is to the final condemnation in 1155. The

absence, not out of his writings but because of his preaching.'[1]

We are then largely dependent for information about Arnold upon his enemies — Saint Bernard, Otto of Freising, John of Salisbury, and the rest, from whom we have already quoted. All these accounts show that Arnold preached evangelical Christianity. They prove that he did more — that he lived the apostolic life himself, and that he owed to his life, at least in part, his great personal influence. 'Arnold,' says another witness, 'was a man ever too stern and detached in manner of life.'[2] Otto of Freising could not condemn his life. The worst he could say of Arnold is summed up in the following statement: 'He was a man not without natural ability, though he was gifted with a flow of words rather than with solid judgment. He was fond of the unusual, eager for novelty. He belonged to that type of man whose mind is easily turned to devising heresies and schismatic disturbances.'[3] John of Salisbury testifies: 'He had the priestly dignity, wore the dress of a regular canon, and mortified the flesh by fasting and sackcloth. He showed himself keen of intellect, but perverse in the interpretation of the Scriptures. He was an eloquent preacher, and inveighed vehemently against the delights of this world.'[4] His doctrine was censured, not his life. According to Walter Map, 'he was noble and great by birth. He excelled in letters, and was first in religion. He allowed himself no indulgence in food or clothing beyond what sternest necessity demands. He went about preaching. He sought not the things that were his own, but the things that are of God. He did always what was amiable and admirable.'[5] Not that his teachings had great value in

first condemnation was in 1137, under Innocent II, the second at Sens, in 1141, under the same Pope. Vacandard, *l.c.*, pp. 63, 67.

[1] *De Nugis*, ed. Wright, p. 43. [2] Cod. Ottob. Lat., *l.c.*

[3] Otto of Freising, *Gesta Frid.*, bk. I, c. 20.

[4] *Hist. Pontif.*, *l.c.* [5] *De Nugis*, *l.c.*

themselves. He seems not to have been a great original thinker; his one unchanging ideal of apostolic poverty for the Church was as old as the institution itself. His significance to his own time and to a later time lies in the value of his effort rather than in the keenness of vision and understanding he brought to the task.

There can be no doubt that Arnold's apostolic life and teaching, aided by learning, eloquence, and magnetism, swayed the people among whom he lived. 'In no place where he dwelt would he allow the people to be at peace with the clergy. He was abbot[1] at Brescia, and while the bishop was on a journey to Rome, he so influenced the minds of the citizens that they would hardly admit the bishop when he returned.'[2] It is not probable that the apostolic doctrine on which this opposition was based failed to find adherents also.

In Paris, after the condemnation of Sens, when Arnold was preaching at Sainte Geneviève, he did not lack hearers: 'Poor men, who openly begged for alms from door to door, and so supported themselves and their master.'

The success of Arnold in winning converts is, however, best proved by Saint Bernard's fear of his influence, expressed in the letters already cited to the Bishop of Constance, and to Guido, the Papal Legate. Some allowance should be made for Saint Bernard's habitually vigorous language, and for his indignation because the French bishops had failed to execute the papal ban which he himself had secured. Still the subject of these letters must have been a man of dangerous power. 'Up to this time,' wrote Bernard, 'wherever Arnold has dwelt, he has left behind him footprints so foul and terrible, that where he once has set his foot, he never dares to return thither

[1] A provost of Augustinian Canons was called abbot in Italy. Giesebrecht, *l.c.*, p. 127.

[2] *Hist. Pontif.*, *l.c.*

any more. Indeed he aroused with exceeding violence the very land in which he was born and threw it into confusion. Therefore he was accused before the Lord Pope as a very evil schismatic and expelled from his native country. . . . Then for a like cause, he was cast out of the French kingdom as a noted schismatic. He had held to Peter Abælard, all of whose errors, attacked and condemned by the Church, he undertook to defend with enthusiasm and energy, with him and for him. Through all these experiences his frenzy has not been diverted; but his hand is still stretched out.'

No man is a dangerous disturber of the established order of things and of the peace founded thereon unless he can command an enthusiastic following. Arnold was a peril to the ecclesiastical order because his attacks upon its inconsistencies and abuses aroused the people to desert the unapostolic clergy for the apostolic prophet of Brescia. Perhaps the Bishop of Constance found out by experiences of his own the power of Arnold. It has already been shown that adherents of Arnold's in Rome may well have been followers won at Zürich. Hausrath believes that a revolt of Augustinian canons at Zürich against the bishop may have been due to his influence. The revolt took place, however, ten years after his departure, and there is no proof that it was an echo of his preaching.

As has been said, no one knows where Arnold was during the two years after he was driven from Zürich. Possibly he remained, protected by the legate Guido, in Moravia and Bohemia — a region which was to become a centre for heretical evangelical Christians later on.

In Rome, Arnold at once became a power. The whole history of the revolutionary movement after his appearance there testifies to his influence. One incident is particularly striking; 'The citizens flocked about him,' says Walter Map, 'and heard him eagerly. It happened they heard how he had preached a sermon about mammon and the scorning of riches in the very ears of the Cardinals and the presence of the Pope. Arnold was cast out by the Cardinals. The people thronged to the Curia and cried out against the Lord Pope and the Cardinals, saying that Arnold was a good man and just, and the others were avaricious, unjust and evil; not the light of the world but defilement.' [1]

He did not win the people by condoning their sins. One writer, it is true, calls him 'flatterer of the people,' [2] but the more trustworthy author of the *Gesta di Federico* gives a very different account of him. 'He chid with equal severity priests and lesser folk thinking that he alone lived rightly, and that others were in error with the exception of those who adhered to his dogmas. He carped at the deeds of the supreme Pontiff, and in short spared no one. He mingled true statements with false, and thus gave pleasure to many. He also cursed laymen for withholding tithes, receiving usury, taking what was not their own, and for gaining wealth by false means.' [3]

The laity followed him in spite of plain-spoken denunciation of their ill-doing, and even the clergy whom he ceaselessly lashed, furnished him with adherents in Rome numerous enough to be deplored by Pope Eugenius.[4] There is one supreme proof of the influence which made him the dread of the prelates: on no account would the Pope suffer him to live in Rome after the downfall of the revolutionary government. Even his dead body was a source of dread. His ashes were scattered on the Tiber, lest his body be

[1] *De Nugis,* p. 43. [2] Gunther, *Ligur., l.c.*

[3] Vv. 767–80.

[4] *Ep.,* Baronius, *Annales Ecclesiastici,* Ann. 1148, vol. XIX, p. 34. '*Fallax et invidus humani generis inimicus per Arnaldum schismaticum, quasi per membrum proprium, hoc effecit, ut quidam capellani unitatem Ecclesiæ, quæ sectionem non patitur, quantum in eis est, dividentes, ipsius Arnaldi sequantur errorem; & Cardinalibus atque Archipresbyteris suis obedientiam & reverentiam promittere & exhibere debitam contradicant.*'

held in veneration by the people.[1] The prelates feared him even in death.

There is then no question that Arnold had a following everywhere he went, although there is no absolute proof that he founded a sect.[2] It is true that a sect called 'Arnoldists' was condemned in various decrees, and mentioned by writers on heresy in the two centuries following his death. Few details are given concerning this body, its origin, or its dogmas. No one can be sure that the name was derived from Arnold of Brescia,[3] although even if it were, it would still be a question whether the sect was founded by him and held the beliefs which he had preached. What are the authorities on these points? The only contemporary writer who states clearly that Arnold founded a sect is the author of the *Historia Pontificalis*, who is believed to have been John of Salisbury, who says that Arnold's followers won popular favour because of the purity and austerity of their lives. 'It is called the heresy of the Lombards.'[4] The *Ligurinus*, written no later than 1186, contains a veiled reference to such a sect.[5] All other twelfth-century accounts are silent regarding any organized following of Arnold's. It should, however, be remem-

[1] Otto of Freising, *l.c.*

[2] Among the authorities who believe that Arnold founded the sect known as Arnoldists are: Preger, *Beiträge zur Geschichte der Waldenser*, p. 220; Dieckhoff, *Die Waldenser im Mittelalter*, p. 163 (ed. 1851); Keller, *Die Reformation und die älteren Reformparteien*, p. 17 (ed. 1885); Tocco, *L'Eresia nel Medio Evo*, pp. 187, 258 (ed. 1884); Comba, *Histoire des Vaudois*, pp. 102 *seq.* (ed. 1901): Gregorovius, *l.c.*, vol. IV, p. 475. The following do not hold that the Arnoldists were derived from Arnold of Brescia: C. Schmidt, in *Real Encyclopédie;* G. Arnold, *Unpartheiissche Kirchen u. Ketzerhistorie* (1740), pp. 378–95: Guadagnini, *Vita d'Arnaldo*, Niccolini, *Arnaldo da Brescia*, p. 34 (1873). For Giesebrecht's view, see above. Hahn, *Gesch. der Ketzer*, does not mention the sect. Breyer, *Arnoldisten*, pp. 389–90, does not believe that Arnold founded it.

[3] There was a group of heretics burned at Cologne, of whom one 'Arnoldus Nomine' was called by the rest '*magistrum suum.*' Cæsar. Heisterbac., *l.c.*, c. 19.

[4] *Hist. Pontif.*, *l.c.*

[5] '*Unde venenato dudum corrupta sapore. Et nimium falsi doctrina vatis inhærans servat adhuc uvæ gustum gens illa paternæ*' (II, 310, *l.c.*).

bered that the *Historia Pontificalis* is an especially reliable source.

Toward the end of the twelfth century the papal and imperial records begin to furnish evidence of the existence of a group called Arnoldists.[1] In 1181[2] Lucius III issued a bull in which he condemned '*catharos, patarenos, leonistas, arnoldistas.*'[3] The condemnation was substantially repeated in 1184[4] and in 1229.[5] Further, Frederick II included the Arnoldists among the heretics doomed to extirpation by his ferocious edicts.[6] The sect is only named, not described; and it must be reiterated that according to the one reliable account which mentions a sect founded by Arnold of Brescia, that sect was not during his lifetime called by his name. 'It was called the heresy of the Lombards.' While these decrees are incontrovertible evidence that a sect existed called Arnoldists, they are not proof that these heretics were followers of Arnold of Brescia.

There is a little further evidence of the continued existence of such a sect. Several thirteenth-century writers mentioned it. Among these are David of Augsburg,[7] Berthold of Regensburg, Stephen of Bourbon, and Durand of Mende. Now David of Augsburg was a Franciscan, of the south German province, who died in 1272. He belongs to the early period of the organized Franciscan labours against heresy.[8] Berthold of Regensburg was his pupil,

[1] Cf. letters of Wezel and '*Quidam fidelis senatus*' for indications that followers of Arnold had formulated his doctrine.

[2] According to Dieckhoff, *Waldenser*, pp. 157, 168. Breyer, *Arnoldisten*, p. 198, gives the date as 1184.

[3] Mansi, vol. XXII, col. 476.

[4] *Ibid.*, col. 477.

[5] *M.G.H. Epist. sœc.*, 13; vol. I, p. 318.

[6] November 22, 1220. *M.G.H. LL.*, vol. II, p. 244. February 22, 1232, *ibid.*, p. 285. May 14, 1238, *ibid.*, p. 326. June 26, 1238, *ibid.*, p. 328. February 22, 1239, *ibid.*, p. 485.

[7] Under the name 'Arnostute,' in *Tractat de inquisicione hereticorum*, given by Preger, in *Kgl. Bay. Akad. der Wissensch. Hist. Cl.*, vol. XIV, pt. 2, p. 216. Also in Martène et Durand, *Thes. Nov.*, vol. V, col. 1778 *seq.*, where it is attributed to Yvonetus. Breyer (*Arnoldisten*, p. 412) says that all the sects mentioned by David are Waldensian.

[8] Breyer, *l.c.*, p. 187.

and was also a Franciscan. He was a popular preacher, and travelled in Austria, Bohemia, and Silesia between 1250 and 1260.[1] Like his master, he simply names the 'Arnoldisti.' If Arnold of Brescia founded a sect, there should have been traces of it, certainly in Switzerland, possibly in Austria and Bavaria. We might then expect to find a more distinctive account of these heretics than the mere reference in one of Berthold's sermons,[2] a reference which might well imply only an acquaintance with the stereotyped lists of heretics given in the condemnatory edicts, papal and imperial.

Stephen of Bourbon was a Dominican monk of Lyons, and an Inquisitor; a genial person, somewhat garrulous, who often gained information by talking with people of various sorts, somewhat as Herodotus did.[3] He writes in a diverting fashion of the multifarious heresies existing in Lombardy, and gives as his authority a man who had studied for eighteen years among the Waldensians.[4] He mentions a bewildering variety of heretics. In a list of sects named after their founders he includes the Arnoldists.[5] He says nothing about their tenets. He has just been speaking of 'those who are called *Communiati*, because they say all things ought to be in common,' in contradistinction to '*Pauperes de Lumbardia*,' who receive possessions.[6] It is impossible to determine who these are. Stephen evidently believes them to be outside the sects, among which he has included the Arnoldists. Yet the reader is at once reminded that, according to John of Salisbury, the sect

[1] Introduction to Pfeiffer-Strohl Edition of Berthold von Regensburg (1862–80).

[2] Speaking of heretics, he says: 'Ein heizent Poverlewe und ein Ariani und Runkeler unde Sifrider unde Sporer und Manachei und Arnolder.' (Sermon, '*Sælic sint die reines herzens sint.*' Ed. Pleiffer-Strohl, vol. I, p. 402.)

[3] Stephen of Bourbon, *Tractatus de diversis Materiis Prædicabilibus*, iv–vii.

[4] *L.c.*, pt. IV, tit. 7, par. 330.

[5] The list reads: '*Arnaldiste, Speroniste, Leoniste, Cathari, Patareni, Manachei sive Burgari*,' *l.c.*

[6] *Ibid.*

founded by Arnold was called the heresy of the Lombards. The doctrine regarding property, suggested rather than stated by Stephen, might conceivably have been derived from Arnold of Brescia. It might, on the other hand, have come from the Humiliati, who certainly existed in Arnold's day, and who, as we shall see, were widely distributed through Lombardy in the thirteenth century.

The last reference to the Arnoldists in thirteenth-century literature is in Durand of Mende's famous little *Rationale divinorum officiorum*, finished in 1286, published first in Mayence in 1459, and very many times afterward.[1] Durand says the Church is 'called a city because of the communion of her citizens; she is defended by the fortifications of the Holy Scriptures, by which heretics are repelled.'[2] Among these heretics, whom he specifies, are the 'Arnoldistæ, blasphemous heretics who say that in no place is it stated that Christ handed over the guardianship of his spouse, the Church, to sensual and unchaste servants, or gave to such the power to perform the sacred mysteries or to bind and loose, or the keys of the kingdom of heaven. Because only those, as says Gregory, even the just men who are still alive, have the power of binding and loosing possessed by the Apostles, if they, together with the doctrine, hold also the life and faith of the Apostles.'[3] This rings like the creed of Arnold of Brescia. No ministry can be a true one except through imitating the ministry of the Apostolic Age. In another place Durand says that the Arnoldists assert that men do not receive the Holy Spirit through baptism, but by the laying on of hands.[4] Do these two passages refer to the same sect? Upon this question no light is thrown by the context. Again, is this last doctrine likely to have been derived from Arnold of Brescia? To be

[1] Note the long list of editions in the British Museum Catalogue.

[2] Durandus of Mende, *Rationale divinorum officiorum*, lib. I, par. 1; '*De Ecclesia*,' ed. Fust & Schöffer, Mainz, 1459, fol. 1.

[3] *Ibid.*, lib. IV. [4] *Ibid.*, lib. I, fol. 16.

sure, he held peculiar views regarding baptism.[1] The doctrine attributed by Durand to his Arnoldists is, however, Catharan,[2] and no proof exists that Arnold of Brescia was influenced by Catharism.

These thirteenth-century writers then prove that a sect called Arnoldists maintained for a time an individual existence among the numerous heretical bodies of that time. They do not prove that this sect had any connection with Arnold of Brescia. The question whether he did or did not leave behind him an organized following is, of course, interesting and significant. The fact that this question cannot be answered does not, however, make any real difference in the estimate of Arnold's influence. There is no doubt that he won everywhere a following large enough to be a danger to the established order. His restless wanderings led him along paths which were to be trodden by many believers in primitive Christianity, in apostolic poverty. His own Lombardy was the home of the Humiliati, of a powerful branch of the Waldenses, of the nameless sects described by Stephen of Bourbon. France gave birth to Waldo, and harbored many communities of his followers. In Germany the Poor Men of Lyons especially flourished. The zeal of some of these enthusiasts may have been kindled by Arnold's fiery words or by their echoes; they may have been inspired by the apostolic life of the Prophet of Brescia to model their lives after the commands of Christ.[3]

[1] *Gesta Frid., l.c., ibid.,* p. 404. *'Præter hæc de sacramento altaris, baptismo parvulorum non sane dicitur sensisse.'* Further, he believed the sacraments were not valid in the hands of sinful priests. Cod. Ottob. Lat., II, 784–85. Cf. Breyer, *Arnoldisten,* pp. 389–90.

[2] Schmidt, *Histoire des Cathares,* p. 150; Lea, *Inquisition,* vol. I, pp. 93–94.

[3] Breyer (*Arnoldisten,* pp. 403, *etc.*) is convinced that the Arnoldisti existed in Lombardy as a separate sect when the Waldenses first appeared there; that the Waldenses were influenced by them, who, however, from this time ceased to exist as a distinct sect. He bases his view on the teaching of the Lombard Waldenses that the Sacraments are worthless in sinful hands, on the fact that Arnoldisti and Waldenses apply to the Church the same unpleasant epithets. This last argument has little force because the epithets in question were habitually applied to the Church by people who were dissatisfied with it.

CHAPTER V

THE HUMILIATI

THE closing decades of the twelfth century throughout western Europe witnessed the transformation of the Age of Faith into an age of doubt, disbelief, and open heresy. The earlier manifestations of religion were proving themselves unable to cope with the restless dissatisfaction with existing economic and social conditions, with the confusion of thought, with the unstable enthusiasm for ill-defined ideals, and above all, with the newly awakened will-power dominating the period, and consequently there developed quite apart from the transcendental formulas of creed, an intensity of virtue, an ardent quest for union with the Almighty, and a return to the practices of the primitive Church. It was not so much that faith disappeared from the consciousness of either priest or layman, of scholar or unlettered pilgrim, as that there were being discovered new channels for its expression which were more consonant with the needs of the times.

As the people emerged from the disasters marking the first half of the century, they seemed to have broken the bonds hampering the spirit, and to have entered upon a nobler heritage of enlarged thought, due in part to a newly awakened confidence in a future promiseful of vast achievement, and in part to the extensive communication with little known lands, one tangible result of the Crusades.

The quickening of religious life, the renewal of faith in the conquering power of the individual, sought immediate outlet in a mighty effort to reform the Church and state, socially, economically, and spiritually. The first half of the century, with its as yet unbroken moral unity, had witnessed innumerable reformers within the Church, who, labouring along conventional lines, had deemed the establishment of new monastic orders, the renewal of asceticism in those already existing, and the increase of almsgiving, adequate cure for the evils of which they were grievously aware and which were most clearly revealed in the undue wealth of the Church as well as in the miserable helplessness of the poor.

Possibly, in that less scientific age, no one went so far as to demand a redistribution of wealth as an amelioration of economic injustice, yet one and all realized that unless the Church renounced her possessions, she was destined to lose her spiritual leadership. Keen-eyed visionaries such as Saint Hildegarde of Bingen (1098–1179), and Saint Elizabeth of Schönau (1164), boldly rebuked the clergy for worldly ambition and thirst for riches, while that sternest of monks, Joachim of Flora, from the mountain fastnesses of Calabria denounced the sins of the Church and predicted that only in its return to apostolic poverty and simplicity would it find a cure for the ills resultant on corruption and luxury. Yet, despite the efforts of well-intentioned mystic or hermit, the Church was doing but little to meet the situation. The earlier efforts at reform, however admirable in themselves, left the mass of the people untouched. They also failed to remedy the glaring shortcomings of the secular clergy. It was inevitable, then, that when new reform movements arose they should be eminently laic and should be organized independently of the Church.

There was a constantly increasing recognition of social evils crying for remedy. Confraternities and hospitals established by the Church were doing their best, it is true, but they made little headway against the misery and disease in crowded towns; indiscriminate charity served then as now merely to encourage idleness; the increase of prosperity among the mercantile class brought into stronger relief the woes of the unconsidered lower strata, always the worst sufferers in an age of transition. Monasticism no longer responded to the needs and aspirations of the times. The ever-increasing wealth of the established orders gave rise to continual intestine discords; envious eyes of the laity were cast on their possessions and, losing their asceticism, they became an incubus on the Church.[1] The realization of the widespread indifference of the clergy and of their general incompetence was fundamentally altering the attitude of the more thoughtful laymen, who gradually began to accept the idea that the only salvation for Christendom as for the Church lay in a return to apostolic poverty.[2] This element, hitherto submissive, and now disgusted with the hierarchy's complete absorption in temporal affairs, was turned by its fervent aspiration for reform into a rebellious proletariat whose intense idealism aimed to overpower the ever-increasing materialism of the priesthood. Hungering for justice and feeling themselves abandoned by the Church, the common people turned to God for help. A new vision of Christ came to them through a study of the Gospels, a vision which they sought to realize in a more austere life and a purified ceremonial. Freed from external influences and limitations and, unlike the clergy, not bound by any vow to respect the institution, little by little they slipped out from under control of the Church. At first, through her traditional and constantly reiterated claim of being the one legitimate dispenser of sacraments and sole custodian of the Faith, she kept a vestige

[1] Jacques de Vitry, *Hist. Occid.*, c. 20, p. 317. This passage refers to the grey monks, but it is an excellent statement of the process by which the very virtues of the orthodox religionists brought about their corruption. S. Bernard., *De Moribus Epis.*, Migne, *l.c.*, vol. CLXXXII, col. 816.

[2] Jacques de Vitry, *l.c.*, p. 270, says the negligence and sin of the clergy are the cause of the evils of the times. 'The world suffers the Moors in Spain, the heretics, schismatics, and false brethren in other lands, because of the dissoluteness, ignorance, and wickedness of the prelates, who are not sleeping but dead, not pastors but dissipators, not priests, but pirates, who joined with wolves in despoiling the sheep.'

of a hold on these restless spirits, but as soon as this claim was reasoned away, the bonds uniting them were severed. From attacking the worldliness of the prelates and the inherent wrong of temporal possessions, it was but a short step to denunciation of the institution itself.

As the changing economic system brought industry out of the monasteries and organized craftsmen and artisans into guilds; as universities rather than the Church became the custodians of the new learning, and scholars, no longer monks, roamed from one land to another; as merchant-travellers, pilgrims, crusaders, and soldier-adventurers brought news of popular efforts to secure world peace, community of goods, and lay preaching; as pedantry was replaced by thought, there is little wonder that from the débris of the old heresies, which Rome tried in vain to stamp out, there arose evidence of new life.

Nowhere was this changing, critical spirit more evident than in Lombardy, ever restive under assertions of papal power, ever a fertile field for freedom either religious or political, ever a comfortable abiding-place for heretics. For more than two centuries the seed had been sown, first by one group and then by another. Early Catharan migrations had deposited their sediment in the Po Valley. The *clerici vagantes* wandered through street and highway, singing their ironic pagan songs, mocking the Church and parodying the Gospel. But the infidelity of these had been coolly received. Rebellious souls might themselves question the efficacy of the mass, but they had no wish to see it offered to Bacchus '*ad Deum qui lætificat cor hominis.*' They would and did renounce the luxury and ceremonials of the Church, but they did not intend to renounce the joys of Paradise. Heretics they might be, infidels, never. They wanted reform such as would make religion abundantly helpful in solving the problems of their daily life. The success of the anti-Catholic movements was due to the earnest attempt to satisfy this aspiration, the cause of their existence. So in this region a number of religious associations, seeking evangelical poverty, sprang up after 1150, one and all appealing to the ideals of the primitive Church and to the simplicity of life prescribed by Christ for his Apostles. Possibly the preaching of Saint Bernard during the time he was in Milan assisted in the crystallization of the movements; possibly echoes of the teachings of such mendicants as Norbert and Robert d'Arbrissel reached them from beyond the Alps; possibly the impulse was but the aftermath of Patarini and Arnoldisti in their midst, whose evangelical austerity, denunciation of tithes and clerical luxury bore evident fruit in this Lombard plain, particularly among the lower clergy.[1] Ignored by their superiors, these became the leaders of the proletariat, whom they accompanied even to the border-lands of heresy, as their sympathy with their own class was stronger than their allegiance to their order. Themselves the victims of the greed and indolence paralyzing the Curia, it was not unnatural that they should ask how the pontiffs could claim their succession from him who had renounced earthly goods — how the Church of Rome, hidden under its burden of ceremonial could be the conserver of the faith of the Apostles.[2]

The social disorders of the century, the rise of new classes, the recognition of economic evils and of political discriminations, the religious revolt against the hierarchy, were dominant, then, at just the time that Rome was preparing to pursue more vigorously the policy of unifying the

[1] Stutz, *Geschichte der Kirch. Benefizialwesens*, vol. I, sec. 21; Golante, *Il beneficio eccles.*, *passim;* Ughelli, *Italia Sacra*, vol. II, p. 110.

[2] Such was the reasoning Moneta of Cremona put into the mouths of his adversaries: '*In ecclesia Romana multi sunt egentes, qui fame, siti, et frigore quasi moriuntur, quibus divites Ecclesiæ Romanæ, non compatiuntur sed affligi prædictis possionibus sinunt; quomodo ergo charitas Dei manet in eis.*' (*Adversus Catharos*, p. 394.)

Church by a definite effort to conciliate the discordant elements destroying its efficiency.

Five years before the first rule was given to Saint Francis and his followers, a group of enthusiasts, who for some time had been practising a conception of evangelical poverty in various towns of northern Italy, appeared before Pope Innocent III at his request, bringing a rule to be sanctioned by the Curia, and asking for recognition as an organized community.[1]

By the end of the twelfth century, the attitude of the papacy toward the constantly shifting groups of idealists appearing in all parts of western Christendom had undergone a marked change. Innocent saw that much of the popular attention and loyalty formerly given to the Church, had been transferred to the heresiarchs, who, despite the anathema against their preaching in disobedience to the conciliar decree, were constantly increasing in influence and who were attracting to themselves those who saw the vast difference between Christ's law and the Church's practice; between the rich self-seeking prelates and the poor fishermen of Galilee who had left all to follow their Master. Keener than his predecessors had been in reading the signs of the times, Innocent also realized that the Church, beset by enemies who fought for conscience' sake, needed to organize all of the enthusiasm and religious zeal she could command within her own ranks. Moreover, he recognized the fact that the same spirit, which a century before had prompted the war against an infidel world to regain the birthplace and sepulchre of Christ, had now become spiritualized and transformed into an

[1] MS. Ambros., S 89 Sup., Puricelli, *Hist. Ord. Humil.*; MS. Bibl. Imper., 11886, Lat.; Migne, *l.c.*, vol. CCXIV, col. 788–89; Spondanus, *Annales Eccles. Baron. cont.*, vol. I, pp. 11, 92; Tiraboschi, *Vetera Hum. Mon.*, vol. II, p. 135. '*Privilegium qualiter ordo Humiliatorum licite potest habere proprium in communi, et de confirmatione regule, et de juramento non prestando directo prelatis ordinis cum certis gratiis.*'

ardent desire to follow literally the Saviour's commands. Seeing all this, he took upon himself the arduous task of turning this enthusiasm for primitive Christianity and evangelical poverty into a means of strengthening the Church itself, which he realized was far enough removed from any similitude of apostolic organization. Far better was it in his eyes to overlook minor deviations from the accepted order than to drive such groups into open heresy and enmity to the Church, as Lucius III had done. So he reversed the latter's policy toward the insistent reformers, conciliating them that they might labour for the welfare of the social and ecclesiastical orders. To this, then, the Humiliati owe their recognition as do the Franciscans and Dominicans.

Of their early history there is no reliable account, and as in the beginning there was nothing to attract attention to them, the date of their origin can only be conjectured. Their own chronicles, the earliest of which appeared in the fifteenth century, give a definite story of the foundation which has been accepted and passed on by most of the later writers down to our own day. According to these, the first Humiliati gave themselves to an evangelical life of preaching and of poverty before Arnold of Brescia dwelt with Abælard at the Paraclete.

'The origin and beginning of the Order of the Humiliati,' so runs the legend, 'was in the time of the Emperor Henry II who came into Lombardy and held under suspicion as conspirators many Lombard nobles, especially of Milan and Como. To prevent their plotting against the Emperor he sent them into exile into Germany in the year 1017 as hostages. After a time, these same nobles, touched by the grace of God in sparing their lives, became inspired by the Holy Spirit to take a vow to serve God with humility, and putting aside all worldly pomp, entered upon a life of penitence, for they thought they would not go to Heaven without humility. Making no delay, they put off the old man, laid aside their costly garments and put on clothing of sackcloth. When they came to speak together, they decided that if by God's help they should return to their native land, they would persevere in the religious life as they conceived it. When these facts came to the Emperor's ears, he summoned them to appear before him in the dress they had assumed, and wondering, he said: "Draw near, best beloved Humiliati. Have you given yourselves to religion as your habit bears witness?" To which they answered: "Even as thou seest, O Emperor." And then he suffered them to return to their fatherland. And they who had been exiles brought their own families in their homes to this same devotion and lived with their wives. Because they would not be idle, they were merchants and established workshops for wool as I know from their successors. They multiplied like fish in Lombardy and outside it.'[1]

The legend then tells how these companies of devout men and women, called Brethren of the Third Order, persisted for more than a century without any recognized rule.[2] Later on, certain of their number separated from their wives and communities of men and women were established. Thus was founded the Second Order to whom, so they said, Saint Bernard gave a rule in 1134. After a time a certain John de Oldrado surnamed de Meda from his birthplace, a town near Milan, established the First or clerical Order.[3]

The earliest version of this picturesque account is found in a chronicle of the Order written by an obscure monk, one Giovanni di Brera.[4] The second is a revision of this made

[1] *Chron. Ord. Hum.*, 1419, cc. 1, 2. [2] *Ibid.*, c. 3.

[3] A deed of gift from Giovanni de Meda, dated 1056, executed apparently by his wife, is one of the documents the compiler of the first chronicle mentions, but did not think it sufficiently important to copy. *Ibid.*, cc. 9, 10; *AA.SS.* VII Sept., p. 343; MS. Ambros., H. 256 Inf., Autogr. Trist. Calchi., *De Rebus Patriis*, f. 6.

[4] Joannis Braidensis, *Chronica Ordinis Humiliatorum.* The oldest and most important copy of this work is that found in the Biblioteca Ambrosiana of Milan,

two years later, probably by the same author;[1] and the third is that of Marco Bossi, head of the Order in Florence, who wrote in 1493.[2] These accounts are brief and unsatisfactory. Even a casual checking-up of their statements with chronicles contemporary with the events they record show many inaccuracies and even more contradictions. Yet with the rule,[3] the necrologies,[4] the breviaries,[5] and a few scattered references in the works of an occasional early historian,[6] they form our sources for the history of the Humiliati, and until the researches of the scholarly Tiraboschi and of his no less scholarly successor, Dr. Luigi Zanoni,[7] robbed their meagre details of most of their value, they were quite generally accepted.

(B S I 19), made by Fra Ottaviano Pizzo (an instructor of San Carlo Borromeo) in the sixteenth century. This contains not a few easily recognizable interpolations. Other manuscript copies are that made by the scholar Pietro Puricelli in the seventeenth century (T 258 Inf.), his Italian translation of the same (C 74 Inf.), and a sixteenth-century copy (V 9 Sup.), somewhat different from that of Pizzo Sup. A fragment of an early transcription is in the Brera at Milan (AD XVI I AB). The chronicle was first published by Tiraboschi in his monumental history of the Order., vol. III, pp. 229, etc.

[1] This *Nova Historia* has been ascribed to various authors. (See *AA. SS.*, VII Sept., p. 347.) Tiraboschi and Zanoni both attribute it to the author of the earlier chronicle. Three copies exist in the Ambrosiana: G 301 Inf., of the fifteenth century, quaintly illustrated in colour; G 302 Inf., of the seventeenth century, with a preface by Puricelli, who also made an Italian translation; C 74 Inf., and C 103 Inf. Another copy is in the Brera (AD XVI I AB). The chronicle is published by Zanoni in the Appendix to his study of the Order.

[2] Marci Bosii *Chronicon Humiliatorum Ordinus.* Copies are found in the Ambrosiana (BS I 12 and C 74 Inf., a translation by Puricelli), and in the Brera (AD XV I AB). It is also published by Zanoni in the Appendix to his work.

[3] An early manuscript of the rule followed by a few prayers, is in the Ambrosiana (D 58 Inf., n. 2); other rules more or less similar to this are in codices A 20 Sup., D 273 Inf., V 9 Sup., E 78 Sup.

[4] MS. Ambros., D 58 Inf., a necrology of obscure names.

[5] A thirteenth-century missal is in the library of the Seminary at Milan and ceremonial for the nuns of the Second Order is in the Chapter Library of the Duomo. Breviaries in the Ambrosiana are in the codices H 267 Inf., I 197 Inf., Z 101 Sup., M 27 Sup. See also Wickham's *The Divine Service in the Sixteenth Century*, London, 1890, for a reformed breviary of the Order.

[6] Notably by the Milanese scholars of the seventeenth century, Pietro Puricelli and Placido Pucinelli, both of whom deserve recognition for their compilation of material rather than for any critical or constructive writing.

[7] Zanoni, *Gli Umiliati nei loro Rapporti con l'eresia, ecc.*

The circumstances as well as the date of the founding of the Order of the Humiliati, as set forth by these early narrators, are open to criticism, although both Giovanni di Brera and Bossi claim to have seen documents proving that the Lombard nobles who were exiles in Germany under Henry II[1] established the Order. Neither, however, cites or quotes his authority.[2] Although the story as told by them was long held to be true, yet there have ever been disagreements as to the name of the emperor under whom the events occurred. Saint Antoninus of Florence says that Conrad II took the exiles into Germany, but that they returned in 1017 with Henry II,[3] and Raphael of Volterra agrees with him.[4] Benedetto Giovio examined documents which convinced him that the Order originated in 1033;[5] others place the foundation in the reign of Frederick Barbarossa,[6] probably, as Tiraboschi has pointed out, because it first became widely known at that time. He himself accepts the version of the chroniclers of the Order,[7] basing his conclusion on the fact that between the years 1002 and 1017 Henry was having trouble with Harduin, King of Italy. The Milanese were involved in the general disturbance as their Count, Obertus, espoused the cause of king rather than of emperor, and, citing the date of the confiscation of the count's goods, Tiraboschi concludes that the nobles went into Germany in 1014, adopted the Humiliant life in 1017, and returned to Italy two years later. It was not very easy, however, to reconcile these con-

[1] Joan. Braid., *l.c.*; Marco Bossi, l.c.

[2] Joan. Braid., *Præf.* (possibly the work of a later writer); Bossi, *l.c.*

[3] S. Antonin., *Chronicon*, par. 2, tit. 15, c. 23, f. clxxviii.

[4] Maffejus, Raphael Volaterranus (1521), *Anthropologiæ*, lib. 21, in *Opera Omnia*, ed. 1540.

[5] Benedict. Jov., *Historiæ Patriæ seu Novo comencis* (written in 1582), lib. 2.

[6] Cavitelli, *Annales Cremonen.*, ad an. 1189.

[7] Giovanni de Brera, less sure in his second chronicle, says: '*quendam imperatorem*' (*l.c.*). M. Bossi says there are many stories of the origin of the Order which are as yet unsolved, and that he has made diligent search to learn the truth. (*Præf.*)

clusions with the lack of their confirmation by contemporary writers, particularly Arnulf of Milan, an eye-witness of events occurring after 1018, and who discusses quite fully the ecclesiastical life of his times. He does mention the fact that certain Lombard nobles were taken into captivity,[1] and he gives an account of King Harduin's renunciation of luxury,[2] but does not associate either incident with the establishment of a religious order. Burchard, Abbot of Ursperg,[3] and Jacques de Vitry,[4] both of whom were living when Innocent's confirmation of the Order aroused new interest in its early history, discuss the Humiliati quite fully, but give no hint of any connection with the nobility, captive or otherwise. Had a tale such as that given two centuries later by Giovanni di Brera been current, it seems incredible that it should have escaped the pen of the garrulous cardinal, ever eager to use an anecdote to illustrate sermon or history. Also Humbert de Romans (+ 1277), general of the Dominicans, who had access to papal bulls when constructing his history of the Order, is equally silent.

Possibly some vague tradition of the Lombards in Germany lingered in the minds of the people and caused them to connect the excellence of the Humiliati in the wool industry with the nation long famous for its superiority in that same art. Possibly the later brethren, trying to satisfy their curiosity as to their early history, seized upon the legend to cement an alliance between themselves and the Milanese nobility by claiming descent from their numbers.

Nor is there any trace of Saint Bernard's connection

[1] '*Henricus vero quid de reliquo gesserit qualiter marchiones Italiæ quattuor Ugonem, Azonem, Adelbertum et Obizonem captione una constrinxerit recitare non expedit.*' *Gesta Archiep. Med., M.G.H. SS.*, vol. VIII, p. 11.

[2] '*Deposito regalibus super altare sumpto que habitu paupere suo dormivit in tempore.*' Arnulf., *l.c.*, p. 10.

[3] *Chron. Ursperg., M.G.H. SS.*, vol. XXIII, p. 377.

[4] *Historia Occidentalis, l.c.*, p. 335.

with the Order to be found in any of his voluminous writings.[1] True, he was in Milan more than once,[2] and in 1134 or 1135 he established a monastery near the city which he called Chiaravalle 'after the valley bright and beloved which was his home.'[3] It is not probable that this alone could have given rise to the tradition of his having provided a rule for the Second Order. Indeed, it is doubtful if the Second Order even existed in his day. The assumption that the adoption of the great Burgundian as patron was the work of some later chronicler seems reasonable. It was difficult to conceive of a religious order that was not founded by a saint or at least under saintly patronage, and if a stray order did happen to find itself unable to give satisfactory and orthodox account of its beginnings, it at once attached itself to some notable saint, by a decidedly apocryphal legend if nothing better presented itself. In this case Saint Bernard's notable activities in Milan made him a more

[1] The earliest extant authority for this connection is Galvan. Flamina, *l.c.*, col. 632, who says: '*Sequenti anno B. Bernardus rediit Mediolanum, Claravallem construxit, Ordinem S. Bernardi ordinavit, qui modo dicuntur Fratres de Conegio. Prima domus istorum Fratrum fuit domus Portæ Orientalis, quam Guido ex Capitaneis Portæ Orientalis construxit. Hic autem Guido vir illustris Roman ivit, et ab Innocentio Tertio in quodam prandio aquam ad manus recepit, et istum Ordinem confirmavit. Et quia iste Papa dicebatur Innocentius Tertius, ideo iste Ordo Tertius appellatus est, et exemptus est ab omnibus graviminibus Communitatis Mediolani. Hi fratres fundaverunt primum et secundum Ordinem Humiliatorum et visitabant ipsos Fratres Humiliatos.*' See also MS. Braid., AE X 10, f. 70t. Puricelli mentions Guido as contemporary with King Arduin. (MS. Ambros., C 74 Inf., f. 455.) He is also mentioned in the earliest known document relating to the history of the Order, a gift of land by Guido de Porta Orientalis (1176), '*Guidonis de Porta Orientali fidejussio pro Vicoboldonensibus Humiliatis.*' (Tiraboschi, vol. II, p. 117.) He was living in 1201 (Potthast, no. 1416). There must have been two of the name connected with the Order. See also Arch. Stato Milano. F. R. Perg. Maria del Monte sopra Varese, n. 213; MS. Ambros., *Raccolta della Croce*, DS IV 11, p. 128, and DS IV 14, p. 50.

[2] An inscription of 1221 in the sacristy of Chiaravalle reads: 'ANNO + Gratiæ McXXV + xi + KI + febb + Constructu + e + hoc + monasteriu + a + bto + bnardo + archiepipo + VI + nonas mai + in onoe + sce mar + careval.'

[3] Bernard transplanted a group of monks from Clairvaux to this his first Italian foundation, but the sterile location and the indifference of the Milanese made it necessary for them to leave. They were recalled, but the monastery never prospered as long as it housed Frenchmen.

than possible choice.[1] The lack of a special Bernardine cult[2] until nearly the time of the suppression of the Order, as well as Pope Innocent's criticism of the early rule as being discordant with orthodox usage, serves to discount the interesting tradition.[3]

John de Meda is indubitably their own saint and the founder of the First Order. But little of his life is known.[4] He seems to have been prompted by regret that so arduous a group as the Humiliati had not their own priesthood, in order that they might labour among souls as effectively as they laboured in wool, and so he established many houses of clerics in Lombardy. He died at the Brera, the oldest convent of the Humiliati in 1159[5] and is believed to have been canonized by Pope Alexander III, although there is no supporting evidence save in his being generally accepted as a saint.[6] According to Jacques de Vitry, the Order spread rapidly up and down the Po Valley, whither the brethren wandered, preaching with much eloquence to the common people, many of whom associated themselves with the Second and Third Orders.

Out of the confusion of evidence and tradition surround-

[1] Jovius says Saint Bernard gave form to what already existed (*l.c.*).

[2] The thirteenth-century missal of the Order at Milan makes no mention of Saint Bernard.

[3] MS. Braid., AD XV 1: Inn. III: '*Privilegium qualiter ordo humiliatorum licite potest habere proprium in commune et de confirmatione regule et de juramento non prestando directo prelatis ordinis cum certis gratis.*'

[4] See *AA. SS.*, VII Sept., pp. 343, etc., for the story of his life. The account given there has but little value, consisting for the most part of general statements and accounts of miracles, 'a mosaic of phrases common to all mediæval saints.' The details of his labours in the third paragraph are the most reliable part. There is no suggestion of the existence of the Order before his time in what is given there.

[5] Joan. Braid., c. XII, *Chron.* 1419; c. XVII, *Chron.* 1421; Marco Bossi, c. V; De Stefano, *Le Origini dell' ordine degli Umiliati, Riv. Stor. Crit. delle scienze teolog.*, vol. II (1906), p. 858, denies his existence; Fumagalli, *Della antichitá longobardico-milanese*, vol. IV, p. 159, says he is a fabulous character.

[6] So Tattus Ludovicus says in his *Martyrologus.* He made a diligent but fruitless search for the Bull of canonization. Giovanni is spoken of as a saint in a breviary of the order which Pope Paul III approved in 1548. Benedict. Jov., *l.c.*; Puricelli, *l.c.*, ff. 135–36; Jacques de Vitry, *l.c.*

ing the establishment of the Humiliati but little can be affirmed with any certainty. It is beyond question that the rule was sanctioned by Innocent III in 1201, and since every movement must needs pass through a period of obscure development before it receives formal recognition, the foundation of this Order was certainly at some previous time. Just how and when it came into existence will probably never be exactly known. All of northern Italy was pervaded by a restless enthusiasm for perfection through poverty, and men and women in Milan had been giving themselves to a life of humility and self-denial for some time before the traditional establishment of the Order. Consequently, it seems safe to infer that the beginnings of the Humiliati rest in the social and religious conditions of the early twelfth century and are a complex resultant of many forces; that at first the community was a cross between a monastic order and an industrial guild with marked characteristics of each, consisting of a considerable number of labourers who had given themselves to the pursuit of a communal life of evangelical simplicity. Nothing, however, in the established facts, nor in the inferences to be drawn from them, suggests even a remote connection with the nobility of Milan, exiled or at home, and the tradition of such an origin is greatly discounted by the fact that their earliest known members were all labourers. Zanoni, the most careful of the later historians of the Order, says: 'I do not know if the Humiliant movement represents for all an heroic vow as did the voluntary renunciation of the Franciscans. These Lombards, poor by origin and by unavoidable necessity, craved a religious life adaptable to labourers and social outcasts, and in the pursuance of an evangelical life they saw a mitigation of the brutality of their times, a solution of the problem of their existence; therefore the poverty, which was in the beginning inexorable, became the poverty of choice and brought with it an unconscious ennoblement of character. Thus they took revenge on that society which despised them as labourers, but which venerated them once they adopted a religious habit.' [1]

The early Humiliati made no attempt to follow the monastic life. In certain sections, particularly in Lombardy, there was arising a revulsion of feeling against such a separation of families as accompanied monasticism and some at least were trying to discover a means of attaining the same perfection of life without distorting Christ's teachings by breaking the unity of the home.[2] Consequently the early groups did not take the vow of chastity, but basing their action on the teachings of Saint Paul, maintained the natural ties. Often the father was the minister and received the obedience of the younger members to whom he gave a fitting example of austere piety.[3] Virginity was never a requirement for admission to the Order. They received every sort and every class of women, who, consecrating themselves to God, laboured as did the early Christians for their daily sustenance.

When Innocent III gave the Humiliati their rule in 1201, he made a careful separation of the community into three orders,[4] along the same lines into which they had already divided themselves, though without any marked consis-

[1] *Gli Umiliati,* p. 107.

[2] S. Barsotti, *Il B. Giov. Cini,* Quarracchi, 1906, p. 155; Tamassia, *L'Affrattelmento,* A. Lattes, *Il Diritto Consuetudinario delle cittá lombarde,* p. 267; *Chron. Laud., M.G.H. SS.,* vol. XXVI, p. 449, ann. 1178. See the First Rule of Saint Francis in *Opuscula S. P. Francisci ad Clara Aquas,* 1904, p. 33. '*Et unusquisque in ea arte et officio in quo vocatus est, permaneat*' (c.VII).

[3] In various places children were given to the Humiliati much as apprentices entered guilds. Whole families entered the Order without severing family ties. Arch. St. Milano, F. R. Perg., S. Eustorgio, sec. XII e XIII, n. 136–38; S. Maria di Brera, cart. 1251–75; Sta. Caterina di Brera, x; Arch. Osp. Magg., Milano, doc., Dec. 12, 1255; MS. Braid. Bonomii, Tab. Clarev., AE XV 28, p. 59; MS. Ambros., Raccolva della Croce, DS IV 18, n. 248; Landulf., Jun., *Hist. Med., R.I.S.,* vol. v, p. 515: '*non solum masculi sed mulieres tonsæ sunt et laneis et ciliciis vilissimis induti ad quæ libet religiosa convertuntur.*'

[4] Pipini, *Chron., R.I.S.,* vol. IX, c. 633.

tency or uniformity of organization. The distinctions had come about gradually as some of the more austere of both sexes proceeded to the First Order, and others, holding an antipathy to the cloistered life, stopped halfway. As time went on, however, all three groups tended to become more monastic, more confined to a definite rule.

The Franciscans divided themselves into groups of friars, nuns, and tertiaries; the Humiliati, on the other hand, were not divided according to sexes, men and women belonging to both Second and Third Orders. In the quaint illustrations of the earlier copy of the *Nova Historia* they may be seen working together, picking, spinning, and carding wool. In some of the illustrations all wear dark *berretti;* in others they are all in white, while in the corner are piles of dark, habit-like cloaks.[1] The sisters of the Second Order were not cloistered, but were not supposed to leave the monastery frequently. Nor were their dwellings closed to the brethren although none could enter without the license of the prelate, nor alone, not except on necessary business, and only in the daytime.[2] After the First Order was instituted, the canons preached once or twice a month to the sisters and visited them when sick.[3]

In other communities the tertiaries were the last to be established; here they were the first; the Second Order consisted of monks and nuns, the First of priests or canons. Throughout their history, however, there was always much confusion between the various ranks. The reversal of the usual procedure was no doubt due to the fact that the Humiliati began as a community of workers of both sexes, usually from the lowest social strata, working from necessity and forming a sort of artisan proletariat without adopting a definite organization. In some places there

[1] MS. Ambros., G. 301 Inf. As these illustrations date from 1421, they do not throw much light on the beginnings of the movement, but being the earliest existing evidence, they are of great value.

[2] MS. Ambros., H 205 Inf. [3] Reg., cc. XLIII, XLIV, in Zanoni, App.

was a distinct separation, but this was not generally true.[1] What few records of the early years of the Order remain to us indicate that the women had direct votes in the election of officers, and suffered few if any of the limitations imposed on the sisters of the regular orders.[2]

The Crusades, the wars with the Hohenstaufen, and the incessant intercommunal strife, all combined to reduce appreciably the male population of the peninsula, leaving a great number of women without their natural guardians and protectors, and that in an age when '*Sine mundualdo mulier vivere non potest sicut piscia sine acqua.*'[3] Feeling themselves unsupported and uncertain of the future, they naturally came to join themselves to others similarly situated, and as associations other than religious were forbidden, they drifted into paths of mysticism and idealism. Hence the middle years of the twelfth century gave birth to many groups of pious women living together without taking vows or leaving the world, devoting themselves to communal labour and charity and in time swelling the ranks of the Humiliati in Italy as they did those of the Beghards and Præmonstratensians farther north.

The desire of the community for a rule of their own was decidedly tepid, and after it was granted them and accepted by them they proved themselves so careless in its observance as to incur a papal rebuke for negligence.[4] The earliest extant version of this '*Omnis boni principium,*'[5] a mixture of Augustinian and Benedictine elements,[6] is so

[1] Jacques de Vitry, *l.c.*, c. 28, pp. 330–31. In Verona the men had an oratory apart from the women, although their houses joined and they held their substance in common. Biancolini, *Chiese di Verona*, vol. III, 390.

[2] Tiraboschi, vol. II, p. 144.

[3] G. Salvioli, *Trattato di Storia del diritto italiano*, p. 365.

[4] Gregory IX.

[5] Another early rule (MS. Ambros., D 273 Inf.) is an obvious adaptation of the Benedictine rule to conditions existing among the Humiliati.

[6] Tiraboschi was so certain that the rule granted by Innocent III was Benedictine that he did not even publish it. He was also convinced that the first order was canonical only in later times, a conclusion discounted by the fact

illogically arranged as to warrant the suspicion that it was written for the occasion and had never been actually used by the community. Moreover, it seemed to have been especially designed for the First and Second Orders, as it provided for the regular offices[1] and for the discipline generally found among religious,[2] dividing the day between labour and prayer. For the Third Order there was a *propositum*[3] which, in its emphasis on humility, obedience, patience, charity, etc., resembles that given by Saint Francis to Brother Cesare of Spira,[4] while in its external form it is not unlike the *Regula Antiqua*.[5] The tertiaries are enjoined to pay tithes, to give alms, to keep fasts, to care for the needy and the sick, to accord the necessary rites to the dead, and to recite with some modifications the canonical hours.

The rule, Augustinian where it makes provision for the daily life of the community and Benedictine where it touches on its organization, is apparently based on the principles and manners of life previously adopted. Until after 1200 the original family grouping persisted despite the growing tendency toward a regular monastic life. The author of the Chronicle of Laon, writing in 1178, says: 'There was at this time certain citizens of Lombardy who lived at home with their families in poverty, following a

that the Bull recognizing the community refers to the delegates as '*preposti et fratres collegium*,' a form in general applied only to those following the canonical life, and also by his granting to the First Order power to celebrate mass, with the assistance of deacons and of sub-deacons, a concession appropriate to regular canons. R. Maiocchi, *Codex diplomaticus Ord. S. Augustini Papiæ*, vol. I, p. xxvii; Helyot, vol. I, p. 50; vol. II, p. 188. Moreover, the phrase, '*Statuentes ut ordo canonices secundum Deum et institutionem vestram per Sedem Apostolicam approbatum perpetuis temporibus inviolabiter observetur*,' is applicable only to canonical orders.

1 In Mantua the Humiliati lived under the Augustinian rule. Biancolini, *l.c.*, vol. III, p. 39.

2 *Regula*, c. XXIII.

3 *Ibid.*, cc. XII, XIV, XVI, XVII, XIX, XXI.

4 *Ibid.*, cc. IX, XI, XV, XVI.

5 Found in a letter of Innocent III, '*Incumbit nobis*,' written June 7, 1201, and printed in Tiraboschi, vol. II, p. 128.

certain kind of religious association'; and Humbert de Romans, nearly a century later, paints the houses of the Order as asylums of peaceful labourers who were at the same time model penitents. The little groups of kinsmen elected one of their number for a head and this '*magister*' continued the paternal exhortation to charity and honest dealing. Lacking the general constitution of the Cluniacs, they came in time to separate according to localities,[1] each of which developed a rule and organization in its own way. That this differentiation did not become more marked is due to the occasional general meetings presided over by the local provosts in turn.

Before receiving the papal sanction, the rapid increase of the Order was largely among the lower classes,[2] including not a few clerics.[3] Houses of Humiliati were found in Florence,[4] in Siena, and even in France,[5] although Lombardy was ever the stronghold of the community.[6] After Milan, Verona, swarming with mendicant monks and new orders, was the most important of their centres. They established themselves here about 1173 under the name of Campagne or Berretani[7] and engaged in wool-weaving with such good results that erelong they had in their charge the churches of Santa Maria della Ghiara, San Leonardo, and San Cristoforo and San Giovanni Evangelista, as well as many others in the campagna.[8] Here, as in Milan and in other Lombard towns, they were given numerous privileges and immunities, and were allowed to act as

[1] The chief divisions were Vibaldone, Como, Lodi, and Pavia. There were also the *Societatis humiliatorum Mediolani et comitatus* and the *Societatis humiliatorum Verone et districtus*. In the thirteenth century they had a magistrate general. Pope Innocent III gave the supreme power to a council of four from each district and made a judicial distinction between preposti, prelates, and ministers. Tiraboschi, *l.c.*, vol. II, p. 44.

[2] Sormani, *Storia degli Umiliati.*

[3] Pipini, *l.c.*, c. 633.

[4] They were the founders of the convent of Ognissanti.

[5] MS. Bibl. Imp. 11886, Lat.

[6] Jacques de Vitry, *l.c.*, p. 334.

[7] Sormani, *l.c.*

[8] Biancolini, *l.c.*

collectors of taxes and tithes at the city gates.[1] They were probably in Bergamo prior to 1171, as in 1370 a contest arose between them and the Croceferi as to which should occupy the more honourable place in a procession. The decision having been given in their favour, it may be assumed that they were in the city before their rivals, who are known to have been there in 1171.[2] The closing decades of the twelfth century saw them established in Pavia,[3] Tortona, Cremona, Lodi,[4] Piacenza,[5] Como,[6] and Vicenza, in all of which places they devoted themselves to their chosen art with more than usual success.

The early division of the Humiliati into two groups, the true and the false, complicates the problem of their origin. Such a division was frequently found in such mediæval associations as included lay members. The two wings, one heretical and one orthodox, originally a single group with a twofold aspiration for immediate union with God to obtain a more richly spiritual life and for the practice of apostolic poverty, became increasingly differentiated as the anti-Catholic excesses of the one provoked a retrogressive movement on the part of the other.

That the true and false Humiliati were originally one, and that they were numerically strong at least two decades before Innocent's rule was given, is indicated by the Chronicler of Laon. In 1178, he says, there were these men who 'abstained from lies, oaths, and lawsuits; they were content with simple clothing: they posed as upholders

[1] Biancolini, *l.c.*, vol. III, pp. 35–36.

[2] Ronchetti, *Mem. Ist. di Bergamo*, vol. III, pp. 147, 22.

[3] Biancolini, *l.c.*, vol. II, p. 635.

[4] A manuscript in the library of the University of Pavia states they were given the church of Santa Maria Maggiore in the campagna near Venarola in 1182: Bossi says they came there in 1200.

[5] In 1180 Pietro Cabacio, a layman and Humiliant, dedicated himself to a hospital near Bardineza on Strada Romea. Campi, *Hist. Eccles. di Piacenza*, vol. II, p. 52.

[6] Porro, G. A., *Storia Diocesana, Arch. Stor. per Lodi*, vol. III, p. 155.

of the Catholic faith: they went to the Pope and asked him to sanction their tenets. The Pope granted that they might carry out their theories provided that they did this in humility and honesty; but he expressly forbade them to hold conventicles, and strictly prohibited their presuming to preach in public. They, however, defied the apostolic command, were disobedient and allowed themselves to incur excommunication. They called themselves Humiliati because they were not clad in dyed garments, but were satisfied with those of a natural colour.'[1]

That the Humiliati whom Alexander II censured were almost certainly of the same origin as those to whom Innocent gave the sanction of the Church twenty-two years later, is evidenced by similarities of rule and of custom. The heretical Humiliati abstained from oaths; the orthodox were according to Innocent's rule to take oath only in case of necessity. Apparently the Humiliati of the rule had wished Innocent to allow them also to refrain from oaths. This the Pope could not do without some qualification; for taking an oath was a necessary part of many business transactions, and jurisdiction over all cases in which an oath was involved belonged to the Church.[2] Here, then, the great statesman was on difficult ground. The Humiliati, in the rule he told them to prepare, had incorporated a principle held by all members of their brotherhood, the disobedient and the wavering alike, which he could not sanction their retaining. They believed that this tenet rested on an incontrovertible command of Christ. Innocent had then to bring them to a different interpretation of Christ's command or lose their loyalty and drive them into the ranks of the too numerous apostolic heretics, among whom were already counted many of their brethren. He began his amended version of this section of the rule

[1] *Chron. Laud.*, *l.c.*, p. 449.

[2] *Corpus Juris Canonici*, c. XXII, qu. 5, c. 7; c. X, bk. II, tit. 1, c. 13.

with a clear, unqualified statement which had doubtless formed a part of what they had submitted to him — the apostolic mandate on which other Christians have based a belief in the sinfulness of all oaths: 'But above all things, my brethren, swear not at all, neither by Heaven, neither by earth, neither by any other oath; but let your yea be yea, and your nay, nay; lest ye fall into condemnation, as saith the blessed Apostle James.[1] Having laid down for the Order as a law for their guidance a precept they had adopted, the Pope proceeded to 'interpret' it. 'For,' he says, 'the indiscreet and impulsive taking of oaths is forbidden, not only by James in his Epistle, but by Christ himself, who said, "It hath been said by them of old time, Thou shalt not forswear thyself, but shalt perform unto the Lord thine oaths; but I say unto you, swear not at all, neither by Heaven, for it is God's throne; nor by the earth, for it is his footstool; neither by Jerusalem, for it is the city of the great King. Neither shalt thou swear by thy head because thou canst not make one hair white or black."'

There follows the explanation by which Innocent tried to prevent these Humiliati from interpreting these commands in the painfully literal way which the Church had reason to dread, because of her experience with other Apostolic Christians. 'When Christ says, "Swear not at all," it is impulsive swearing that he prohibits. And, indeed, we should take oaths not from impulse, but from necessity. When he adds "neither by earth nor by heaven" he forbids indiscreet swearing, because we should not swear by the creature, but rather by the creator. "But let your communication be yea, yea; and nay, nay," that is, whatever you utter, in affirmation or denial, should be the thought of your heart. For not only affirmation or denial is involved, but rather the truth itself, as

[1] James, 5:12.

Christ according to John frequently says in the Gospel, "I say unto you Amen, Amen." All that goes further than this leans to the side of evil; its nature, however, is not so much that of *culpa* as of *pœna*. Furthermore, the burden of the oath rests less on him who takes it than on him who requires it, because it proceeds from that weakness which is ever a matter of *pœna* rather than of *culpa*.'

Innocent would have the Humiliati understand, moreover, that Christ and the Apostles did not, as they had supposed, prohibit the taking of oaths, but on the contrary sanctioned the practice. 'It is permitted,' proceeds the rule, 'to swear under the compulsion of necessity. This is taught by the Apostle when he says, "For men verily swear by the greater and an oath for confirmation is to them an end of all strife." The angel also, whom John saw in the Apocalypse, who stood "upon the sea and upon the earth and lifted up his hands to Heaven, sware by him that liveth for ever and ever. And thou shalt swear, the Lord liveth in truth, in judgement, and in righteousness," saith Jeremiah the Prophet.'

The disobedient Humiliati abstained from lawsuits. The Order authorized by Innocent were told: 'Patience is also necessary, especially in adversity, to bear evils inflicted upon you by others. As the Lord saith in the Gospel: "It hath been said, an eye for an eye and a tooth for a tooth; but I say unto you that ye resist not evil; but whosoever shall smite thee on the right cheek turn to him the other also; and whosoever shall compel thee to go with him a mile, go with him twain, and if any man will sue thee at law and take away thy coat, let him have thy cloke also." Again the Apostle: "Dearly beloved, avenge not yourselves, but rather give place unto wrath; for it is written, Vengeance is mine, I will repay saith the Lord." Again he saith also: "Now therefore there is utterly a fault among you, because ye go to law one with another. Why do ye not rather take a wrong? why do ye not rather suffer yourselves to be defrauded?" And again the Lord in the Gospel: "In your patience possess your souls." Again, "Forgive, and ye shall be forgiven." Imbue yourselves also with fervent charity which is summed up in two precepts, that is to say, in the love toward your God and your neighbour, as it is written: "Thou shalt love the Lord thy God with all thy heart and with all thy soul and with all thy mind and thy neighbour as thyself." Charity should be shown even to thy enemies, for the Lord saith: "Do good to them that hate you, and pray for them that despitefully use you and persecute you, that ye may be the children of your father which is in Heaven; for he maketh the sun to rise on the evil and the good, and sendeth rain on the just and on the unjust." Also the Apostle saith: "If thine enemy hunger, feed him, and if he thirst, give him drink."' One of the reproaches cast upon the Church by the apostolic reformers was that, contrary to the commands of Christ and the Apostles, her prelates engaged in lawsuits and contentions. For this Arnold attacked the clergy, as did the apostolics of Cologne and Waldo, as well as many earnest Churchmen who remained loyal to the institution despite the faults they saw and lamented.[1] It may well be, then, that the Humiliati who defied the Church had decided on the basis of these very texts cited in Innocent's rule that Christ had intended his disciples to abstain from lawsuits.

The disobedient Humiliati lived at home with their families; the Third Order, approved by Innocent, were to remain with their families and were forbidden to put away their wives except for Scriptural causes. Both groups wore simple clothing of undyed wool.[2] Both believed them-

[1] See the reproach by Alexander II to the clergy of Lucca in *Memorie di Matilda*, vol. II, p. 133. Also Peter Damian, *Ep.* 1, 15, col. 225, Migne, *l.c.*, vol. CXLIV.

[2] Cipolla, *Un amico di Can Grande, Memorie R. Accad. delle Scienze di Torino*, Ser. II, pp. 39, 44, vol. for 1909.

selves to be champions of the Church. Both wished to preach, although permission to do so had been refused to those who first sought the papal sanction.[1] They seemed, however, to have been ardent preachers, particularly in the cities, where they not only laboured for religious reform and for an increase of spiritual fervour, but where they became ardent partisans of some political movement.[2]

Preaching was one of the characteristic practices of the Humiliati, and persistence in preaching in the face of the unqualified uncompromising prohibition of the Pope had been the form of disobedience which brought about the condemnation of the 'false Humiliati.' This obligation, believed by so many apostolic Christians to have been laid by Christ upon his servants, was incorporated in the rule for the government of their life submitted to Innocent by the Humiliati in 1201. Innocent treated the subject with caution. The rule runs: 'It shall further be your custom to come together in a suitable place every Lord's Day; and then shall one or more of the brethren of proved faith and tried religion, powerful in deed and word, with the permission of the bishop of the diocese, utter the word of exhortation, warning his hearers and leading them to honest habits of life, in such a way that no word shall be said about the articles of belief and the sacraments of the Church.'

The license to preach could not be altogether withheld in the face of the insistence of the Humiliati and the risk of antagonizing them. It was therefore given and carefully qualified. On the other hand, Innocent provided against trouble which might be caused by over-zealous bishops.

[1] See letter of the pontifical legate Girardo di Sessa, 19 April, 1211, Tiraboschi, *l.c.*, vol. II, p. 154. *Ad hæc nostra,* in which the Church first uses the name Humiliati authoritatively. Earlier documents speak of them as humble before God.

[2] Jacques de Vitry, *l.c.*, defines Milan as '*fovea hæreticorum,*' and says the Humiliati were in the first ranks of the doctrinal disputants. After the separation of the orders, the true Humiliati, orthodox defenders of the faith, became the more active.

'Beyond the limits heretofore stated,' says the rule, 'we forbid any bishop to hinder brethren of this sort from uttering the word of exhortation: since according to the Apostle "the Spirit ought not be quenched."' It may well be that Innocent's carefully guarded license in the rule of 1201 was the result of the action of the first set of humble brethren in response to the unqualified prohibition of his predecessor. They had proved that the denial of right to preach turned into heretics, men who were disposed in all things else to serve the Church faithfully, and Innocent enlisted champions wherever he could.

There is further evidence that both branches of the Humiliati sprang from the same trunk. In 1181 the Council of Verona issued a decree against various heretics. Among them were named 'those who falsely pretended to be Humiliati or Poor Men of Lyons.'[1] The execution of this decree was evidently found to be difficult as far as the Humiliati were concerned; for in 1197, Innocent wrote to the Bishop of Verona: 'We understand that on the authority of our letter[2] sent to our beloved sons the clergy of your Church against the Zazari, the Poor Men of Lyons and the Humiliati who have not followed the papal command, one of the aforesaid clergy has issued sentence of excommunication against the Humiliati and all heretics, without the distinction we established in our letters. Acting on the precedent of this sentence, some have shunned certain men who are called by the people Humiliati, perhaps against their will, and who savour not of heresy, but of orthodox faith, and who in all humility of heart and

[1] Bull '*Ad abolendam*,' Mansi, vol. XXII, col. 476; D'Argentré, *l.c.*, vol. I, p. 71, gives 1183 as the date. Cf. Mansi, *l.c.*, col. 477, for repetition of the edict in 1184. '*In primis ergo Catharos, et Patarinos et eos qui se Humiliatos, vel Pauperes de Lugduno, falso nomine mentiuntur, Josepinos, Passaginos Arnoldistas, perpetuo decernimus anathemati subjacere.*'

[2] No such letter appears in the *Regesta* of Innocent III, nor is any cited by Tiraboschi nor by Spondanus nor by Zanoni. What his qualifications were it is therefore impossible to determine.

body are anxious to be servants of God, and who may even have sworn to you that they remain faithful to the rule of the Church. . . . Since it is truly not our intention to condemn the innocent with the guilty, we command that you call such men to your presence and inquire of them and of the others about their life and conversation and anything else which you think should be investigated.' [1]

Two years later, Innocent made overtures and gave a rule to men who styled themselves Humiliati. May it not be true that in the letter just quoted he distinguished between these men, who did not wish to be numbered among the heretical Humiliati, and those obdurate people who had persisted in the face of the papal prohibition in obeying Christ's command as they interpreted it and preached the Gospel? The obedience of the Humiliati whom he conciliated had been questioned on precisely the points which constituted the contumacy of the 'false Humiliati.' The whole body had not disobeyed to an equal degree; but the tendencies which had made heretics of some of its members were at work among the rest. Innocent had then written to the Humiliati to suggest that, in order to put an end to certain scandals which had been circulated regarding them, they draw up for his approval a rule. It was in accordance with this command that the representatives of the Order went to Rome in 1201, and the rule approved by the pope was a modified version of that which they themselves prepared.[2] The rule, then, as finally conceived is based on the

[1] *Ep. Innocentii III Veronensi Episcopo.*, lib. II, no. 228, Migne, *l.c.*, vol. CCXIV, col. 788.

[2] '*Et scandalum extinguendum, quod contra vos fuerat obortum, vobis dedimus in mandatis ut . . . proposita vestra conformaretis in unum propositum regulare.*' (*Literæ ad præpositos primi Ordinis*, Cod. Pur. 1201.)

'*Cum ad sopiendum vel sepeliendum potius scandalum, quod contra vos fuerat suscitatum non paucis credentibus, vos constitutiones Ecclesiasticas non servare, ad nostram presentiam certos nuntios misissetis, mandatis vos apostolicis exponentes, nos proposita vestra de consilio venerabilis fratris nostris Vercellensis Episcopi, et dilecti filii Lecodiensis et bone memorie de Cerreto Abbatum mandavimus in unum*

principles and the manner of life which the Humiliati had adopted. The modifications made by Innocent and his arguments in support of those modifications are evidence bearing on the attitude of the Curia toward the apostolic movement after the 'false Humiliati' and the followers of Waldo had proved how strong a hold that movement had over the people.

There are really three separate rules: for the First, the Second, and the Third Orders respectively.[1] The first two show most clearly the circumstances under which they were adopted; the third throws most light on the character of the whole movement. The Biblical extracts cited as authority for the regulations are, it is most probable, those by which the Humiliati themselves had been influenced to their conviction. 'You propose,' runs the rule, 'to seek humility of heart and gentleness in life by God's aid. As the Lord says in the Gospel: "Learn of me for I am meek and lowly in heart, and ye shall find rest unto your souls."' Then, doubtless having in mind the stiff-necked behaviour of those other Humiliati, as well as the doubtful position of those to whom the Church's sanction was to be given, the writer of the amended rule proceeds: 'You propose to render obedience to the Church's prelates, as the Apostle says: "Obey them that have the rule over you and submit yourselves; for they watch for your souls as they that must give account," for that is not true humility which lacks obedience as a yoke-fellow.'

The entire document shows the great anxiety of Innocent to retain these apostolics within the Church. Starting with an apparent agreement that they may keep a tenet

regulare propositum conformari. Cumque ipsi presentatam sibi a vobis vite vestre formulam et regulam, quam propontis profiteri, examinassent diligentius, et in aliquibus correxissent, nos eam tandem per dilectos filios . . . examinari fecimus, et tandem correximus per nos ipsos, et correctam curavimus approbare.' (*Literæ ad dilecti filiis de Braida,* Cod. Braid.

[1] *L.c.*

and a practice itself a fundamental belief not only of all the Humiliati, but of other evangelical Christians, whose influence the Church had reason to dread; which would, if liberally interpreted, inevitably lead to conflict with the civil and ecclesiastical authorities, the Pope 'diligently corrected' and qualified the original, unequivocal statement, 'Swear not at all,' until there was no longer any controversy or difficulty. That they accepted the papal interpretation of their own doctrine seems unquestionable; there is no record of disobedience.[1]

The Third Order, from whose rule the above quotations have been made, were like the legendary founders of the movement, laymen living not apart from the world, but at home with their families. According to the Chronicle of Laon, the heretical Humiliati resembled them. Whatever can be learned concerning the manner of life of the Third Order bears directly on the 'false Humiliati.' Involved as they must be in secular affairs, they were nevertheless, so runs the rule,[2] to obey the laws of Christ. '"All things whatsoever ye would that men should do to you, do ye even so to them." "Strive to enter in at the strait gate: for wide is the gate and broad is the way that leadeth to destruction and many there be that go in thereat; because strait is the gate and narrow is the way which leadeth unto life, and few there be that find it." Further, keep peace with all men and return all money taken in usury and all ill-gotten gains.'

All three orders of the authorized Humiliati held pro-

[1] This part of the rule admits of another interpretation, less plausible than the one adopted above. It is possible that the prohibition of oaths had been found by the Humiliati themselves, already wavering from their first intention to follow literally, regardless of what it might cost, the Gospel commands, to be inconvenient. They were not ready to cast aside altogether the tenet regarding oaths, but they were ready to explain away its rigour. Still, even if this interpretation be the true one, it does not disprove their connection with the heretical Humiliati who also held this tenet.

[2] Tiraboschi, *l.c.*, p. 131.

perty.[1] Although in the beginning they chose a life of poverty and refused all possessions, yet erelong their industry brought them such rich returns that they could no longer hold themselves to their pristine austerity. Gifts of land and of houses were made as early as the definite records of the community exist and all three orders seem to have shared in the benefactions. The members of the Second Order were communists.[2] Apparently those of the Third Order held possessions as individuals, for the rule provided that they were to supply the needs of those disabled by sickness.[3] If property had been held in common, all would have shared alike as a matter of course, and no such provision would have been necessary. The rule lays certain restrictions on the use of all property possessed by the Second and Third Orders as communities or as individuals. The First Order was to pay no tithes, quite naturally, as they were priests. The Second Order paid tithes on property, but not on products. The Third or secular Order was laid under strict obligations as to the duties of its members to contribute to the support of the Church. They were to pay tithes and first fruits, but they were on no account themselves to possess tithes. Nor was their property really their own after tithes were paid. 'Of the first fruits that remain to you, you ought to give alms. Give to the poor all that is left after your just and necessary expenses are paid. "Give alms of such things as ye have; and behold all things are clean unto you." Again, "Lay not up for yourselves treasures upon earth, where moth and rust doth corrupt, and where thieves break through and steal; but lay up for yourselves treasures in

[1] By 1176 they were holding property in Milan. Spedale Maggiore, *Archivi Speciali. Enti Civili e Religiose, Sottoclasse Sesto.* In this year they were given the vineyard called La Brera. MS. Ambros., H 205 Inf. '*Et scias quod domus Brera fuit una de primis domibus huius ordinis. Cuius religiosi fratres de Guercio dicebantur.*' (Bossi, c. IV.)

[2] Tiraboschi, *l.c.*, pp. 136–37.

[3] *Sciatis autem, quod vestri moris existit, si quis de vestra societate.*

heaven where neither moth nor rust doth corrupt, and where thieves do not break through and steal.'''

Innocent's rule becomes the more intelligible when the resemblance between the false Humiliati and those who came for his approval is considered. The great statesman reversed the policy of his predecessor toward the apostolic reformers, and conciliated, so far as he could, enthusiasts who might otherwise have become enemies of the Church. It is probable that these of Lombardy were received by the pope at the very council to which Waldo had gone to win sanction for his attempt to lead the evangelical life and from which he went forth to strengthen not the Church but heresy.[1]

The Biblical commands cited in the rule as authority for the tenets and practices of the brethren were probably the original sources of their conviction that those customs and practices were enjoined by Christ upon his followers and maintained during the apostolic age. So considered, they form another reason for considering the true and false Humiliati to have been originally one, since they were both seeking evangelical poverty.

Of the orthodoxy of the Humiliati before the twelfth century it is difficult to speak with any degree of certainty, since the disorder of sects in upper Italy at this time makes any accurate enumeration of them impossible. Before the Inquisition their doctrines were not generally known. Even in 1238, when this tribunal had made great strides in discrimination between heretics and near-heretics, the decretal of Frederick II presents a singular confusion of ideas and names.[2]

[1] Breyer, *Arnoldisten,* p. 404. But the *Chronicon Laudunense* gives 1178 as the date of Waldo's mission to Rome and 1179 for the Humiliati. Walter Map, in his account of the appearance of the Waldenses at the Third Lateran Council, does not mention the Humiliati; but he might have failed to distinguish among the humbly clad men who came thither on much the same errand.

[2] *M.G.H. LL.*, vol. II, p. 238.

The early Humiliati seem to have held the Christian faith as true, 'but where is it to be found or what is pure?'[1] The later members, whose reconciliation with the Church was assured by Innocent's careful policy, departed from the essentially apostolic spirit of the early movement.[2] The other group, false according to Innocent III, though true to their convictions at great cost, were lost to sight among the apostolic heretics who abounded in Lombardy. They had much in common with Arnold of Brescia and may easily have coalesced with his disciples. Like him, they believed in a life of poverty, not destitution. With him they agreed that tithes and first fruits should be given to the clergy. On the other hand, like the followers of Arnold, they were naturally swept along, losing their separate identity in their fusion with the Waldenses to whose rapid progress in Lombardy both sects largely contributed. They are referred to by name as late as 1213,[3] but they are coupled with the Poor Men of Lyons together with whom they are accused of preaching in secret, of assailing the priesthood and the Church of God.[4] Stephen of Bourbon names the heresies of Lombardy, quoting as his authority a certain man who for eighteen years had studied among the Waldenses in Milan, but he does not mention the Humiliati. Perhaps by that time they had become amalgamated with the Poor Men of Lombardy 'who receive possessions.'[5]

[1] Jacques de Vitry, *l.c.*

[2] The papal approval of the Franciscans and Dominicans is here definitely ascribed to the existence of the Humiliati and to the Poor Men of Lyons, whose influence, it was hoped, might be counteracted by the Mendicant Orders.

[3] *Chron. Ursperg.*, *l.c.*, p. 376.

[4] '*In occultis quoque predicationibus, quas faciebant plerumque in latibulis, ecclesiæ Dei et sacerdotibus derogabatur.*' Stephen of Bourbon, *Tractatus*, pt. 4, tit. 7, par. 330.

[5] In support of the theory that the rapid growth of the Waldensian movement in Lombardy was due to the presence of the Humiliati, see among other authorities: Comba, *Valdo ed i Valdesi*, pp. 99, etc.; *Real Ency.*, vol. VIII, p. 477; Lea, *Inquisition*, vol. I, p. 76; Breyer, *Arnoldisten*, p. 405; Zanoni, *Gli Umiliati*, etc. For the missions of the Lombard Waldenses in Germany see Müller, *l.c.*; Haupt., *Waldenserthum und Inquisition im Südöstlichen Deutschland.*

For if the practice of the heretical Humiliati is revealed by the rule, they owned property, but yet were poor, since they reserved for themselves only enough to supply actual needs, giving what remained as alms. That the Lombard Waldenses, as well as the German converts won by Lombard missionaries, differed from their French brethren is due, in part at least, to the influence of the earlier apostolics, the Humiliati and the Arnoldisti.

CHAPTER VI

THE CATHARI AND ALLIED SECTS

THE Cathari, the arch-heretics of the Middle Ages, are best known through the successful crusade which Simon de Montfort waged against the powerful, militant community of them in southern France, the Albigensians, in the thirteenth century. Presumably an offshoot of the great Manichæan movement which originated in the east [1] early in the Christian era, they spread westward into the African and Asiatic provinces of the Empire,[2] and were transferred, we know not how, into Bulgaria and Hungary, from whence they gradually filtered into southern Germany, France and northern Italy.

As early as 372, the Emperor Valentinian was alarmed at their numbers in the west and forbade their meetings.[3] More stringent decrees from his successors declared their faith to be a public crime, and they themselves enemies of state and Church [4] — futile legislation for the most part, as they continued to grow in numbers and in hostility to the established order. The presence of a strong community of them in Rome about the middle of the fifth century so alarmed Pope Leo the Great that he caused them to be condemned by a synod and banished by the Senate,[5] measures which checked them for the time being in that city, but which, by dispersing them to other parts,

[1] Possibly in Persia. Their own legends trace their origin no further than their appearance in the Slavic countries, but their faith bears a strong imprint of the Oriental.

[2] Schmidt, *Histoire des Cathares*, vol. I, pp. 1–8; *Real Ency.*, vol. XIII, p. 762.

[3] *Cod. Theod.*, lib. XVI, tit. 5, l. 3.

[4] Theodosius the Great, in 381, 382, 389. *Ibid.*, tit. 5, 11, 7, 9, 18. Honorius, in 399, 405, 408. *Ibid.*, 11, 33, 40, 43. Theodosius II, in 423, 425, 428. *Ibid.*, 11, 59, 62, 65.

[5] In 444. *Mansi*, vol. IV, col. 729, etc.

enabled them to establish new centres for the promulgation of their doctrines, traces of which might be found almost anywhere in western Christendom, in the Middle Ages. The organization of judicial machinery for the extirpation of heresy was not to be achieved for some centuries, and, failing that, effective persecution was impossible to the popes. However, the emphatic commands issued by Gregory the Great to bishops of dioceses where this dualism was known to exist, adjuring them to exterminate it,[1] were sufficiently effective to keep it from appearing above the surface of society for about four hundred years. Just when it reëmerged cannot be definitely determined, as the different outcroppings appeared under various names,[2] but by the tenth century it was quite well organized in districts as far north as Champagne and as far west as Aquitaine.

Although the missionary activities of the Cathari began shortly after they reached Bulgaria, yet before 1000 the spread of their doctrine seems to have been the casual result of the extensive commercial relations of the Slavs with occidental peoples.[3]

In the eleventh century their missionaries became more active in the west. Their zeal in proselyting, their dauntless courage in the face of all obstacles, danger, and persecution,[4] their loyalty to the faith they deemed essential,

[1] Mansi, vol. VI, cols. 746, 782, 1174, 1197.

[2] Their own name for their heresy, Cathari or Pure, is Greek and indicates their Byzantine origin. It was by this they were widely known, but as they moved westward they were called Bogomils, Bulgars, Paulicians, Paplicans, or Orientals. In southern France they were known as Albigensians, or Albigeois, from the town of Albi near Toulouse, their headquarters in this section. Here they were also given the name of Texerants, as so many of them were weavers. In Lombardy they were known as Gazari, a corruption of Cathari. The Inquisitors generally referred to them as Manichæan, because the sinister association of the word aroused the detestation of the orthodox and brought down on them the severest penalties of Church and state.

[3] *Real Ency.*, vol. VII, p. 466.

[4] In 1025 one Gerald de Montfort was burned alive in Milan for heresy. Mansi, vol. XIX, col. 424; *Recueil des Historiens des Gaules et de la France*, vol.

attracted many who were discontented with the lack of spirituality found in the Church. During the next two hundred years they increased with alarming rapidity, becoming the dominant heresy of the age, with well-organized communities in a thousand towns,[1] and bishops in Lombardy, Tuscany, Toulouse, and Carcassonne.[2] Italy being on the highway between Bulgaria and the west, and permeated with the spirit of political and intellectual independence, offered an especially fertile field for their labours; Milan was their headquarters,[3] while Viterbo, Verona, Mantova, Brescia, Bergamo, Vicenza, Rimini, Treviso, and Piacenza were infested with them. In Ferrara they were so numerous that the bishop was unable to cope with them and appealed to the civil powers;[4] in Modena they made a pact with the Catholics and lived among them with equal privileges.

From Italy they spread through Languedoc, sending missionaries north and south.[5] In Orleans they made converts even among the clergy, including the queen's confessor. At their trial before the king and a synod of prelates, the refusal of this priest to recant so angered Her Majesty that as he passed her on leaving the hall, she plucked out one of his eyes.[6] By the twelfth century they had their own bishop in Cologne,[7] and were established in

x, p. 540; Roger de Hoveden, vol. II, p. 273 (Rolls Series); Lami, *Antichità Toscane*, p. 480; Cæsar. Heisterbac., *Dial. Mir.*, Dis. v, cc. 21–25; Evervinus, *Epistola ad S. Bernard.*, Migne, *l.c.*, vol. CLXXXII, col. 677; *Epistola* Ecclesiæ Leodiensis ad Lucium, Papam II, Martène et Durand, *Amplis. Coll.*, vol. I, col. 776–77; *Gesta Epis. Leod.*, *M.G.H. SS.*, vol. VI, p. 228; Petrus, Vallium Sarnii Monachus, *Hist. Albigens.*, *Recueil*,, vol. XIX, p. 32.

[1] Cæsar. Heisterbac., *l.c.*, c. 9; Döllinger, *Sektengeschichte*, vol. I, pp, 212–13.

[2] *Notitia Conciliabuli apud S. Felicem de Caraman*, *Recueil*, vol. XIV, pp. 448–49.

[3] *Cod. Ottob. Lat.* 136, Biblioteca Vaticana. Ex Cod. Joannis Angeli, *De vitiis et virtutibus.*

[4] Muratori, *Antiq. Ital.*, diss. 60.

[5] Mansi, vol. XIX, col. 742, 424; *Gesta Epis. Leod.*, *l.c.*, p. 228; Cæsar. Heisterbac., *l.c.*; Ademarus, *Historiarum*, *M.G.H. SS.*, vol. IV, p. 142; Rad. Glabrius *Historiarum*, *Recueil*, vol. x, p. 27, p. 35, note b.

[6] Rad. Glabrius, *l.c.*, p. 38.

[7] Cæsar. Heisterbac., *l.c.*, c. 19.

Flanders, Switzerland, Suabia, Bavaria, and Hungary, but had been unable to enter England.[1]

Naturally their spread was most rapid in those parts where the clergy were slothful and corrupt, partly because they met with less opposition, and partly because the vigorous austerity of their lives, the rationalism and general helpfulness of their teachings, delighted those who sought relief from a slack and sunken hierarchy. Their understanding of the hidden forces of the century may have been accidental, but their stern morality gave them a consciousness of strength, a straightforwardness of spirit which enabled them to resist anathema and edict,[2] and which won for them disciples among nobles powerful enough to render considerable material assistance, particularly in their earlier years.[3]

The tenets of the Cathari which attracted the attention of the clergy were for the most part doctrinal. Like the Manichæans they taught that since Christ had refused all sacrifices the idea of sacrifice in the mass was heretical.[4] Nor could any priest, good or bad, create the body of God.[5] Indeed, it was preposterous to imagine that Christ would wish to change bread and wine into his body, or to permit that body to enter a man's stomach or be devoured by rats and mice.[6] To them, believing as they did, that matter in

[1] Wm. of Newburg, *Historia Rerum Anglicarum*, lib. II, c. 3 (Rolls Series).

[2] Ademarus, *l.c.*, pp. 143, 148; Rad. Glabrius, *l.c.*, p. 35; Synod of Saint Carroux, 1028, Mansi, *l.c.*, col. 485; Synod of Arras, 1125, col. 423; Second Lateran Council, 1139, *l.c.*, vol. XXI, col. 525; Council of Rheims, 1148, col. 717; Council of Tours, 1163, col. 1167; *Gesta Syn. Aurel.*, ann. 1017, in d'Achéry, *Spicilegium*, vol. I, p. 604.

[3] *Gesta Syn. Aurel.*, *l.c.*; Ademarus, *l.c.*, p. 436.

[4] *Coll. Occitan.*, vol. VII, p. 193; Eckbertus, *Sermo* XI, *Bib. Max. Vet. Pat.*, vol. XIV, p. 478; Ebrardus, *Liber Antihær.*, in Gretser, vol. XII, pt. 2, p. 145; Reinerius Sacchonus, *Summa*, Martène et Durand, *Thes. Nov.*, vol. V, col. 1763; *Gesta Syn. Aurel.*, *l.c.*; Moneta, *l.c.*, p. 300.

[5] Eckbertus, *Sermo* XI, p. 478.

[6] *Coll. Occitan.*, *l.c.*, p. 201; Moneta, *l.c.*, p. 301; *Disputatio inter Catholicum et Hær.*, Martène et Durand, *Thes. Nov.*, *l.c.*, col. 1729; Ebrardus, *l.c.*; Ermengardus, *Opusculum contra hæreticos*, Gretser, *l.c.*, p. 232.

any form was the expression of the evil spirit,[1] this doctrine of transubstantiation was the worst of abominations and all who gave Christ's words a literal interpretation were in error.[2] Infant baptism was also rejected, since those whose faculties were undeveloped could not receive the Holy Spirit.[3] Water baptism they held as useless; only that baptism of the Spirit, whereby every good man became the vehicle for the Paraclete, had virtue.[4] The cross, symbol of Christ's suffering, should be hated rather than reverenced.[5] Saints had no more power over mortals when dead than when living;[6] nor did these ascend to heaven before the day of judgment.[7] The existence of an inferno was questioned by them,[8] as were purgatorial fires,[9] the efficacy of indulgences,[10] and the remission of sins after death.[11] Oaths were regarded as mortal sins as surely as adultery or homicide and were absolutely forbidden. Their yea should be yea, and their nay, nay.[12] An oath, they said, was out of keeping with their faith, as it implied pride in one's word.[13] This alone was enough to render the Cathari a dangerous element in the eyes of their contemporaries whose social order was based on the feudal oath.

Since they held that all flesh originated from evil, it was inevitable that they should reject the doctrine of the resur-

[1] Moneta, *l.c.*, pp. 10, 295; Alanus de Ins., *Adv. Hæret.*, Migne, *l.c.*, vol. CCX, col. 360; Cod. 13, Biblioteca Mugell. de Salvi Burce Placent., in the Biblioteca Laurenziana, Florence, *Prologus; Cod. Vat. Lat.* 4030, *Inquis. Lang.*, f. 252.

[2] *Cod. Vat. Lat.*, *l.c.*, ff. 284 etc.

[3] Moneta, *l.c.*, pp. 284, 237; Limborch, *Liber Inquis. Tholos.*, p. 37; Eckbertus, *Sermo* VIII, p. 464; *Coll. Occitan.*, *l.c.*, ff. 193, 221; *Cod. Vat. Lat.* 4060, ff. 49–60. Some of the sects taught that baptism was not instituted by Christ, but by John the Baptist, whom they considered a false prophet. Moneta; *l.c.*, p. 394.

[4] Evervinus, *l.c.*, col. 676; Eckbertus, *Sermo* VII; Moneta, *l.c.*, p. 282; Mansi, vol. XIX, col. 444.

[5] Bonacursus, *Vita Hæret.*, in d'Achéry, *Spicileg.*, vol. I, p. 209; *Coll. Occitan.*, *l.c.*; *Cod. Salvi Burce, l.c.*; *Cod. Vat. Lat.* 4030, ff. 69t–73t.

[6] Luca Tudensis, *De Altera Vita*, cc. 1, 22. [7] *Ibid.*, c. 2.

[8] *Ibid.*, c. 3. [9] *Ibid.*, c. 4. [10] *Ibid.*, c. 18. [11] *Ibid.*, c. 7.

[12] Reinerius, *Summa*, *l.c.*, p. 486; Moneta, *l.c.*, pp. 469–70; Bonacursus, *l.c.*; Doat, vol. XXXVI, f. 37; Matt. v, 37.

[13] Bernard. Guid., *Pract. Inquis.*, p. 239.

rection of the body.[1] Further, as a result of such a tenet, if not indeed the cause of it, they shared with the liberal branch of the Gnostics the belief that Christ had no real body, and therefore was neither born nor crucified.[2] Such natural deductions from the primary principle of most Oriental religions, that of the malignity of all matter, led to the proscription of many Christian tenets based on the Old Testament, and to the substitution for them of a confusion of paganism and gospel teachings which they offered to the world as a sort of reformed Christianity.

The dualism of the Cathari recognized the equality of the powers of good and evil, and their eternal opposition, but unlike the Manichæans, the western sect believed in the ultimate triumph of good and recognized the Trinity, which they invoked in their benedictions.[3] Apparently they had turned to the earlier heresy to illuminate the origin of good and evil, just as the Church turned to the Greek philosophers to explain the relation between the visible and the mystical in the sacraments.

The difference existing among the various branches of the Cathari were so marked as to make any generalizations as to their doctrines rather difficult. The fundamental dogma of the dual nature of man and the universe was later subjected to a variety of interpretations and modifications in different localities, so that unity of faith and of practice among the different communities was all but impossible.[4] Unlike the Gnostics, with whom dualism was a fundamental doctrine, the Cathari tended to subordinate it to conduct, regarding the conflict between good and evil rather as a necessary consequence of apostolic Christianity,

[1] Moneta, *l.c.*, p. 371.

[2] Bonacursus, *l.c.* Some of the sects said that demons had feigned to die in his stead. *Cod. Reg. Paris*, 4269.

[3] Eckbertus, *Sermo* I, p. 449; Bonacursus, *l.c.*, p. 208; Reinerius, *Summa*, col. p. 1768; Moneta, pp. 5, 24; Doat, vol. XXXIV, ff. 95, 99; vol. XXII, f. 96; Alanus, *l.c.*, pp. 6, 7; *Disputatio*, *l.c.*, p. 1707.

[4] Bonacursus, *l.c.*; Moneta, *l.c.*, p. 105; Pet. Vall. Sarn., *l.c.*, p. 5.

in practical protest against a corrupt hierarchy, than as a warfare between opposing spirits. They shared the tendency, everywhere prevalent in this century, to analyze, dissect, and reorganize the Church. Unlike the Waldensians, whom they resembled in many respects, their revolt was aimed at the doctrine of the institution rather than at the discipline.

Generally speaking, they recognized 'the two equal principles, God and Satan, of whom the former created the invisible, spiritual and eternal universe; the latter, the material and temporal which he governs. Satan was the Jehovah of the Old Testament; the prophets and patriarchs were robbers, and consequently all Scripture anterior to the Gospels is to be rejected. The New Testament alone is Holy Writ; Christ, however, was not a man but a phantom — the Son of God who appeared to be born of the Virgin Mary and who came from Heaven to overthrow the worship of Satan.' [1]

They taught that men were spirits fallen from Heaven, clothed in a material body, the work of the Evil One, and were here subjected to a probation, ending at the receiving of the rite of the *Consolamentum*, or laying on of hands, a rite committed to the true Church by the Apostles. That part of the Old Testament which describes the beginning of the world and its development into kingdoms and hierarchies has Satan for its authority and inspiration, while its poets and philosophers are divinely inspired. The Mosaic law is from Satan, the god of darkness, who created the body; the intellect and will are the work of Light and partake of the essence of those angelic, immortal creatures who express the fullness of God's love.[2]

When their manner of life was questioned, it was found

[1] Lea, *Inquisition*, vol. I, pp. 24, etc. See also Bonacursus, *l.c.*; Doat, vol. XXXVI, f. 257.

[2] Moneta, *l.c.*, p. 105.

that they considered marriage sinful. True matrimony, they said, was not between male and female, but between soul and spirit. 'For in Paradise there was never a corruption of the flesh, nor anything not simply and purely spiritual, and God designed this higher union for those souls which had fallen from Heaven through pride and ignorance that they might return to eternal bliss by matrimony with the Holy Spirit, by good works and by abstinence from sins.'[1] The stricter Cathari taught that none could be saved except virgins, and they admitted to the *Consolamentum* only those who had renounced all conjugal relations.[2] However, there was not absolute agreement on this point. Among some, virgins alone could marry; among others, only the Perfecti were obliged to live celibate lives.

They forbade the use of all animal food including milk, cheese, and eggs, as these had to do with the propagation of matter and were consequently evil:[3] they taught the sanctity of human life, declaring that no civil power had the right to condemn a man to death: neither internal nor external interests of a country ever justified warfare, which was inspired by demons and contrary to the law of God.[4] The soldier, the judge who sentenced a criminal to death, and the preacher of a crusade were all murderers;[5] and the Cathari were in this regard consistent followers of their own teachings, as in their most prosperous days they never put to death either opponent or persecutor.[6]

In creed, ethics, ritual and ecclesiastical government,

[1] Doat, vol. xxxvi, ff. 251t, 252.

[2] *Acta Inq. Carc., Cod. Reg. Paris,* 4269; *Cod. Salvi Burce, l.c.*; Doat, vol. ii, f. 115; vol. iv, f. 204.

[3] Bonacursus, *l.c.*, p. 209; Doat, vol. ii, ff. 22, 27, 30, 145, 146, 152, 234–35; Eckbertus, *Sermo* vi, p. 458.

[4] Moneta, *l.c.*, pp. 506, 513, 515.

[5] Matt. 26: 52; Doat, vol. xxiii, f. 100; vol. xxii, f. 89; Ebrardus, *l.c.*, pp. 157, 159.

[6] Moneta, *l.c.* In 1052 Henry II declared some people in Gosslar guilty of heresy because they refused to kill a chicken. *Gesta Epis. Leod., l.c.*, p. 228.

they opposed the Church and cast aside its machinery, rejected its sacraments, its saints, its relics, images, indulgences, tithes, and oblations, holding it to be the synagogue of Satan in which salvation was impossible. 'All of its rites were futile or worse than futile. Asceticism and the prohibition of marriage were the logical consequences of a belief which recognized the body as the handiwork and servant of Satan, hampering and striving to ruin the soul, the child of God.' [1]

The Church having been repudiated, the dualists formed their own organization, their own hierarchy, claiming to have the sole Church of Christ whose members were the true successors of the Apostles,[2] with the power to 'bind and loose' and to reconcile the sinner with God, which was the basis of the hold of the Church over the people. Their anti-sacerdotalism was not democratic; a wide difference distinguished their two classes, the Perfecti and the Credentes.[3]

The latter formed the lower rank; they had fewer obligations and fewer religious privileges, but more social. As they were only partially initiated, they could live in the world, could eat meat, marry, hold property, and engage in trade. Nor were they obliged to keep the fasts.[4] The Perfecti, chosen only after a long probation, were the elect in whom the Spirit dwelt,[5] the official class from whom the priesthood was drawn.[6] The duties of the Perfecti were both administrative and sacerdotal. They had charge of the finances and attended the monthly *Apparallamentum;* they alone could recite the Lord's Prayer, which they did thrice daily before meals; they alone could administer the

[1] Bernard. Guid., *l.c.*, pp. 237–38; Moneta, *l.c.*, p. 508.

[2] Eckbertus, *Sermo* III, *l.c.*, p. 450.

[3] *Ep. Eccles. Leod.*, *l.c.*; Doat, vol. II, f. 280; vol. IV, f. 205.

[4] Molinier, *L'Église et la Société Cathares*, *Revue Hist.*, vol. XCIV, pp. 345–46.

[5] *Cod. Reg. Paris*, 3371; Doat, vol. XXIII, f. 201.

[6] Bernard. Guid., *l.c.*, p. 239.

Consolamentum, the reception of which was the prime condition of admission to their rank. They were forbidden to marry and to hold property; what they did not earn was supplied by the Credentes. Three times a year, they observed rigorous fasts: from Saint Brice's Day (November 13) to Christmas, Lent, and from Pentecost to the feast of Saints Peter and Paul.[1]

Their hierarchy consisted of four orders set apart by the laying on of hands: Bishop, Filius Major, Filius Minor, and Deacon. Unlike the Roman priesthood, that of the Cathari was executive rather than sacramental, although the heretics claimed powers of absolution and the gift of the Holy Spirit. They also held that the gift of apostolic succession had been bestowed on them rather than on the Roman priests.

Admission to the sect was conferred by promising the *Convenenza* or assembly of the Cathari to renounce the Catholic faith, to pay homage to the Perfecti, and before death to receive the *Consolamentum*,[2] a rite conferred by two Perfecti and by far the most important in their eyes, as it wiped out sin and assured the entrance of the Holy Spirit. If either ministrant were guilty of mortal sin, its efficacy was invalidated. The life of the consoled was so austere that few had the courage to undertake it, postponing the ceremony until the last illness, so that consequently the form of administration was often altered to suit some especial need.[3] As the sect did not believe in eternal damnation, those dying unconsoled were forced to undergo transmigrations of the soul until the absolution had been finally

[1] Bernard. Guid., *l.c.*, p. 241; Moneta, *l.c.*, p. 313; *Ep. Eccles. Leod.*, *l.c.*; Doat, vol. xxv., f. 3; vol. xxxii, 102t; vol. v, f. 246.

[2] Doat, vol. xxii, f. 170; *Cod. Reg. Paris* 4269; *Cod. Vat. Lat.* 4030, ff. 117t, 213; *Cod. Casanat.*, A III, 34, f. 24t; *Lib. Inq. Thol.*, p. 29; Bonacursus, *l.c.*; p. 210. For the administration of this rite, which could be given by men or by women, see *Le Nouveau Testament traduit au XII siècle en langue provençale, suivi d'un rituel cathare* (ed. Clédat), Coll. Occit., *l.c.*

[3] *Lib. Inq. Thol.*, pp. 104, 179; Doat, vol. xxxii, f. 170.

received.[1] The life of the Perfecti to which this rite gave access was so rigorous that those who received it were urged to end their lives lest on their recovery they commit the unpardonable sin of breaking the vow they had taken. This voluntary suicide, either by suffocation or by starvation was known as the *endura*, and was a logical outgrowth of their doctrine of the inherent evil of matter as well as of the belief that death by illness or by senile decay showed Satan's mastery over man's divine spirit.

They had few sacraments beside the *Consolamentum*, and all were far less important, serving for little but to make more universal their appeal. Confession was required,[2] even for very slight offences, and was made in public; for the mass, they had substituted the breaking of bread, a remarkably literal reproduction of the Gospel account of the Last Supper.[3]

The Cathari claimed that they were not heretics destroying the Church, but rather that they were purifying it and infusing into it a new strength, a claim more or less justified by the simplicity of their ritual and their emphasis on perfection of life instead of reliance on the sacraments for salvation. Apparently the great body of the sect did not understand the subtleties of their faith, for neither they nor their contemporaries give much emphasis to these in their writings. Their version of dualism had probably originated in speculation over mystical and transcendental doctrines, their heritage from the Orient, but even in southern France, where they were strongest in numbers and keenest in argument, the philosophical possibilities and eventualities of their creed seem not to have been recognized, nor the frequent contradictions between faith and practice noted.[4]

[1] *Cod. Casanat.*, A IV, 49, f. 288. [2] Eckbertus, *Sermo* IX, p. 466.

[3] *Cod. Vat. Lat.*, *l.c.*; *Lib. Inq. Thol.*, p. 160; Doat, vol. V, f. 188; vol. XXIII, f. 204t; Reinerius, *Summa*, *l.c.*, p. 1763; S. Bernard., *Sermo in Cantica*, 66; Mansi, vol. XIX, col. 423.

[4] Eckbert of Bonn, who talked with them, says they were unlearned in Chris-

Their nobler tenets, those with a universal appeal, such as that of the eternal conflict between good and evil, were so weakened and limited by what was morbid and unbalanced — their denunciation of marriage, for example — that, even without the atrocious crusade urged against them in the thirteenth century, it seems doubtful if they could have long endured. The greater part of their members, the Credentes, were exempt from the austerities imposed on the Perfecti as a substitute for purgatorial fires to prepare them for the life to come. So long as they promised the *Convenenza* to renounce the Catholic faith, pay reverence to the Perfecti, and to receive the *Consolamentum* before death, they might indulge in whatever pleasure they desired. Such an arrangement naturally gave rise to tales of their insincerity, hypocrisy, and licentiousness, tales generally without foundation, as the Believers were for the most part simple-minded, hard-working artisans, weavers, smiths, etc.

Catharism was largely a negative heresy, denying the doctrines, hierarchy, and worship of the Catholic Church, its claim to apostolic succession, the doctrine of Petrine supremacy, and the right of the Church to hold property.[1] In their efforts to gain converts the Catharan preachers more than probably emphasized their own asceticism, contrasting it with the worldliness of the clergy whom they explicitly and implicitly attacked as modern Pharisees,[2] at the same time denouncing the Roman Church as the woman of the Apocalypse, drunk with the blood of saints; the Pope as the Anti-Christ and Sylvester as the beast of the Apocalypse, son of perdition in whose time the Church was lost.

tian doctrine. *Sermo* II, *l.c.* William of Newburg calls them '*sine litteris et idiotæ.*'

[1] Moneta, *l.c.*, pp. 390–96. They were among the first to denounce the Donation of Constantine.

[2] Moneta, *l.c.*, p. 397; Bonacursus, *l.c.*

Their attraction for the multitudes who joined their ranks lay not in their opposition to the Church nor in their philosophical systems, but rather in the concrete facts of their lives, in their extreme asceticism, and in their austere virtue.[1] Idealists in an age dangerously materialistic, they taught the freedom of the spirit, the sacredness of life, and the inalienable right of all men to seek salvation each in his own way. The *endura* was the legitimate outgrowth of this idea of the fundamental rightness of self-guidance. When one felt himself ready for the glories of the next world, let him cast aside the body, the spirit's unclean prison, and enter upon the joys of Paradise.

Popular enthusiasm was generally aroused by their exhortation to simplicity and purity of life such as Christ enjoined on his early followers.[2] If literal adoption of their asceticism was impossible, their ethics were admirable. Reinerius Sacchus, once a member of their sect and later an inquisitor, says they were distinguished by conduct and by conversation, were temperate in meat and drink, industrious, and, generally speaking, a conspicuous protest against an age and a people dominated by a keen pursuit of the joys of this world.[3]

To the rank and file of the sect their fundamental doctrine was perfection of life based on literal obedience to the commands of Christ, and their especial task, the revival of the primitive Church and of apostolic customs, long overlaid by excessive sacerdotalism.[4] Why, they asked, when Christ had nowhere to lay his head, should his successor live in a palace and claim that worldly dominion which he had denounced. Under the insignia of the purple mantle and jewelled crown of the successor of Sylvester it was difficult to recognize a disciple of Christ. The thirst of the Curia for riches and honour had nothing in common

[1] Doat, vol. xxxvi, f. 60. [2] *Ibid.*, f. 37. [3] *Summa, l.c.*
[4] Evervinus, *l.c.*; Eckbertus, *l.c.*

with the desires of the Evangelists. In some communities this attempt to follow Christ literally led to the practice of communism, but it never found expression in mendicancy. Even their ministers were obliged to labour, although they were forbidden to engage in trade or in any occupation where lying and stealing were possible.[1]

The superbly decorated churches then being built called forth their criticism, as they held that the heart of the believer was the true house of God.[2] Their own meeting-places were at first the houses of the Credentes, but, as they grew more prosperous, they erected churches which they kept simple and unadorned, forbidding images,[3] stone altars, candelabra, incense, and even hymns.

In their emphasis on the doctrine of salvation through poverty, certain branches of the Cathari were not far removed from Arnold, Waldo, or Francis, although it is not easy to distinguish between the numerous heretical bodies of the eleventh and twelfth centuries. The records of the Inquisition, even where most complete, are often quite lacking in dates and localities and fail entirely to trace changes or development in doctrine. Popular preachers arose now and then whose teachings savoured more or less of Catharism, although they were not outwardly members of the sect. Such were Peter of Bruys and his disciple, Henry of Lausanne, curious shadowy figures, appearing suddenly, like many another apostle in the Middle Ages, against the gay Provençal background, playing a brief but stormy part, fleeing hither and thither before persecution, and crying out a message to all who would hear, until they were silenced by death.[4] Pilgrims and mendicants, they won many converts in the rich towns of southern France,

[1] Evervinus, *l.c.*; Moneta, *l.c.*, p. 451.

[2] Moneta, *l.c.*, p. 461.

[3] *Ibid.*, p. 480; Ebrardus, *l.c.*, c. 4; Ermengardus, *l.c.*, c. 9.

[4] Petrus Venerab., *Tractatus contra Petro Brusianos*, Migne, *l.c.*, vol. CLIX, col. 723; S. Bernard., *Ep.* 241, Migne, *l.c.*, vol. CLXXXII.

already impregnated with Catharan heresies and too consciously independent, too vigorously alert, to be orthodox.

So little is known of their lives or their doctrines that it is difficult to place them with any feeling of certainty. Peter is said to have been a native of the hamlet of Bruys in the diocese of Embrun in Narbonne and was a priest in Vallonise,[1] from whence he was expelled because of his antisacerdotal ideas. Finding a refuge among the more liberal Gascons and Provençals, he wandered twenty years (*circa* 1106–26) among them preaching in obedience to the divine command, 'Go ye into all the world and preach the Gospel to every living creature,' which he maintained was laid upon him as directly as it had been on the Twelve.[2] More akin to the eighth-century iconoclasts than to the dualists, he denied dogmas and condemned ceremonies and corrupt practices without at any time setting forth positive doctrines alien to Christianity; reviving, perhaps unconsciously, the teachings of Claude of Turin in his desire to return to the primitive cult of apostolic Christians.[3] In the confutation of his tenets by Peter the Venerable, Abbot of Cluny, written to the Archbishops of Arles and Embrun and certain bishops, may be found the best account of the dogma.[4] An apocryphal preface to this epistle gives the following summary of his teachings:[5]

The baptism of infants was rejected on the ground that those under years of discretion could not possess the faith on which salvation depends, nor could they profit by the vicarious faith of their god-parents. Baptism of adults by sprinkling was permitted, however. Catholic converts

[1] P. Abælard., *Introductio ad Theologiam,* lib. II, c. 4, Migne, *l.c.*, vol. CLXXVIII, col. 1056; Alphonsus Castro, *Adv. Hæreses,* lib. III, p. 168 (ed. 1571).

[2] Pet. Venerab., *l.c.*; Gieselea, *Kirchengeschichte,* vol. III, pp. 390–91.

[3] P. Abælard., *l.c.*

[4] Claude was Bishop of Turin in the ninth century and an ardent opponent of relic and image worship. An account of his teachings may be found in Jonæ Aureliens, *De Cultu Imaginum,* Migne, *l.c.*, vol. CVI, col. 30, p. 305, etc.

[5] This tractatus or epistle is printed in Migne, *l.c.*, vol. CLIX.

were rebaptized, whether because the rite was first administered in their infancy, or whether because it was administered by priests, is not stated.[1]

Sacred places for worship, such as temples and churches, were useless and should be pulled down lest they be overestimated.[2] God hears everywhere those who deserve to be heard, whether they pray in tavern or temple, in market place or sanctuary, before an altar or before a manger. The true Church of God was not a multitude of stones piled together, but rather, the spiritual union of those who believed.

Crosses, the instruments and symbols of Christ's torture, were senseless things, unworthy of adoration, and should be burned. Not only should they be rejected because they were associated with Calvary, but they were doubly, or trebly accursed because Saint Peter and Saint Andrew had met death by crucifixion. A cross should not be reverenced any more than the stones by which Saint Stephen suffered martyrdom, or the gridiron on which Saint Laurence was roasted.[3] Sacrifices, prayers, and alms for the dead were derided; each soul was to be judged on his own merit, and life once over, the account was closed and unalterable.[4]

The doctrine of transubstantiation was absolutely denied and the sacrament of the mass rejected,[5] the Lord's Supper being considered but an historical incident.[6] This rejection of the Eucharist is the most important of his errors, and it is the only one of his doctrines concerning which Peter's own words have been preserved:

'O people, believe not the bishops, the priests, and the clerks, who, as in much else, seek to deceive you as to the

[1] Pet. Venerab., *l.c.*, col. 752; Saint John, IV; Saint Mark, V, IX, XVI; Saint Matthew, XV, XVII.

[2] Pet. Venerab., *l.c.*, col. 742.

[3] *Ibid.*, col. 771; *Ex Gestis Pontificum Cenomannensium Recueil*, vol. XII, p. 547.

[4] Pet. Venerab., *l.c.* [5] *Ibid.*, col. 787.

[6] *Ibid.*, Præf., col. 732; d'Argentré, *Collectio Judiciorum*, vol. I, p. 14; *Gest. Pont. Cen.*, *l.c.*

office of the altar, where they lyingly pretend to make the body of Christ, and give it to you for the salvation of your souls. They plainly lie, for the body of Christ was but once made by Christ in the supper before the Passion, and but once given to the disciples. Since then it has never been made and never given.'

Hymns in the Church were but mockery. Loud voices and musical notes do not appease the wrath of God, whose chief delight is in the pious desires of his own children. Nothing but the faith of man and his personal righteousness avail for his salvation; neither symbol nor sacrament has any efficiency.[1]

That Peter practised some of his teachings seems evident from the abbot's complaint that in their parts people were rebaptized, churches profaned, altars destroyed, and priests and monks scourged, imprisoned, and forced to marry. When on Good Friday, 1124, he showed his contempt for the Church and the priesthood by burning a pile of consecrated crosses and fed the bystanders with meat roasted in the ashes, active fermentation was directed against him and he was burned as a heretic in Saint Gilles in 1126.[2] A small sect survived him and continued to promulgate his doctrines either as Petrobrusians or as Henricans until they were finally merged with the Cathari or the Waldensians.[3]

Henry, a monk of Lausanne, more formidable than Peter[4] because of his greater eloquence and learning, is first heard of at Le Mans in 1116. His arrival was heralded by two of his disciples who came to the bishop asking that he be allowed to preach. Here, as in most places, mendicants were hospitably received by the clergy and Heribert,

[1] Pet. Venerab., Præf., *l.c.*, col. 719.

[2] *Ibid.*, *l.c.*, col. 729; *Annales Benedic.* vol. VI, pp. 318–19; d'Argentré, *l.c.*, vol. I, p. 14; Pet. Venerab., *Ep.*, *Recueil*, vol. XV, p. 640.

[3] Gieseler, *l.c.*

[4] Matt. Paris, *Chron. Maj.*, ann. 1151 (Rolls Series), vol. 57, part 2, p. 188.

the bishop, who was on the point of departure for Rome, gave the desired permission.[1] Attracted by the austerity of his life no less than by his denunciations of the vices of the clergy and the defects of the established faith — themes ever welcome to the vulgar crowd — multitudes flocked to hear him and whole congregations became his followers.[2] Courtesans repented of their evil ways, and casting aside their luxury, married youths of position, who, like themselves, assumed the coarsest of garments as an expression of their desire to embrace the apostolic life. On his return, Heribert was understandably dismayed at the factions rending his diocese, and he called Henry to account for sowing discord between the clergy and the people. He challenged him to a public disputation, but, failing to prove him a heretic, had to content himself with forcing him to leave.

Little is known of Henry's teaching at this time beyond his anti-sacerdotalism, but his career shows the activity of the preachers of his type, as he was heard of in Tours, Rheims, Bordeaux, Albi, Perigord, and in various parts of Gascony,[3] everywhere condemning the worldliness of the Church. The clergy were powerless, as the nobles hated them too cordially to interfere in their behalf and the people were only too glad of the excuse the new doctrines gave them for pillaging the churches.[4] Alberin, sent by Pope Innocent II to meet him at Toulouse, was unable to accomplish anything[5] until he was joined by Bernard of

[1] *Gest. Pont. Cen.*, *l.c.*, p. 548.

[2] *Ibid.*; d'Argentré, *l.c.*, vol. I, p. 16. In the trial Henry claimed to be a deacon.

[3] Mansi, vol. XX, col. 224; S. Bernard., *Ep.* 241, Migne, *l.c.*, vol. CLXXXII, col. 434; Evervinus, *l.c.*, col. 876. Saint Bernard says that when the Pontiff himself visited Toulouse, the people of a certain suburb refused his blessing, saying that they had their own father, pope, and advocate greater than he.

[4] *Gest. Pont. Cen.*, *l.c.*

[5] D'Argentré, *l.c.*, vol. I, p. 16. S. Bernard., *l.c.*: '*Basilicæ sine plebibus, plebes sine sacerdotibus, sacerdotes sine debita reverentia sunt, et sine Christo denique Christiani*'; *Ep.* 242, *l.c.*, *Ad Tolosanos:* '*Hoc etiam moneo vos, charissimi, quod*

Clairvaux, who, fearing that Christianity would be absolutely banished from the south of France, threw himself most gallantly into the work of reclamation and challenged Henry to a disputation. When the latter refused, the nobles, hitherto his supporters, turned from him and he was obliged to flee. After about a year, spent we know not where, he reappeared, was captured and brought in chains to the Archbishop of Arles, who charged him with heresy before the Council of Pisa in 1134.[1] He was convicted and given in charge of Saint Bernard at his convent at Clairvaux. Whether he really entered the community and left later, or whether he refused to go, is not certain, but soon after the Council he is heard of preaching, and later was seized and put in prison, where he is supposed to have died after ten years.[2]

At first Henry seems to have confined himself to denouncing the worldliness of the clergy, but in the last years of his life he adopted the tenets of Peter of Bruys, adding to them a prohibition of second marriage and a disapproval of any conjugal relation.[3] It was not long before the doctrines of these two mendicants spread from the Garonne to the Rhine.[4] The austere lives of their followers, their zeal for purity and for piety, won popular favour especially near Cologne. They lived by the labour of their own hands,[5] they advocated clerical poverty, they rejected the sacraments, and they kept the fasts of the Cathari, but apparently they made no use of the *Conso-*

et dicebam vobis cum præsens essem, ut nullum extraneum sive ignotum prædicatorem recipiatis, nisi qui missus a summo seu a vestro permissus pontifice prædicaverit. "Quomodo," inquit, "prædicabunt nisi, mittantur?" (Rom. 10 : 15.) *Ipsi sunt qui induentes sibi formam pietatis et virtutem ejus penitus abnegantes: profanas noviatates vocum et sensuum tamquam melli venenum, verbis, cœlestibus intermiscent.*'

[1] Mansi, vol. XXI, col. 485.

[2] In 1145, *Gest. Pont. Cen.*, *l.c.*, p. 547; Albericus, Monach. Trium Font., *Chron.*, *M.G.H. SS.*, vol. XXIII, pp. 840, 845.

[3] S. Bernard., *Serm. in Cantica*, 64, Migne, *l.c.*, vol. CLXXXIII, col. 1084.

[4] *Ibid., Serm.* 65. [5] *Ibid., Serm.* 64.

lamentum, nor did they adopt the organization into Credentes and Perfecti, yet, except that the baptism of adults is not expressly denounced, their doctrines were Catharan, and they succeeded in pruning away many rites of the Church that were of post-apostolic origin.[1] There is scant positive evidence to show whether their return to primitive Christianity was conscious or whether it was merely born of the desire generally prevalent at this time for a purification of the Church. There does seem to be presumptive evidence, however, for the conclusion that these heresiarchs had compared the existing order with the early Christian practices in so far as they knew them. They seem to have felt also that they were actual disciples of Christ, preaching in obedience to the command given by him to his Apostles. Moreover, their doctrine of baptism seems to have been founded on Christ's own words.

Further evidence exists of the apostolic character of heretics discovered at Cologne between 1144 and 1147 by Everwin, Provost of Steinfeld, whose account of them, written to Saint Bernard, indicates that they were Petrobrusian.[2] Saint Bernard acceded to Everwin's request to preach against them, and he attacked them in two sermons which, however, follow the account of his disciple too closely to be of much independent value.[3]

Just where and under what conditions this group originated cannot be determined. They seem to have been Henricans, but with a stronger tinge of Catharism than were those found in southern France. Even before the date of Everwin's letter, heretics more or less similar had been found in various parts of France, notably in Flanders and

[1] *Real Ency.*, vol. I, pp. 701, etc.; *Kirchen Lexicon*, vol. I, p. 1142.

[2] Evervinus, *l.c.*; Huffer, in *Historischer Jahrbuch des Görres-Gesellschaft* for 1899, p. 765, n. 4, says the letter must have been written after 1147, as it suggests a personal acquaintance between Everwin and Bernard not likely to have been formed before the latter's journey to Germany in 1147.

[3] S. Bernard., *Serm. in Cantica*, nos. 65 and 66, *l.c.*

in Brittany, around Limoges, Bonn, and Gosslar, as well as in the valleys of the Rhone and the Rhine.[1] The account given by Everwin of those at Cologne reads like an expansion of Peter the Venerable's digest of the Petrobrusian errors. Like Henry and Peter, these rejected infant baptism and for the same reason.[2] Like them they retained the rite for adults, but condemned entirely all other sacraments.[3] Fully convinced that the Church had lost its primitive character, they no longer regarded it as that founded by Christ. 'They say that all the priests of the Church are not consecrated, claiming the apostolic dignity has been corrupted because the clergy have been involved in secular business. He who sits in the chair of Peter is no soldier of God like Peter, and has deprived himself of the power which Peter had in so great a degree, and which he has not at all. The archbishops and bishops who in the Church lead secular lives do not receive from the Pope power to consecrate others. This belief they base on the words of Christ, "the Scribes and Pharisees sit in the seat of Moses." [4] . . . All the observances of the Church which were not founded by Christ and the Apostles in direct succession from him, they call superstitions.[5] . . . In the intercession of saints they put no trust. They hold that fasts and other methods of mortifying the flesh, imposed for sins, are unnecessary for the just and even for sinners. For in whatsoever day a sinner shall repent, all his sins shall be remitted unto him. Nor do they admit

[1] *Histor. Trever.*, *M.G.H. SS.*, vol. VIII, p. 193; *Ep. Eccl. Leod.*, *l.c.*, col. 777; Guib. Nov., *Opera*, ed. d'Achéry, app., p. 690; Hugo. Metell., *Certamen papæ*, in Hugo, *Sac. Antiq. Mon.*, vol. II, p. 349; *Gesta Epis. Leod.*, *l.c.*, p. 117; *Gall. Christ.*, vol. II, col. 523; Caesar. Heisterbac., *l.c.*, dis. 5, c. 19.

[2] Evervinus, *l.c.* [3] *Ibid.*

[4] *Ibid.* Cf. this attack upon the worldly clergy with the accounts of the effect of Henry's preaching at Le Mans: '*Qua hæresi plebs in clerum versa est in furorem, adeo quod famulis eorum minarentur cruciatus, nec eis aliquid vendere, vel ab eis emere voluissent; immo habebant eos sicut Ethnicos et Publicanos.* (*Gest. Pont. Cen.*, *l.c.*)

[5] Evervinus, *l.c.*

there is purgatorial fire after death, but hold that the souls of men when they go forth from the body, pass at once into eternal rest or everlasting punishment. So they count as of no avail prayers and offerings of the faithful for the dead.' [1]

The sacrifice of the mass was rejected because the priests of the 'Church are none of them validly ordained, the apostolic dignity having been contaminated by contact with the world,' and the pope, having lost the divine power bestowed on the Prince of Apostles, cannot bestow this on the clergy, all of whom they hold to be sinners.[2]

In their desire to restore the simplicity and purity of the primitive Church, these people were apostolic, but they show, in addition, traces of Catharism quite pronounced enough to banish them from the ranks of the orthodox. For example, they call all marriage, save that contracted between virgins, fornication — a doctrine derived from the words of Christ with which he answered the Pharisees, 'Whom God hath joined let no man put asunder'; they held oaths to be sinful; they refused to eat meat; they kept the Catharan fasts, and they declared themselves to be the only true successors of the Apostles, claiming that their heresy had existed secretly from the first century.[3] However, they were not wholly in accord with Cathari of southern France, neither in their attitude toward marriage nor in their acceptance of the Old Testament, which they cited in proof of their belief in immediate reward or punishment after death.[4] So far as Everwin's information went,

[1] Evervinus, *l.c.*

[2] *Ibid.*; *Histor. Trever.*, *l.c.*; *Lib. Inq. Thol.*, pp. 360–63.

[3] Cf. S. Bernard., *Serm. in Cantica*, 65, *l.c.*: '*Nec enim in cunctis assertionibus eorum (nam multæ sunt) novum quid aut inauditum audisse me recolo, sed quod tritum est, et diu ventilatum inter antiquos hæreticas a nostris autem contritum et eventilatum.*'

[4] '*Non credunt ignem purgatorium restare post mortem; sed statim animam solutam a corpore, vel ad requiem transire, vel ad damnationem. Quærant ergo ab eo, qui dixit quoddam peccatum esse, quod neque in hos sæculo, neque in futuro re-*

they had no hierarchy. 'They hold the pope of no account,' he said, 'but they do not say they have any other beside him.'

Still these nameless heretics of Cologne must be counted among the sects allied to the Cathari, and it is not impossible that they owed their origin to Peter of Bruys.[1] Their attempt to restore apostolic Christianity gave them a decided hold on the popular mind of their day and rendered them formidable opponents of the established order.

Contemporary with these, but not in agreement with them, were those who called themselves Apostolics and who were likewise discovered by Everwin at Cologne 'as if boiled up from the depths of hell.' More clearly Catharan than the first group, they not only forbade the use of all animal food, but they recognized the characteristically Catharan ceremony of a spiritual baptism administered by the laying on of hands, a rite which they claimed was that 'baptism with the Holy Ghost and with fire' which John the Baptist promised would be given by the one mightier than he who was to come after him.[2] Toward baptism as administered by the Church their attitude cannot be determined. Everwin believed that they accepted adult baptism, but it is possible that he was misled by their purposely equivocal statements.[3]

Those to whom the spiritual baptism was administered were set apart as the Elect. They alone had the power to

mitteretur, cur hoc dixerit, si nulla manet in futuro remissio purgatiove peccati. L.c., 66.

[1] It is, however, possible that the formation of these sects was aided by the Cathari, the Tauchelmites, and other anti-sacerdotal manifestations of the north. *Epistola Trajectensis Ecclesiæ ad Federicum Archiepis. Colonien.* 1112, in d'Argentré, vol. I, p. 11.

[2] In the baptism of Saint Paul, according to Saint Luke's account, no water was used; and 'whatever is found in the Acts of the Apostles about the laying on of hands, they would apply to baptism.' Evervinus, *l.c.*

[3] This study is not concerned so much with the relation of the Apostolics to the Cathari as with their teachings on primitive Christianity. Therefore the question of their attitude to adult baptism is of but passing moment.

baptize others, and to consecrate the bread and wine. Ranking below them were the Believers from whom the superior class was chosen, and a lower order known as Hearers.[1] Apparently they had no doubt that Christ founded a hierarchy not dissimiliar to that of the debased Roman Church; that he instituted sacraments of which baptism and the mass as administered by the Church were a travesty. Everwin says they have their own pope,[2] and that one of those captured was a bishop. Certainly they made no effort to copy the simple democracy of the early Church.

Like the Cathari, the Apostolics were accustomed to consecrate all food and drink at their daily meals, following the custom of Christ and the Apostles. The consecration was effected by means of the Lord's Prayer, '*in corpus Christi et sanguinem*,' as they believed '*ut inde re membra et corpus Christi nutriant*,' statements which may easily be interpreted to indicate their acceptance of the doctrine of transubstantiation. If this conjecture be true, then the Apostolics were not genuine Cathari, as the latter believed that Christ was not a man, but a phantom.[3] On the other hand, Everwin, who does not give the impression of one gifted with unusual powers of discrimination, may have given undue significance to a very simple and purely apostolic rite which he was incapable of separating from the doctrines in which he himself believed.

Like the Cathari, they condemned marriage, 'but for what reason,' said Everwin, 'I have not been able to ascertain — either because they have no reason to give or

[1] The sects in Dauphiny near the Rhone and in the region where Peter of Bruys laboured had practically the same organization and held generally the same tenets as to baptism, oaths, and the Church. *Ep. Eccles. Leod., l.c.*

[2] Evervinus, *l.c.*

[3] Everwin apparently thought the Apostolics believed in transubstantiation, for after describing them he turns to his 'other heretics' with the words: '*Omnino ab istis discordantes. . . . Isti negant in altari fieri corpus Christi, eo quod omnes sacerdotes ecclesiæ non sunt consecrati.*'

because they dare not avow it.' They were not obliged to live apart from women, however. Bernard, relying evidently on hearsay, says they administer the Eucharist, and live outwardly like Christians, fulfilling the forms of the Church, giving tithes, making confessions and attending divine service, but refuses to attach any virtue to this, condemning them as wolves in sheep's clothing, full of obscene practices, and teaching doctrines which appeal to women, peasants, and idiots.[1]

True Cathari the Apostolics may or may not have been, but evangelical Christians they undoubtedly were, founding their customs on a literal interpretation of the commands of Christ and on the usages of the early Church in so far as these could be determined. Particularly was this true of their effort to restore primitive Christianity through the practice of poverty. Like the Cathari they maintained that the papacy had lost its pristine power at the time of the Donation of Constantine, having been so perverted by the possession of temporal wealth and secular honours that they no longer served the Church of Christ.[2] That such monastic orders as the Benedictines and Cistercians undertook a life of poverty, added nothing to the sanctity of the institution as a whole, since they practised it so imperfectly. Losing evangelical poverty meant the loss, as well, of holiness of life and turned the temple of the living God into the dwelling-place of Satan. As a result, since the time of Sylvester there had existed a double Church, the one part being spiritual, consisting of those who, in imitation of the Apostles, lived in absolute, Christlike poverty; and the other carnal, the Roman Church, the Beast of the Apocalypse, the woman with the golden cup of abominations.[3]

This poverty being interpreted as literal destitution, the Apostolics received nothing save alms, refusing to receive,

[1] *Serm., l.c.,* 65. [2] Evervinus, *l.c.* [3] *Lib. Inq. Thol., l.c.*

hold, or carry money, and living for the most part as mendicants without settled homes.[1] '"You," they told Everwin, "add house to house and field to field. You seek your own and the things of this world. Even those who are held most perfect among you, the monks and the regular canons, though they do not hold property as individuals, but possess it in common, have all things. . . . You love this world and are at peace with this world because you are of this world. . . . Christ possessed nothing and allowed his disciples to possess nothing." . . . They [the Apostolics] say they are the Church because they alone walk in the footsteps of Christ and follow truly the apostolic life. They seek not the things which are of this world; they possess nothing, neither house nor lands nor any money, just as Christ possessed nothing and allowed his disciples to possess nothing. . . . "We," they say, "are poor men of Christ, having no permanent abiding-place, fleeing from city to city; like sheep in the midst of wolves, we suffer persecution with the Apostles and martyrs. Yet we lead a life holy and very strict, persisting in fasting and abstinence, in prayers and labours day and night, seeking only the necessities of life from our followers.[2] All these things we bear because we are not of the world. Pseudo-apostles have misinterpreted the word of Christ, and have sought their own, and have made you and your fathers proud and worldly. We and our fathers are born of the Apostles. We have remained in the grace of Christ, and we will so remain until the end of the world. To separate you from us, Christ said: By their fruits ye shall know them. Our fruits are the footprints of Christ."'[3]

In addition they vowed obedience to no mortal man, only to God alone, and after the manner of the early Christians they preached and taught in the market-places.

[1] Doat, vol. VII, f. 610.

[2] '*Tantum necessaria ex eis vitæ quærentes,*' *l.c.*

[3] Evervinus, *l.c.*

Nor were they idle, for they laboured to obtain their daily bread, accepting alms only when their own efforts failed to supply their needs. They retained the *Pater Noster*, the *Credo*, and the *Ave Maria* of the Catholics, but rejected the ritual; their songs seem to have been the Psalms of the Old Testament, as they disapproved of the hymns and chants used by the orthodox. Carrying the doctrine of apostolic poverty to its logical conclusion, they held that a hierarchy which rejected the command given by Christ to the group of men from whom that hierarchy claimed to derive its authority could never be recognized as the Church of Christ, a deduction also made by Arnold and Waldo, but avoided by Saint Francis.

Just how the sect is to be classified is not easy to say. Their belief in their own apostolic character might easily be emphasized in the mind of some members of the Catharan body and in that case would quite naturally develop into the doctrines of the heretics at Cologne. But it is equally true that any company of men setting out independently to create a manner of life conformable to the usages of the early Church might find in the Catharan belief in their own apostolic origin a common resting-place. Indeed, in districts permeated by Catharism, as much of western Europe seems to have been at this time, such men would be drawn both by the logic of their reasoning and by the pressure of events toward the Catharan organization.

On the whole, the Apostolics of Cologne are most easily accounted for on the assumption that they were a branch of the Cathari, who, influenced by the spirit of the age, had become enthusiastic for evangelical poverty, without severing their connection with the dualists, a conclusion supported by circumstances. They do not speak of a heresiarch and usually a sect begins with adherence to a leader. They refer to persecutions endured. Prior to the time of

Everwin, there is no record of any persecution save the attempts to put down Catharism and to check the Petrobrusians in southern France.

Everwin tells, though, of their being seized 'against our will' by an over-zealous populace and put on the fire and burned. What is more marvellous, they entered the flames and bore the torture not only with patience, but with joy. 'Whence,' he naïvely inquires, 'do these children of the devil obtain a steadfastness in their heresy such as is scarcely found in believers in the faith of Christ?'[1] While Saint Bernard seems to have heard of persecutions other than these which were endured by the sect, his statement is far too vague to serve as evidence.[2]

The Apostolics certainly had Catharan beliefs, whatever their origin or for whatever reason they adopted the name by which they were known. Their own statement that 'they have a great multitude scattered almost everywhere throughout the world' may easily be taken as referring to dualists in general. Heretics that were unmistakably members of the larger organization were found at Treves in 1122,[3] at Toul in 1130,[4] and in Champagne in 1144.[5] There seems to be not the slightest evidence that these were Apostolics.[6] Everywhere heresies existed that were not Catharan, but were decidedly apostolic and anti-sacerdotal. Since these were of independent origin, there is perhaps

[1] Evervinus, *l.c.*

[2] '*Quæsiti fidem, cum de quibus suspecti videbantur, omnia prorsus suo more negarent; examinati judicio aquæ, mendaces inventi sunt. Cumque negare non possent, quippe deprehensi, aqua eos non recipiente; arrepto, ut dicitur, freno dentibus, tam misere, quam libere impietatem non confessi, sed professi sunt, palam pietatem astruentes, et pro ea mortem subire parati. Nec minus parati inferre qui astabant. Itaque irruens in eos populus novos hæreticis suæ ipsorum perfidiæ martyres dedit.*' *Serm. in Cantica*, 66, *l.c.*

[3] *Gesta Trever.*, *l.c.*, p. 193.

[4] Hugo. Metell., *Ep.*, *l.c.*

[5] *Ep.* Eccles. Leod., *l.c.*, p. 777.

[6] Hugo writes of the heretics of Toul: '*Pestilentes homines, qui veriori nomine, bestiæ appellari possunt, quæ bestialiter vivunt, coniugium enim detestantur, baptismum abominantur, sacramenta Ecclesiæ dirident, nomen Christianum abhorrent.*'

reason for believing that the Apostolics may also have developed independently of the Cathari. In Perigord, for example, the followers of Pons or Pontius, an illiterate rustic whom Saint Bernard opposed in Toulouse,[1] claimed to be returning to the apostolic life and to the poverty of the early Christians. They eschewed meat and wine,[2] rejected all alms and possessed nothing of their own. Of their doctrines but scanty information exists. Their refusal to venerate the cross [3] as well as their rejection of most of the ritual [4] suggests some connection with the Petrobrusians, particularly as Henry of Lausanne is known to have taught in that region after his adoption of Petrobrusian doctrines. Their austerities and external holiness drew numerous adherents, including nobles, priests, monks, and nuns as eager to embrace a life of poverty as a means of salvation as were the followers of Francis a century later. Of the fate of Pons and of his disciples nothing is known, but their apparent numbers and zeal bear witness to the discontent with the existing order so common in the eleventh century.

Quite as little is known of that weird zealot, Éon de l'Étoile, who during the last years of the first half of the twelfth century troubled the faithful in Brittany, Aquitaine, and Champagne, and his place in the history of the movement for evangelical poverty is not easy to determine. A hermit of little or no learning,[5] he conceived the idea that he was the son of God and went up and down the land preaching incoherent doctrines and inciting his followers to despoil the churches that the poor be fed,[6] a procedure which hints of apostolic socialism. Sermons and tracts

[1] S. Bernard., *Itineraria*, Migne, *l.c.*

[2] In certain cases a modicum of these was allowed every third day.

[3] Heribertus Monachus, *Ep. de hæret. Petragoricensibus*, *Recueil*, vol. XII, p. 550.

[4] Instead of the Gloria they said: '*Quoniam regnum tuum et tu dominari universis in sæcula sæculorum amen.*'

[5] '*Pene laicus*,' Mansi, vol. XXI, col. 720.

[6] Wm. of Newburg., *l.c.*

were directed against him and soldiers were sent to capture him and his followers. In 1148 he was led before the Council at Rheims, and, unable to defend himself from the charge of heresy which his accusers were equally unable to prove,[1] he was given over to a monastery,[2] where he was detained until his death. Perhaps the judgment of his superiors at the trial that he was mentally irresponsible is the safest to adopt; in any case, after the lapse of centuries he has sunk into such utter oblivion that any independent estimate of him seems impossible. His many disciples, illiterate rustics though they were, preferred death at the stake to recantation,[3] but just what the tenets were to which they gave such loyal adherence is not known.

It is true that the influence of these heresiarchs, if heresiarchs they were, on the Apostolics is doubtful, save as they added to the discontent already existing in western Europe. Scarcely less conjectural is that of the Tauchelmites of the Netherlands, followers of a gifted and somewhat arrogant preacher named Tauchelm[4] or Tanchelm.[5] He appeared early in the twelfth century, in the vicinity of Antwerp,[6] where he preached secretly at first, then, as his influence grew, from housetops and in open fields to great crowds of eager listeners.[7] His first disciples were, it is said, women and idiots, but it was not long before important citizens joined him and, banding themselves together as a guard for their leader, enabled him to go from place to place unmolested by either civil or ecclesiastical

[1] Mansi, *l.c.*, col. 722–23.

[2] Otto of Freising, *Gesta Frid.*, *l.c.*, says he was at Saint Denis, while in Rob., *App. ad Sigeb.*, the place is given as Rheims. *M.G.H. SS.*, vol. VI, p. 498.

[3] Otto of Freising, *l.c.*

[4] Lea says he was an apostate monk, *Inquisition*, vol. I, p. 64, but Tocco calls him a layman, *L'Eresia nel Medio Evo*, p. 157.

[5] Also called Tanklin, Tandemus, and Tanquelm.

[6] Sigebertus Gemblacensis, *Cont. Valcellensis.*, ann. 1115, *M.G.H. SS.*, *l.c.*, vol. VI.

[7] *Ep. Traj.*, *l.c.*

authorities, 'seducing the people as if he were an angel of God.'

In 1112 he went to Rome to secure papal sanction for his self-imposed mission. This being refused, he returned home by way of Cologne, where he was seized by the German soldiers and handed over to Archbishop Frederick, who imprisoned him and his followers.[1] A synod was then called to sit in judgment on him, but before it met he escaped to Bruges accompanied by a few disciples.[2] Here he attempted to gain a hearing, but was driven out of the town by clergy and laity. Returning to Antwerp, where his influence was strongest, he preached up and down the Rhine and in the diocese of Utrecht. In 1115 he was ejected from Louvain by Godfrey, Duke of Lorraine, and shortly afterwards is supposed to have been killed by an angry priest when in a boat trying to escape his enemies.[3]

The sources of information for Tauchelm's activities are written by his persecutors and are therefore not to be accepted as final evidence.[4] They bear witness, however, to his eloquent zeal and to his influence, particularly in Antwerp, then an especially promising field for any earnest teacher. Rich and populous through her commerce, she is said to have had but one priest who, living in luxury and sin, was naturally but little interested in his flock.

Tauchelm was anti-sacerdotal enough to satisfy the most exacting of the Cathari, but beyond that he seems to have had little in common with the dualists. Indeed, his first

[1] *Ep. Traj.*, *l.c.*

[2] Sigebert, *l.c.*; *Ep. Traj.*, *l.c.* Those left in Cologne purged themselves by the ordeal of water.

[3] The author of the *Vita S. Norbert* gives 1126 as the date of his death, manifestly an error. *M.G.H. SS.*, vol. XII, p. 690; Madelaine, *Vie de S. Norbert*, p. 271; *Annal. Fland.*, lib. IV, ann. 1113–35, *M.G.H. SS.*, vol. VI, p. 459; *La Grande Ency.*, vol. XXX, p. 909. Three of his followers who refused to recant were burned at Bonn.

[4] *Ep. Traj.*, *l.c.*; *Vita S. Norbert*, *l.c.*; *AA. SS.*, 1 Jun., p. 918; and Fredericq, *Corpus Inquisitionis hæreticæ pravitatis Neerlandicæ*, vol. I, pp. 22–29; P. Abælard., *Int. ad Theol.*, *l.c.*

efforts, directed against the Augustinian doctrine that the gifts of God are bestowed only on those who receive them with faith, savoured rather of the Donatists than of any branches of the Manichæans.[1] However, he taught the nullity of all hierarchical dignities from pontiff to clerk[2] and inveighed against the luxury and corruption of the clergy.[3] As for the sacraments, he held that these were polluted in unworthy hands, and that, owing to the degeneracy of the clergy, they had become useless if not altogether harmful.[4] Moreover, he said that they could be administered by any good man, whether he was consecrated or not. Whether he himself administered baptism and the Lord's Supper, or whether he substituted other rites for these, is not known. He denied the right of the Church to exact tithes,[5] although he is accused of having demanded and received rich gifts from his followers and to have clad himself in all the pomp and majesty of a king.[6] Just how much of this can be credited is hard to say, but the austere lives of his followers, their voluntary poverty, their quest for apostolic righteousness,[7] throw doubt on the authenticity of these tales of Tauchelm's arrogant pride,[8] as well as on the accusation that he taught that Christ was the Son of God only because he was filled with the Holy Spirit, and for the same reason he himself was able to claim the same mark of divinity.[9] Equally incredible is the tale that he wed the image of the Virgin in the public square by touching its hand,[10] or that he urged his followers to drink

[1] '*Contra has sententias ille declamans dehortabatur populum perceptione sacramenti prohibens etiam decimas ministris Ecclesiæ exhiberi.*' *Ep. Traj.*, *l.c.*

[2] *Ibid.*, *l.c.*; *Vita S. Norbert*, *l.c.*

[3] *Ibid.*, *l.c.*; *AA. SS.*, *l.c.*, p. 918.

[4] '*Ex meritis et sanctitate ministrarum virtutem sacramentis accedere.*' *Ep. Traj.*, *l.c.*

[5] *Ibid.*, *l.c.*

[6] *Ibid.*, *l.c.*; *AA. SS.*, *l.c.*

[7] They call themselves Pauperes Christi, or Apostolics. *AA. SS.*, *l.c.*, p. 832.

[8] Mansi, vol. XXI, col. 320; *Vita S. Norbert*, *l.c.*; '*Cum pretioso apparatu, in vestibus deauratis, triplici funiculo crinibus intortis et auriphrygii ligamine triplicatis, incedebat. AA. SS.*, *l.c.*, p. 844.

[9] *Ep. Traj.*, *l.c.*

[10] *Ibid.*

the water in which he bathed, that they might be healed of all disease.[1] Certainly he did claim the inspiration of the Holy Spirit, and that he was the one true successor of Saint Peter,[2] but beyond this it is difficult to speak with certainty. His journey to Rome suggests that he did not consider himself a heretic.

A rude organization of his followers was worked out by an ironmonger named Manasses who instituted a fraternity called a Gilda, consisting of twelve men representing the Apostles,[3] but just what their offices were is not known. Beyond this there is nothing constructive in his teaching.

After Tauchelm's death, his followers lived on in Zeeland, Thuringia, Alsace, Bohemia,[4] and in the diocese of Cologne. In Antwerp, where they were most numerous, Bishop Burchard of Cambrai established twelve canons in the Church of Saint Michael,[5] to convert them, but these accomplished nothing. In 1125, the bishop urged Norbert of Prémontré to conduct a mission there, which he did, his efforts proving so successful that in that city, at least, the heresy was uprooted,[6] although traces of it were to be found elsewhere throughout the century. In Flanders the Tauchelmites were noticeably active, and as there was at various times an influx of heretics from this county to Cologne,[7] there is a vague possibility that even if the erratic doctrines of Tauchelm did not actually influence the Apostolics, the habit of independent thinking they inculcated and their attitude of indifference to the clergy were not without their results on the growth of this heresy.

None of these men, Pons, Éon, and Tauchelm, were avowed Cathari, although Éon's claim to be son of God

[1] Sigebert., *l.c.*, p. 328. [2] *Ep. Traj.*, *l.c.* [3] *Ibid.*, *l.c.*

[4] Hugo, *Vie de S. Norbert*, pp. 126–27.

[5] *AA. SS.*, *l.c.*, p. 918.

[6] *Vita S. Norbert*, *l.c.*

[7] *Annales Colonienses Maximi*, *M.G.H. SS.*, vol. XVII, p. 778.

has been interpreted as being Manichæan,[1] since his argument that the Prince of the World was the God who had filled it with the light of his spirit must have implied the existence of an opposite kingdom. No one of them is in himself worthy of consideration as an advocate of evangelical poverty; yet each typifies some phase of the excess of religious feeling which dominated that age; each manifested a fanaticism, an erratic emotionalism, which might well baffle the most astute psychoanalyst, and because they were all able to draw unto themselves great numbers of disciples, who eventually became ardent Apostolics, they are not to be ignored if only because of the impetus they gave to the development of certain tendencies characteristic of the age — dissatisfaction with the Church and the hierarchy, the desire for a return to apostolic simplicity of creed and ritual, the importance of the individual in the achievement of his soul's salvation, and the right of man to follow the dictates of his own conscience in the development of his religious life, some tenets at least of which were held by the Franciscans.

That there is no record of any discovery of apostolic heretics in Germany from the time of Everwin to the days of the Waldensians is no proof that they did not exist. During this interval the great prelates of the Rhine Valley were absorbed in an effort to determine the relation of Church to empire to the exclusion of all else. Whether the Concordat of Worms should be rejected, or, if accepted, how they should adjust themselves to its terms in a way best adapted to the ultimate increase of their own power, seemed to the Prince-bishops a matter of far greater moment than the pursuit of a few unlettered heretics.[2] More-

[1] Hahn, *Geschichte der Ketzer*, vol. I, pp. 463, etc.

[2] On the preoccupation of these prelates with worldly affairs and the resulting tendency of heresy to increase unmolested, see Röhrich, *Die Gottesfreunde und die Winkeler am Oberrhein*, in Illgen, *Zeitschrift für die Historische Theologie*, vol. X, pt. 4, pp. 118, etc. For an interesting contemporary account of the clergy, es-

over, had they been ever so zealous in their efforts to maintain the purity of the faith, the detection of the Apostolics might well have been difficult. Those discovered by Everwin partook of the sacraments and conformed outwardly to the customs of the orthodox.[1] The secret growth of the sect in the twelfth century was the more possible, as the Church had, as yet, no organized system for ferreting out heresy. Nor does the fact that the group is not mentioned by name in the great contemporary works of inquisitors, prove that the Apostolics ceased to exist. To one not actually in their midst, they might easily appear quite indistinguishable from the Cathari on the one hand or from the Waldensians on the other. The same reasoning applies to the absence of their name from the papal and imperial edicts against heresy, issued in the latter part of the twelfth and the beginning of the thirteenth centuries.

While there is no definite proof that the Apostolics maintained their sect and diffused the 'poison of their doctrine,' it seems quite probable that they did so, since the district 'infested with their heresy' came to be a fertile ground for Waldensianism forty years later, and the practical teaching of the earlier heretics resembled that of the later to a remarkable degree. In only one other locality did the preaching of Waldo gain so quickly a large following, and that was in Lombardy, where Arnold and the Humiliati had previously aroused an enthusiasm for primitive Christianity and evangelical poverty. Therefore it seems not unreasonable to assume that the Apostolics of Everwin furnish an explanation for the remarkably rapid growth of the German Waldensians into an organization decidedly formidable to the Church. Their creed had doubtless lived on, ever gaining strength in the popular

pecially in the diocese of Treves, see Potho of Prüm, *De statu domus Dei*, in *Bib. Max. Vet. Pat.*, vol. XXI, pp. 489, etc.

[1] S. Bernard., *Serm. in Cantica*, 65, *l.c.*

mind by constant contemplation of the wealth and luxury of the clergy in that region, and their absorption in the pursuit of pleasure and of temporal power, to the exclusion of any realization in their own lives of the teachings of the Founder of their faith.

CHAPTER VII

THE WALDENSIANS

THE great movement for the restoration of primitive Christianity manifest in Germany, Italy, and southern France in the twelfth century, found expression not only in the teachings of individual reformers and in the foundation of new religious orders, but also in the establishment of sects forced by conviction or by circumstances to separate themselves from the Church. The names of such ardent leaders as Peter of Bruys, Henry of Lausanne, and Arnold of Brescia have come down to us, but doubtless there were many others of equal fervour, though possibly of less power, who have sunk into oblivion; for example, those who inspired the Apostolics of Cologne and the Humiliati of Lombardy, and those whose influence is manifest in the enthusiasm which made their followers such earnest workers and joyful martyrs.

Before the twelfth century closed there appeared a new prophet of primitive Christianity, one who became more widely known than any of his predecessors save possibly Arnold of Brescia. This was Peter Waldo. He began seeking to restore the organization of the early Church after the Apostolic movement was well established. Therefore he and his followers formed a centre around which gathered the Arnoldisti and the Humiliati of Italy, the Petrobrusians and Albigensians of France, and perhaps the Apostolics of the Rhine Valley. The sect resulting from the fusion of these elements, so strong that the whole force of the Church did not avail to crush it, mirrors the trend of the twelfth-century movement for evangelical poverty. From the beginning the Waldensians were better known than were most of their contemporaries. Before the movement was many years old, the Church was on her guard against those who were trying to follow the life marked by Christ for his disciples and who were making a strong appeal to such Catholics as realized how far the hierarchy had drifted from the apostolic ideal. There are, accordingly, accounts of the doctrines and practices of the sect in the polemics directed against its members,[1] while a fair amount of contemporary evidence exists as to its origin.[2] Thanks to the thoroughness of the Inquisition, the writings of the earliest Waldensians,[3] whatever they were, have all perished. A few now extant are of a later date than the chronicles in which the sect is first mentioned, and represent the ideas of men embittered by years of persecution and influenced by heretics who like them were at war with the Church, but who differed from the Poor Men in many details of philosophy and custom.[4] It is therefore

[1] The various codices relating to heresy and to the Inquisition found in the Vatican Archives, in the Biblioteca Casanatense in Rome, in the Bibliothèque Nationale, and in the various places where the Inquisitors held forth are the most valuable manuscript sources for the history of the Waldensians. In 1665, Jean de Doat, president of the Chambre des Comtes de Navarre, was charged by Colbert to seek out in the different archives of Languedoc, Guyenne, and Béarn, documents of historical interest. He spent five years on the task and the resulting two hundred and fifty-eight volumes form an important source of mediæval history, since most of the documents antedate the sixteenth century. This collection is now in the Bibliothèque Nationale. As some of the copyists were poorly qualified for their tasks, the results of their labours are not above criticism.

[2] Bernardus, abbas Fontis Calidi (+ 1190), *Adv. Walden.*, *Bib. Max. Vet. Pat.*, vol. XXIV; Walter Map, *De Nugis Curialis* (ed. Wright), dis. 1, c. 31. Map saw Waldo and his followers at Rome in 1179. Alanus de Insulis, *l.c.*; Moneta, *l.c.*; Stephen of Bourbon, *Tractatus* (ed. Lecoy de La Marche); *Chron.* Anon. Laud., *M.G.H. SS.*, vol. XXVI; Reinerius, (+ 1250), *Summa*, *l.c.*; Davide de Augusta, (+ 1274) *Tractatus de hæresi pauperum de Lugd.*, (ed. Preger.) *Anon. Pass.*, Gretser, vol. XII, pt. 1.

[3] *Ep. Frat.*, Döllinger, *l.c.*, pt. II, p. 359, laments the destruction of books: '*propter persecutiones innumeras, quas passi sumus, unde multoties perducti sunt libri quasi in nullum, ita ut vix sacram possemus paginam reservare.*'

[4] The oldest Waldensian document in existence is the *Rescriptum hæresiarcharum*, written about the year 1230 by the Lombards to their German brethren. Two copies of this are in Munich and one in Vienna, all fourteenth-century codices. The Strassburg MS., a sort of tract written in 1404, was destroyed by

almost entirely from the testimony of their enemies that their history must be written.

Contemporary authorities agree that this particular aspiration after evangelical Christianity was given definite form by a merchant of Lyons. 'In 1173,' says the anonymous author of the Chronicle of Laon, 'there was at Lyons in France a certain citizen, Waldo by name,[1] who had heaped up for himself much money by sinful usury. One Sunday he had joined a crowd which he saw gathered around a troubadour; he was smitten by his words and took the singer to his home that he might give himself over to hearing him attentively.'[2] The passage he was reciting was the story of the blessed Alexis,[3] a favourite subject for wandering minstrels and one which must have been often sung in the market-places of the French villages and towns. By good fortune there still exists an eleventh-century manuscript which well may have been the version heard by Waldo and the men and women who followed him.

'Alexis,' so runs the song, 'was the only son of a certain Euphemius, a nobleman of high degree, who lived in Rome in the fourth century. At his birth he was dedicated to the

fire in 1870. It gave some interesting though traditional information of the origin of the sect. An account of it appears in the *Zeitschrift für die hist. Theol.*, for 1852. In the Bibliothèque Nationale at Paris are a thirteenth-century New Testament in Waldensian dialect, some tracts, poems, and translations of the Fathers, while the Bibliothèque de l'Arsenal has a translation of the Gospels, Epistles, and an exposition of Haimon in the dialect of Lorraine, written in the late thirteenth or early fourteenth century. At Geneva are five fifteenth-century manuscripts, sermons, tracts, poems, and commentaries, all in Waldensian. Cambridge University possesses the Morland Manuscripts, similar to those of Geneva. Other copies are in Trinity College in Dublin. These are written in Waldensian and in Latin and consist of translations and tracts in prose and verse. They give us very little of value concerning the beginnings of the sect and little of their earliest doctrines. Waldensian Bibles are found also in Grenoble and Zürich.

[1] For speculations as to Waldo's name and probable birthplace, see Comba, *Histoire des Vaudois*, p. 10.

[2] Doat, vol. xxxvi, ff. 44, *etc.*

[3] *La Vie de Saint Alexis, Poème de XI siècle*, (ed. Gaston Paris, Paris, 1887) For an account of the manuscript, see Pref., pp. 2 *etc.*

Celestial King. Like others of his class, he went to school and then entered the service of the emperor. When he was grown his parents having no other son, disregarded their vow to God and affianced Alexis to the daughter of a nobleman. The marriage was celebrated, but after the ceremony, he remembered that he had been given to the service of God and decided to live the life of a celibate and to embrace poverty. So he fled from his father's house and from his native city, wandering eastward until he came to Odessa where he gave alms to the poor wherever he could find them. He did not wish to be encumbered by any property, and when he had shared with the beggars all he possessed, he sat himself down in their midst, receiving alms to whatever amount God passed over to him. He kept for himself just what was necessary for the care of his body and gave the rest to his companions. And thus Alexis, the well-born, in the city of Odessa, heartily served his Lord. His enemies never succeeded in entrapping him and for seventeen years he lived there wearying his body in the service of God.

'Neither his affection for man nor woman, nor desire for honours made him willing to give up this life. When he had so subjugated his body that he never of his own desire went beyond the city, God caused a sacred image on the crucifix to speak for love of him to the servitor at the altar, who was commanded to call the Man of God into the monastery, since because of his service, he was worthy to enter into Paradise. At first the servitor was unable to find him and returned to the image for further instruction. "It is he who sits by the door," was the answer. "He is near to God and to the Kingdom of Heaven." So the servitor went forth again, and finding him, brought him into the monastery. Now consider the example through all the country when it was known how the image spoke on behalf of Alexis. All honoured him, both high and low, and all prayed to him to show them mercy (i.e., to pray for them). But when Alexis saw they wished to do him honour, "Certes," said he, "I have no business here. I do not wish to be encumbered by this homage." So he fled from Odessa and returned to Rome, where he went to his father's house, and, all unknown to his parents, became their pensioner. Under the stairs he lay on a bit of carpet and fed on the leavings of the table. From his great position he was reduced to abject poverty. As he loved God more than all his kinsmen, he did not wish his mother to know he was there. He kept only what would support his body from the food given him. The rest he handed over to those poorer than himself and passed his days in cheerful poverty under the stairs where he held intercourse with all who passed by.

'So he lived for another seventeen years. Then infirmity came upon him. When he felt that his end was near he obtained from one of his father's servants ink and parchment and wrote down the story of his life. In the week destined to be that of his death, a voice was heard in the city issuing from the sacristy at the command of God, who called out to all his faithful in that place, saying the glory he purposed to give them was near at hand. A second time the cry was heard and they were summoned to hunt up the man of God dwelling in Rome, if they did not wish their city to be engulfed and all its inhabitants to perish. Those who heard the voice remained in great doubt, for they knew not where to seek. So they went for counsel to the Pope and the Emperor, and all the people, uniting their prayers, implored the Lord to give them knowledge of that holy man by whom they were to be saved. They begged him that of his pity he would tell them where he could be found. They sought and sought, but no one knew where the holy man dwelt. While they were seeking, the soul of Alexis went to Paradise. Then the good servant who had cared for him went to Euphemius. "Sire," said he, "dead is the man who lived on your charity and this I dare maintain, that he was a good Christian. For a long time I have come in contact with him. I know nothing for which I could blame him and it appears to me that he is the man of God."

'Quite alone, Euphemius turned him about. He came to his son where he lay under his stairway; he lifted the clothes wherewith he was covered; he saw the clear, fair countenance of the holy man. In his clenched hand was the parchment wherein he had written the story of his conversion. Euphemius and the others tried to take this from the dead hand, but to none would it open until the Pope touched it. The papal chancellor then read the document. In it were set forth the name of father, mother, and family, the story of his wanderings overseas, of his life in Odessa, of the miracle wrought there by the image of God and of his return to Rome. Euphemius made lament over the body of his son. "O son! to whom were to go my great hereditary possessions, my wide, broad acres of which I had so many, my huge palaces in the city of Rome! On your behalf, O son, I laboured for these things. After my death they would have brought you honour. White is my beard and hoary my head. My high distinction I had preserved for you my son, but you did not care for it. So great sorrow I lay in store for me this day. Son, may your soul be absolved in Paradise. It was your privilege to have donned helm and cuirass, to have girt on a sword like your peers; you should have ruled over a great establishment and carried the standard of the empire as did your father and all your relatives. To such suffering and such great poverty, O son, you brought yourself in distant lands; and these possessions which should have been yours, you denied yourself entirely in your poor lodging. Had God so willed, you should have been lord of all."

'Saint Alexis had a rightly directed will. For this he has been honoured up to the present day. His body lies in the city of Rome and his soul is in Paradise with God. Very happy may he be who wins similar praise!'

So vivid an account of the honour given by God and man to voluntary poverty set Waldo to pondering deeply.

'When morning had come,' continues the Chronicler of Laon, 'the citizen of whom we have been speaking hastened to the school of theology to seek counsel for his soul. He was taught many ways of going to God and he asked the master what way was more sure and more perfect than all of the others. The latter answered him with these words of the Lord: "If thou wouldst be perfect, go sell what thou hast," ' etc.[1]

According to the legend, he returned to his wife and gave her leave to choose what she would keep, his personal property or his real estate: i.e., what he possessed in ponds, groves, and fields, in houses, rents, vineyards, mills, and fishing rights. Although she was very sorrowful at having to make such a choice, she kept the real estate. From what remained, Waldo made restitution to those from whom he had taken unjust gains. A greater part of his money he settled on his two little daughters, whom, without their mother's consent, he had placed in a convent;[2] the rest he spent on the poor, for a very great famine was then wasting all France and Germany.

The same citizen gave bread, vegetables, and meat to all comers three times a week until the feast of Saint Peter's Bonds; at the feast of the Assumption he scattered money among the poor in the village, crying out: 'No man can serve two masters, God and mammon.'

The bystanders, thinking he had gone mad, came

[1] *Chron.* Anon. Laud., *l.c.*; Doat, vol. xxxvi.

[2] At Fontevrault, founded by Saint Robert d'Arbrissel, a twelfth-century apostle of evangelical poverty.

running up to him, but he said: 'O citizens! I am not insane as you think. I have avenged myself upon my enemies who made me their slave so that I was ever more careful of my money than for the glory of God. I served the creature rather than the creator. I know many will blame me because I have done this openly. But I do it for my sake and for yours; for mine so that if any man sees me owning money henceforth, he may say that I am mad; and I have done it for your sakes that you may learn to place your trust in God and not in riches.'

'On the next day as he came from church, he asked a certain citizen for food. The man took him to his house and promised to give him all that he needed as long as he lived. When Waldo's wife heard of this, she was not a little troubled, and, half beside herself, she ran to the archbishop and asked that he restrain her husband from begging from any one but herself. So great was her distress that the prelate and all who were present were moved to tears. Then the woman seized her husband by the coat and said: "Is it not better, husband, that I should redeem my sins by giving alms than that strangers should have the privilege?" From that time, by command of the archbishop, he was not suffered to take food from any one but his wife.

'So in the year of grace 1173, this Peter Waldo, the citizen of Lyons, having made a vow to Heaven that he would possess neither gold nor silver, nor take thought for the morrow, began to have sharers of his manner of life, who, following his example, gave all to the poor and professed voluntary poverty.'

Waldo was possessed of a keen desire to read the Scriptures. Though not illiterate, he did not know Latin,[1] so he bargained with two priests[2] to translate and copy for him

[1] Doat, vol. XXXVI, says he was uneducated, but eager to learn.

[2] Stephen of Bourbon, a Dominican inquisitor in Lyons early in the thirteenth century, says he knew these priests. *Tractatus, l.c.*

parts of the New Testament,[1] which he committed to memory as a guide for right living as well as a basis for preaching. It is not improbable that this association with the priests precedes the events given by the Chronicler of Laon and that the story of Saint Alexis was but the decisive influence which led him still further on the way he had already chosen.

As others came to share his ideals, he taught them what he himself had learned,[2] and sent them to preach in the market-places and even in the churches of the neighbouring villages, where, unlearned though they were, they won many converts. Quite early they adopted a distinctive dress, consisting of a dark outer garment, resembling that of a religious, and sandals from whence they derived their name of Insabbatati or unshod.[3]

'And because he and his followers presumed to interpret the words of the Gospel in a sense peculiarly their own, not perceiving that there were any others, they said that the Gospel should be obeyed according to letter, and they boasted that they wished to do this and that they only were the true imitators of Christ. In scorning the power of the Church lay their first heresy. By their zeal they led others astray, as they could so easily do by dressing up their sacrilegious doctrine with fair phrases from the saints, but they passed over in silence whatever contradicted their own ideas. They taught their docile and fluent disciples to repeat the words of the Gospels and the sayings of the Apostles and other saints by heart, in the vulgar tongue so that they might know how to teach others and lead the faithful astray. They seemed to be more learned than other men because they were able to say by heart certain portions of the Scriptures; for this reason they

[1] Doat, *l.c.* [2] *Chron.* Anon. Laud., *l.c.*

[3] Burch. et Cuon. Ursp., *Chron.*, p. 376. Pet. Vall. Sarn., *l.c.*, p. 6; Ebrardus, c. xxv; *Cod. Vat. Lat.* 2648, f. 71, t.

esteemed themselves superior to our people, and not only to laymen, but even to those who were literate, for they were fools and did not understand that a schoolboy of twelve often knows more than a heretical teacher of seventy; for the latter knows only what he has memorized, while the former, having learned the art of grammar, can read a thousand Latin books and to some extent, understand what he has read.'[1]

So far the conversion and career of Waldo are quite similar to those of Francis. Each was convinced that for him the true life was to be found in absolute, literal obedience to Christ's commands, particularly those regarding poverty, and in preaching to all men the gospel which could transform life. Both men were devout sons of the Church. Waldo had found in the theological schools the law of his life; he had placed his daughters under the care of the Church; he had obeyed the archbishop; in many respects he was in the position of the early Humiliati before their application for papal sanction, and strongly akin to the founders of the monastic orders of that century, although, unlike them, he was forced by circumstances to cross the line, so difficult for religious enthusiasts to discern, which separated the devout churchman from the active heretic.

Canon law at that time forbade all preaching in public save by those licensed by the Church,[2] although the prohibition had fallen into desuetude because of the apathy of the clergy. No attempt, therefore, was made to stop Waldo until he and his followers became too conspicuous for their zeal as well as for their many converts to be longer ignored. However, by the end of the year 1178, reports of grave errors reached the ears of the archbishop, and Waldo was ordered to refrain from all public discourses.[3] Apparently

[1] Davide de Aug., *l.c.*, p. 212.

[2] For the laws regulating preaching and the clergy's neglect of this duty, see Lecoy de la Marche: *La Chaire Française*, pp. 21–25.

[3] Stephen of Bourbon, *Tractatus*, p. 292; Doat, vol. XXX, f. 202; vol. XXXVI, f. 45.

he was puzzled to account for the unwillingness of the Church to allow him to follow literally the commands of Christ. He quoted in his defence Saint Peter's response to the chief priests: 'It is better to obey God than man.' He also reminded his accusers that Christ told his Apostles to 'preach the Gospel to every living creature.'[1]

Even after the archbishop had silenced him, he hoped to gain the sanction of the Church to serve God according to his convictions. Therefore, he journeyed to Rome with a small band of disciples in order that he might attend the Third Lateran Council and present to the Pope himself his petition to continue to preach and to practise evangelical poverty as he had done the past six years.[2]

This Council, summoned by Pope Alexander III in 1179[3] to take action against the heretics of southern France, was one of the most magnificent diets of the Christian world. Over a thousand bishops and clerics were present, as well as monks, senators, and important laymen.[4] Among the number was Walter Map, the friend of Becket and Henry II, a canon of Saint Paul's and Archdeacon of Oxford.[5] A brilliant scholar, a bitter satirist of the very evils Waldo was unconsciously attacking, he has left us what is, perhaps, the best account of this first appearance of the Poor Men.

The impression they made on the Englishman was

[1] *Chron.* Anon. Laud., p. 449.

[2] Another account is that given by Bernard. Abb. Font. Cal., *l.c.*, col. 1590. According to Müller, Bernard died in 1193 so that his tract must have been written before this time.

[3] Reuter, *Geschichte Alex. III*, vol. III, p. 778. Hefele, *Conciliengeschichte,* vol. V, p. 717, n.2, says Waldo was at the Fourth Lateran Council instead of the Third, but this is manifestly an error, as the Waldensians were specifically condemned at Verona in 1184 by Pope Lucius III for preaching without permission and this could not have happened before they applied for papal sanction. See also Davide de Aug., p. 219.

[4] For an account of the members of the Council see Comba, *l.c.* p. 41.

[5] In England he had presided over some important ecclesiastical councils and he had also served as ambassador to France.

definite enough; he has very little to say in their favour and does not hesitate to call them crude and ignorant.

'They were simple and illiterate men named after their leader, Waldo, who was a citizen of Lyons on the Rhone, and they presented to the Lord Pope a book written in the French tongue, in which were contained a text and gloss on the Psalter and on very many other books of both Testaments. These besought with great urgency that authority to preach should be confirmed to them for they thought themselves expert when they were scarcely learned at all and really knew less than school-boys. For in every small point of the sacred page, so many meanings fly on the wings of virtue, such stores of wealth are accumulated, that only he can fully exhaust them whom God has inspired. Shall not therefore, the word given to the unlearned be as pearls before swine when we know them to be fitted neither to receive it nor to give out what they have received? . . . They never have settled homes, but two and two they travel about with bare feet clothed in wool, possessing nothing as individuals, but holding all things in common.'[1]

He then goes on to relate how he himself was set to examine two Waldensians and soon exposed their lack of theological learning by entrapping them into giving answers to one of his questions, which, although they did not know it, was heretical and Nestorian.

Further examination, however, quite cleared the Poor Men of any suspicion of heresy. They professed to draw their doctrines entirely from the Bible and the writings of the Church Fathers; they denied holding any unorthodox opinions; they asserted their belief in transubstantiation although they refused to take oaths to support their professions, as even then they held these to be sinful. Their arguments apparently carried weight, for Alexander em-

[1] *De Nugis, l.c.*

braced the suppliants and approved of their vow of voluntary poverty, although he forbade their preaching without the consent of their local clergy.[1] He realized that the increasing number of unlicensed preachers, their fervour and the eagerness with which the people listened to them, constituted a menace to ecclesiastical discipline and one which the Church was forced to meet, and that soon. But it seemed to him necessary to stimulate the religious activity of the priesthood rather than allow further liberties to their critics. Alexander was not blind to the clerical laxness which had fostered the growth of such itinerant preaching, but he was slow to act and slow, too, to arouse the Church to action,[2] although one definite reason for calling this Council had been to deal with this very situation.

Before he went to Rome, Waldo had attracted little attention outside of Lyons itself, but after his return his followers seem to have spread rapidly in all directions. Since they touched a common and vital need, they met with such marked success that they soon drew to themselves the notice of ecclesiastical authorities. The little group of enthusiasts who had been sent forth derided and bewildered from the Lateran multiplied until they seemed capable of menacing the institution itself. In 1181, at the Council of Verona, Lucius III[3] condemned, along with the Cathari and Patarini, 'those who call themselves Poor Men of Lyons, because they preach without authority of the Church and deny the sacraments.' That they were guilty of the first offence is beyond doubt, but it was not for many years afterward that they as a body questioned the doc-

[1] Moneta of Cremona says they were allowed to preach, but he knew more of their doctrine than of their history, p. 443.

[2] Jacques de Vitry, *Hist. Occid.*, c. 5, p. 270: '*In confusionem autem et ignominiam prœlatorum et qui populum instruere debuissent per malignum spiritum, veritatem Evangelii Dominus prœdicabat.*'

[3] Alexander III died August 30, 1181. Mansi, vol. XXII, col. 493. The condemnation was repeated in 1184.

trines of the Church. Had Alexander or Lucius been wise enough to treat these first Waldensians as Innocent treated the evangelicals of his day, who desired, as did these, to remain in the Church, it is conceivable that the Catholics might have won an army of zealous champions and the heretics lost many obscure but steadfast martyrs. To be sure, the step is short from the conviction that Christ commanded his disciples to live in poverty to the belief that clergy living in luxury are not a true priesthood of Christ. Yet Norbert never took this step, nor Stephen Harding, neither Francis nor Dominic; and the Waldensians might never have taken it had the pontiffs adopted a more conciliatory policy and by some easily contrived interpretation of ecclesiastical law, allowed them to preach. On the other hand, the breach might have been merely postponed, for while Waldo considered himself a son of the Church and was possessed of a strong desire to be of service to her, he had boldly withstood the Archbishop of Lyons, telling him it was better to obey God than man.[1] While the decision of the Councils that it was neither wise nor feasible to sanction the preaching of laymen, seemed at the time a necessity, the Church was still to realize that men inspired by enthusiasm for evangelical Christianity could not be suppressed, and that multitudes would hear and follow those who were obeying literally the commands of Christ which her own clergy were so obviously disregarding.[2] She was slow to comprehend that the dominant enthusiasm of the age was not for great ceremonials and stately festivals, nor for magnificently robed priests living in luxurious palaces, but for the simplicity and purity of

[1] Alanus de Insulis quotes this doctrine as proof of their heresy.

[2] Burch. et Cuon. Ursp., *Chron.*, *l.c.*, gives the slight grounds on which the Waldensians were enrolled among the heretics: '*Eo quod supersticiosa dogmata et observationes in eis reperirentur; in occultis quoque predicationibus, quas faciebant plerumque in latibulis, ecclesiæ Dei et sacerdotio derogabatur*'; but this refers to their later disregard of the decree of 1179.

primitive Christianity. In the great battles against heresy in which she was soon to engage, she needed to enlist on her side all of that religious fervour which the uncompromising attitude of the hierarchy turned against her. Up to that time and for some years later, the Waldensians as a sect were not anti-sacerdotal. They had not criticized the unapostolic lives of the clergy nor did they insist that these follow evangelical poverty as necessary to their salvation; for while like Saint Francis, they considered that for themselves literal obedience to Christ's commands to live in poverty and to preach the Gospel to every living creature was the right, the ideal life, they did not consider it as essential to all Christians. It would have been so easy to conciliate them, but the Church preferred to ridicule and reject them and so lost them forever.

The decade following the condemnation of the Waldensians at Verona was marked by doubt, indecision, and even disagreement within the sect. It was a period in their growth when doctrines were being established and new practices adopted. In 1181, Humbert, Archbishop of Lyons, died and was succeeded by the capable and cultured Jean de Bellesmains,[1] who was far too jealous of sacerdotal authority to tolerate in his fold those whose orthodoxy was open to suspicion. Consequently, the Poor Men were banished. They fled southward to Dauphiny, Guyenne, and Provence, northward to the Rhineland, and eastward to Lombardy, wherever tolerance and freedom of thought seemed to assure them a refuge. Tradition says that Waldo went to Picardy,[2] a not incredible legend, as even then that province was noted for its independence of thought and avidity for disputation. Those who found refuge in Metz attracted no little attention to themselves because of their zeal in studying the Scriptures and ex-

[1] '*Vir magnæ litteraturæ et eloquentiæ.*' *Gall. Christ.*, vol. IV, col. 130.

[2] He is said to have died in Bohemia in 1217. Perrin, *Hist. des Vaud.*, p. 223.

pounding them privately to the citizens. The bishop, Bernard, tried to expel the offenders, but they had found prominent patrons[1] who defended and encouraged them in their opposition to the authorities. They not only refused to leave, but even went so far, it was said, as to maltreat the bishop himself.[2] In 1199, Innocent III wrote the Catholics in that city as follows:

'Our brother, the Bishop of Metz, tells us that in his diocese and especially in your city, a great number of laymen, men and women, have made translations in French of the Gospels, Epistles and Psalms, etc., which they read together and expound resisting the priests who would restrain them. Now the desire to know the Scriptures is not reprehensible, but what is condemnable with you is to hold secret assemblies and to abrogate the right of preaching[3] and to rail at the simplicity of the priests.'

Although the exact origin of the Waldensians of Piedmont is still largely a matter of conjecture, it seems reasonably safe to infer that they were strongly influenced by the refugees from Lyons even if they were not established by them.[4] It is possible, even probable, that these found in the valleys where they settled many evangelical sects, and that they developed more or less secretly in their mountain fastnesses,[5] forgetting their French ancestry and devising new legends of their origin. Some claimed Claude, Bishop of Turin (822–39),[6] as their founder; others held

[1] Cæsar. Heisterbac., *l.c.*, dist. v, c. 20.

[2] '*Injurias contumeliasque hac de re perpessus.*' *Gall. Christ.*, vol. XIII, col. 754.

[3] *Ep.* 141, Migne, *l.c.*, vol. CCXIV.

[4] Boyer, *L'Histoire des Vaudoise*, MS. from the Royal Library at Turin, f. 1; Stephen of Bourbon, *Tractatus*, *l.c.*; Davide de Aug., c. 20, p. 216.

[5] Rorengo says they lived secretly that followers might be attracted to them through curiosity or that they might come the more readily if there were no danger of their apostasy being known. *Mem. Hist.*, p. 7.

[6] Cod. Garola, vol. I, f. 320, in the communal library at Pinerola. Monastier, *Histoire de l'Église Vaudoise*, p. 21; Gay, *Histoire des Vaudois*, c. I. Muston, *Hist. Vaud.*, bases his theory of their separate origin on a difference in dialect and writing which he says are indigenous to the places in which they are found, but

that they were the successors of a small group of good men who had protested against the degradation of the Church in the days of Sylvester and Constantine.[1] Later historians think the nucleus of the Italian Waldensians was the False Humiliati,[2] while still others have connected them with the followers of Arnold of Brescia.[3] It is certain, at all events, that the later Waldensians of Piedmont were a fusion of various sects and that they were a formidable group.[4] Any claim to an existence prior to the twelfth cen-

his theories have been disproved by Forster, who says their language is Provençal, not Italian, in origin. (*Rivista Cristiana*, Firenze, 1882, pp. 97, etc.) As early as 1235 they were evidently claiming connection with the Apostles, as a Catholic polemic of that year attempts to show the stupidity of such a claim: 'But you were born yesterday. Thirty years ago, in 1205, you had your first chief, and before you were with Waldo some time, and many have seen your submission to Rome.' '*Pauperes Lombardi exiverunt a Pauperibus de Leono, et hoc est circa trigenta annos, et surrexit Joannes de Roncho, qui eorum erat ancianus, et ipse erat idiota absque literis.*' '*Eratis cum eis sub regimine Gualdenses, et stetistis aliquo tempore sub suo regimine.... Sed, vos Pauperes Lombardi, non potestis probare quod vestra sit de trigenta sex et ideo positus est millesimus in isto libro, quia multi viderunt vos esse in ecclesia Romana, et ivistis cum Pauperibus Leonistis et exiistis de congregatione eorum et fecistis pro vobis congregationem et adhuc dicitis, quod ecclesia Dei stetit amissa multis annis usque ad vos et vos restitutis. Major stultitia non potest credi.*' Cod. Salvi Burce, *l.c.*

[1] The oldest authentic document relating to the Italian Waldensians is found in Pinerola and is dated 1220. '*Liber statutorum . . . civitatis Pinerolii* . . . Aug. Taurin . . . 1602. *Statuta et ordinamenta facta per illustr. D. Thomain comitem et sapientes Pinerolii . . . currente millesimo ccxx Inditione vii*, p. 84. *Item statutim est quod si quid vel si qua hospitaretur aliquem vel aliquam Valdensem vel valdensam se sciente in posse Pinerolii dabit bannum solidorum decem quoties cumque hospitaretur.*' The next is dated 1334 and the next 1476. Between 1188 and 1206 the monks of San Martino in Pinerola complained of an invasion of the Waldensians. Charvaz, *Delle Vicende e della Condizione Attuale dei Valdese*, MS. from the Royal Library at Turin; Caffaro, *Notizie e Documenti della Chiesa Pinerolese.*

[2] Preger, *l.c.*, p. 206, rests his argument on the fact that both sanctioned matrimony and abstained from oaths, and Müller, p. 56, says the solidarity of the Poor Men of Lombardy would have been impossible unless they had come from the existing organization of the Humiliati, about this time divided into two groups, thanks to the vigorous policy of Pope Innocent III; but he overlooks the fact that the Poor Men had a very different organization from the Milanese sect.

[3] Breyer, *Die Arnoldisten*, p. 409. Archivio di Stato, Torino, Mazzo, I, n. 4.

[4] Stephen of Bourbon says he talked with a heretic returned from Lombardy, where he had lived for eighteen years, who told him that there were no less than seventeen heretical sects existing there, the majority of whom followed evangelical poverty. Each claimed to be the true and Catholic faith and each excommunicated all dissenters. *Tractatus*, *l.c.*; Doat, vol. XXX, f. 202.

tury, however, seems to be without adequate foundation. Even the long-supported theory that they might be traced to 1120 has now been disproved.[1]

In a body which spread so rapidly[2] and whose membership consisted for the most part of poor and simple folk, forced to conceal their faith for their own safety, it was inevitable that differences of organization and doctrine should creep in. The Lombard branch and their offshoots in Germany, for example, tended to more drastic criticism of the Church than did the Lyonnais, and they also had a more definite and complete hierarchy.[3]

It was but natural that they should spread most rapidly in those regions where the heretical sects had prepared the ground for the reception of any new doctrines based on an appeal to reason rather than on obedience to authority. So far as is known, there were no Cathari in Lyons, although the rapid growth of the Waldensians in that locality may have been due to some unrecorded congregations of the

[1] This claim was based on the interpretation of a line in *La Nobla Lecyzon*, an early doctrinal poem, copies of which are found at Cambridge, Dublin, and Geneva.

'*Ben ha mil e cent ancz compli entierament.*'

Raynouard thought this meant that the poem was written in 1120 (*Choix de poèsies*, vol. II, p. cxlii), but a later and more accurate scholar, the Honourable Algernon Herbert, has proved that the line refers to the Antichrist and that the poem was written about the thirteenth century. (*British Magazine*, vol. XVI, pp. 605–10.)

[2] The Inquisitors gave as the reason for their growth their vainglory, i.e., wishing to be honoured as the Catholic orders were; their great zeal, for they taught day and night; their translations of the Scriptures into the vulgar tongues and using them in their sermons: and the scandals arising from the bad example of the priests as well as the insufficient teaching of the doctrines of the Church. (Martène et Durand, *Thes. Anec.*, vol. V, col. 1783.)

[3] Cod. Vat. Lat. 6216, f. 262; Reinerius, *Summa*, col. 1775: '*Pauperes Lombardi concordant cum primis in juramento et justitia sæculari. De corpore vero Domini sentiunt etiam pejus quam primi, dicentes quod concessum est cuilibet homini sine peccato mortali existente consecrare illud. Item, dicunt quod Ecclesia Romana est Ecclesia malignantium et bestia et meretrix, quæ leguntur in Apocalypse . . . de hæresi Leonistarum seu Pauperum de Lugduno. Dividitur autem hæresis in duas partes. Prima pars vocatur Pauperes Ultramontani, secunda vero Pauperes Lombardi. Et isti descenderunt ab illis.*'

heretics, as generally it was where they were most numerous that the followers of Waldo established themselves most securely.

However, Lyons was not overdistant from Provence, the land of the Albigensians, a branch of the Cathari, against whom the Church had long waged ineffectual warfare. One of the richest districts in all Europe, it was attached nominally to the French crown, although it differed widely in language, customs, and institutions from the more northern counties. It was a gay and pleasant land and its luxury-loving rulers devoted themselves to the cultivation of music, poetry, and the kindred arts. At this time it was under the rule of Raymond VI, one of the most picturesque counts of all history, who combined in himself the refinements of his age and also its many weaknesses. He was a friend and protector of heretics. His attitude toward the Church was a queer combination of open aggression and sudden submission, of dogged resistance and dramatic, purposeless repentance. But few of his subjects were Catholics. In the thriving cities, Jews and Moors lived on an equality with Christians. Nowhere was the Church more despised by the people, most of whom had come to embrace views that may be termed prematurely Protestant. Apparently it was but a question of time when the Church should disappear entirely in the Mediterranean provinces. Toleration of heresy was leading to destruction of the Faith, and when persecution did come, it was prompted by an instinct of self-preservation as well as by a sense of duty.

About 1190, at a disputation held at Narbonne[1] at the instigation of the Archbishop, who evidently feared their influence on the faithful, the Waldensians set forth their views on lay preaching and obedience to the clergy in no unmistakable terms. Apparently they were less bewil-

[1] Disputations were quite characteristic of the religion of this day.

dered at the attitude of the Church than they had been when defending their position before Pope Alexander III, and they accepted with some eagerness the opportunity to explain their doctrines. They quoted the New Testament account as given in the ninth chapter of Saint Matthew, 'Wherefore if we preach the name of Christ even though we do not follow the bishop and other priests, yet they ought not forbid us,' and Phil. I: 15–18, 'Wherefore then do not the bishops likewise rejoice when Christ is preached by us; why do they forbid us?'

They further said, when asked why they refused to render obedience to the bishops, that if the bishops were obedient to the command of Christ, there would be no necessity for disobeying them, but if, on the other hand, they were failing to observe such commands, why, then, should others follow them in their sins? — and finally, they definitely refused to give up preaching.[1] From this time on even the French Waldensians realized that a break with the Church was imminent. Two years later, Alphonso of Aragon, also Count of Provence, expelled them from his realm.[2] The decree was not enforced, apparently, for during the next fifteen years the Poor Men were especially active in that part of France. In 1206 Innocent III sent a number of Cistercian monks to Pamiers to convert the heretics if possible, or at any rate to check their preaching. A short time after they arrived, Diego, the Bishop of Osna, returning from Rome, met these missionaries, who were so disheartened that they were quite ready to relinquish their task. The heretics, they alleged, were so obdurate that little or nothing could be done with them, especially since they cast up to the monks the disgraceful habits of the regular clergy. The Cistercians declared that

[1] Guil. de Pod. Laur., *Hist. Alb.*, *Recueil*, vol. XIX, p. 191; Bernard. Abb. Font. Cal., *l.c.*; *Gall. Christ.*, vol. VI, p. 267.

[2] Alph. reg. Arag., *Edictum Contra Hæreticos*, *Bib. Max. Vet. Pat.*, vol. XXV.

unless the priests reformed, all attempts to convert the heretics or to limit their influence with the people were futile. Diego declined to consider the case hopeless. He gave them wholesome advice, admonishing them to exert themselves even further and to close the mouths of the malignant by themselves following the example of their blessed founders, Robert and Stephen, in word and deed, and by proceeding in all humility on foot, without gold or silver, to imitate the Apostles more closely than the heretics were doing.[1] Soon afterwards a disputation was held at Pamiers which resulted in the more orthodox wing of the Waldensians being reunited to the Church under the name of Poor Catholics. The leader of this movement was Duran de Huesca, one of the converts. Their Order received the sanction of Innocent, who showed toward them the same conciliatory policy he manifested toward the orthodox Humiliati.[2]

In his letter to the Archbishop of Narbonne in which he asks clemency for the Order, Innocent said he had examined Duran and his fellows, and that he was satisfied as to their orthodoxy. They accepted both Old and New Testaments, the doctrine of transubstantiation, and the *ordo* of the Roman Church, including alms and prayers for the dead; therefore, he said, they should be free to practise as rigid a poverty as they pleased, providing they did not attack the clergy; he further stipulated that they should be excused from military service and from oaths.

Not a great deal is known of the Poor Catholics, but

[1] Guil. de Pod. Laur., *l.c.*, p. 193; Guil. de Nang., *Chron.*, d'Achéry, *l.c.*, vol. III.

[2] See Innocent's letter approving of the Rule of the Poor Catholics, Migne, *l.c.*, vol. CCXVI, col. 1510; also his letter of reproof to the Bishop of Narbonne and others, called forth by complaints that the Poor Catholics did not readily forsake their Waldensian practices, *l.c.*, col. 75; also a letter to the Bishops of Tarragon and Narbonne, desiring lenient treatment for the Order, *l.c.*, col. 256; also in similar vein to Duran himself assuring him of the support of the Bishops, col. 274; also to Alphonso of Aragon, col. 608.

they seem to have been allowed to keep whatever customs did not actually conflict with the Church.[1] They said some of the offices, kept the canonical hours, refused the Sacrament when administered by a sinful priest; they were self-supporting, giving all of their surplus to the Church; they kept the fasts and feasts of the calendar; no mention is made of a peculiar dress nor of any ordained priests among them, but they were set apart for missionary work among the heretics and were allowed to maintain schools.[2]

The Order was short-lived. Soon after its foundation the fury of the Albigensian Crusade ravaged southern France. After it had passed no traces of the Poor Catholics were discovered.[3] They may have relapsed into heresy or they may have joined the Mendicants, who soon after made their appearance. No more striking illustration of the fact that the Church was finally forced to adopt the methods of the evangelical heretics exists than in the story of these Poor Catholics, significant as embodying Innocent's recognition of the popular demand for preachers who followed literally the commands of Christ and the example of the Apostles, especially as regards poverty and lay preaching. While they did not last long enough to make any imprint on their century, yet in them lay the possibilities of all that Francis and Dominic were later to accomplish. It is worth noting, in this connection, that while Innocent sanctioned this Order, he was reluctant to grant the same recognition to the Penitents of Assisi, hesitating to encourage too far the principle of lay preaching and doubting the value of aggressive poverty, possibly because he feared the

[1] *Ep.* Inn., *l.c.*, col. 73; Cod. Vat. Lat. 8634, f. 61.

[2] Innocent's letters do not agree with the accounts found in the chronicles, nor in the letters of the local prelates, on the subject of the orthodoxy and compliance of these Poor Catholics.

[3] A group of them existed in Milan under the leadership of Bernardus Primus. They had a school there which they had held as Waldensians. Pet. Vall. Sarn., *l.c.* Helyot says they were incorporated with the hermits of Saint Augustine. *Hist. des Orders Monastiques*, vol. II, p. 238.

results of so striking a comparison with the lives of the clergy.

While the Poor Men began as orthodox Catholics, they gradually developed into schismatics after they came into contact with the more numerous heretics in the various parts where they chanced to go. As in many cases these bodies were already practising poverty and were preaching as they believed, in accordance with a divine command, just as Waldo and his disciples were doing, it is not surprising that after the second and third generations of Waldensians appeared among the older sects, they came to adopt some of their other doctrines, especially after the opening of organized persecution on the part of the Church. After the Albigensian Crusade, the Poor Men of southern France are more and more associated with the Cathari by the inquisitors, although the older chroniclers did not confuse the two groups. The later Waldensians seem to have shared with their dualistic neighbours their denunciation of a wealthy priesthood, of the temporal power of the Church, and of certain doctrines and practices which seemed to them to be unapostolic, such as indulgences, purgatory, prayers and alms for the dead, the consecration of vestments, water, salt, ashes, the veneration of the saints, the Virgin, and relics. Like them, too, they rejected oaths and held all shedding of blood, even when on a crusade, to be murder.[1]

When the break with the Church finally came and the Waldensians accepted it as inevitable, they threw themselves into missionary work, showing a boundless zeal for

[1] Luc. Tud., *l.c.*; Cod. Vat. Lat. 2648, f. 48; *Ibid.*, 4030; Cod. Cas. A IV 49; *ibid.*, D III 18; Cod. Dub., class C, Tab. 1, no. 6, *La Nobla Lecyzon;* Doat, vol. XXVII, f. 221; vol. XX, f. 9; vol. XXXVI, f. 47; Alan. de Ins., *l.c.*, lib. 11, c. IX; Pet. Vall. Sarn., *l.c.*; Davide de Aug., *l.c.*, p. 208; Moneta, *l.c.*; Cod. Monac. Lat. 544: '*Quærunt etiam hæretici quare credamus nos Christiani panem fieri corpus Christi, cum in Symbolo Apost., sc. credo in Deum, nihil de isto pane dicitur, et in illo symbolo Credo in unum Deum item nec in eo; quicunque vult salvus esse; in istis enim symbolis tota fides nostra consistit, et nulla mentio fit ibi de corpore Christi.*'

proselyting, spreading their doctrines on every hand and meeting everywhere a cordial response, especially among the lower classes, who were eager to escape the vices and oppressions of a corrupt and indifferent priesthood. Despite the divergent details of ceremonial and doctrine marking the divisions of the sect, their appeal had everywhere the same psychological basis, an enthusiasm for literal obedience to the commands of Christ.

By the thirteenth century, a consciousness of their differences in creed and in ritual led the Lombards and French to hold conventions to bring about unity, but the only apparent result was to give each faction new opportunities for altercations and to establish each the more firmly in its own peculiar belief. On the whole the French branch was less democratic than the Lombard and more in harmony with the Church, and as it was in closer accord with the established order, it was slower to complete a separate organization.

Waldo had taught and practised a poverty that was not only absolute, but which was also voluntary: to be embraced with all one's heart; a poverty of the spirit as well as of material possessions, after the example of the Apostles of old, who had only their boats and their nets, or of the poor widow who had but the mite she laid on the altar. Why should any man desire more than these holy ones had claimed? Such a doctrine was neither new nor heretical, at least not until it was joined to criticism of the clergy or claims to apostolic succession.[1]

Preaching, however, was quite another matter. Their insistence on teaching the people everywhere, with the sanction of the Church if it could be secured, without it if

[1] *Glosa Pater*, Morland MS., B, f. 8: '*Li paure per sperit son benayta. . . . Ben di pane per sperit co es de volunta non forca ni de besogna en la vita.*' Doat, vol. xxi, f. 200; vol. xxix, f. 210; Cod. Vat. Lat. 2648, f. 77; 4030, f. 37; Moneta, *l.c.*, p. 448; *Cantica*, Morland MS., 4, 14, warns against hypocritical poverty and condemns the Church for trafficking in poverty.

this were denied, was bound to bring them into conflict with the ecclesiastical authorities sooner or later. Naturally, their ignorance as well as their independence of thought soon involved them in error,[1] which, although involuntary, was sufficiently marked to call for decisive action on the part of the clergy, who first forbade their preaching and later persecuted them when they disobeyed. But not even the fear of death could make the Poor Men abandon what their conscience dictated, convinced as they were that in this they were obeying a divine command. In apostolic days, they argued, all could preach freely. By what right, then, could they be forbidden to do so now? Laymen had preached before and their efforts had been blessed; the Apostles were not learned doctors nor saints, yet Christ had entrusted to them the spread of his Gospel. When these objections reached the ears of the Pope, he sent word to them that, while it was true that laymen of good life and orthodox views might preach to their neighbours in their own houses and exhort them to follow a godly life, they could not do more, else they would teach amiss and lead others astray.[2]

After the establishment of the Inquisition, the opposition of the Church developed into persecution, and the mild disapproval of the Waldensians for the wealth and corruption of the Romanists became active denunciation, although on the whole the sect never showed the bitterness felt by the Cathari and by the heretics of northern Italy. They considered the organization useless; any assembly of good men was equally potent. They rejected the theory

[1] Davide de Aug., *l.c.*, p. 202. Mansi, vol. XXII, c. 477: '*Et quoniam nonnulli sub specie pietatis virtutem ejus juxta quod ait apostolus denegantes authoritatem sibi vindicant prædicandi.*' The author of the *Chron. Laud.* gives an account of a sermon by Waldo.

[2] Alan. de Ins., *l.c.*, col. 377; Bernard. Abb. Font. Cal., *l.c.*, col. 1597; Davide de Aug., *l.c.*; Stephen of Bourbon, *Tractatus*, p. 280.

Doat, vol. XXXVI, f. 60, says the infallible test of a Waldensian was his preaching and his knowledge of the Scripture, especially of the New Testament.

of tithes, alms, parishes, and all forms of benefices, although their own ministers were dependent on the gifts of the Credentes. Since their most positive tenet was their reliance on the Bible as the one all-sufficient guide to perfection of life, they felt that it provided for all necessary ceremonial and organization,[1] particularly the New Testament, which they held to be more important than the Old, although they did not reject the latter. As most of them could not read, they attached unusual importance to memorizing passages from the Scriptures, which they prided themselves on knowing better than the orthodox priests.[2]

As the Waldensians grew more numerous, it was impossible for them all to preach, so the first division into orders was the separation of the ministers or Perfecti from the laymen or Credentes. The latter had no organization, and in cases where a strict adherence to the practices of the sect would have meant conflict with the authorities they were allowed so many compromises that it was difficult to distinguish between them and the orthodox.[3] After the earliest days they wore no distinctive dress, and to all intents and purposes lived the lives of ordinary citizens. They did receive the Perfecti into their homes, which of course no Catholic would have done, and they attended their own services, though often this was done secretly. They also contributed to the support of their ministers.[4]

[1] Cod. Cas. A IV 49; Cod. Geneva, 209 a, *Sermon Zacaria;* Davide de Aug., *l.c.*; Doat, vol. XXVIII, f. 23t.

[2] *Anon. Pass.*, *l.c.* The inquisitors agreed that the use of the Bible by ignorant laymen was the mainspring of their heresy. 'Multitudes' of heretics in Metz had their own Bibles. (*Ep.* Inn. III, *l.c.*, 235; Alan. de Ins., *l.c.*, col. 395.)

[3] Davide de Aug., p. 216; *Index Errorum quibus Wald. Infesti sunt,* in Gretser, *l.c.*, vol. XII, pt. 2, pp. 95–96; Cod. Vat. Lat. 4030; Cod. Vat. Lat. 4336, f. 305.

[4] For example, they were allowed at times to take oaths and were encouraged to attend the orthodox services. Davide de Aug.: '*Quamvis sine causa gladios et arma ferant pro simulacione, tamen dant complicibus suis intelligere, prestari sibi in hoc obsequium, si occidant aliquando tales, per quos tement exterminari*' (p. 217). Cod. Barb. Lat. 2645, f. 149.

The Perfecti existed in the sect from the early days, although the name was not given them until the thirteenth century. Not a great deal of information is to be found concerning them. The field of their effort seems to have been very wide and they themselves peculiarly energetic and successful, since their converts were soon numerous enough to invite persecution.[1] Upon them lay the obligation of literal obedience to the teachings of Christ and the interpretation of evangelical Christianity by poverty and preaching. In France they constituted the sect proper, and before a half-century had passed were organized into a hierarchy.[2]

As they differed among themselves as to talents and abilities, separation into orders similar to those of the early Christians was inevitable. Prompted by the same need for leadership, they gradually worked out a rather definite gradation of bishops or majors, priests and deacons, whose powers differed in various localities; although everywhere they seem to have had all charge of preaching and of the disposal of whatever money was given to the organization.[3] Aside from their black coats and sandals, they wore no distinctive dress; like the later friars they went forth two by two throughout the land. Just how long was the period of probation before one entered the priesthood is not known, nor how long one must serve as a deacon or priest before becoming eligible for the bishopric. All Perfecti took the vows of poverty and of chastity.[4] After the establishment of the Inquisition most of their preaching was done at night and in secret places;[5] in some

[1] *Statuta Synodalia.* Odonis Episcopi Tullensis (1192), c. 9, Mansi, vol. XXII, col. 647–70.

[2] In Germany and in Lombardy the Credentes seem also to have been organized at a later time.

[3] Cod. Vat. Lat. 2648, *l.c.*

[4] This custom varied in Lombardy and Germany.

[5] Doat, vol. XXIX, f. 217. In some cases it was necessary to undergo a probation of one year before being received as a Perfectus; six or seven years more

sections, at least, they practised communism. Elsewhere the priests received the gifts of the faithful, which they turned over to the bishops, who divided them among their fellow labourers according to their several necessities.[1] From early times, in Lombardy and in Germany and later in France, general councils were held at which posts were assigned to preachers, new members received, and the finances arranged.[2]

The ritual likewise varied in different localities and in this also the authorities are so confused that any definite statement is difficult. Like most of the evangelicals, the Waldensians refused to administer baptism to infants and after the fourteenth century they substituted for water baptism the laying on of hands; what they did in the days of Waldo is not known, but the fact that no ceremony is mentioned makes it reasonable to assume that if the sacrament were administered, it was in the orthodox way. Laying on of hands was also the rite used for the ordination of their bishops, to whom they rendered homage by genuflection.[3]

For the Eucharist they substituted a blessing and breaking of bread which was then distributed to all present[4] and after this came a benediction in the vulgar tongue: 'Blessing and charity, wisdom and grace, honour and virtue of the strength of God be yours, century of centuries, Amen.'[5] Before the meal they bowed themselves in prayer while he who presided over the hospice pronounced a blessing over the food, saying, '*Benedicite*,' while the rest of the congre-

before being ordained as a deacon, and seven years more before admission to the priesthood. *Inq. Carc., Cod. Reg. Paris,* 4269. This was in the fourteenth century, however.

[1] '*Viri diligite uxores vestras sicut Christus dilexit ecclesiam. . . . Quicunque reliquerit patrem aut matrem suam aut agros aut uxorem centuplum accipiet.*' Cod. Monac. Lat. 544, *l.c.*

[2] Doat, vol. xxx, f. 214.

[3] Cod. Vat. Lat. 4030; Doat, vol. xxi, f. 69; vol. xxii, f. 13t.

[4] *Rescriptum Lomb.*

[5] Doat, vol. xxx, f. 210.

gation made answer, '*Deus*.' And then the *Pater Noster* was repeated, after which the major of the hospice said in his native tongue: 'O Lord, who blessed the five barley loaves and the two fishes in the desert, bless this food and drink and all the persons who participate in it in the name of the Father, Son and Holy Ghost.'[1] Sometimes during the dinner or supper, a sermon was preached by the director of the hospice, after which thanks were paid to the preacher by some one of the audience and his preaching was given formal approval. After the meal they again returned thanks in the native tongue, and again bowed themselves as before.[2]

In some cases this supper was preceded by that of the major washing the feet of all present; at times the meal included fish and wine. The ceremony was one of remembrance not of sacrifice.[3] 'Lord God of Abraham, Isaac and Jacob, God of our fathers and Father of our Lord Jesus Christ, who by the hands of the bishops and priests, your servants, and by their multiple prayers; Lord Jesus Christ who blessed the five loaves and two fishes in the desert, and blessing, turned water into wine, bless in the name of the Father, Son and Holy Spirit this bread, fish and wine, held not in sacrifice nor holocaust, but in simple commemoration of the most holy supper of Jesus Christ and His disciples.'

Before or after the breaking of bread there was held a general confession of sins followed by a remission pronounced by the Bishop,[4] not, however, as a priestly function, for they seem to have quite definitely agreed that remission was a divine prerogative never delegated to men. The benediction of bread was restricted to those of godly life. The first point of departure from the orthodox faith

[1] Cod. Dub. Class C, no. xiii, *Processus contra Wald.*
[2] Cod. Vat. Lat. 2648, *l.c.*; Strassburg MS.
[3] Cod. Vat. Lat. 4030, f. iv.
[4] Doat, vol. xxx, f. 234; Cod. Vat. Lat. 2648; Cod. *l.c.*

was in most instances the refusal to accept the ministrations of those of vicious lives,[1] and the French Waldensians were slow to deny the efficacy of good priests or even laymen, regardless of their religious affiliations. They went so far as to urge their brethren to make their Easter confession to the Roman clergy if one of good life were at hand, and the rest of the time to come to their own teachers.[2]

Their services were simple, unaccompanied by chants or ceremonial. According to Stephen of Bourbon they said that God laughs at those who sing to him what they wish to say.[3] Likewise they opposed elaborate houses of worship, saying that God did not dwell in a house made of hands and therefore it was not necessary to go into a church to adore Him. 'They also say that Latin prayers do laymen no good as they do not know what they were saying; also what is not proven by the text of the Bible is fabulous. They say too that the Scripture has the same effect in the vernacular as in Latin, wherefore they consecrate in the vulgar tongue and administer the sacraments, and they despise the decretals, decrees, sayings and expositions of the Saints and adhere only to the Bible. And they refuse to acknowledge the mystical sense of the Holy Scriptures.'[4]

All accounts of the Perfecti show a certain fundamental uniformity of life in the various countries where they extended their missions. In one respect, however, those of

[1] Cod. Cas. 3217, f. 124; Cod. Vat. Lat. 4030, vii; Doat, vol. XI, f. 2t. (1209).

[2] The Morland MSS. at Cambridge include a manual of confession in Latin.

[3] '*Hæretici vero nec domum Dei, nec domum orationis vocant nec in ea cum electis orare curant; sed malunt in domibus suis, quam in domo Dei orare. . . . Quare ergo impii hæretici jactant se servare evangelium et sequi apostolos; cum non in templo orent sed in thalamo, nec ibi doceant sed in foro et quidam clam in domu. . . . Et inquiunt si excelsus non habitat in manufactis; non habitat ecclesiis factis manu hominum. Si autem ibi non habitat, cur iremus illuc ad orandum?*' (Bern. Abb. Font. Cal., pp. 212–13.)

[4] *Max. Bib. Vet. Pat.*, vol. XIII, p. 298.

the French group differed from the Lombards and Germans; they did not engage in any manual labour.[1] The others were expected to contribute to their own support, though they were not to work for gain.[2] Both groups claimed that their practice rested on apostolic authority: the French quoting in their defence Saint Paul's argument (1 Cor. 9:7–11), while the Lombards and Germans claimed to be following the example of the Apostles themselves.[3] All felt, however, that to secure the attention of the multitude the preachers of evangelical poverty must themselves be poor. This condition, apparently, all Perfecti fulfilled and maintained through persecution and other dire vicissitudes.[4] Accounts of them in the thirteenth, fourteenth, and fifteenth centuries agree on this point and show them to be wanderers from place to place often accompanied by neophytes, possessing nothing, having no settled homes and living on the charity of the Credentes.

Whether the poverty maintained by the Perfecti was actual destitution or not is impossible to prove. Some isolated statements point to a contrary conclusion by implying that the Waldensians held a certain amount of property for the benefit of the sect as a whole. David of Augsberg

[1] Alan. de Ins., *l.c.*, col. 399; Cod. Vat. Lat. 2648, *De Pauperibus;* Dieckhoff (p. 190) says the Church censured the Waldensians for this prohibition of work until the principle was adopted by the Mendicants.

[2] *Anon. Pass.*, p. 64. The *Rescriptum Hæresiarchorum* seems to have little bearing on this point. The question dealt with there concerns the *congregationes laborantium*, which Waldo wished to break up. There is no reference to Perfecti. These associations might well be Humiliant communities whose members could not be entirely assimilated by the Waldensians as long as the older organizations remained. See Müller, pp. 51–54, for the view that these societies were forbidden by Waldo because the brethren joined them and thus transgressed the rule that the Perfecti should not work. He also says that the Perfecti used the trades as disguises. This they would scarcely have done had labour been forbidden.

[3] *Anon. Pass.*, *l.c.*

[4] Potthast, Regesta, 11818; 16819. Albericus, *Chron.*, p. 878; Cod. Vat. Lat. 2648; Cod. 4030, f. xxxvii.

says that they collected money for their own needs and for the support of the poor and of students, a statement which suggests an interesting parallel with the early Apostles whom they tried to copy literally in all ways, since the Church's first property consisted of alms collected for the relief of the poor of the community. It seems possible that the Waldensians felt the workings of the same social and economic laws which later made the primitive Church a rich and powerful institution.

However, they did not pursue the same course as the early Church, for there is little doubt that they maintained unbrokenly the practice of evangelical poverty, although it may not have involved destitution. The strength of their hold on the religious life of Europe points to this conclusion, as does the fact that their greatest success came after the days of Francis and Dominic and in the localities where the Mendicant Orders were not represented.[1]

Furthermore, after the Inquisition was organized, the inquisitors hunting them out were instructed to ask those suspected of this particular heresy, 'if he sells what he possesses, if he takes no thought what he shall eat or wherewithal he shall be clothed; if he does not provide for his journey money, nor bread, nor two coats, nor shoes; if he renounces all things, if he has nothing of his own.'[2] At all events, as late as the opening of the sixteenth century, the Perfecti claimed that they still followed poverty. 'The Barbes[3] say that they are poor men of Christ, going about the world as imitators of the Apostles.'[4] They also inveighed against priests who were not poor, saying that popes and clerics who have possessions are not of the true Church nor are they true pastors or governors, but wolves, and that God did not commit the Church to them,

[1] Davide de Aug., *l.c.*, p. 212.

[2] Cod. Vat. Lat. 4030, f. iii; Bernard. Guid., on the contrary, lays no stress on this point, but does emphasize their abstention from oaths. *L.c.*, p. 244.

[3] A later name for a teacher.

[4] Doat, vol. xxx, ff. 214, etc.

and that through their disobedience they have lost all power to bind and loose and are in the way of perdition.[1]

The Credentes seem nowhere to have maintained absolute poverty if indeed they ever practised it, but by their labour they supported the Perfecti and the organization. Indeed, it seems impossible for any group under the ban of the Church to have long maintained such a practice. A religious organization countenanced by the institution might find mendicancy a practicable way of earning a livelihood, for the rank and file of people gave to holy beggars willingly for their own salvation. Those under interdict, liable on every hand to persecution, could not count on such support; gifts to them brought not a blessing, but a share in their condemnation. Other influences, of course, may have been present to make poverty unfeasible for the Credentes, but whatever the factors there is no doubt as to the result. The great body of believers earned their living and gave to their preachers the necessities of life; the Credentes abandoned the strict and literal observance of evangelical poverty that the Perfecti might be free to observe it.

Little evidence exists on which to found any idea of the social rank from which Waldensians drew their converts. While it is generally assumed that the great majority of them were from the class of manual labourers,[2] yet any generalization is of necessity rash, not only because the known facts are so scanty, but because the movement was so widespread. Waldensian communities were numerous throughout western Europe in lands where conditions varied widely. Although on the whole they seem to have been unskilled labourers, shoemakers, weavers, swordmakers, there are found in the documents concerning

[1] *Cantica, Glosa Pater, Vergier de Consolation,* in Morland MS., *l.c.*, and Geneva MS. 209a.

[2] Haupt., *Die Wald. Ursprung,* p. 7; Alan. de Ins., *l.c.*, p. 225.

them the names of advocates, physicians, and even certain of the nobility.[1]

A disputation was held in the palace of Raymond of Foix in 1207 for the purpose of reconciling the Waldensians with the Church, and the wife and sister of Raymond are numbered among the heretics.[2] David of Augsberg mentions a powerful prince in Germany who joined their ranks and says they had such influential friends that no one dared to molest them.[3]

Most of the accounts speak scornfully of them as simple, illiterate '*idiotæ*,'[4] but there is no little evidence that in Germany they maintained schools and that in Lombardy they had a fairly well-organized educational system.[5] The Perfecti seem to have been well skilled in disputation, and certainly the elaborate arguments of Moneta of Cremona could not well have been called forth by illiterate men.[6] As some of their converts were from the priesthood, and as some lay nobles became bishops in their Order, it seems that there were evidences of intelligence among them quite as marked as among the general run of people. While it is likely that a school such as that at Milan which they maintained[7] afforded teaching more advanced than what was to be had in their meetings, yet the sect as a whole never gained the hold at the universities that characterized the

[1] Doat, vol. XXIX, f. 4, 10, 11.

[2] Pet. Vall. Sarn., *l.c.*, p. 10; Guil. de Pod. Laur., *l.c.*, p. 200.

[3] *Anon. Pass.*, p. 399.

[4] Davide de Aug., p. 213: '*Ad simplices et rudes solent accedere.*' Bern. Abb. Font. Cal., *l.c.*, p. 1595: '*Accitis itaque pluribus tam clericis quam laicis religiosis ac sæcularibus,*' but he adds that they seduce the weak, simple, and innocent, especially the women, and through women, weak men.

[5] See Steph. of Bourbon, *Tractatus*, p. 280, for an account of a man who for eighteen years had studied in '*secta hæreticorum Valdensium.*' Cf. Inn. III, *Ep.* 296, *l.c.*

[6] Moneta, *l.c.*; Davide de Aug., p. 218: '*Student diligenter attrahere sibi aliquas potentes et nobiles feminas ut per eas etiam viros vel cognatos earum sibi faciant faventes, ut sic liberius in terris illis se dilatent et nullus audeat eos tangere sub illorum tuicione munitos.*'

[7] *Ep.* Inn., III, lib. XII, no. 17, Migne, *l.c.*, col. 29.

Dominicans at Paris and the Lollards at Oxford. Such a thing would scarcely have been in accordance with their ideas of humility. All through Lombardy and Provence more schools for heretics existed than for theologians and very many of those trained in them were holding disputations, preaching in the fields and in the market-places when no churches were to be had, and presiding over meetings in the houses of the faithful in order to give instruction to their converts.

As persecution developed anti-sacerdotalism among them and they came to assume that a church which held property could not be that founded by Christ, their next step was to claim for themselves sole right of apostolic succession. The Roman Church had not only lost this right, but had become the whore of Babylon, and no laws passed since the time of Constantine now had any force. In proof of this they called attention to the pride, avarice, incontinence, drunkenness, and envy of the priesthood, at the same time comparing with such sins their own virtues of humility, generosity, chastity, and sobriety.[1]

Again, Christ had expressly forbidden murder; therefore a church whose prelates shed blood in his name were not truly his followers.[2] The pope and the Roman clergy had been guilty of bloodshed, for they had preached crusades, carried on war against the empire, and persecuted the Waldensians themselves. Christ had sent out his Apostles 'as sheep in the midst of wolves. Now the Church has become a wolf,' said they, 'and we are the sheep; for we are persecuted by the Church and whoever heard of a sheep killing wolves?'[3] Then, they concluded,

[1] Cod. Barb. Lat. 2645, f. 145; Cod. Strassburg, ed. Schmidt, written 1454.

[2] Moneta, *l.c.*, p. 513. The heretics quote Matthew 10:23. Then they say: '*Papam non fugere imo bellum indicere Imperatori*' (p. 513). Then Matt. 5:44–45 and then, '*Quomodo istud observat judex Ecclesiæ Romanæ cum occidit malefactorem.*' Cod. Vat. Lat. 2648, f. 67t.

[3] Moneta, *l.c.*, p. 514: '*Objiciunt etiam illud quod habetur Mat.* 10:16 "*Ecco ego mitto vos sicut oves in medio luporum;*" *Se mones oves dicunt, non autem lupos.*

'we who follow the law of Christ and the example of his Apostles are the true Church and it is our priests who have the power to bind and loose.'[1]

In order to support this claim they adopted the Sylvestrine legend to explain their origin and also the fact that the Roman Church was not that founded by Christ.[2] According to this account the Church fell when Sylvester accepted from Constantine the gift of lands and of secular power. The primitive institution did not altogether disappear; but it was hidden until its revival by Waldo.[3] The form of the legend as accepted in the thirteenth century by the Waldensians is brief and bare of all picturesque details, although later versions were more evidently designed to appeal to the multitude. The circumstances of Constantine's gift to Sylvester are reproduced as they are set down in the Donation and the continuity of the primitive Church down to the time of Waldo was specifically asserted. The Roman *ordo*, they said, was originally derived from the Apostles and, until the time of Constantine, the Church remained true to the commands and teachings of Christ. In the fourth century a certain man named Sylvester was rector of the Church. He with his companions dwelt on Mount Sirachus near Rome and led a life of poverty because of persecution. Constantine, then a leper, had a vision or dream; he summoned Sylvester, who baptized him in the name of Christ and cured him of his miserable infirmity. The Emperor, thinking to honour the man who had made him whole, offered to Sylvester the crown and dignity, which the bishop accepted, and from that time the

Ecclesiam autem lupum esse, non autem oves. At quod dicunt hoc esse mirabile cum non inveniatur, quod oves persequantur, vel occidant lupos nos e contra accidimus et persequimur eos.'

[1] '*Primo ergo dicent quales deberent esse Christi discipuli ex verbis evangelii et apostolorum, dicentes illos tantum esse apostolorum successores es, qui eorum vitam sequuntur.*' Davide de Aug., p. 206; Doat, vol. XXXVI, f. 50.

[2] See Wezel, *Ep. Wib.*, *l.c.*; Bonacorsus, *l.c.*, p. 64.

[3] Davide de Aug., *l.c.*, p. 207; Moneta, *l.c.*, pp. 402, 405.

episcopacy increased in honour, and evils multiplied over the earth. Both the Waldensians and Cathari declared that when Sylvester accepted this gift, the primitive sanctity was lost and the Church fell.[1]

However, certain of Sylvester's companions refused to follow him in the new life of prosperity, saying: 'We have this commandment from God that we have no earthly possessions.' To whom Sylvester replied: 'Unless you remain with me I shall forbid you the earth'; but they, rejoicing, said: 'Therefore we give thanks to God, for if you forbid us the earth because we observe his commandments, you will open to us Heaven by our merits.' As they disputed with Sylvester, that same night they heard a voice from Heaven saying: 'To-day poison has been poured out within the Church of God'; and this gave them courage to carry out their undertaking boldly, and so they were excommunicated that the Word of God might be fulfilled. As they went forth they said to Sylvester: 'We leave to you the earth; we seek rather Heaven.'

They were allowed to depart and they followed the way of poverty and, multiplying, endured for a long time. Persecution vexed them sorely and they were forced to retire to secret places where they kept the true faith alive until the time of Peter Waldo and his companions, who brought it to light again.[2] The story as the Waldensians told it in the thirteenth century was likely to appeal to the un-

[1] Moneta, *l.c.*, p. 397; Stephen of Bourbon, *Tractatus*, p. 297. *Dicunt Ecclesiam romanam Babylon meretricem de qua legitur Apoc.* XVII; Dante, *Inferno*, XIX, ll. 106–11:

> Di voi pastor, s'accorse il Vangelista
> Quando colei, che siede sovra l'acque,
> Puttaneggiar coi Regi a lui fu vista:
> Quella, che son le sette teste nacque
> E dalle dieci corna ebbe argomento,
> Fin che virtute al suo marito piacque.

[2] *Ep. Frat.*, *l.c.* Later in the account is the statement that all this cannot be proven. '*Propter testium absentiam, nemo enim hodie est qui audierat seu viderit proprium rei principium, quia multum tempus jam est elapsum.*'

critical multitude even as that of Saint Alexis appealed to Waldo.

Poverty then they preached always. Upon the practice of it their *ordo* rested.[1] Their observance of it constituted their claim to be considered the true heirs of the Apostles and was the chief means by which they secured converts from a Church burdened with wealth.[2] The methods by which the Perfecti sought converts can only be conjectured, but their success may be attributed in a large measure to their constant use of the Gospels, which the common people could understand more easily than the more subtle Epistles and Psalms; the multitudes of the twelfth- and thirteenth-century folk listened with willing ears to those who told them in simple and definite terms what Christ wished his disciples to do. Moreover, their position as opposed to that of the priests of the Church was impregnable, for they lived the poverty they preached.

The attitude of the Church to this movement points to the conclusion that the Waldensians remained in very truth Poor Men of Christ. The ecclesiastical authorities assumed that the strength of the sect lay in the rigid obedience of its preachers to the commands of Christ, especially in their literal interpretation of that which concerned the practice of poverty. In order to satisfy what was apparently a very definite popular demand, the Church later sanctioned the very tenets it had earlier denounced, but the reason for the denunciation lay undoubtedly in the fact that this practice was combined with others less objectionable. It was certainly to counteract what seemed to be one of the most popular practices of the heretics that the Church encouraged the friars to preach and to practise poverty so long as they held to the fundamental doctrines. Their special task was to induce Christians, whom belief in these doctrines

[1] Cod. Vat. Lat. 2648; Doat, vol. XXXVI, f. 50t; Davide de Aug., *l.c.*, p. 210.
[2] Stephen of Bourbon, *Tractatus*, p. 290.

had led into schism, to return to the fold. The successful efforts of Innocent III in winning back a section of the Humiliati and one of the Waldensians prove the wisdom of such a policy.

It is the life of the Poor Men and their appeal to the popular mind of the late twelfth and early thirteenth centuries that must be understood in order to estimate their influence as a world power. They neither knew nor cared for philosophical subtleties; their movement was essentially ethical and practical. The life which they themselves led and which they urged others to lead made the same appeal logically and psychologically as that advocated by those arch-saints, Francis and Dominic. Unlike their contemporaries, who held in the beginning tenets similar to theirs, these found it possible to continue to follow literally the commands which they had originally adopted as their rule; commands which had perforce been put aside by the Church and by most of the monastic orders, and which were to be adopted and then relaxed by the followers of Saint Francis, as the developing institution inevitably conformed to economic laws. There is no way of knowing whether the Arnoldisti and Humiliati remained true to the principle of primitive Christianity and apostolic poverty. In the case of the Waldensians, some fragmentary material exists which bears on their history after the first enthusiasm had given place to complications. The later generations of the sect seem to have obeyed literally their original rule. Possibly persecution made possible what canonization prevented.

CHAPTER VIII

CONCLUSION

The closing years of the twelfth century witnessed the culmination of the temporal power of the Church as her victory over the emperor secured to her those rights and privileges she had claimed for herself since the days of Charlemagne. Not only was she the spiritual head of Christendom; she had become also a quasi-political organization, wealthy, powerful, and outwardly united. So completely had her prelates identified themselves with affairs of state that the government of the civilized world, if not in their hands, was to all intents and purposes under their guidance. The wrangling disputations of the Schoolmen had resulted in the superimposition of a theological system which in its universality supplemented the unification achieved by the Hildebrandine policy, while ceremonials and sacraments controlled every phase of human activity from the cradle to the grave.

At the very time, however, when her moral grandeur and ecclesiastical absolutism were at their apex, there appeared from time to time, amid the pomp and majesty of the papal court, uncouth figures bent on strange errands. Neither monks nor priests, but humbly clad citizens, they spoke the simple language of the common people, as inspired by a courage not easy to appreciate in this more audacious age, they not only pointed out the defects of the all-powerful institution, but asked permission to take in hand the task in which they claimed the Church had so manifestly failed, that of interpreting the will of God and the mind of Christ.

Visionaries they were, all of them, and they made demands which could not be fulfilled: demands to which the pontiffs at first paid no attention, engrossed as they were in what seemed to them to be affairs of far greater moment. While the suppliants differed among themselves as to doctrines and as to practices, yet, because they represented the widespread insistence for a reform of the Church through the practice of evangelical poverty, they at last gained a hearing and some of them gained also the papal sanction for which they had come.

This aspiration for a return to the simplicity of the early Church and for the practice of evangelical poverty as a means of attaining a more perfect life on earth, and to render more certain the hope of eternal happiness, was one decided manifestation of the restless spirit dominating western Europe in the twelfth and thirteenth centuries, and was a product of native energy, awakened by contact with new ideals. As life, wealth, and industry advanced, and the mind of the people displayed a new receptivism, there was put forth a widespread effort to reconstruct the social order on the ruins of the ancient civilization, an effort which resulted in a sincere dissatisfaction with existing conditions and a feeling that all was not well with the world. Consequently, every established institution, social, political, or religious, was challenged to show some reason for its continuance. Decades of persistent effort at self-expression and self-assertion had developed shrewd hatreds. Barons and merchants, bishops and heretics, courtiers and townsmen, visionaries and scholastics, each realized that his own existence depended on the subordination of his rival, and the fierce clashing of individual interests made competition and coöperation equally impossible. The old order must justify its existence or be cast aside.

In the fifth century, in some complex and obscure way, the feudal system had superseded the old municipalities. Now these were regaining the prestige they had lost and at the same time new towns were developing, peopled with craftsmen who were organizing themselves into guilds, and by their organization were able to seize and exercise great influence in local affairs. The roads to the east, recently thronged with hostile armies bent on conquest, were now filled with merchants invading the west, a far more powerful host than the Crusaders had been. The changing economic order was bringing a new spirit into religion just as surely as the Crusades brought a new spirit into the commercial world. Crusaders were becoming merchants, and merchants, religious leaders.

Politically, this restlessness was uprooting the feudal system and creating the rich, ambitious, liberty-loving communes; socially, it was replacing the landed nobility with an eager, sceptical middle class, whose power rested on material achievements rather than on inherited rank or established class privilege; religiously, it was producing a multitude of reformers whose appeal to reason and intelligence endangered the very foundations of the established Church, already weakened by a priesthood intellectually lazy and spiritually corrupt. All three phases of this movement, the political, the social, and the religious, represented heresy or the breaking away from the established order, and all manifested a common tendency to seek some remedy, material or spiritual, for the all but intolerable prevalent disorder.

The list of those who questioned the teachings of the Church is longer in the two centuries just preceding the establishment of the Mendicant Orders than at any time since the Council of Nicæa. Never were such elements more vigorous, more complex, more inherently able to bring about the transformation they were seeking. In the towns where political liberty was most developed, they had swept all before them. The heterogeneous population fostered freedom of thought, while the misery existing in the crowded streets aroused a general recognition of the necessity for reform of some sort, although no one knew just the nature it should take. The crusading spirit was as manifest in a desire to consecrate one's self to some great cause near at hand as it was in the willingness to cross the sea in order to fight the infidel.

Had the Church been spiritually united, had the clergy been spiritually competent, she might easily have turned this restless enthusiasm to a happy conclusion, but, despite the earnest efforts of reforming monks and pontiffs to maintain her spiritual leadership by stemming the rising tide of heresy, she was far too handicapped by the results of her long alliance with the temporal powers to take advantage of the situation. Her peace with the empire was made. Outwardly majestic, nominally the custodian of all virtues, tolerant of those who menaced her very existence,[1] she was torn by internal dissensions; her ideals were flaunted by a corrupt and ignorant priesthood who had taken God from the hearts of men and had substituted instead an army of saints; for faith, she taught superstitions; she had replaced prophecies by hallucinations, and the Scriptures by stupid and impossible stories of pseudo-saints from which the industrial classes turned in contempt.

The twelfth-century reforms within the Church manifested in the establishment of new monastic orders had not been permanently effective, and while the most austere heretic that ever lived was no more eager for the reëstablishment of the purity of the Church than was Stephen of Grammont, Bernard of Clairvaux, or Norbert, all of whom tried by warning no less than by example, to bring about the needed reform, their work scarcely survived them

[1] Even the sternest of prelates showed a remarkable tolerance to heretics. None of them were charged with the judicial murder of those whose opinions were at variance with their own. Those who were put to death had been condemned by the civil powers or suffered at the hands of the mobs; in most cases the bishops tried to rescue them. Arnold's crime, it will be remembered, was political, not religious.

and the evils they strove to remedy increased. By the middle of the century, the monastic idea of absolute surrender had been replaced by a desire for a more positive expression of individualism. The average man of that day wanted a religion more active than mere devotion to saints and martyrs, to the person of Christ in the crib or on the cross.

Even the most rigid of the monastic orders had proved themselves unable to maintain their pristine simplicity. The gifts of their admirers were constantly defeating the aims of their founders. They did not realize that such a system could never long remain inviolate because of the very humanity of the monks. The corruption that crept in was a natural result of the interaction of their vices and virtues. Few of them could 'see life steadily and see it whole,' and each quality that meant the advance of the monastic ideal had a complementary quality that led to its overthrow. As the orders became wealthy, they lost their popular appeal, for while they gave abundantly to those in need, they were no longer their friends, as they shared neither their lives nor their necessities.

There was nothing fundamentally new in the general insistence on a return to apostolic poverty as a means of ridding the Church of its corruption, although the wealth of the clerical orders and their absorption in affairs of state gave it a rather marked emphasis in the years between the establishment of the monastery at Citeaux by Robert of Molesme and the coming of Francis of Assisi. The earliest advocates of the ideal, however, did not go so far as to insist that the alliance between Church and state be utterly abolished. Indeed, Bernard and Norbert often left their monasteries to participate in secular affairs. Nor did they insist on absolute poverty for the whole priesthood. Only for themselves and their disciples was it to be adopted as a means of attaining spiritual perfection. Each had shared with Saint Benedict a desire to escape worldly careers in order to work out a philosophy of life in the midst of solitude, and all, save possibly the earliest Cistercians and Stephen of Grammont, had definitely withdrawn from active participation in a Church burdened with an excess of temporal power and its attendant evils, and had established their orders as a protest against the corruption and wealth left behind, thus differing from the earliest founders of monastic orders and approaching in spirit the Evangelicals and Mendicants.

As the monastic fervour ran its course, the middle class, the merchants and scholars, undertook what pope and monk had alike failed to accomplish, and because of their lack of theological training inevitably developed ideas which the Church was not slow to designate as heretical. All of the new movements, heretical or orthodox, were born of a desire to return to apostolic Christianity and were marked by an intense devotion to the Scriptures. In contrast to the monastic movements they were based primarily on an appeal to reason rather than to emotion, and because of the austere simplicity of life advocated by their leaders, they drew both laymen and clergy to their ranks. They differed widely in doctrine, some of them dissenting merely in matters of ceremonial and others professing dogmatic errors on subjects fundamental to the faith. While all of these movements were characterized by independence of thought, they lacked the metaphysical subtleties of the Manichæans and Nestorians and concerned themselves with matters of daily living and of their duties to their neighbours rather than their relation to an unseen, omnipotent power. It was in their practical application of the teachings of Christ to the evils of their times, their applying religious remedies to social evils, that they may be considered as forerunners of the Franciscans.

Francis of Assisi was in no way a rebel against the existing order, but he undoubtedly put himself in emphatic contrast with the Roman Catholic Church and particularly with the secular dignity of the hierarchy, whether secured through temporal office and power as in Italy, through great holdings as in Germany, or an intermixture of these and feudalism as in France. Like Arnold of Brescia, he protested definitely against the tendency of the Church to absorb the affairs of state and their accompanying enjoyments and luxury and profligacy; against the penury of Christian virtues, the enslavement to temporal things, the almost pagan craving for honours and wealth, he placed the recognition of the needs of the unfortunate as the supreme duty of the Church.

With the Cathari he had little in common save for the occasional reformer who came from their ranks to preach clerical poverty, yet the Apostolics in their renunciation of earthly goods, Peter of Bruys and Henry of Lausanne in their efforts to turn Christian worship to its original purity, were rather more spiritually akin to him than to the learned, audacious sect from which they sprang.

He was in accord with the spirit of the early Humiliati, for, while they were rather more careful of the needs of daily life than he wished his disciples to be, and possibly not so eager to relieve the necessity of others less fortunate than themselves, they did forecast the gentleness and the simplicity of the Minores rather more strongly than they reflected the spirit of monasticism.

Of all of these various groups of aspirants after apostolic poverty, the Waldensians seem to have been most similar to the Franciscans in spirit and in practice and a rather definite connection between the two is suggested. Later than the other movements in time of organization, they were in their first enthusiasm when Francis began his mission. As Assisi was by no means an isolated hamlet and as the Poor Men had by then begun to spread southward from Lombardy, he could not have been wholly ignorant of them. Then, too, the shrewd, observant Bernardone must have brought back news of their activities in southern France.

The careers of Peter Waldo and Francis were curiously alike: both came from the newly arisen merchant class; both were converted in a peculiarly dramatic way; both gave themselves up to the new life in order to relieve the necessities of the poor. It would be easy to consider Francis as a follower of the merchant of Lyons, so similar were they in faith and in practices. However, certain fundamental differences appear upon closer examination, and, on the whole, it seems more reasonable to consider them as individual products of the spirit of their times and of their respective communities.

Their later careers vary. With Waldo the Bible became the one supreme guide for faith as for conduct; with Francis an inner miracle pointed the way. While the Waldensians were driven into heresy, the Franciscans received the sanction of the Church. Yet the former never strayed far from the fold. In both France and Italy it was difficult to distinguish the orthodox branch of the sect, the Poor Catholics, from those branded as heretics. They form a direct and close connection between the Mendicants and the earlier Evangelicals who desired the reform of the priesthood by relighting the religious fires which a careless priesthood had all but extinguished.

It is impossible to disjoin the Franciscan movement from those heretical ones which Innocent III arrested by crusade and inquisition, for it is not apart from the tendencies of the age which produced them all. Rather it is the soul of these, the diviner essence, the permanent and eternal part of them, that which gave them the right to exist and which carried their fundamental doctrine of self-abnegation to so extreme a form that it became in very truth a revolt against human nature itself. That the Mendicant Friars existed and continued to exist even in this modern age which has so absolutely rejected the theory of salutary effects of poverty, holding that this and not wealth brutalizes mankind, is due to the one feature which is Saint Francis's great contribution to his age and to all civilization, that capacity of caring so intensely for one's fellow men that all questions of doctrine and of dogma sink into relative unimportance.

PART II

STUDIES IN THE SOCIAL HISTORY OF THE MIDDLE AGES

Part II

STUDIES IN THE SOCIAL HISTORY OF THE MIDDLE AGES

CHAPTER I

REFUGEES OF ANOTHER DAY

Early race memories, preserved in epic tradition, sing of the arms and the hero, and History, the heir of the Epic, has not outgrown the habit of gathering her tales from the feats of a Cæsar or a Beowulf, a Hector or a Godfrey — from the deeds of those who, whatever the immediate occasion, were always dominated by the primitive instinct of seizing by might that which they desired, of overcoming by force that which threatened what they valued. Seldom, indeed, has she been able to look beyond the fluttering garments of king or of baron to the multitude of humbler folk whose fate poet and chronicler alike have so drearily summarized and so constantly reiterated: 'The men were killed, and the women and children were sold into slavery.'

True, the tragic poet saw the great dramatic situation outside the broken walls of Troy, lit by the flames of her vanished splendour, but Euripides, who thus gave voice to the woes of war-sufferers and exiles, and who preserved for us their lament over their dead, heard only the cry of the women of the palace. Yet then, as now, war meant countless ruined homes, meant the loss of humble treasure, stolen, burned, or abandoned in flight, as the desolate procession of helpless, guiltless, and homeless fared forth from the city gates as forlorn as the later refugees of Belgium or of Poland, of Serbia or of Armenia. Of these and of their fate, epic history neither knew nor cared, for since the songs must needs be of the arms and of the hero, what mattered a handful of nameless followers?

Our modern age, with the wounds of warfare still fresh, sees the people, not the leader; the tales celebrate the prowess of Sammy and Tommy and M. Poilu; the pictures are of burned villages, of ruined orchards, of huddled groups of war-orphans clustered about the castle gates. We to-day are learning to think in terms of modest homes and of simple farmsteads; to feel with the poor the loss of what their pathetic thrift amassed; to consider the effect of war on the non-combatant; and to see that the history of a nation is written, not in the wars and crusades of her rulers, but in the sufferings and aspirations of her commoners.

Occasionally, however, in the past there has arisen, above the clanging spears of Troy or the battle-cries of Agincourt, the voice of these lesser folk, and a very notable example is found in that court of claims held by Louis IX in 1247,[1] in which a group of villagers of northern France were given opportunity to make known to their king the wrongs they had suffered at his hands some eighteen years before.

All through the late summer and autumn of the year 1228 men and women were busily gathering in the harvest from the wide fields and hillsides of the fair province of Le Perche.[2] Mowers with their long scythes cut the ripened

[1] King Louis IX, anxious to clear his conscience before embarking on his Crusade in 1247, sent monks, priests, friars, etc., to various parts of France to learn what injuries or unjust exactions his people had suffered at the hands of king or baron and to make recompense. Of the inquest held in Normandy, only a few fragments of the record are preserved. These are published in volume XXIV of the *Recueil des Historiens des Gaules et de la France*.

[2] Le Perche, situated thirty-five leagues northwest of Paris in the diocese of Séez, had belonged to the crown of France, at least nominally, since before the time of Clovis. Charles the Simple gave it to Raoul the Dane as a royal fief, and from this time on it was held by the Dukes of Normandy, who divided and subdivided it until it was reduced from its original large and flourishing state to one of the smallest counties in France. Even so, its counts held an important

wheat, while the women, following down the swathes, bound the sheaves, keeping a watchful eye on the rosy-cheeked babies tumbling about in the sunshine on the grain-strewn ground at their feet. Stout horses, such as give Le Perche fame in our own day,[1] drew the creaking, broad-wheeled carts along the narrow lanes. The beat of flails on the threshing-floor came through the drowsy air. Among the shadows at the edge of the forest,[2] swineherds tended the ungainly beasts fattening on acorns. Sharp blows of steel on wood told that some one near by was gathering his yearly share of fuel. A deep content settled over the countryside, for the crops were unusually abundant. Bins full of golden grain and ricks of hay and straw, bronzing in the hot autumnal sun, gave promise of enough and to spare, even after taxes had been collected by bailiffs of my lord the count, and tithes by stewards of my lord the bishop. No need, then, for anxiety in the months that should elapse before the next harvest, and in sign and token of their thankfulness, villagers and burghers alike burned holy candles before the shrines of the good saints who had delivered them from the misery a short crop brought. Plenty crowned the peace which blessed their days.

Yet was it peace? There, ever before their eyes on the heights above the sunny fields, was the grim old castle of Bellême,[3] a symbol and threat of war. Mistress of the west,

place in all assemblies of princes. Possibly this importance of Le Perche was due to its three royal villes, Mortagne, La Perrière, and Bellême with their strongholds, and to its many religious houses. Courtin, R., *Histoire du Perche*, p. 11; de Romanet, O., Géographie du Perche, pp. 23 ff.; Bry, G., *Histoire des Pays et Comté du Perche*, pp. 3, 7, 114. Bart des Boulais, *Recueil des Antiquitées du Perche*, p. 14.

[1] Ardouin-Dumazet, V. E., *Voyage en France*, vol. I, ch. XXV.

[2] The great forest of Bellême excelled all others of that region in the quantity and quality of its wood. It was also famous for its medicinal springs. Bry, p. 11; Courtin, p. 14; de Romanet, p. 8.

[3] The castle of Bellême was one of the finest in Normandy. It was built on a steep hill, enclosed by a high wall surmounting a deep moat; towers garnished

it stood haughty and isolated, rearing against the blue October sky its menace of pitiless walls and battlemented towers, from which the banner of the count dangled idly in the motionless air. But happy in the daily routine of humble labour and of simple pleasure, and content with their bountiful harvest, the Bellêmois regarded it with as complete indifference as the Belgians paid to the forts of Liège and Antwerp before the tempest broke over their heads in 1914.

For both, war was inevitable. The storm-clouds had been gathering over Le Perche for half a century and more, ever since Philip Augustus had conceived and partially carried out his relentless policy of welding the tumultuous feudatories into a great state by external expansion and internal organization, strengthening the power of the crown without destroying the feudal system, which he aimed to subordinate to the monarchy. By force or by cunning, by clever diplomacy or by wise statesmanship, this vigorous monarch had brought fief after fief under his direct suzerainty, despite the resistance of lord and lordling who sought to keep castle and fortress as centres of misgovernment. Time and again under Philip and under his successor, Louis VIII,[1] this resistance had threatened to express itself in revolt. Time and again these Capetians had been made to feel that they were merely Counts of Paris, holding their kingship, not by any right divine, but by consent of their vassals — a consent only too easily

the sides, and in the centre a huge dungeon crowned a small mound. Within the walls was the sumptuous church of Saint Léonard, one of the most famous sanctuary churches in that part of France. It was founded in 1092 to hold the relics of Saint-Léonard de Vandœuvre, and was destroyed in 1562 by the Huguenots. In the time of Henry I of England, the Counts of Bellême lost their castle to the Counts of Le Perche. Guillaume de Nangis, *Vita Sancti Lud.*, in *Recueil*, vol. xx, p. 316; Bart des Boulais, pp. 71 ff.; Bry, pp. 18, 45, 48; Hommey, *Histoire de Séez*, vol. I, p. 413.

[1] Petit-Dutaillis, *Étude sur la Vie et le Règne de Louis VIII*, ch. IX; Le Nain de Tillemont, *Vie de Saint Louis*, vol. I, ch. 91, 94.

withdrawn should they wax arrogant. Now, in the face of such monarchical self-assertion, feudal rebellion was a foregone conclusion, and the old order of feudal barons saw, in the apparent helplessness of child-king [1] and regent mother, an opportunity to return to the unrestrained liberty of that earlier day whose joys some of the barons then living had shared. The coronation of Louis [2] was the signal for the outburst of a perfect plague of conspiracies: [3] conspiracies to supplant the queen-mother as regent; [4] conspiracies to kidnap the little king; [5] conspiracies to dethrone him and to crown in his stead either his uncle the shock-headed Philip,[6] or else that Sire of Coucy, Enguer-

[1] There seems to be some uncertainty as to the age of Louis IX at the time of his accession. Not having been the heir-apparent, his birth was unrecorded. M. de Wailly, however, has proved quite conclusively that Louis was born April, 1214, and therefore was twelve and a half years old when he was crowned. *Mémoire sur la date et le lieu de Naissance de Saint-Louis.*

[2] Louis was crowned at Rheims, Saint Andrew's Day, 1226. Among those absent were the Counts of Champagne, Bar, Brittany, La Marche, and Saint Pol. The last four were helping Richard of Cornwall, brother of Henry III, ravage the king's lands in Poitou. The Count of Champagne, Theobald, was in disrepute because he had deserted Louis VIII at the siege of Avignon the previous August. When he sent his squires to engage lodgings at Rheims, Blanche ordered the provost to refuse him admission to the town. Roger of Wendover, *Flores Historiarum*, vol. II, p. 315; Mousket, *La Chronique Rimée*, in vol. XXII, *Recueil*, ll. 27508, 27559 ff., 27590 ff., 27690 ff.; *Chronique de Reims*, in vol. XXII, *Recueil*, p. 304; Guiart, *La Branche des Royaux Lingnages*, in vol. XXII, *Recueil*, l. 8980; *Chron.* Baudoin d'Avesnes, in vol. XXI, *Recueil*, p. 161.

[3] Roger of Wendover, *l.c.*; Mousket, *l.c.*, ll. 27735 ff.; Rymer, *Fœdera*, vol. I, p. 289; Chantereau, *Traité des Fiefs, Preuves*, pp. 169, 170; Guil. de Nangis, *Vita*, p. 312; Baudoin d'Avesnes, *l.c.*; *Chron. St. Denis*, vol. XXI, *Recueil*, p. 104; *E Mari Historiarum*, vol. XXIII, *Recueil*, p. 107; Guiart, l. 9070; Joinville, *Histoire de St. Louis*, ed. Ducange, p. 16; *Chron. de Reims*, p. 306; Berger, *Blanche de Castille*, p. 71; Le Nain de Tillemont, vol. I, p. 328 ff.

[4] Joinville, p. 15; *Chron. St. Denis*, *l.c.*; Le Nain de Tillemont, vol. I, p. 445.

[5] Mousket, l. 27995; Guil. de Nangis, *l.c.*; *Chronicon* Girardi de Fracheto, in vol. XXI, *Recueil*, p. 3.

[6] Philip, it will be remembered, was the son of Philip Augustus and Agnes of Meran, and had been legitimatized by Pope Innocent III. Potthast, *Regesta*, nos. 1499–1500, p. 132. His loyalty to his nephew fluctuated. At one time (1228) he went so far as to fortify Calais as the centre of an attack on the throne, but he was won over by judicious gifts from the regent. *Chron. Andrensis Monasterii*, D Archéry, *Spicilegium*, vol. IX, p. 659; Guil. de Nangis, *Vita*, p. 312; Le Nain de Tillemont, vol. I, p. 437.

rand,[1] of unsavoury memory whom even the great Philip Augustus himself had not dared discipline.[2] A great number, lay and ecclesiastical, went over to the group of brilliant, disorderly barons who were lightening their intrigues by gay cavalcades, and *chansons amoureuses*.[3] Though varying in detail and in immediate object, the underlying purpose of the conspirators[4] was always the same — to bring about a reversal of the policy of the last two reigns, to restore baronial rights, to maintain the independence of the lords against the crown.[5]

These efforts were futile, thanks to the hated foreigner,[6] Blanche of Castile, whom Louis VIII, acting upon a confidence born of years of experience with her energy and

[1] Enguerrand, surnamed the Grand, although not in direct line of succession nor even of near kinship, was powerful because of his great ability and because of the many marriage alliances which connected him with most of the peers of the realm. *Chron. de Reims*, p. 308; *Récits d'un Ménestrel de Reims* (ed. de Wailly), p. 179; Duchesne, *Histoire de Coucy, Preuves*, p. 367. 'Je ne suis roy, ne prince, ne comte aussy: je suis le sire de Coucy,' was his proud boast.

[2] When the canons of Rheims complained to Philip Augustus of Enguerrand's deeds of violence, the king could only say: 'I can do no more for you than pray the Sire of Coucy to leave you unmolested.'

[3] For poems written by them see Raynouard, *Choix des Poésies Originales des Troubadours*.

[4] Guil. de Nangis, *Chron.*, p. 517. The chief of the conspirators were the Counts of la Marche and Brittany and the King of England. Other barons were with them intermittently, but could not be counted on for much help. La Marche was the wealthiest baron of France and Blanche was zealous in her efforts to win his allegiance. But his marriage to Isabel, mother of King Henry, led him to espouse the latter's cause, until even he saw further resistance to royal power was futile.

[5] The barons demanded a restitution of the lands which they said Philip Augustus had taken illegally, that is, without consent of the twelve peers. Blanche categorically refused to accede to this request, saying she had no right to alienate any part of the royal domain, a rather inconsistent position since she had advocated Louis VIII's bestowing great appanages on his younger sons. They also insisted on the release of Ferrand of Flanders and Renaud of Boulogne, both of whom had been imprisoned in the Louvre since the battle of Bouvines. This request was granted. (Albericus, *Chron.*, *l.c.*, 595; Mousket, ll. 27500, 27758; Baudoin d'Avesnes, p. 161; Joinville, p. 16; Roger of Wendover, vol. II, p. 315; *Chron. de Saint-Magloire*, l. 7.)

[6] There was a general feeling among the barons that a woman could not rule in France, even as regent. 'It was not her place to do so.' *Chron. S. Denis*, p. 104; Guiart, ll. 9115–16.

ability,[1] appointed as regent, deeming his brother Philip Huripel too young[2] and inexperienced to cope with the organized anarchy then threatening the central power. He chose wisely, for Blanche had already served a worthy apprenticeship in affairs of state.[3] Although the thin, haughty, grimly stubborn Spaniard was understandably antagonistic to the peers, the burghers, lesser nobles, and clergy rallied to her support most valiantly, thus declaring in favour of order and national unity as against turbulent feudality.[4] The perils confronting her daunted her not at all; she determined to maintain the tradition of royalty established by Philip Augustus, cost what it would. Surrounded by a small group of loyal barons[5] whose numbers were increased from time to time as the astute queen beguiled others into temporary quiescence, and by a complete staff of well-tried officials,[6] a legacy to the royal power from Philip Augustus, she was able to thwart the efforts of the malcontents to wrest power from her hands,[7] though not until many petty wars had scarred the land and ruined multitudes of non-combatants by the pitiless

[1] Mousket, *l.c.*, ll. 27145 ff.; *Chron. de Reims*, p. 304; Robert de Sancerre, *Sermon en vers*, *Recueil*, vol. xxiii, p. 127, ll. 75 ff.; Petit-Dutaillis, p. 8.

[2] Philip was then twenty-six. *Chron. de Hain*, clx, 102–03.

[3] Mousket, ll. 27142, 27144; Roger of Wendover, vol. ii, 220–21; Joinville, p. 15; Guil. de Nangis, *Chron.*, p. 517; *Vie de St. Louis par le Confesseur de la Reine Marguerite*, *Recueil*, vol. xx, p. 64.

[4] *Chron. S. Denis*, p. 109; Mousket, ll. 27237, 27266; Robert de Sancerre, *Sermon*, *l.c.*; Guil. de Nangis, *Vita*, p. 314.

[5] Before his death, Louis VIII secured from those barons with him at Montpensier, oaths of allegiance to his young son. These barons, largely ecclesiastics, remained for the most part loyal. Aside from the variable Enguerrand, Theobald, and Philip, Blanche could count on the support of Robert of Dreux, and Henry, his brother, Archbishop of Rheims, and of the lords of Montfort, Montmorency and Beaumont. Mousket, ll. 27234, 27251, 27567; *Chron. de Reims*, p. 303; Le Nain de Tillemont, vol. i, pp. 426–27; Dom Morice, *Histoire de Bretagne*, vol. i, pp. 153–54.

[6] Chief among these was Guérin, the venerable Archbishop of Senlis, who died in 1227. After his death, Blanche's dependence on the papal legate, Romani of the famous Frangipani family of Rome, gave rise to unpleasant rumours. Mousket, ll. 27257, 27299, 27897; Roger of Wendover, vol. ii, p. 315.

[7] Guil. de Nangis, *Vita*, p. 314.

ravaging of their lands, farms, and villages.[1] The allies put forth a brave fight.[2] Aided by the English king,[3] who was casting longing eyes toward Normandy,[4] they harried the royal domains in western France,[5] sending the peasants scurrying into the shelter of walled towns from whence they sent word to their king as to how it was with them,[6] until Louis accompanied by the regent, the cardinal-legate, and the Counts of Boulogne and Dreux, set out for Tours[7] where he summoned the conspirators to meet him. There Theobald of Champagne capitulated,[8] whether because of his romantic love for 'the queen with the fair name,'[9] whether because the recent ravaging of his lands had somewhat subdued his adventurous spirit, or whether fighting itself was too revolting to his poetic soul, certain it is that he made separate terms[10] and shamelessly betrayed the plans of his confederates.

[1] Notably the wars in Champagne, waged first by the king to punish Theobald for his disloyalty, and then by the barons to punish him for deserting their cause. Guil. de Nangis, *Vita*, pp. 312, 314; Guiart, l. 9120; Baudoin d'Avesnes, p. 162; Mousket, ll. 27735, 27965; Dom Morice, *Preuves*, vol. I, pp. 856–57.

[2] La Borderie, *Hist. de Bretagne*, vol. II, p. 311. The allies were strongly established in Poitou, where they held Thouars, and where was the greater part of their forces; in Le Perche, where they held Bellême, and in lower Normandy, where they held the fortress of Saint Jacques de Beuveron. For the letters of confederation, see Chantereau, *Acts* 169–70, and Dom Morice, *Preuves*, vol. I, pp. 856–57.

[3] Duchesne, *History of Coucy*, p. 229; *Chron. St. Denis*, p. 104; Guiart, l. 9134; Rymer, vol. I, p. 289; Mousket, ll. 27742–43; Roger of Wendover, vol. II, p. 316; Baudoin d'Avesnes, p. 162.

[4] In 1228, Henry sent legates to Normandy bearing gifts and entitled to make promises of great privileges should the duchy return to him. Roger of Wendover, vol. II, p. 316. During most of this time, Richard of Cornwall was leading a predatory army across the border of Gascony and Aquitaine.

[5] *Chron. St. Denis*, p. 105; Guiart, l. 9136.

[6] Guil. de Nangis, *Chron.*, *l.c.*, Labbé, *Mélange*, p. 653; Duchesne, *Hist. de Dreux*, p. 327; Lobineau, *Hist. de Bretagne*, vol. I, p. 220.

[7] *Chron. St. Denis*, p. 108.

[8] Guil. de Nangis, *Vita*, p. 314; Mousket, l. 27837; Guiart, l. 9094; Le Nain de Tillemont, vol. I, p. 453. Louis was at Tours, February 20, 1227.

[9] Blanche at this time was about forty, and Theobald not much over twenty-five.

[10] On March 2d. Dom Morice, *Preuves*, vol. I, p. 859.

Poor, fat, slow-witted Theobald! During the next few years he sighed in vain for some token of favour from his elderly lady-love, pouring out his soul in tenderest verse, until even he saw that he was kept dangling merely for policy's sake, and in a fit of temper went over to the allies, who, unable to understand his vacillations and intolerant of his feeble ambition, welcomed him coolly enough. So he was soon back in the royal army, and when the barons were finally forced to submit, he retired to his kingdom of Navarre,[1] where he devoted himself to piety, crusades, and religious poems.

The Counts of Brittany and la Marche refused to pay homage to the king at Tours, but signified their willingness to meet him at Chinon.[2] Arrived at Chinon the next day, the royal party found no one. A message from the barons suggested that the meeting be held at Charrière de Curçai, and there, by means of ambassadors, they spent twenty days in blind conference and rode away.[3] Realizing that he was being trifled with, the king sent so sharp a summons to them to meet him at Vendôme that even they dared not disobey, and a treaty was signed[4] March 21, 1227, with mental reservations on the part of at least two of the barons that it should be broken at the first possible opportunity.[5]

By 1228, Blanche had weakened the league against her,

[1] Theobald inherited Navarre from his mother's brother in 1234.

[2] Guil. de Nangis, *Vita*, p. 314; Mousket, l. 27834; Guiart, l. 9100; Dom Morice, *Histoire*, vol. I, 155.

[3] *Chron. de Tour*, p. 319; Guil. de Nangis, *Vita*, p. 312.

[4] This rather ambiguous treaty is accredited to Blanche. By its terms, Peter was given Bellême and La Perrière, which he promised not to fortify, but to yield to his daughter Yolande as part of her dowry when she married Jean, the brother of Louis IX. As Jean died the next year, the marriage never took place, but Peter kept the castle. De Romanet, *l.c.*, *Pièce Just.*, no. 16, p. 13; Robert of Sancerre, *Serm. en Vers*, l. 229; Mousket, ll. 27851, 27873 ff.; Guiart, ll. 9111 ff.; Guil. de Nangis, *Vita*, p. 314; La Borderie, *l.c.*, vol. III, p. 315; Dom Morice, *Histoire*, p. 155; Lobineau, vol. I, p. 226; Roger of Wendover, vol. II, p. 319.

[5] The Counts of la Marche and Brittany.

although her chief enemy, Peter of Dreux, was again in arms.[1] Peter was Count of Brittany,[2] which fief he held as regent for his son, but he is most generally known as 'Mauclerc' from his renunciation of the priesthood.[3] It is doubtless due to his defection from their ranks that the clergy, the historians of the time, have overemphasized his faults and have quite ignored his natural abilities which were decidedly in evidence, even though they were employed in an unworthy cause.[4] He was quarrel-loving; he was easy at making promises and equally easy at breaking them; he was absolutely regardless of the rights of other men if they stood in the way of the end he sought;[5] and he was disloyal[6] in a time when disloyalty marked the uttermost depths of depravity. But he was also one of the ablest men of that century; valiant, adroit of spirit, clear of mind and unwavering in purpose, generous and high-hearted as a king.[7] Nor does he suffer particularly by contrast with most of the feudal magnates of his day, least of all with his predecessors in Le Perche, who were quite generally held in horror for their lawlessness and for

[1] '*Illius malitiæ caput esse videbatur.*' (Guil. de Nangis, *Vita*, p. 316; Le Nain de Tillemont, vol. I, p. 444.)

[2] Peter married Alix, daughter of Constance of Brittany by her second husband. Alix died in 1221, leaving a minor son for whom Peter held Brittany. Duchesne, *Hist. de Dreux*, p. 327.

[3] Dom Morice, *Histoire*, vol. I, p. 993, note 16.

[4] Peter was continually quarrelling with the priests of Brittany, and was even accused of having murdered one. During most of this period he was under the ban of excommunication. Matt. Paris, *Chron. Maj.*, vol. III, p. 192; *Chron. Tour*, p. 318; Actes de Bretagne, vol. I, p. 86; Duchesne, *Histoire de Dreux*, p. 200.

[5] Matt. Paris, vol. III, p. 191.

[6] Peter was especially bound to support the descendants of Philip Augustus, since that king had arranged his marriage with Alix, thus raising him from the rank of a cleric without a benefice to that of a peer of the realm. He took an oath of loyalty to Philip and his heirs, promising to receive the homage of the lords in Brittany only 'Sauf la fidélété du roi de France, notre Sire.' (Dom Morice, *Histoire*, vol. I, pp. 138, 140.)

[7] Fauchet, *Des Poet. Fran.*, livre 2, CXIII, pp. 107–08; *Hist. Litt. de la France*, vol. XXIII, p. 684; Dom Morice, *Histoire*, vol. I, p. 140; d'Argentré, *Hist. de Bretagne*, p. 189.

their oppression of their subjects.[1] In the autumn of 1228, he was in an evil mood. Many of his fellow barons had been won over to the support of the crown;[2] it became increasingly evident that he was on the losing side, and Peter was not a good loser. The submission forced from him at Vendôme was humiliating enough, and even more galling to his proud spirit was the ignominious frustration of his plot to kidnap the little king[3] the spring before. Enraged by these failures and unable to bring himself to submit to the rule of a woman counselled by a priest and a doddering *vieillard*,[4] he determined to throw the remnants of the Treaty of Vendôme to the winds by fortifying Bellême as a first step towards asserting his independence of the crown.[5]

Now, in 1226, just before Louis VIII started southward on his ill-fated crusade, Bishop William of Châlons-sur-Marne, the last Count of Le Perche, died.[6] Louis took over the fief and then gave La Perrière[7] and Bellême with its castle, as well as Saint Jacques de Beuveron in lower Normandy, to Peter Mauclerc *en garde*,[8] a most unwise move and one bound to create trouble. Peter seldom relin-

[1] Matthew Paris, p. 191. [2] Guil. de Nangis, *Vita*, p. 312.

[3] In the spring of 1228, the barons, under the leadership of Peter, met at Corbeil and made plans to seize the king. The Count of Champagne, then on the side of the regent, took Louis to Orléans from whence he went to Montl'héri or to the neighbouring castle. The presence of the conspirators at Corbeil kept him from proceeding to Paris. Blanche, then in the city, appealed to villagers and burghers for aid, whereupon a volunteer host appeared and escorted him to the door of Notre Dame. Joinville, p. 13; Guil. de Nangis, *Vita*, p. 314; Duchesne, *Hist. de Dreux*, p. 828; *Chron. St. Denis*, p. 104.

[4] This was Barthelmi de la Roie, whose intellect was enfeebled by his great age. For over twenty years he had controlled the Exchequer.

[5] Dom Morice, *Histoire*, vol. I, p. 157; La Borderie, vol. III, p. 311.

[6] De Romanet, p. 63.

[7] La Perrière was situated on the extremity of the forest of Bellême, seven kilometres northwest of the castle. Bart des Boulais, p. 85; Bry, p. 19.

[8] Guil. de Nangis, *Vita*, p. 316: '*Illud castrum a rege Ludovico defuncto autem ut dictum est, idem comes acceperat in custodia.*' *Quer. Norm.*, 113; Guiart, l. 9081; Teulet, *Layettes du Trésor des Chartes*, vol. II, p. 120; *Chron. St. Denis*, p. 105; Dom Morice, *Preuves*, vol. I, p. 852; La Borderie, vol. III, p. 311.

quished what was once in his hands, and castles such as these, not only rich in tithes and forest dues, but also a vantage-ground against Normandy as well as a first line of defence for Brittany, were possessions to fight for. Yet valuable as they were to Peter, they were even more valuable to the ambitious regent, who saw in Mauclerc's leadership a menace to the security of the royal power, and she beset herself to acquire them, regardless of the treaty which gave them to the count. Her father, Alphonso of Castile, had been a cousin of Count Thomas,[1] the predecessor and nephew of Bishop William. On the strength of this kinship, she put forth her claim to Le Perche as the next in line of succession. Peter had nine points of the law in his favour. They were in his hands and he meant to hold them. If the regent wanted them, let her take them if she could; and he gave vent to his anger by renewed devastations in Poitou.[2]

So matters stood in that fruitful year of 1228. But of all of this the Bellêmois knew nothing. Even when Count Peter and his soldiers appeared in the castle early in 1229, they were slow to grasp the situation.

The rocky mass which holds the sea from France along the Breton coast, here in Le Perche dies down into rolling tablelands from which low hills rise gently to rocky crests, and then fall abruptly away to the plain below, their craggy summits furnishing to the mediæval architect an ideal site for strongholds.

As Count Peter looked down from the battlements of the castle crowning this natural fortress, he felt a pardonable confidence that so paltry an army as he planned would rally to the support of the regent [3] would be helpless before

[1] De Romanet, p. 62. [2] *Chron. St. Denis*, p. 105.

[3] Guil. de Nangis, *Vita*, p. 316. The council of barons called by Peter at Corbeil the previous spring had agreed to furnish only two knights each when summoned for service. Theobald of Champagne's appearing with three hundred, then, rather upset Mauclerc's plans.

Bellême. From the southern wall, there was a drop of a sheer hundred feet to the plain below; surely no human power could scale that height. Nor did there seem any imminent danger from the north, where at the foot of the courtyard the strongly walled town came to the very gate of the castle, thus forming a sort of ante-fortress. True, to the east and west, where the *faubourgs* of Saint-Sauveur [1] and Saint-Pierre [2] lay beyond the fortifications, there was less room for security. Indeed, as Count Peter knew, a century before a besieging army had established itself on the very site of Saint-Pierre,[3] and from that vantage-ground had reduced the castle. This was in 1118. In 1202, Count Geoffrey had strengthened the fortress most admirably. Still, that was a quarter of a century ago, and time enough then as now for military architecture to make considerable progress. Peter was sufficiently astute to realize that it behooved him to anticipate every possible contingency a siege might offer. The castle was considered impregnable. It must be made absolutely so. Then it must be well-provisioned. The first thing to do was to replace the overhanging wooden galleries outside the battlements with just such stone corbels as his uncle,[4] Enguerrand the Grand, was building to support the machicolations at Coucy. While the wooden galleries were good points of vantage for hurling missiles directly upon an enemy who might be driving heavily weighted rams against the lower wall, or attempting to loosen the stones with their insidious metal-pointed picks, yet being of wood they were vulnerable to fire-tipped arrows, as many a castle guard had learned to his

[1] The *faubourgs* each contained churches, hospitals, etc. Near the *ville*, the houses were crowded closely, but towards the open country they grew more sparse. The church of Saint-Sauveur is present parish church of Bellême.

[2] The church of Saint-Pierre fell into ruins about 1711. Bart des Boulais, p. 76; Bry, pp. 11, 12, 18, 34; Lobineau, vol. I, p. 225; Teulet, *Layettes*, vol. II, p. 120.

[3] In the reign of Henry I of England. Bry, p. 22.

[4] Peter was the son of Enguerrand's sister, Yolande.

sorrow when the structure had burned away beneath his feet.

Then a foregate on the north between castle and town was even more necessary than the stone corbels. At present there was only a single gate, and although it was built of stout oak heavily faced with metal, it was hardly strong enough to resist those mighty siege engines which Count Peter had seen the royal army use so effectively at Avignon.[1]

And now the troubles of the non-combatants began. In the first place stone had to be provided at once for the masons, and, as there was no time to quarry and shape it, it must be had ready-cut. But where? Count Peter's men cast appraising eyes over town and suburbs. Nothing there. They looked farther and were more fortunate. At Saint-Quentin-de-Blauvon, a thrifty and prosperous village beyond the forest, a miller named Herbert was planning to build a new house. The piles of stone and wood were all ready. To Herbert, these represented years of toil and of self-denial; to Peter's soldiers, non-home-builders as they were, they represented nothing beyond an easy solution of their problem. The change of ownership was rapid and informal. Naturally there were indignant protests from Herbert and his friends. Indeed, the resistance might have been more than merely verbal had not the soldiers suggested reimbursement at a vaguely future day.

The stone was carried off to the castle in Herbert's own stout cart, his very excellent horse and his new harness being requisitioned for the purpose.[2] It seems hardly necessary to add that the promised payment was never made. Herbert appealed to the king's men for redress at the time the court of claims was held, although it was not the king's army that had worked him ill.[3]

[1] *Chron. de Reims*, p. 303. [2] *Quer. Norm.*, no. 122.

[3] Claims were presented for injuries received from Louis VIII as well as from Peter and Louis IX. *Quer. Norm.*, no. 119.

The new gate was built within the *ville*, just beyond the old one, and a most elaborate structure it was, with the portcullis flanked by round towers from which the watchful porters might challenge all who crossed the drawbridge. A new moat, a new barbican, and new palisades were all added, as necessary precaution against a surprise attack. A considerable fortress in itself, it had called for space beyond the castle walls — and in Bellême there was no space. Every foot of the old town along the narrow, tortuous streets was occupied; houses and little shops were built all of the way up to the old gate, the nearest of them leaning against the very castle wall.[1] These were for the most part of timber and valueless to the count and to his engineers. However, they occupied land that was not valueless, and therefore they must be razed. No sooner said than done, for these men of arms were wreckers of houses by vocation and by avocation. The tearful protests of the dispossessed families, who stood by watching the destruction that made them homeless, were to the cynical soldiers but a by-product of the necessary business of war, and no more to be regarded than the cries of birds whose nests are crushed among the broken branches of felled trees.

Rumours of Count Peter's building projects soon spread through the countryside, for all bought and sold in the same markets,[2] and those from other towns heard much from their neighbours of Bellême these wintry days. Apprehension began to disturb the ease resulting from their plentiful harvest. If the count needed to strengthen his defences, it meant war, and war meant the provisioning of the castle. Nearly every village in France had learned by bitter experience by what method or from whose stores

[1] *Quer. Norm.*, no. 127.

[2] The Thursday markets of Bellême were, and still are, noted, as are its fairs held four times a year. Bart des Boulais, p. 79 n.

a castle was likely to be stocked, and the people of Le Perche knew Peter Mauclerc!

The burghers in the *ville* of Bellême were not seriously alarmed. Their stores were within the walls, so the count's servants would not be apt to levy on them unless the town itself were threatened. Therefore, when armed men rode in and out of the castle, those gathered along the streets or leaning out of the narrow windows were less anxious than curious.

But the situation was not so hopeful for their neighbours of Saint-Sauveur and of Saint-Pierre, who in these years of comparative peace had developed into prosperous communities of skilled artisans, workers in iron, weavers and tanners — self-supporting and industrially necessary to their overlords. Their homes were well-furnished and well-provisioned. In most of them might be found just such tiny hordes of money [1] against a rainy day as one would find among their descendants to-day. Conscious of their superiority over the peasants, they had settled down into a comfortable and orderly existence, far removed in their thoughts from the terrible catastrophe of war which even now was hammering at their gates.

As mediæval warfare was largely a matter of endurance on the part of the besieged, preparedness meant the provisioning of the castle with plenty of food — bread, salt-meat, and wine, enough to last for at least a year and a half.[2] The immediate duty, then, of Count Peter's stout Breton soldiers [3] was to secure this provender, and to them the suburbs seemed the logical first source of supply. Not only were they near at hand, but it was necessary that they should be emptied of their stores for, when the enemy came, he would encamp there, seize all moveable property,

[1] *Quer. Norm.*, no. 185.
[2] Guiart, l. 9076; Courtin, p. 269; Le Nain de Tillemont, vol. I, p. 531.
[3] *Chron. St. Denis*, p. 105; Duchesne, *Histoire de Dreux*, p. 329.

and use the land as the base of operations against the castle.

In such an event the inhabitants would be driven within the walls for refuge. Even they might be expected to see that they would have a better chance to enjoy their own grain if Count Peter took it than if they kept it; but, alas! they reckoned in no such way! The supplies were theirs; the count's men said nothing of payment. Furthermore, they did not want war; they saw no reason for war; the enemy's coming was uncertain, while winter was certain, and certain, too, were hunger and cold. Voluble and hot-headed as their descendants to-day, they filled the lanes with their clamour and fought for their own rights, but they had no chance against the count's soldiers who were ready to extort their property from them by violence.[1]

So forced contributions were levied from every home and carried into the castle.[2] Wine, dried peas, cheese, oats, wheat by the cartload, stacks of hay for the horses and of straw for bedding were commandeered on the spot, together with the wagons and horses necessary for transportation. As for the droves of swine which had fattened in the forest during the summer and autumn, these were unceremoniously driven within the castle walls without even a question as to their ownership.[3]

There was one particularly large hoard of grain which rumour said was stored either in the *ville* or in one of the suburbs and which belonged to the Brotherhood of Saint Peter, a local charitable organization. A faithful search of the suburbs failed to disclose its whereabouts; finally it was discovered in Bellême itself in care of Theobald le Faveth, the steward of the Brotherhood. He fought valiantly, and only when he was struck down were the count's men able to secure the nine sextaria of oats and the even

[1] *Quer. Norm.*, nos. 113, 126, 182, 206.

[2] *Ibid.*, nos. 126 bis., 134, 206.

[3] *Ibid.*, nos. 206, 239.

greater quantity of wheat which had been stored away for the relief of the poor.[1] And there were many poor before Count Peter had done preparing for war. What privation war itself would bring men hardly dared think.

After the destroyers departed, the suburbs settled back into life's normal pursuits as men do everywhere after excitement or disaster. True, household cares were heavier because stores were lighter and daily human needs must be met and the day's work done as before. Erelong, beggars were whining out their usual monotonous appeals; pedlars and pilgrims wending their way down the snowy lanes were tarrying at hamlet and sanctuary; alms-gatherers were collecting their mites for the lazar house beyond the walls,[2] and housewives in market-place and men in the tavern were recounting the details of Peter's latest misdeeds. Within the castle walls, artisans and ironmongers, armourers and smiths, tailors, brewers, and butchers were busy adding to the count's stores. The winter set in early that year and was bitter cold. Long afterwards stories were told of its rigour — of the snow that never melted; of wolves made so bold by hunger that whole packs of them entered village and town for food; of wild beasts that perished in woods and fields; of birds lying dead under the hedges and of beggars freezing to death in their corners.[3] But undaunted by the weather, Count Peter busied himself — once the castle was provisioned — laying waste the king's lands until he should appear to take revenge.[4]

He came at last, heralded by rumours, hurried but insistent. Then, shortly after, the dark, slowly moving army was descried in the far distance by the watch on the town wall, the black line gradually turning, as it drew near, into

[1] *Ibid.*, no. 113. The value of this grain was one hundred *sous* equivalent to about three thousand gold francs.

[2] A dependency of Saint Martin's-of-Old-Bellême, founded 1026.

[3] Guil. de Nangis, *Vita*, p. 316; *Chron. St. Denis*, p. 105.

[4] Guiart, l. 9136; *Chron. St. Denis*, *l.c.*

a brave array of glinting lances, enamelled helmets and shields, bright-coloured surcoats and fluttering pennants. However, the russet-clad peasants, watching in sullen despair from behind the hedgerows, saw in this pageantry of war only the cruel force that should rob them of what their industry had created. The medley of armoured knights, of *jongleurs* in parti-coloured mantles, of priests, of sober-clad villagers, of light-armed cavalry, varlets, engineers, sappers, and cross-bowmen guarding the rumbling carts laden with camp-equipage, were to the country-folk merely despoilers of hearth and home, while the formidable supply of machines and siege engines, mangonel, trebuchel, and battering-ram, seemed veritable instruments of the Evil One himself.

There was little time to watch, however. On sight of the army the air became charged with the excitement that anticipation of danger always brings. The blue and gold banner of the Count of Brittany fluttered a haughty défiance from the dungeon tower, and the great bell clanged out an ominous warning. Soldiers were set to cover the hoardings with rawhides; the storehouses of weapons were opened and arms were distributed; messengers were sent to the suburbs to order the inhabitants to bring their cattle and moveables within the walls for shelter. All was noise and confusion. Men and women hurriedly collected what they could carry and stumbled up the hill, a pitiful procession of terror-stricken refugees. Haste was imperative, and the *faubourgs* emptied themselves pell-mell into the *ville*, leaving their houses to the tender mercies of a troop of Count Peter's men, who armed with axes and flaming torches, came rushing through the streets and lanes, battering in closed doors, and setting fire to thatched roofs, so as to make the buildings useless to the enemy, who might otherwise find in them protection against the cold, the most effective ally of the besieged.[1]

[1] *Quer. Norm.*, nos. 126 bis, 127.

As the fugitives pushed through the gate, they stood huddled together uncertain as to what to do next, when along came the soldiers fleeing from before the king's vanguard ere the work of destruction was done, and, forcing a passage through the dense crowd, struck down and trampled all who happened to be in their way.

The kindly burghers did what they could to give comfort to the homeless. After every house was filled, many found shelter in the parish church, never more truly a sanctuary. Little family groups occupied the corners and the floor around the pillars. Bundles were unpacked and children put to bed by the dim light of altar lamps. In a few hours, all had settled down to the grim routine of war. Outside the walls, over toward Sérigni, but in full sight of the castle, the army sat down before Bellême [1] and began to prepare for the siege. Gay tents and pavilions were erected for the soldiers; what few houses had escaped Count Peter's men were put in order for the nobles,[2] and the engineers from Falaise [3] organized their workmen and began the construction of breastworks across the suburbs. From the walls of the town, grim-eyed men watched in impotent rage the ruthless destruction of what their toil and self-denial had accomplished — just as the men of Attica, fifteen hundred years earlier, from behind the Long Walls of Athens had watched the Spartans destroy their farms — just as seven hundred years later, refugees from the villages of France, Belgium, and Italy were to see their houses burned and their treasures scattered.

In 1247, a group of men from Saint-Sauveur and Saint-Pierre appeared in the king's court and claimed forty-six hundred *livres* for the damage they suffered that night at the hands of count or king — for houses burned

[1] *Chron. St. Denis*, p. 105. From Bellême to Sérigni, the land extended in a long plateau.

[2] *Quer. Norm.*, no. 126 bis.

[3] *Chron. St. Denis*, *l.c.*; Guiart, l. 9142.

or destroyed, for vines, trees, and crops trampled to earth, for household goods seized, and for the provision extorted by violence,[1] since what was taken that night was never restored.

The attacking force realized that Count Peter had allies with whom he might communicate by means of the underground passages which had been made under their very feet to undiscovered outlets a considerable distance away. So shifts of varlets, lighted by flickering torches, laboured all through the night, and when morning dawned, the watchmen peering over the battlements saw, in place of the prosperous suburbs of the day before, a newly constructed ditch [2] behind which formidable earthworks faced the frowning walls and towers of Bellême.

Nor did the work of destruction stop here. The king's host must be fed, and, like all mediæval armies, it had brought little or no food in the baggage train. The immediate surroundings of the castle had been levied on to furnish provision for the garrison. Now the outlying hamlets for miles around must give of their stores, not of food alone, but of all that should find favour in the eyes of these battle-scarred veterans, who, in the armies of Philip Augustus and Louis VIII, had foraged from Lincolnshire to Palestine. Along highway and riverbank, one little village followed another in close succession, and each in its turn, Mortagne, the seat of the Counts of Le Perche,[3] prosperous Nogent-le-Rotrou, poverty-stricken Corbon,[4] beautiful Longny, Vaunoise, rich in vineyards,[5] Dame Marie,[6] with its famous priory, the forest village of Eperrais,[7] and Mauves, twelve kilometres away, now felt the heavy hand

[1] *Quer. Norm.*, nos. 114, 146, 149, 169, 198, 200.

[2] Guil. de Nangis, *Vita*, p. 316; *Quer. Norm.*, nos. 114, 136 bis.

[3] *Quer. Norm.*, no. 226.

[4] *Ibid.*, no. 208.

[5] *Ibid.*, nos. 174, 191.

[6] *Ibid.*, nos. 170, 171, 179.

[7] *Ibid.*, no. 198; Bart des Boulais, p. 30.

of the soldier of fortune. Sérigni,[1] already raided by Count Peter, was swept bare as a hermit's cell. Even before camp was pitched, the depredations began, the soldiers carrying off sacks of grain across the backs of their horses,[2] driving herds of swine before them,[3] and guarding with watchful eyes the carts filled with wine-casks, hay, or straw,[4] whose sullen owners knew full well that neither carts nor horses would ever be returned.

Twice as far away as Sérigni, in the heart of the forest, lay the monastery of Saint-Martin's-of-Old-Bellême; hard by was the clean, prosperous little village where well-filled barns and storehouses were a tempting sight for greedy-eyed soldiers. If they had no conscientious objection to laying hands on church property — and few had — a monastery was well worth visiting in any case, and Saint-Martin's was especially so.[5] The village was sacked first — stripped of its stores, of all the small possessions, houschold and personal, in which the genius of home and family seem incorporate, and the loss of which can never be computed.[6] The soldiers turned then from the village to the monastery, where prior and brothers waited, as helpless to save themselves as they had been to save the villagers, and soon the tramp of heavy feet broke the quiet of dormitory and of refectory, even of the very church itself. Rude hands seized vestments and tapestries, enamelled reliquaries and carvings — all that was portable, stopping not even at the desecration of the sacred altar

[1] *Quer. Norm.*, nos. 118, 130, 136, 145, 153, 169, 176, 179, 180, 186, etc. Over fifty complaints for losses of wood, money, houses, grain, etc., were brought in.

[2] *Ibid.*, nos. 114, 120, 126, 136, 143, 169, 181, 208.

[3] *Ibid.*, no. 122.

[4] *Ibid.*, nos. 126, 131.

[5] The priory was a dependency of Saint-Martin-de-Marmoutier, and existed in the eleventh century. The exact date of its foundation is not known, though tradition says the founder was that William of Bellême who was living in 980. Its charter dates from 1050. *Cartulaire de Marmoutier pour Le Perche*, p. 13. Bart des Boulais, p. 30.

[6] *Quer. Norm.*, nos. 126, 129, 143, 185.

vessels. Sadly the monks watched their own carts piled with loot disappear down the road towards Bellême. To them the king kept his promise to pay them for what they had lost, though of the one hundred *livres tournois* which he sent only eleven reached them.[1]

When the hundred and more villagers from Saint-Martin's presented their claims eighteen years later, they spoke only of property damage.[2] What they suffered in the way of personal injury, mutilation, outrage, or death can only be inferred. No compensation could be made for these, and the object of the king's inquiry was to discover wrongs possible of redress. However, between the lines of the accounts of the siege and of the records of the court, one may read how deeply the cruelties and atrocities of this war cut into the lives of the people.

Nor is it difficult to reconstruct the story of privation and hardship in those other villages between Bellême and Mortagne from which supplies were taken. Seldom did mediæval folk store away more than enough for their own needs, even in the years of a plentiful harvest. Now all of that was gone and the villeins stood to learn how very long to hungry folk are the weeks between January and harvest-time and how hard tillage must needs be for those whose horses have gone over to the king.

All the while that the foragers were thus engaged, the royal army was pressing the attack on Bellême. Within a short time they secured possession of the *ville*, although just how the chroniclers do not say, possibly because the burghers were so easily overcome that the incident went unrecorded. At any rate, the town soon became part of the royal camp and the base of operations against the castle. Lodgings were found for the regent, the king, and

[1] *Quer. Norm.*, no. 135.

[2] *Ibid.*, nos. 125, 126, 131, 132, 134, 140, 143, 147, 155, 158, 161, 166, 170, 175, 179, 183, 185.

the tag-ends of the court in abandoned houses near the outer walls of the town. The more fortunate ones, those who could pick and choose, took those well-supplied with food and fuel for which they quite forgot to pay.[1]

Young Louis, outside of lesson hours, had a happy enough time hunting and exploring the country with his knights and squires. To him the gay round tents and wide pavilions had all the aspect of a holiday, and despite the cold and discomfort, he was inclined to look on the siege as a jolly lark. Nor were the soldiers too overburdened with cares. Lacking the ready-made amusements which modern organizations furnish through canteen work, they were forced to provide their own diversions, which they seem to have been quite able to do. On one occasion there was a fire in the camp. Some houses were burned, and apparently the regent was in danger. As a token of gratitude for her escape, they made a snow queen and crowned it with holly. Then they danced about it until the watchers on the wall thought they must have Saint-Guy's dance.

The marshal, however, did not encourage merry-making. He was prepared for a short siege, although he hoped to take the castle by assault. Siege meant delay; delay endangered supplies; in a siege the army was at a disadvantage, for while the garrison could hold out as long as food lasted, the army was extremely likely to diminish as contingents completed the terms for which they owed service, and often enough not even the promise of *deniers* for additional time was potent enough to hold them. For instance, there was Theobald of Champagne whose three hundred knights formed no insignificant part of the army before Bellême.[2] Both marshal and regent remembered well that two years before he had marched away and left Louis VIII in a critical position before Avignon, saying that his forty

[1] *Quer. Norm.*, nos. 135, 126.
[2] Joinville, p. 16.

days' service was rendered.[1] Moreover, the besieging army rarely had food enough to hold the troops together until the castle supplies were exhausted.

Assault was decidedly best. But before it could be attempted the new camp within the walls of the *ville* must be secured against a sally from the garrison by a second wall just before the castle gate.[2] What few houses had escaped Count Peter's ruthless hand could easily be torn down to make way for the fortifications,[3] and enough peasants had been brought in from the neighbouring hamlets to put the work through in short order. If either siege or assault were to succeed, however, something must first be done to protect men and horses from the bitter cold.[4] It was Queen Blanche who devised the plan that saved them, though not a way particularly helpful to the countryside. 'She sent criers through the army to make known to the soldiers that all who desired a reward should cut down trees — nut trees, apple trees, all they could find, and take them to the camp.'[5] For the time being, the rank and file of the army became wood-choppers, hacking down anything they could find to feed the great fires before tents and pavilions. At first they set themselves to felling trees,[6] but a little of such strenuous labour was enough, and when a squad of enterprising varlets, as ingenious as they were lazy, seized and sold her a pile of timber which had been the home of Godfrey the Little,[7] it occurred to the others that the tearing down of houses was more interesting than cutting down trees, besides being more in their line. So house after house in the ville of Bellême and in Sérigni was razed to feed the fires of the king. Nor did they stop at houses. Whatever was

[1] *Chron. de Reims*, p. 307; Mousket, l. 27955; Guil. de Nangis, *Vita*, p. 312; Guiart, l. 9093; Le Nain de Tillemont, vol. I, p. 404.

[2] Duchesne, *Hist. de Dreux*, p. 329.

[3] *Quer. Norm.*, no. 117.

[4] *Chron. St. Denis*, p. 105; Guil. de Nangis, *Vita*, p. 316.

[5] *Chron. St. Denis*, p. 105.

[6] *Quer. Norm.*, nos. 161, 208.

[7] *Ibid.*, no. 130.

inflammable, whatever could be obtained with least effort, was eagerly appropriated.

The first assault on the castle was unsuccessful. 'Those within defended themselves so vigorously that the king's men could accomplish nothing that way. On the morrow the marshal of the host called together those who knew how to mine, and ordered that they construct a mine beneath the foundation of the castle,' [1] for they lacked the modern explosives which have so simplified destruction.

Peasants and sappers were set to work in all haste to dig a great chamber beneath the castle walls, under the shelter of a roof covered with rawhides, and in the meantime, the marshal undertook to draw the fire of the garrison by a cavalry attack. His tactics failed. Before the miners had gone as deeply as they must to force an opening through the walls, they were driven out [2] by the rapid fire of the Bretons, though not until they had filled the hole they had dug with all they could lay their hands on, and had kindled a fire which greatly weakened the castle from below before it was extinguished.[3] As a second attempt seemed out of the question, the besiegers gave up the idea of taking the castle by undermining its walls. Another night of labour by the varlets and engineers, and the next day two siege engines were ready, huge poles hung on pivots between massive uprights. The larger of the two, the powerful Petraria, was the '75' of its day, and so accurate was its aim and so long its range that the lesser engines within the walls were powerless against it. All that the garrison could hope to do was to scatter, by rapid fire of the cross-bowmen, the engineers who loaded the sling, but even here they accomplished little, as the king's bow-

[1] *Chron. St. Denis*, p. 105; Guil. de Nangis, *Vita*, p. 316; Courtin, p. 269.

[2] *Chron. St. Denis*, p. 105; Lobineau, vol. I, p. 226.

[3] Guil. de Nangis, *Chron.*, p. 532; Guiart, ll. 9138, 9144; Le Nain de Tillemont, vol. I, p. 532.

men, stationed near the castle walls, retaliated by charges of small stones from the lesser engine, material for which was amply furnished by the ruined houses of the *ville*.[1] The final day of the siege dawned clear and cold. Hardly was the sun above the horizon when the attack began by a hurricane of stones from trenchbuts and catapults — those vicious little engines so curiously like our own machine guns in their maddening persistency. Then *beffroi* were pushed across the ice-covered moat to shelter the troopers, who were hurling lighted torches and Greek fire over the walls, and the arbalists whose rapid fire of arrows was fast clearing the parapets of their defenders. Above the inferno of the detonation of stones from the Petraria [2] and from the crumbling of houses in the range of Count Peter's engines — above the blare of trumpets ran the royal battle-cry 'Mont-joie Saint-Denis!' answered from behind the walls by the brave 'Saint-Malo! Saint-Malo!'

The Bretons fought with a ferocious valour worthy of a nobler cause, but their courage was outmatched by the superior equipment of the besiegers. Every man within the castle was pressed into service; those who would not fight at the loopholes, supplying fresh armour and dragging off the dead and wounded. Even the women aided by throwing stones and hoops of burning pitch over the walls and by twisting the casting engines. The forces were too unequal for the struggle to last long. Finally a huge stone hurled by the Petraria crashed into the courtyard killing scores of warriors and civilians,[3] for stones discriminated as little as do bombs and shrapnel. The great keep was in flames. Cries of old men and of little children filled the air. Even the indomitable Mauclerc saw that further resistance was impossible, and he surrendered on promise of life and

[1] *Quer. Norm.*, no. 117.
[2] Guil. de Nangis, *Vita*, p. 316; Ducange, pp. 44–45; Sismondi, vol. VII, p. 57.
[3] Guil. de Nangis, *l.c.*

limb for all and courteous treatment of the knights. The gates were opened; the royal troops marched in; king and count took oath on the sacred relics of Saint-Léonard to preserve the peace;[1] and so the castle fell.

The blue and gold standard of Mauclerc, which a few days ago had waved so valiantly from the dungeon tower, now lay torn and dishonoured at the bottom of the moat. In its place the royal standard, the oriflamme, fluttered its red glory against the pitiless grey sky. Above the snow-burdened fields the castle walls stood marred and broken. The great gates, through which the king and his gaily caparisoned knights had ridden in triumph, opened, and the defeated Bretons came out, following their leader dejectedly down the road that led to Brittany:[2] opened again to allow the king's army to pass out, through the village streets, strewn with the wreckage of war, and across the black and desolate plateau of Le Perche:[3] opened yet again, this time to emit a forlorn procession of peasants and burghers for whom there was no longer room in the castle. A piteous sight they were as they stood huddled together, shivering in the icy winds, awed by the deathlike silence brooding over lanes and byways. Indeed, they looked more like hunted animals than like human beings, so dirty and grimy were they, so bedraggled and mud-caked from their days in the crowded castle. Perplexed and bewildered,

[1] Guil. de Nangis, *l.c.*; *Chron. St. Denis*, p. 105; Duchesne, *Hist. de Dreux*, p. 329; Dom Morice, *Histoire*, vol. I, 160; Le Nain de Tillemont, vol. I, 532.

[2] Mauclerc continued his rebellions, aided by various barons and by the King of England, until 1234, when he made a most humiliating submission, entering Paris with a halter around his neck, 'unkempt, dejected, sick with fear and white with shame.' He surrendered Brittany, which was returned to him *en garde* for his son, and promised to accompany Louis on a crusade. He kept this promise, and won great praise from Joinville for his piety and loyalty. In 1248, he accompanied Louis IX to Egypt, was taken prisoner at Mansourah, and died on the way home.

[3] The royal troops stayed long enough to repair and extend the fortifications by piling heavy stone walls on the site of vanished houses, and then withdrew, leaving the castle in charge of a garrison. *Quer. Norm.*, nos. 120, 122, 128, 137, 138, 164, 181, 211.

they felt they must be in an alien land. The new stone walls and ditches extending across *faubourg* and *ville* robbed the scene of all trace of familiarity. Broken glass from the church windows crackled under foot as they stumbled down the slippery roads, trying to distinguish fragments of their own property among the stone-peppered heaps of rubbish.

Erelong, men and women from neighbouring hamlets came hurrying along the muddy lanes, eager for details of misfortunes greater than their own. There was Lucas Bernout of La Perrière;[1] there were Colin de Chevalier and Jean de Moulons and his mother from Appenai;[2] there was the widow Laroise from Igi;[3] there were a score from Saint-Martin's, and even more from Sérigni — all gathering about the homeless ones in the ruined market-place. A moment of dumb wonderment at the devastation before them, and then tongues were loosened. They had tales of their own to tell! Over in Sérigni not a stick was left of Roger Barbin's new house, which had cost all of twenty livres just that year;[4] Jerome Girard's well-stocked barns were now as empty as air;[5] Matthew of Mauves had lost his new cart, harness, and horses,[6] and Gervase of Longpont was 'at the same sign-post';[7] Jean Calabré's best field was turned into a swamp;[8] the good Père Étienne of Saint-Ouen-de-la-Cour had suffered as many damages as if he had been no better than the rest;[9] the widow Emmeline's farm between Sérigni and the *ville* had disappeared in a ditch which also engulfed her house;[10] and the same ditch had spoiled three fields for Raynard Cheverulle;[11] but what could one do?

Gervase of Belloner's mill, not yet paid for, was burned to the ground, and he, poor fellow, unable to face the con-

1 *Quer. Norm.*, no. 144.
2 *Ibid.*, no. 189.
3 *Ibid.*, no. 194.
4 *Ibid.*, no. 130.
5 *Ibid.*, no. 136.
6 *Ibid.*, no. 211.
7 *Ibid.*, no. 206.
8 *Ibid.*, no. 184.
9 *Ibid.*, no. 193.
10 *Ibid.*, no. 137.
11 *Ibid.*, no. 128.

sequences, had disappeared. Sad news this for the Provost Nicholas who had gone Gervase's security; he must now bear a double loss.[1] Verily, a misfortune seldom comes alone!

When the dungeon bell sounded the curfew, the peasants hastened down the hill to reach their homes before dark, while the poor villagers settled themselves as best they could for the night, sheltered by rude camps erected among the débris. What the future held in store for them, they could but dimly guess. However, they knew that out of those heaps of blackened rubbish they must reconstruct their homes, their towns, their old routine of life, and must do it too, without horses, carts, implements, or seeds. Their pastures were empty; their fine horses had been taken over to the king's camp;[2] their implements had gone to feed the king's fires;[3] their seeds treasured for the spring planting had gone to make porridge for the soldiers,[4] while their craftsmen had lost shops, tools, and materials for their labour. Fortunately the siege had been short,[5] so that hunger and the crowding in the castle had not carried pestilence, but this was about the only misfortune they escaped. Ah well, they were not the first to suffer thus, nor would they be the last. Moreover, they knew that they would be powerless to prevent a recurrence of this disaster should the interests of their superiors again clash in their vicinity, and, as best they could, they forgot their sorrows while they slept.

Well for them that they knew only their present misfortunes; that the trials the future would bring as aftermaths of war were as yet unguessed! The coming months were fraught with manifold changes — small in themselves, perhaps trivial to modern eyes, but important enough then.

[1] *Quer. Norm.*, no. 115.

[2] *Ibid.*, nos. 112, 117, 120, 122, 126, 136, 143, 181, 187, 191, 206, 208, 211, 289.

[3] *Ibid.*, no. 198. [4] *Ibid.*, nos. 114, 120, 136, 143.

[5] 'Paucos dies.' Guil. de Nangis, *Vita*, p. 316.

Rights which had come down from father to son, based on custom rather than on definite law, were to be disregarded, partly because there was no proof for the claims, partly because it paid to ignore them.[1] Feudal customs were changed and feudal dues were increased without warning or compensation. There was Robin Hilloin, for instance, who for years had collected certain dues for the royal treasury. He was still to render his thirty *livres* per annum, although he could collect nothing from the impoverished peasants.[2] There were the poor lepers at Mauves, who for well-nigh a century had been allowed the privilege of a collector, that is, some one man who had been freed from all *tailles*, etc., in order that he might solicit alms for them. This privilege was now revoked. Their agent had to pay the same dues as his fellow men. To meet them he must seek regular employment, leaving the lepers to manage as best they could.[3] There was Thomas Calabré, the royal forester, who had inherited his office and dignity from generations of ancestors. He had to surrender both to a newcomer appointed to represent the king in the management of the forests.[4] Over in Sérigni was Colin Marcion whose mill had been destroyed by the king's men in their search for fuel. It would take him three years to rebuild, and then his customers, who during this time had gone to the king's mill at Monte Restout, would not be allowed to return.[5]

The forest, hitherto profitable to peasants, a source of pleasure to the nobles,[6] and fundamentally useful in the economic life of all classes,[7] was henceforth under a new régime. No longer could the nuts and herbage furnish pasturage for pigs, goats, and cows,[8] nor could fagots of dead boughs be carried home on the backs of donkeys for fire-

[1] *Quer. Norm.*, nos. 116, 121, 131.
[2] *Ibid.*, no. 223.
[3] *Ibid.*, no. 225. See also nos. 111, 156.
[4] *Ibid.*, no. 141.
[5] *Ibid.*, no. 118. See also nos. 123, 124, 159, 182.
[6] *Ibid.*, no. 163.
[7] *Ibid.*
[8] *Ibid.*, nos. 120, 208, 221, 222, 227, 229, 238.

wood;[1] nor — and this was truly serious in days of reconstruction — could its timber be used to repair damaged property. Neither could they foresee the new taxes they must pay — taxes on what they bought and taxes on what they sold;[2] nor that their buying and selling would be restricted to the royal markets. They were even to be taxed in order that the hall given them by Count Geoffrey in payment for land he had taken from them might be rebuilt.[3]

Such are a few of the traceable results of a siege of seven hundred years ago, on the people of this little district of northern France. It was not long nor famous, yet its effects on the non-combatants were so great that in 1247, four hundred and five out of four hundred and eighty-two complaints made at Mortagne were connected with it. It cost more than fifteen thousand *livres* in damage to land,[4] grain, timber and vineyards; in the loss of carts, horses, mills, forests, household goods, pigs, wine, peas, straw and hay.[5] It meant the confusion of feudal rights,[6] the loss of privileges,[7] the imposition of new taxes and duties.[8]

In the history of the growth of the French monarchy, the war was a matter of slightest importance, but it brought to these happy-hearted peasants, who in the preceding autumn had reaped their plentiful harvest in tranquillity, a supreme disaster, teaching them that in the royal plan neither they nor theirs counted in the least.

[1] *Quer. Norm.*, nos. 135, 139, 208, 221, 222, 229.

[2] *Ibid.*, nos. 111, 134, 160, 219, 223, 226, 228. [3] *Ibid.*, no. 135.

[4] *Ibid.*, nos. 112, 125, 126 bis., 127, 131, 140, 142, 164, 184.

[5] *Ibid.*, nos. 115, 117, 120, 122, 125, 126, 126 bis., 131, 132, 135, 136, 140, 141, 143, 155, 161, 163, 169, 189, 198, 208, 211, 218, 219, 223, 225, 229, 230, 289.

[6] *Ibid.*, nos. 126, 131, 159, 182, 219, 223, 229.

[7] *Ibid.*, nos. 116, 121, 160, 162, 163, 165, 166, 167, 185, 206, 219, 226.

[8] *Ibid.*, nos. 134, 160.

CHAPTER II

GLIMPSES OF MEDIÆVAL LIFE

(Among the fragments of studies found with Miss Davison's papers was this incomplete account of the adventures of a thirteenth-century merchant of Marseilles at the Fair of May at Provins. She had taken him no farther than his arrival, however, and, as she left no suggestion as to what was to follow, it has seemed best not to add what would be a purely conjectural and arbitrary conclusion. What is given here has been rewritten, but nothing has been added to her sketch; all that is new material is included in the notes. G. R. B. R.)

1. *A Merchant Prince of Long Ago*

It was early spring in the year 1234, busiest of all seasons in Marseilles. The port was full of vessels [1] awaiting their cargoes for the Levant,[2] for Tunis and for Spain. The Fair of May at Provins,[3] most important of those held in the north, was about to open. For weeks, Bernard de Manduel and his brother Jean,[4] young merchants of the city, had been preparing their wares to send to Champagne. Now the huge bales of rich Oriental silks and brocades were corded; [5] the boxes filled with sandal from Tripoli, coral from Acre, alum from Aleppo, indigo from Bagdad, aloes from Arabia, azure (powdered lapis-lazuli), precious drugs and preserved fruits, had all been sealed; vases of enamel and rare glass were safely wrapped in cotton and hemp; dyestuffs, so desired by the weavers of Flanders, were sorted and labelled; invoices were finished; experienced and reliable carriers, able to guard the caravan along the way, had been engaged. To-morrow at sunrise the pack-mules would be loaded for the journey.[6]

It was in truth a great adventure, this taking of eastern merchandise to the great fairs, exchanging it for iron, wood, and cutlery to be shipped to the Mediterranean ports. It was Jean's first trip,[7] and on its success depended his career as a merchant. In a way it marked the end of the apprenticeship he had begun under his father, Stephen, founder of the house of de Manduel, and had continued under Bernard's able leadership.[8] But he knew well what profit the goods should bring and what he should pay for those he took in return, so he felt no qualms as to his success.

It was from just such enterprises wisely undertaken that Stephen had acquired his wealth.[9] In the closing years of the preceding century, he had come from Arles to Marseilles with less than a hundred pounds.[10] His first trip had been to Messina,[11] whither he had sailed with Pierre Vital and Barthelmy Mazellier, investing in a cargo of bacon, hides, licorice, jewels, and enamels, which had sold to such advantage that he had made further ventures in Sicily and in Italy, sometimes going himself, sometimes lending money to others.[12] At the end of ten years he had been drawn into the great tide of Levantine trade with Pierre,[13] by that time master of his own ship, de Olivia. God was ever good, and the fortunes of the sea favoured them, so that they brought back their own with increase.

At first when Stephen's capital was limited, he was forced to make quick sales; later, as he grew more prosperous and could afford to wait for his money, he took cotton or spices and sold them to Ceuta, Oran or Bougie, receiving amber, camphor, hats, and horses, leather, grain, and cloth.[14] In 1219, he owned a share in the Santa Cruza, and a little later had his own warehouse near Poissoner, a centre of Mussulman trade.[15]

When he died in 1230, his sons stood high among the burghers of Marseilles as men of dignity and influence. There were many such merchants there then, living in the closely packed, narrow streets of the vicomte's town,[16] and with their wealth[17] they had purchased[18] freedom so that they dealt with the world according to their own pleasure. The last year had been difficult for the city; for three long months it had been besieged by Raymond Bérenger, during which time no vessels had entered or left the port. But now, since peace was declared, prospects were brighter, and Bernard and Jean were anticipating years of prosperity in which they should build their own fortunes to the advantage of the city and should leave their sons in a position to uphold and increase its power and fame. A treaty with Arles had secured for Marseilles consular rights there,[19] which meant added advantages, as that was the most important imperial city in that region.

All things seemed to promise a prosperous trip, and Jean set forth that mid-April morning with a high heart. At daybreak the cavalcade of merchants and their followers passed through the *porte*[20] and took the highway that led to Arles. Since carts and wagons were difficult to defend and inconvenient where the roads were bad and the fords deep, the carriers engaged for the transportation of goods were bound by contract to use only sumpter beasts, so the line was long.[21]

However, these merchants felt no anxiety about themselves, since both the King of France and the Count of Champagne saw to it that the safe conduct of fairs should be observed.[22] Indeed, as such travellers were a source of income[23] to the lands they crossed, it was decidedly to the advantage of the barons to protect them.

Following the hill-road to Arles, they were joined by merchants from Montpellier, and here they rested long enough to organize themselves into a '*universitas*,'[24] electing a captain from the Montpellier group[25] who should assume responsibility for the trip, represent them in the cities through which they passed, and act as their advocate at the fair.[26] Then they set forth for Provins.

They did not find the roads from Arles to Champagne

in good repair despite the tolls collected for their maintenance,[27] but they were fairly safe.[28] At each ford or bridge, the great opportunities of highwaymen, stood a cross symbolizing the peace of the road.[29] As the guarantee of safety ended at sunset, they were forced to travel only by day, but, since this was one of the main thoroughfares into central France, the inns were frequent. True, they were not always comfortable,[30] and at this season were very crowded, but Jean found his fellow lodgers merry and good-natured and full of strange tales of adventure.

Following the Rhone to Lyons they crossed to the Loire Valley, went north to Nevers, then across country to Vézelay on the Yvonne, thence to Sens,[31] where they branched eastward from the Paris road and soon entered the open pastures and wooded hills of Champagne. It was late one afternoon in May that they caught their first glimpse of many-towered Provins,[32] so beloved of her counts, rising above the turreted walls. At the foot of the hill nestled between the Voulzie and the Duretin was the little daughter city, the *ville basse*.

Entering the Porte de Troyes, they passed along the narrow streets, past Saint-Ayoul,[33] Notre-Dame-du-Val,[34] and the newly built Sainte Croix,[35] crossed the old stone Pont-au-Poisson which connected the upper town with the lower, and joined the procession of merchants who like themselves were hurrying to secure places during the first eight days of the fair when ingress was free.[36] They wended their way up the slope of the hill to the Place du Châtel, sought out their *halle*, unloaded their wares, and with their horses returned to the lower town, where they were to lodge in the great *maison* reserved for those from the south.

Then followed busy days, arranging their merchandise that it might be inspected before the formal opening. Provins had no one *camp de foire*, as had Paris, for example;

all operations were confined to the *places* and *ruelles* of the *ville.* Stalls were in the Place des Changes, the Place du Châtel, and the Place Saint-Jean, in the upper town and in the Place Saint-Ayoul in the lower. Before the Grosse-Tour,[37] the churches, the *halles,* the Bourg-Neuf, and down the side-streets, tanners, pastry-cooks, jewellers, were busy setting forth whatever seemed likely to please the passer-by.[38]

Like the Flemish merchants and others who came regularly to the fair,[39] the merchants from Toulouse had permanent quarters in which to exhibit their wares,[40] and Jean was soon engaged in storing his bales in the great subterranean vaults of the Hôtel Forcodas [41] and in arranging for exhibition, in the lofty vaulted hall above, his drugs, spices, and rare craftwork from the Orient.

Then he went forth to inspect the stalls and shops of the other merchants and to make his selections. The cloths were exhibited first; in the *halle* of Ypres he found the finest textures and the brightest colours: scarlet, pale rose, purple, grey, and green; the weavers from Douai had sent quantities of brunette cloth;[42] the silks of Cevennes were what he needed for Tunis; and the *étamine* from Arras, the metal, leather, and iron from the north were for Sicily and Spain.

Descending into the lower town, he found the products of Provins already widely famed for their quality.[43] Here, too, were the stalls for food,[44] the horse market,[45] in front of Saint-Ayoul, and on the Pont-au-Poisson every known variety of fish.

At every step in the old town and in the new were the large, round stones and plates on which were paid the rents of the fair; those due the abbey of the Paraclete were in the rue Saint Nicholas; those for the fief of Bonne Aventure in the rue Murot; those of the Cordelières at the corner of the rues Sire-Hugues and des Lions.[46]

On the ninth day the cry of 'Hare! Hare!'[47] signalled the formal opening of the fair, and from the loggia, where the *changeurs* were seated behind their money tables,[48] the *règle de fer* was deposited and other weights and measures.[49] Time and manner of payment[50] were announced. Here, too, as the days passed, the guardians of the fair heard complaints and administered justice.[51] It was no easy matter for so many different nationalities[52] to transact business without misunderstandings, and, accustomed as Jean was to the babel of tongues in the port of Marseilles, he found them even more confusing here: Lombards, Genoese, Flemings, English, Spaniards, all bargaining at once and each in his own currency as well as in his own language. More than once it was necessary to apply for assistance to the *courrier*, a disinterested functionary belonging to none and to all, whose business it was to act as interpreter and to bring together all who desired to barter their commodities.

Along with the inspecting and bargaining, there was no end of revelry: buffoons and *baladins* established themselves before the loggias; strange tropical animals, dark-skinned women, human monstrosities, veritable *filles du diable*, were exhibited. Trained dogs and monkeys[53] were put through their tricks; poets and minstrels sang their lays or recited old *fabliaux* loved by the crowd, and pilgrims related their adventures. The *Confrères de la Passion* erected rude sheds and gave a mystery. Many there were, especially the young nobles,[54] who had come simply for the amusement provided; others, whose aims were less innocent, came and remained as long as they could elude the watchful guards who patrolled the streets day and night accompanied by a sort of military music, which at the close of the day sounded the curfew.[55]

(Another incomplete study centering about the fairs is that of Hervis de Metz, drawn from the romance of that name, one of the Lorraine Cycle and composed by the trouvère, Jean de Flagy, at the close of the twelfth or opening of the thirteenth century. Miss Davison left no record of the manuscript or edition of this poem she consulted, but, in preparing it for publication, the manuscript in the Bibliothèque de l'Arsenal, no. 181, was used. As it is not overlong, no references are given to the verses. G. R. B. R.)

2. *Hervis of Metz*

In the seventh century, the old Duke of Lorraine, being heavily in debt owing to his thoughtless generosity, found himself unable to provide a *dot* for his only child, Ayelis '*au cler vis*.' He consulted his friends who advised him to offer her to the wealthy merchant Thierri, also his *prévôt*, and to promise him the succession to the duchy. Thierri was at first so overcome by the great honour that he declined, but was finally persuaded to accede to the proposition. Immediately after the wedding took place, the Duke departed for the Holy Sepulchre.

In the course of time a son was born to Thierri and Ayelis, who was given the name of his father's brother, Hervis. His mother supervised his education and saw that he was taught to read, write and abbreviate. He was also instructed in the game of checkers and in feats of horsemanship in which he distinguished himself far more than he did in intellectual pursuits.

When he was fifteen, his father planned to send him to the fairs to seek his fortune by buying and selling cloth. The boy was apparently unwilling to follow in the footsteps of the plebeian Thierri, and protested that he knew nothing of such matters; he suggested that his father equip him with horse and arms and let him go to the tourneys of France where his knowledge of horses and falcons would bring him high renown. Thierri was very angry and would have beaten him had not Ayelis interfered. Yielding to his mother's entreaties rather than to his father's threat to put him on less than bread and water if he did not go and return with good success, Hervis rather sullenly assented, saying, however, that he would buy '*mon boin et mon plaisir*.' His father took him to the castle gate, gave him four thousand marks of gold and silver, and, charging him to be economical, sent him forth with his uncle.

Arriving at Provins, Hervis showed as little interest in the cloth of Flanders and jewels of Paris as might have been expected. He secured quarters at the best hostel, one in the lower town, and began to entertain lavishly. The first night he had eighty guests, the next, one hundred and sixty, the next, two hundred and forty, and the next, three hundred and twenty. In eight days he had spent over a thousand marks on wine, women, and falcons, Arab steeds, and a greyhound, 'more white than a *fleur-de-lys*,' for which he had bargained most cleverly, as became the son of a merchant father.

His uncle sent news of his prodigality to his father, who ordered him home, a command he took his time in obeying. Then followed another noisy quarrel in which Ayelis again acted as peacemaker. Hervis was kept at home all through the summer, but what his fare was is not told.

By Christmas time, his father's ire had cooled somewhat and he sent the boy forth again, this time with three uncles, to the Fair of Lagny near Paris with sixteen thousand marks to purchase '*vair et gris*.' Hervis promised his mother that this time he would obey his father and not squander the money, but, alas, almost as soon as he arrived, he was riding outside the city walls and met ten squires with a beautiful damsel whom they were taking to the fair to sell as a slave. Enflamed by her beauty, he asked the men who she was.

'A maiden,' was the reply.

'That I perceive is true, but where did you find her?'

'Far from here; more than sixty days' journey, and we are going to sell her at this fair.'

'But who is her father? What is her name?'

'We know neither,' they said.

So Hervis dismounted, went to the damsel and asked who she was. She told him that her name was Biautris, but would say nothing of her family save that she was a chaste maiden.

After some parley, Hervis paid her ransom, fifteen thousand marks, and returned to the hostel. Three youths, the son of the *prévôt* of the *ville*, the nephew of the abbot, and the third who is unnamed, had seen the transaction, and themselves desiring the maiden, undertook to fight Hervis for her. He purchased weapons from the innkeeper, fought them in the market-place, and killed two. By this time he had barely enough left of his money to get him back to Metz. Biautris was unwilling to return with him and tried to persuade him to remain at the fair, but he told her he was going to take her to his castle and marry her and that eventually she would be a duchess.

After many conventional adventures, they arrived at the castle. Not even his mother could save him this time from his father's wrath, and the two were turned from the door. Fortunately, Hervis had a half-sister, married and living in the village, a woman full of *bonté*, who received them and arranged their marriage.

All of this time Biautris had refused to reveal her identity. As she saw her young husband wasting his brother-in-law's substance with as great indifference as he had wasted his father's and realized the hardships the worthy pair were enduring on their account, she took matters into her own hands. She sent Hervis to the fair at Senlis to buy her some thread of gold and rich silk and some samnite, and while he wasted time in a tournament, he did not go so far as on the previous occasions. Hiding herself from all, Biautris made four beautiful pieces of embroidery and wrapping them in a scarf sent Hervis with them to the fair of Tyr, trusting to his penniless condition to keep him out of mischief. She gave him minute directions; she told him what to buy and what to pay; he was not to patronize those merchants whose stalls were near the gate, as their prices were too high. He must lodge with one Baudris, and he should pay but thirty-two silver marks for six weeks' entertainment. If Baudris noticed his shabby clothes, he must say that he had dressed so purposely in order to make the robbers think he was a pilgrim; if Baudris seemed troubled because he had no wares, he was to say they were on the way, and he must buy Arab horses and cloth, to be paid for at the close of the fair. Her embroidery was to be displayed in a stall near the centre of the town. The first day he was to ask two thousand marks for it; if any one objected to that as being exorbitant, he was to double the price; and to continue doubling it at every objection.

Hervis obeyed her instructions rather better than he had his father's. His propensity for entertaining, however, got the better of him and he dined the dignitaries of the town at Baudris' expense until that worthy man declared he was ruined. He said that ever since the loss of his dear mistress, Biautris, he had had nothing but bad luck. Hervis, much surprised, questioned him and found out that his wife, whom he had been disinherited for marrying, was the daughter of the King of Cyprus and Tyre and sister of Flores, King of Hungary. She had been promised in marriage to the elderly King of Spain (then almost forty years old) and her father had engaged to send her to him after two months. Then, leaving her in charge of Baudris, he had gone to Hungary to consult with his son regarding the terms of the alliance. One morning while Biautris was in her garden, her maidens heard voices beyond the walls which they recognized as those of their own lovers, and got her permission to leave her while they visited with the young men. As she sat alone, listening to the nightingales, ten armed knights appeared, bound her and carried her off. This was all that Baudris knew. However, Biautris had embroidered her portrait on one of the pieces of cloth and this proved to Hervis the identity of his wife.

The next day he put his cloth on the market, and one of the first to pass by was King Flores, who also recognized the embroidery. To his urgent questioning as to where it had come from, Hervis explained that he had bought the cloth from Seville in Spain, but as he was a mere merchant he had no way of knowing who had made it. Flores found the price too high, but when he returned the next day, Hervis had doubled it. Flores was at his father's castle where he had been ever since his sister's disappearance. When he told the king of the embroidery, the latter went to the fair in order to see it and was so overcome at the sight of his daughter's handiwork that he paid Hervis his price, then thirty-two thousand marks.

Of course he learned who the merchant was, and had news of his daughter. Hervis returned home by way of Rome and was joyfully received by Biautris. Nor did Thierri withhold his blessing when he discovered that his son was now wealthy and that Biautris was of even higher lineage than her husband. After a long series of insipid adventures, the chief of which was the deliverance of Metz from Pepin, he died while in the Holy Land. All of the details of the fair at Tyr are very similar to what is known of those held in Champagne, even to the beggars at the gate asking alms for the love of Christ.

(The following sketches are simply a compilation of the material Miss Davison had collected for a background of some studies she intended to make of personages who to her embodied certain neglected aspects of thirteenth-century life. G. R. B. R.)

3. *Paris in the Thirteenth Century*

DESPITE the squalid hovels and the low houses huddled over the narrow streets which characterized thirteenth-century Paris, there were signs and manifestations of an increasing refinement in the daily life of the upper classes. Windows were glazed or at least were covered with semi-transparent horn; fresh rushes were strewn daily in the halls; dogs slept in kennels apart from the common rooms of the family; such domestic offices as pantries and butteries were provided for the managers of the household, and in the palaces, at least, the old stone walls were whitened or covered with tapestries.

Paris was no longer the little village of the early Capetians, although it was still distinguished for the mud which had given it its original name; Philip Augustus had endeavoured to pave the main thoroughfares, but it proved to be a rather larger task than he supposed, and even the most important streets were unfinished at his death and were impracticable for carriages during the bad season throughout the whole thirteenth century.

This was an age of building. Churches, monasteries, and hostels for scholars were erected by private individuals and by the churches. Philip of Dreux, Bishop of Beauvais, who died in 1217, willed to the poor clerks of Saint Thomas of the Louvre fifteen pounds to aid them in building a church; and to those of Saint Nicholas, he gave fifty pounds to erect a house. As the two groups of scholars were near the Louvre, it was thought that they could use the same church, but the plan caused so much trouble that they were finally separated and the scholars of Saint Nicholas obtained from the Bishop of Paris permission to have a chapel and cemetery for themselves and their domestics in the neighbouring parish of Saint-Germain l'Auxerrois. In 1226, they formed a confraternity with the abbeys of Saint Denis and most of the monastic houses of the diocese, which lasted until 1540.

The Cistercian church of Saint Antony was enlarged and decorated by the piety and munificence of Louis IX in 1233. These monks claimed to have been given the fourteen arpens of land on which the monastery was built, as well as two hundred arpens between Paris and Vincennes, by Louis VIII, as a thank offering on the occasion of the birth of his second son.

In 1202, the Hôpital de la Croix de la Reine, later Trinity, was founded by two brothers, Jean Pale and Guillaume Estuacol, in the parish of Saint-Germain l'Auxerrois, under the superintendence of the dean and chapter of the church. The Bishop of Paris gave them permission to build a chapel for the use of pilgrims and the poor. It was not to have a bell, nor was it to exercise any curial function without the consent of Saint-Germain, to which church it was to pay six shillings per annum, as well as three shillings to the dean, three to the curé, and five to the chapter. The chaplain was installed by the bishop to whom he had to take oath not to usurp the rights of the collegiate church. Five years later, finding their poverty oppressive, they petitioned for a bell. The dean and chapter of Saint-Germain objecting, they submitted the request to the bishop, who granted it on condition that they double their rent, a burden which one Robert Ferpier and his wife assumed out of mercy for the poor brethren.

About the same time, Saint-Honoré was founded by Renold Chereins, who gave nine arpens of land outside the city walls on the road to Clichy for that purpose. Estienne Bélot and his wife Ada, *bourgeois* of Paris, built a house by Saint-Honoré to aid thirteen scholars; this was the origin of the college or hospital of Bons Enfants. They also furnished the beds and set aside a certain amount of their property to secure the foundations of a prebend. On the greater festivals, these scholars sang for the king and helped him to distribute alms.

The Trinitarian monks, called Mathurins from their founder, Jean de Mathieu, a Provençal, were established in Paris before 1209. At first they were a most austere order, rode only on a donkey, from whence their name, *Frères aux Aines*. Their chief function was to buy Christian slaves from the hands of the infidels.

Paris was divided into three sections: the *cité*, on the island; the *ville*, that part north of the river; and the university, to the south. The *cité*, which contained the Hôtel Dieu, Notre Dame, and the Palais, was connected with the mainland by bridges: the Grand Pont or Pont au Change on the north was defended by the castle, the residence of the *prévôt*, who rendered justice in the king's name. On the south was the Petit Pont, on which had existed from ancient times the *bureau de péage*. At the end of this bridge was a gate for the defence of the city, while in the centre, by the Petit Châtel, was held the *marché aux graines*. The Petit Pont was bordered with shops and houses, twenty-eight book-sellers being listed among them. The banks of the Seine were peopled with artisans grouped around church and chapel. In 1206, a great inundation submerged these, and one ten years later broke all bridges. The semi-circular walls, on which Philip Augustus spent twenty years, enclosed monastic lands and vineyards as well as buildings. To the south of the river were the Dominican monasteries, the church of Saint-Étienne, then merely a chapel, Saint-Severin, Saint-Julien-le-Pauvre, and Sainte-Geneviève. This last church belonged to the old abbey. Three hundred years before, it had been burned by the Normans and the walls had fallen into ruins. Stephen de Tournay, abbot from 1177 to 1192, restored the edifice, rebuilt the walls, and covered the roofs with lead. He also reëstablished the chapels, cloisters, refectory, labouring at the same time with equal zeal to restore the discipline and to create a love of piety and of letters.

Three circles of walls, the outer one a mile in diameter, enclosed the *ville* and the university. The inner wall surrounded the island. It was higher and more beautiful than either of the others; the second, some remains of which are still standing, began at the Porte de Paris near the Grande Ponte, crossed the rue Saint-Denis, and from there ran between the rue des Lombards and the abbey of Saint-Magloire, where it turned to the rue Saint-Martin, disappeared behind the cloisters of Saint-Merry, and reissued at the port of Saint-Médéric, opposite the *Maison du Fléau*. Then following the rue de la Verrière to rue des Deux Portes, it was joined to a huge tower still standing, crossed the rue de la Tixeranderie past the cloister of Saint-Jacques, ended in the Tour de Pet au Diable, and so on to the river between Saint-Jacques and La Grève.

The outer ramparts commenced at the bridge of the old Louvre near the middle of the court of the new building, ran to rue Saint-Honoré, across the house of the priests of the oratory, passed between the rue d'Orléans and rue de Grenelle, then to rue Coquillière, and from there crossed to the Hôtel de Soissons. After this they extended to rue Montmartre between rue de Jour and rue Plasterie on to the Pointe Saint-Eustache and rue Quiquetonne. At last it wandered between the rues Mauconsel, Paver, du Petit-lion, aux Oues, Grande and Petit Heulin, Grenier, Saint-Ladre and Cour de Mose, Michel, comte Geoffrey l'Angevin, and, having crossed the Blancs Manteaux and Sainte-Anastase, ended at the river.

On the south side the walls began at La Tournelle, continued behind the Collèges des Cardinals de Moine and des Bons-Enfants along behind Sainte-Geneviève. Four towers at the extremities of the walls formed an extra defence: the Tour de Bailly and Tour de Bois on the north and on the south, the Tour de Tournelle and Tour de Nesle. Great chains across the river added to the defence of the city. Beyond the ramparts was the strong squat tower of the Louvre built by Philip Augustus from the onerous taxes levied on all church lands. Here famous prisoners were lodged, among whom was Ferrand of Flanders taken captive at Bouvines.

The schools to which Paris owed her fame were never more prosperous than they were under Philip Augustus and Louis IX, both of whom called hither the most erudite scholars to give instruction in science and arts. The public schools were born in the episcopal mansion and in the royal palaces, the one for clerks and the other for nobles. By the twelfth century they had made such progress that more spacious quarters were needed than the close or the palace court provided. Despite the fact that new ones were set up at Sainte-Geneviève and at Saint-Victor, the canons and bishops found themselves uncomfortable by the great number of students, who disturbed their peace and prevented the full exercise of their piety. Gerbert, bishop in the early twelfth century, tried to remedy this by passing disciplinary laws, but his efforts were futile. His successor solved the problem to a certain extent by decreeing that all scholars not clerics were not to lodge in the cloisters reserved for canons nor were they to have classes there, but were confined to the region between the episcopal palace and the Hôtel Dieu, a division confirmed later in the charter of 1257.

The schools were not confined to the isle and Saint-Victor and Sainte-Geneviève; famous doctors began teaching in the quarter later called the University even before the twelfth century. Here the youth could lodge more comfortably and breathe a purer air than in the *cité,* facts which contributed to the health of the body and to the vigour of the spirit.

The church of Saint-Julien-le-Pauvre divided with Notre-Dame the honour of sheltering letters and arts. The rectors were elected there, and while theology was restricted to Notre-Dame, it seems fairly certain that the humanities were taught at Saint-Julien, and later on, medicine and law as well as the courses leading to the master of arts. The Bishop of Paris long retained jurisdiction over the doctorate in theology and ordered those teaching this subject on pain of ecclesiastical censure to teach between the two bridges. The monks of Saint-Germain contested this privilege and claimed to have the right of teaching all sciences within their own walls.[56]

While Paris was never preëminently a commercial city, the increase of population in the latter half of the eleventh century, after Philip Augustus had brought the provinces under royal control, encouraged fairs and markets and the movement was aided by the patronage and protection afforded merchants by the crown. The rivers flowing into the Seine near Paris had opened the interior of the country to navigation as early as the Roman days. All through the Middle Ages goods were sent and received by the river. Although no sailing vessel came into the Seine, the arms of the city was a *bateau. Marchands de l'eau* were early instituted, who came in time to be considered as *prévôts* of all commerce. Land trade developed more slowly and was always less important than that of the rivers.

La Grève, with its rows of piles, on the right bank, was the most ancient port. In 1141, the land had been given the *bourgeoisie* by Louis VII for this purpose.[57] Another port was on the left bank below the Petit Pont, and still another at the western extremity opposite the École Saint-Germain. In 1213, a charter of Philip Augustus levied a tax on the wines taken by the merchants to pay for this port.[58]

The chief *prévôt* of the merchants was regarded as representing the *bourgeoisie.* With four others he judged breaches of rules, supervised pilots, and those who sold wine, salt, carbon, wheat, wood, etc., and fixed the salaries of their employees.

The first market was between the monastery of Saint-Éloi and the street or road leading from one bridge to the other, and called, until the very eve of the Revolution, the rue de la Marché Palu. Other markets were soon established at *Les Halles* and at La Grève. In all, each branch of commerce had its appointed stalls for produce of the town, of the *faubourgs* and of the neighbouring villages. While the articles sold varied widely, there were few luxuries, as the Parisians were very frugal. Many documents exist to prove that the wares sold in markets could not be sold elsewhere on those days.

The artisans lived on the streets near the *halles,* as some of the names still in use bear witness; e.g., the rue de la Tisseranderie, rue de la Mortillerie, rue de la Tannerie, rue de Boulangers, etc. Those industries needing water were naturally near the river or some brook emptying into it. The mills were for the most part under the Grande Pont and the bakeries were not far away. The great abbeys had their own ovens, and the residents of those parishes had to bake there, a requirement difficult to enforce, as very often there was confusion as to who owed this right, since the parish lines were not distinctly drawn.

The more important fairs held at Paris were those of Saint-Germain, Saint-Ladre, and La Lendit, each of which lasted a fortnight. The first of these was held in the *bourg* of Saint-Germain. The abbot of the monastery controlled the administration of justice and the revenues. That of Saint-Ladre was held by the leprosy of Saint-Lazare outside the city until Philip Augustus bought it and transferred it to the great market at *Les Halles*, in 1181. Here there was a great space of enclosed sheds surrounded by walls and with huge gates. The king added appreciably to his revenue by taxing all who attended, *changeurs*, furriers, merchants of silk, of wax, salt, etc. Apparently the amount levied was considered an extortion, for while some of the *métiers* found their gains compensated for the charges of removal of their business and for the taxes, others, such as the butchers, paid the king for the privilege of not attending.

The fair was sometimes farmed by the king to officials, who collected imposts and administered justice, acting as a sort of monarch of *Les Halles* with powers as absolute as those exercised in the royal domain.

During this fair the royal standard of weights was kept in the neighbouring rue des Lombards. The use of this was obligatory, and the user was liable to an impost. In the fourteenth century these standards were turned over to the *bourgeoisie*.

The June Fair, La Lendit, was held in the plain of Saint-Denis. It was most popular with the Parisians and drew immense crowds of merchants, foreigners, scholars of the university, *baladins*, *cabaretiers*, courtesans, and felons.[59] All products of industry were exposed for sale; mothers bought household utensils; students, parchment; and strangers exhibited proofs of their skill in mechanical arts. And there were not lacking the customary amusements, debaucheries, tricks of *jongleurs*, and other contrivances to delude the innocent.

The increased aggrandisement and prosperity of Paris brought advantages both civil and commercial to the citizens, particularly if they belonged to the corporation of merchants, advantages which seem to have been short-sighted, as there is no record of grain being stored against famine, although in such times the *prévôt* gave commissions to the burghers to seek grain in the environs of the city.

Most of the commerce was in the form of a monopoly, particularly in salt, cloth, hides, grains, beasts, muttons, all of which were subject to imposts, as were the Jews, who had to pay extra if they brought a lamp to the city, probably the seven-branched candlestick for the celebration of their Sabbath. Hebrew books were also taxed. The Jews were not molested until the close of the next century. They were located in the rue de Petit Saint-Antoine, on Mont-Sainte-Geneviève, in a *cul-de-sac* of the rue de la Tisseranderie, in the rue des Lombards, rue de Quinquenpaix, rue des Jardins, rue de la Harpe, and rue de Saint-Bon. Most of them were very poor. They had two synagogues, a cemetery, and a mill. At the other mills they had to pay an extra tax of five shillings a hundred measure.

The *prévôt* of the merchants was an important official under the late Capetians. His jurisdiction extended over the territory surrounding Paris for a distance of six or eight leagues. If a merchant from out of town sent his ship up the Seine, he was stopped at Pont de Mantes. Nor could he proceed on his way until he had declared his intention to sell. This formality complied with, the *prévôt* designated a merchant of Paris as *compagnon,* whose duty it was to accompany him to the city, to see that his prices were fair, and to seize his cargo in case he violated any requirements. This right was enforced even after the annexation of Normandy had given the king the lower Seine. The same oversight was levied on those who were simply passing through in order to sell in the provinces.

The Parisian merchants tried to get a monopoly of the commerce of the upper Seine, especially in Burgundy, an especially important province, as it alone exported wine to a great distance, but the most they could do was to prevent such wine from being unloaded in the city. It must be sold from the boats if at all.[60] They also excluded the Burgundians from ascending the Marne to sell wine. The Parisians prevented the Normans likewise from sending sea salt and fresh fish upstream unless they paid for the privilege.[61]

Naturally the cities retaliated. Auxerre prevented Paris from unloading salt from Normandy at her port until 1200, when the king forced the count to yield. When Normandy came under Philip Augustus, an attempt was made to secure commercial advantages that would counterbalance the pretensions of the Paris Hanse and which would prevent the merchants from having direct communication with the sea. Rouen was by far the most troublesome in this respect and maintained her position so absolutely that Paris at last felt the necessity of making concessions and granted her rival the privilege of sending empty boats as far as Saint-Germain-en-Laye, to be laden without duty.[62] Rouen was not satisfied with this concession, however, as she wished unrestricted commercial privileges on the Seine that she might draw from the interior provinces what she needed, but Parlement refused to accede to her request when it was made,[63] and the case was not settled until much later. Another contest arose with Rouen about 1200 over the measuring of Norman salt in the port of Paris, and a commission was appointed to bring about a reconciliation. The Rouen merchants lost the case.

Police duty on the banks of the Seine was rigorous and unceasing. Any attempt to unload merchandise did not escape the vigilance of the sergeants. When an offender was caught, his boat was seized and he was cited before the *prévôt* of the merchants to hear the sentence of confiscation. He might plead in his own defence or he might employ an advocate. In either case he was given a patient hearing, but the conclusion was always the same: he had broken the privilege of a merchant and his goods were confiscated. The numerous judgments still existing prove the viligance of the officers as well as the determination of the foreigners in eluding laws which they felt were prompted by commercial egotism. Protection by a powerful man in the *ville* sometimes secured grace for the guilty man, but even then he had to appear and state that he had offended and had incurred confiscation. Some merchants were complacent enough to lend their names as *compagnons* of foreign speculators, themselves taking no part in the speculation, but the penalty for this was expulsion from the corporation and the loss of all honours and privileges. Eventually the merchant could be reinstated, but until he was, he had only the rank of the lowest class. Ordinarily the courts were no respecters of persons. Wine was seized which the abbot of Saint-Germain l'Auxerrois wished to have disembarked at Paris to be placed in his residence there for his own use. The abbot appealed to the king for redress, and, while the Parlement decided the case in his favour, the Hanse refused to give up the wine. On another occasion the Bishop of Paris was forced to surrender a boatload of figs and other luxuries brought him by Spanish merchants as a gift up the Seine.

Shops were usually closed in the afternoon when the bell of Notre-Dame, Sainte-Merri, or Sainte-Opportune sounded the curfew. In all crafts work by artificial light was forbidden, as it lowered the standard of production. On Sunday and on the numerous feast days all shops were closed and the people went to church, and in the afternoon walked *en famille* outside the walls.

4. *Commerce and Industry*

AFTER the Fall of Rome commerce declined in all parts of the Empire, not only because of the barbarian invasions, but because of the teachings of the Church Fathers, who condemned it as being fraught with dangers to the soul. Tertullian, for example, pointed out that since all trade was prompted by a desire for gain its basis was avarice, one of the deadly sins.[64] Saint Jerome thought that one man's gain in trading must be another man's loss, and as all bargaining offered chance for fraud it was dangerous to the soul. Saint Augustine condemned all business as evil, since it turned men's minds from seeking the true rest which is to be found only in God.

Of course such teachings could not, in the nature of things, survive, and it was not long before the attitude of the Church became more tolerant. Leo the Great said that trade was not in itself either good or bad; the evil lay in the way in which it was conducted. The scholastics condemned commerce on the authority of patristic texts as well as on Aristotelian grounds.

After the Crusades, commerce developed so rapidly that it had to be justified and accepted; it was too widespread to be condemned. Among those realizing its necessity was Saint Thomas Aquinas, who made the motive with which it was carried on the test of its legitimacy. 'There are two ways,' he says, 'in which it is possible to increase the prosperity of any commonwealth. The more worthy is the production of an abundance of necessities by virtue of the fertility of the land; the other is by means of commerce by which what is necessary is brought to a common market from different places. The former is the more desirable condition, since it is better that a state should possess an abundance of riches from its own soil, for when merchants are necessary to maintain the people, injury may result to them in time of war when communications are checked. Also the coming of foreigners is apt to corrupt the morals of any people. If the citizens devote themselves to commerce, there is opportunity for many vices. For when merchants desire to increase their gains, the others are also filled with cupidity. The calling of a merchant is widely different from that of a soldier. The former abstains from manual labour, enjoys the good things of life and becomes soft in body and flabby in mind. For this reason a state should restrict its commercial pursuits.'[65]

This teaching was generally accepted throughout the Middle Ages, at the time when the merchant class was becoming more and more a vital part of the social organism.

In Gaul the coming of the Germans checked whatever of commerce had existed under the Empire. Traces of a revival appear in the Merovingian period, and under Charles it may be said to have flourished. There are records of cheese, wine, oil, horses, Spanish mules, hunting dogs, and Frising cloth being sent to the East from Marseilles, Arles, and Narbonne, and of spices, silks, linen, wine, Arab perfume, and Byzantine and Italian works of art being introduced. Even before the Crusades, kings and churches imported artists; the Benedictine monks not only employed foreign workmen, but they sent their own monks East to learn foreign crafts, and the prelates all sought to attract to their churches *ouvriers d'élite*.[66]

With the establishment of feudalism, commerce and industry localized as surely as did social institutions and became component parts of the hierarchy. It is in the great religious establishments, however, the monasteries and cathedrals, that it first developed; its beginnings in town and hamlet are insignificant and obscure.

The feudal estates were generally self-supporting, producing their own grain, wine, wood, meat, wool, and whatever was used on the place. Trade in necessities was forbidden by the barons, who sought to prevent all exports from the fief lest there be want later on, a normal and universal practice peculiarly similar to that of modern warring nations whose governments seek to control foodstuffs. The mill, oven, and winepress, which later furnished opportunity for gross abuses, were in these early days maintained for the convenience of those too poor to have their own, quite similar in fact to the present-day coöperative movements; e.g., dairies in Ireland.

Whatever was needed was made on the fief by the local carpenters, masons, potters, blacksmiths, armourers, weavers, tailors. Imported articles were few and precious, usually of gold and of silver, and were handed down as heirlooms or kept until some special need, such as ransom, forced their sale.

Of course the difficulty of transportation for goods as well as for men was one of the great obstacles to commercial development. All roads, bridges, ferries, etc., as well as the policing of the same, were strictly local affairs, since in the absence of a central government there was no other power to assume the obligation. This led to an indefinite multiplication of tolls, such as were to be found in the United States in the days when well-built roads depended on private enterprise. In the Middle Ages the amounts levied were arbitrary and often in kind; as time went on there was an ever-growing tendency to regulate these.[67]

In northern France the Norman invasions in the ninth and tenth centuries brought rural population to the *villes*, fostered the construction of castles and fortified towns, and gave a new importance to the urban population, which the Crusades in the following centuries stimulated. The late eleventh and early twelfth centuries, notwithstanding the darkness enveloping them, abound in beginnings of important movements, not the least of which was the introduction of the Latins to the Orient and the opening to the one new vistas of luxury, and to the other, new sources of supply of raw materials.

The latter part of the twelfth century witnessed the transition from domestic industry of the courtyard of the castle to free and privileged industry behind the walls of the *villes*.

Corporations began with the grouping of artisans of the same craft in the *atelier* of the barony and was followed by voluntary association of similar groups in the subject towns. The movement was not always favoured by the lords, especially the ecclesiastics, and very early in their history the towns witnessed conflicts of *métiers* and their insurrection against the domination of the barons. The general trend, however, was toward the enfranchisement of the crafts and their organization into corporations, especially during those years when the barons were absent on crusades.

By the time of Philip Augustus, a considerable number of artisans were free, working for themselves, although an occasional evidence exists of an attempt on the part of the nobility to limit their independence.[68] Even when the *métiers* were technically out from under baronial control, they were to a certain extent subject to the overlord by virtue of the *corvée*. The progress of the labourer, however, was steadily upward, and even those craftsmen left on the fief and working for the barons were treated rather as vassals than as serfs.

The monarch not infrequently helped in the emancipation of the labourers and in their organization. For example, prior to 1182 any one might make and sell bread. To promote public health, the king forbade any save those members of the *métier* of bakers to bake their own loaves or to sell to others. Then he constituted a monopoly of bakers, promising them a master who should judge all cases of violation of their rights, in return for which each member of the *métier* was to give the King a measure of wine.

The *corps des métiers* multiplied and gained sanction through the laws of the sovereign whom they paid well for all privileges. Under Philip Augustus, they began to write their own statutes, erect chapels, even churches, give windows in which they were portrayed working at their various crafts, etc. There seems to have been no especial proof of ability required of those who would practise an industry. Possibly the local reputation of the applicant was enough.

The *métiers* may in a way be considered as *fiefs bourgeois.* Certainly they were the municipal aristocracy in many places, an aristocracy based on intelligence as well as on wealth. Each group had its master, and in towns not communes these paid to the lord a *redevance* for the right of exercising their profession. Besides this official there were valets, working-men, apprentices, all of whom were under oath to observe the regulations and to respect the authority of their superiors. The *métiers* had full powers over those who worked in their craft and controlled the standard of production. No foreigner could work in a *ville* unless he put himself under the jurisdiction of the *métier.* The same restriction was laid upon the inhabitants of the *ville.* There was, in fact, no free and independent labour, in the modern sense of the term, save perhaps in a few exceptional cases. No man had more than one kind of employment save those whose *métier* could be exercised but part of the time, such as *crieurs du vin*, etc. Usually, the manufacturer sold his own goods. In the regulation of labour, imposts, and policing, the industrial class had its own hierarchy. In some instances, nobles were members of a *métier;* they were exempt from commercial imposts and from the formalities by which the rest were governed.[69]

An interesting example of a *métier* was that of the *Pois-*

sonniers de l'eau du Roi. The king reserved for himself the right to fish from the point of the Île Notre-Dame to Saint-Maur-des-Fosses, but he conceded this privilege to the *métier*, giving it as a fief to the family of a certain Guérin du Bois, who had the revenues and justice thereof. The *métier* then had to pay five shillings rent, four shillings to Guérin and one shilling to the king. The size of the fish one might catch was also regulated; the nets used had to conform to a certain model given by *Le Queux du Roi* for the size of its meshes. These restrictions, however, were not to infringe on the right of the Bishop of Paris to fish in the river alongside of Notre-Dame.

Fish could be sold only from the stalls at Pierres-aux-Poissonniers at the side of the Grand Pont; no fishing was allowed in spawning time, between the middle of April and May; fish must be brought directly to the market, not sold on the way, nor must the duty due the king be avoided by détour or by hiding. The fish must be examined by *Le Queux du Roi*, who selected what he wished for the royal table. All members of the *métier* were obliged to fish on Wednesday, Friday, and Saturday, and every day in Lent, a most unpopular service. In the summer months fish must be sold the day it was caught, and in the winter, within two days.

In principle, the *métier* was an open community with its own officials. An entrance fee was usually levied and all new members had to give a banquet to the corporation. The price of labour was sometimes fixed by their own regulations, sometimes by the overlord, sometimes by the grand master of the *métier*.

Charitable organizations or religious *métiers*, also called confraternities, though rarely met in the statutes, existed in great numbers after the middle of the thirteenth century. In some of the wealthier *métiers*, these were formed as an inner circle or collateral organization, and both groups united in adopting a patron saint, choosing a chapel, establishing a *fête* with special ceremonies, thus giving the corporation a religious and charitable character, quite unlike what the Roman trade corporations had been. The confraternities had charge of funerals, of indigent orphans of the masters, of apprentices and apprenticeships, of the distribution of alms, and the care of the aged. They also saw that confiscated food must be given to the poor, to hospitals, and to prisoners.

Of religious guilds, pure and simple, France never had as many as did Germany, for example. These were organized to provide candles for services, prayers for the unfortunate and for those, such as sailors, who had to travel on Sunday; to provide alms for the sick and needy, to bury the indigent dead, and to present religious plays. Such organizations were established by the Dominicans in Mantua, in 1255; in Perugia, in 1258; in Pavia, in 1288; in Lucca, in 1272; in Orvieto, in 1288; in Douai, in 1470. The common obligation met by all was to say three rosaries, two *credos*, five *Pater Nosters*, and fifty *Ave Marias* weekly, and to attend the Association held every spring. In the early years of its development, industry was limited to the supplying of local needs. Then the returning crusaders brought knowledge of metal-work, of textiles, especially silk, and of glass, so that after the twelfth century, labour grew more skilled. The opening of mines in Champagne was followed by the establishment of a *fabrication de fer;* other industries, such as building of cathedrals, also opened the hitherto undeveloped resources of the country.

Allied to the *métiers* were the companies or corporations of merchants, originating in the eleventh and twelfth centuries as a means of defence against the exactions of masters, and in a desire to prevent strangers from buying and selling in the city. While the *métiers* were active behind the city walls and within the towns, the merchants controlled whole regions such as river basins; e.g., the *Marchands de l'eau* of Paris, the *Vicomte de l'eau* of Rouen, the *Communauté des marchands de la Loire et ses affluents*, etc. In Paris and Rouen these corporations were identical with the municipality. Elsewhere they seem to have had nothing to do with the government of the city.

The merchants, unlike the artisans, did not group themselves around the great proprietors. Some of these were engaged in extensive, even international, operations, the scope of which is not clearly known. They apparently existed in the time of Charlemagne. When the central power declined, they did not seek asylum with the barons, but proved themselves to be self-sufficient. With the later rise of industry and the growth of commerce, they established themselves at the ports of entry of merchandise in whatever *villes* were well situated for commerce. In many cases they absorbed the life of the growing municipality, shaping its development, and as a natural consequence they became the body politic of the commune, and were indirectly, if not absolutely, invested with the administration of the city.

There was little or no formal taxation even in the communes, which were practically outside the feudal system; most of the expenses were met by levies, so much per day per man for a war, or any emergency, which was collected by the *prévôt*.[70] This *prévôt* was responsible for the collection of all revenues, which were paid weekly. They were farmed out to him, and in case he could not pay them he was put in charge of an agent. While little remains to throw light on municipal expenses, the list of royal expenditures under Louis IX is quite complete and very illuminating. It includes such items as kitchen expenses, wine, fruit, wages of employees, liveries of pages, gifts, jewels, travelling expenses, etc. A chief item found therein is the bounty paid for the destruction of eagles and wolves which devoured not only animals but persons.[71] Record is also made of state expenses, such as the entertainment of ambassadors, diplomatic missions, communal militia, etc. The accounts of the queen and of the queen-mother were kept separate.[72] From 1202 to 1295, the treasury was at the Temple; after that time, it was at the Louvre.

5. *The Parish Priest*

(These notes on the parish priest were taken largely from the *Regestrum Visitationum* of Eudes Rigaud, Archbishop of Rouen in the reigns of Philip Augustus and Louis IX. They were evidently meant for the projected chapter on 'The Bishop's Workshop.' G. R. B. R.)

I

Chronicles, poems, *fabliaux*, canons of the Church, councils, reports of ecclesiastical visitations, sermons, all that have come down to us from the Middle Ages, bear abundant testimony to the vices and shortcomings of the clergy. Parish priests, pope, bishop, abbot, monk, forgetting their high calling in Jesus Christ, stand forth as the chief sinners of their time. They entered the priesthood from the basest of motives; their careers were stained by simony, avarice, indifference, and neglect of duty. Their '*grant richesse*,' which should have been given to the poor, they used to satisfy their own selfish desires. Every privilege of the order was turned into an abuse; the right of hospitality, due to clergy alone, they demanded for a cavalcade of followers so licentious that they corrupted the abbey which sheltered them. The sacraments of the Church were sold to gratify their base desires; the very altars were despoiled to add to their ease and comfort; they were too ignorant to teach; too indolent to bestir themselves to feed their flocks.

And as the list of their shortcomings grows, it gives as distorted a picture of their times as one would have today should he attempt to reconstruct our social order from the criminal laws and records of trials. Behind this very tirade, however, may be found proof of the existence of godly priests who served God and man with as sincere devotion as might be found in any age. Such are not mentioned; they are taken for granted, dismissed with a '*cetera bene.*' Only from the omission of vices may the virtues be inferred. Yet, had there not been this leaven of efficient pastors, the fabric of the Church would have soon decayed.

Of the doings of the delinquents, we have abundant record; but what of the priest who sought to fulfil his duty; what were his peculiar difficulties, his trials, his labours, his relaxations, his rewards?

The most important figure in the social life of the Middle Ages was the parish priest. He shared all the concerns of the village; his relation to his people was one of peculiar intimacy. The wonder is not that in sharing the interests of his flock he should share their shortcomings and wrongdoings, but that he should be criticized for so doing; it would have been impossible for him to have done otherwise. The ecclesiastical organization of the day was universal and pentrated every temporal institution — the commune, the fief, the *métier*, and the developing monarchy.

The priest had above all the cure of souls. He was responsible for all the inhabitants of the parish, as all save Jews were subject to the Church. He must conduct them with a firm hand in the way of salvation by seeing that they attended the offices of the Church, particularly mass and confession. He must spread such information as was necessary to all — must act as journal and public bulletin, must publish and enforce sanitary and police regulations and excommunications, and must make the acts of councils and the will of the bishop known to his flock.

Many priests were of humble origin; the Church was the one possible career for peasants. The majority of the lower clergy were very poor, as the individual or monastery with the right of presentation to the benefice took most of the tithes. Indeed, this was so general that Alexander II complained of abbeys which leave but the merest pittance to the *curés*, and the Fourth Lateran Council condemned those who take from the priest all but one sixteenth of the tithe. In some cases the abbot took the whole, leaving the incumbent only the alms.[73]

Moreover, these tithes were most difficult to collect and were evaded in every way known to man mediæval or modern. Often even the threat of excommunication was not enough to enforce their payment.

Sacraments were to be administered free of charge according to statute; afterwards, however, the *curé* might accept with thanks any good-will offering, although these were limited in amount and might be offered in oil and candles as well as in money. They might be accepted after any special services on the part of the priest, such as baptism, viaticum, marriage, reconciliation of enemies, or burial. In each case the *curé* was forbidden to receive too much! There is more than one record left to us of a priest refusing to administer these special services, notably that of burial, until the payment had been made.

The *curé* could be paid in kind or in money, not only by his parishioners, but by the bishops. During an ecclesiastical visitation, the bishop often demanded a certain amount of food for entertainment of himself and his cortège and then stopped at the nearest monastery. Often the priest was unable to collect as much as the prelate desired; in this case he was in the position of a debtor and his income was seized as payment. At times the bishop demanded money in place of entertainment, and, when this had been given, made his visit, thus imposing a double burden on the poor *curé*.[74]

Of the education of the parish priest little is known unless he attained high dignity; of the many who lived and died in obscurity, one can only conjecture. The Church itself usually educated free of charge those who wished to take orders. A boy whose father wished to make a priest of him sent him to school in his own village, where in all probability he was badly taught, as the license to teach was often given carelessly or sold to '*clercs complètement ignorante en grammaire et ne point l'art d'enseigner les enfants. Car ils pensent plutôt aux misérables intérêts d'un seul qu'a l'utilité publique.*' So the efforts and sacrifices of the parents went for nothing. The bishops many times tried to control and improve education, but they seemed to have been rather unsuccessful, at least if one judges by the records of the examination given by Eudes Rigaud, Archbishop of Rouen. In the twelfth century the Bishop of Autun prescribed that two of the most capable *curés* be sent from each archpresbyteriat into the *grandes écoles* to learn theology so that they might learn more completely the science of preaching.[75]

It was probably due to the lack of education among the lower clergy that provision was made for the absence of a priest from his parish whenever he was studying.[76] Occasionally one is found in school or at the university after his installation.[77] In the latter case, however, the temptation to a life of pleasure was so great that it very often frustrated all serious purposes. In the twelfth century schools for clergy were held in fief; certain high clerics had the right to give license to travelling masters who should instruct particularly the clergy. Regular training in music was provided for the clergy rather generally in the cathedrals, where there were *écoles de chant*,[78] but also by the skilled musicians who went from one church to another to provide the music on special occasions.[79] The priest was charged to avoid such faults in the Church offices as abbreviating or running the words together.[80] He must take care to sing distinctly, and when there was an antiphonal chant by two choirs, there must be no '*tuilage*'; that is, one beginning before the other had finished like '*tuiles sur un toit.*'[81] There must also be a definite pause in the Psalter.

In the examination of candidates for the priesthood, music played an important part, and a candidate was sent down quite as often for inability to sing or read music[82] as for ignorance or evil life; in the former case, however, he was allowed to try again. The Visitation made by Eudes of Rigaud mentions one youth who tried and failed twice. His father had spared no expense on his education, but the village master to whom he was entrusted knew but little. When the bishop discovered his incompetence, he administered a sharp rebuke to the patron who had appointed him. This particular student went elsewhere to school and learned to read and write Latin and was taught songs anything but sacred by his fellow students.[83]

Plenty of relaxation was furnished the priests by the feasts of the Church and by the carnivals and pageants. The old Roman Saturnalia coincided with the great Christian festivals of Christmas and the new year, and the people kept many of the customs and ceremonials belonging to the older time, even imitating the wearing of skins of beasts until prohibited by the Church councils.[84]

II

(The following fragment seems to merit a place in this collection, although there is nothing to indicate its purpose. It is apparently part of some study of a young priest in Rouen. G. R. B. R.)

He knew what his duties would be: to say mass, and vespers, to hear confessions, to give last unction to the dying, to bury the dead, to perform the marriage ceremony, to keep his church in order, and to see that it was not profaned.

Just that morning he had said his first mass in the little

grey stone church. Now, as the sun reddened the sky below the evening star, he peered into the dusk of the church to where the red altar lamp glowed among the shadows. To him the prayers of the faithful had sanctified the place and it was filled with the beauty of holiness, even as it was consecrated by the presence of the Host. He went softly into the twilight to kneel in prayer and to dedicate himself anew to the service of God and the cure of souls. So his life as a priest began — coloured by the enthusiasm and idealism of his youth. He was kindly, energetic, enterprising, of good mind and strong body. He loved people and the society of his fellows, and he was looking forward with pleasure to his life with his flock. He would learn to know them well, to work with them and for them, and join in their innocent pleasures, for surely he could be a priest and a Frenchman at once. The archdeacon had instructed him well in the extra-religious parochial duties. He knew he had undertaken wide responsibilities and varied functions as well as the cure of souls. With the optimism and blessed inexperience of youth, he felt that all of these tasks would be easy. Energy and good-will would make light work of them. It seemed so easy to renounce family life, variety in dress, social pleasures in order to consecrate himself the more absolutely to his work. He was only twenty-five; before him stretched the long years of his life in which he must daily renounce in the presence of what he had set aside. No monastic fleeing from any reminders of temporal things, but constant living among the joys of the world without once partaking of them. And he knew full well how sweet these things could be.

A month went by, and the lines of care began to show in his face. Life was becoming such a tangle. For one thing he had been having unexpected trouble with the excommunicate. The archdeacon had told him time and again that not one service must ever proceed in the presence of one cut off from the fold. He himself would not willingly permit such a sacrilege. He would go any length to prevent it. But until he actually tried it, he did not realize what a difficult thing it would be to prevent. It seemed simple enough to keep a list of the excommunicate and post it on the walls of the church, and if one of these persons came into the church to stop the service. But last Sunday he had been so absorbed in the mass that he had not seen Nicholas enter and had proceeded with the sacred office. He had not foreseen that contingency.

To keep track of those cited by the bishop would be possible, but what about those who automatically joined the excommunicate because they would not boycott them? He had heard that Robin the miller still ground Nicholas's corn for him. Perhaps others, of whom he had not heard, would likewise disregard the ban. And even if he could keep track of the black sheep, it would be hard to turn one's own people away from the church when he so longed for their presence. Of course it could be done. He knew of one parish so well-disciplined that an excommunicated merchant had been well-nigh ruined because his neighbours refused to trade with him. What another priest had done he could surely do.

Another thing troubled him. A fortnight before, the bishop had sent him notice to serve upon Monseigneur Comte de ——. He had taken it and had been most notoriously beaten by the count's servants. Now there was another notice to be served. This time he was not going unarmed. Was the servant of the Holy Church a dog or an ass?

However, he must go into the sacristy now, for here came the children to school. A *socius* had been promised to help in this work of teaching, but as yet the patron had not selected him. So for some hours he must give himself up to teaching the elements of grammar, numbers, and a little plain chant.

After the children had gone, he tried to collect tithes from some especially obstinate men. One fought him; he defended himself; another he gave up; the bishop must excommunicate him. Then he worked for a little time at his vines; he was late to vespers and hurried somewhat through the service.

6. *Fulque of Neuilly*

In those dark and evil days and in that perilous time, Paris, like other cities, was darkened by crimes and defiled by unspeakable filth. Her clergy, more dissolute than laymen, resembled nothing so much as a mangy goat or a bad egg. By their evil example, they corrupted the guests who came to the city from far and near; moreover, she preyed upon all who dwelt within her walls, dragging them with her into the depths. Men who basely wasted their substance in riotous living, were praised and held in high repute; all considered them virtuous and liberal, while any who would live in soberness, justice, and piety were speedily condemned by the shameless voluptuaries as misers and superstitious hypocrites.

As for the students here, they could find leisure for nothing more than to hear or learn something new. Some studied just to know, which is curiosity; other to be known, which is vanity; others for profit, which is avarice and akin to simony. But few laboured to be edified or to edify others. They wrangled and argued about diverse sects; they bitterly disagreed and abused each other because they came from different countries; they shamelessly cast manifold affronts and abuses at each other. The English were called drunken men with tails; the French, haughty, weak, and effeminate; the Germans, violent and obscene at their feasts; the Normans, vain and boastful; the Poitevins, traitors and opportunists (*fortunes amicos*); those who came from Burgundy were brutish and stupid; they deemed the Bretons fickle and shallow and were always casting in their teeth the death of Arthur. They called the Lombards avaricious, vicious, and cowardly; the Romans, factious, turbulent, and given to evil speaking; the Sicilians, tyrannous and cruel; the men of Brabant, incendiaries, brigands, ravishers; the Flemings, fickle, prodigal, slothful, and as yielding as their own butter. Abuse like this was often followed by blows.

We do not speak of the logicians before whose eyes were ever flying the lice of Egypt; that is, their subtleties were so involved that none could catch the drift of their reasoning, in which, as Isaiah said, there is no wisdom. The doctors of theology sat in the seat of Moses; science had puffed them up, but wisdom had not taught them. For they taught but *did* not; they were become as sounding brass and a tinkling cymbal and as a stone which remains itself dry, but carries water to the beds of spices. They were envious of one another and by smooth speaking drew students away from each other because they sought their own glory and took no thought for the good of souls.

Their ears were not deaf as they listened to these words of the Apostle, — 'If a man desire the office of bishop, he desireth a good work'; and so they piled up prebends for themselves and sought after promotions; and it is the preferment they desired, not the work. They would fain have the uppermost rooms at feasts and the chief seats in the synagogues and greetings in the market-place. Notwithstanding the Apostle James says, 'My brethren, be not many masters,' they did make such haste to be made masters that they could not gain students save by gold. Yet it is safer to hear than to teach, and a humble listener is better than an unlearned and presumptuous doctor.

Yet among them the Lord kept for himself a few honest men who feared him and stood not like the rest, in the way of sinners, nor sat in the seat of the scornful. . . .

One of these was Peter, the venerable poet of Paris, who was as a lily among thorns, as the angel of Pergamos before the seat of Satan; as the fragrant incense in days of summer; as a vase of solid gold, adorned with all manner of precious stones; as the olive putting forth leaves and the cyprus lifting itself on high; as a heavenly trumpet and a player on the zither before the Lord. He was a man mighty in deeds and in speech . . . of a surety, for he began to act as a burning and shining light, as a city placed upon a hill, and as a golden candlestick in the house of the Lord.

Now Fulco the priest did desire to drink of this spring exceeding clear, and did humbly enter into his school, bearing tablets and stylus to receive and gather together sayings, moral and commonplace, from the lips of the master, so far as his natural perts would allow. These sayings he pondered without ceasing and stored them securely away in his memory. But on feast days he went back to his church and earnestly gave forth to his flock the wisdom he had gathered throughout the week.

And since he was faithful over a few things, the Lord made him ruler over many things. At first, when he was called and summoned by neighbouring priests, he did fearfully and modestly begin to preach the things he had heard, to simple laymen in the vulgar tongue. But his wise and venerable master took heed of the zeal of this poor and unlearned priest, his disciple, and he esteemed his faithfulness and devotion and he did compel him to preach to the learned scholars of Paris in the church of Saint-Severin. And the Lord gave of his grace and strength to his new soldier in such full measure that his master and all who heard him marvelled and bore witness that the Holy Spirit spoke in him and through him. And thereafter others, teachers and students alike, flocked to hear his rude and simple preaching. One invited another and one circle of hearers brought another circle, saying 'Come hear Fulco, the priest like to another Paul.' But he was made strong in the Lord and clothed with virtue from on high, as Samson was when he slew the beasts of Ephesus with the jawbone of an ass. When, therefore, on a certain day in an open space in the city which is called, in the vulgar tongue, Champel, a great throng of clergy and people was gathered together before him that he might sow in the field of God the seed of divine preaching, he opened his mouth and the Lord filled it as it is written. The Lord opened his mind that he might understand the Scriptures and added grace to his words that many were filled with remorse and contrition. They cast off their garments and the shoes from their feet, and bearing scourges or thongs in their hands, they threw themselves down at his feet, placing themselves and all that they had at his will and behest. But he gave thanks to God who has power to raise up from the stones sons of Abraham, and received them all with the kiss of peace. He did enjoin soldiers that they should do violence to no one, but be content with their wages; robbers and usurers, he did charge that they should make restitution to all so far as they were able; abandoned women, that they should cut their hair and forsake their wonted shameless life. And some sinners did renounce Satan and all his train and begged him to grant them absolution.

Not only did his speech, inspired of God, arouse them to contrition, but, as many say who saw with their own eyes, the Lord did through him restore to health many sick and oppressed with various diseases. And Fulco did not accept the grace of God carelessly, but made haste diligently and zealously to increase the talent given him. And so he did suffer hunger like a dog and, urged by the Spirit, went about the city. Yea, he did even run about throughout all the kingdom of France and a great part of the empire. Mighty in spirit, he did waste the ships of Tarsus; vehement in season and out of season, as if unmindful of what was past, he pressed forward to what lay before him. He did not hold back his sword from blood, but girded it upon his thigh and, coming from gate to gate through the midst of camps, he fought the Lord's fight armed with justice on the right hand and on the left. And as a live dog is better than a dead lion, he did not give over driving the wolves from the Lord's flocks with continual barkings. He did feed the untaught with the word of doctrine, comfort the desolate with the word of consolation, the doubtful with the word of counsel, the hardened with the word of chiding, the erring with the word of reproach, the sluggish with the word of exhortation, the beginner with the word of friendly counsel.

And because he cared so vehemently, he did with few and simple words kindle all people, not only humble folks, but even kings and princes; for no man dared to resist him. Moreover, men did eagerly flock from far countries to hear him and to see what marvels the Lord wrought through him. And many sick were brought on their beds and put in the streets through which he was like to pass, so that when he came they might touch the hem of his garment and be made whole from their disease. And he, whensoever he touched them, or when, for the press of the crowd, he could not come nigh them, was used to bless them or to give them to drink of water he had blessed. And so great was the devotion and faith of the sick and of those who brought them, that they did desire to be healed, not only through the merits of the servant of God, but for the zeal of their spirit and the greatness of their faith. And they did deem themselves blessed who prevailed to tear away a part of his garment and keep it for themselves. Wherefore his vestments were so rent by the multitude of the people that nearly every day he had to have a new cape. And since ofttimes the crowd did press upon him so sore that he was not able to bear it, he pushed the rude people away by laying about him stoutly with the staff he bore in his hand lest he be stifled by those who sought to touch him. But even when he wounded those whom he struck, they took not offence, neither murmured, but out of their great devotion and steadfast faith, kissed the blood as if it were made sacred by the man of God. And when on a certain day, one did wantonly tear his cape overmuch, he spoke to the throng, saying: 'Do not rend my garments, for they are not blessed. But I will bless this man's cape.' And he made the sign of the cross, and the folk did tear in pieces the cape of that man, and did keep the parts for relics.

He was the scourge of the covetous and confounded the robbers and eke those who through avarice had stored up much riches, especially in those days; for there was great scarcity of food. And he did often cry out: 'Feed those who suffer!"

On a certain day he was saying in his sermon that men are accursed who store away grain and how they should sell it for a low price before the harvest is come; and that suddenly on a time the scarcity will have an end; and they had faith in his words as if the Lord had spoken, and made haste to bring forth the grain they had hidden away to sell it. And so it befell that through his word food could be had everywhere at a fair price.

And he was moved with such zeal against hardened sinners and those who made delay in seeking the Lord, when he saw how they lied he did often curse them or seemed to curse them. All men feared his curses like thunder and lightning, especially when they told him how certain ones whom he had cursed had been seized by a demon, and how others like them who suffered wasting sickness, suddenly fell to the ground and foamed at the mouth.

But worn out by the severity of his penances and by the harsh sackcloth — yea and even a leathern cuirass thereto, in which, it is said, he was ever clad, and by too great vexation, he was often stirred to wrath. But right as he was cursing those who pressed upon him and those who did interrupt his sermon by speaking among themselves, they all fell to the ground, and there was a great silence. And he did follow up the unchaste priests and their concubines, whom he did call yoke-fellows of the devil, with such reviling and cursing that they were confounded with fear. And he cried out after all who were of the ilk and pointed the finger at them, wherefore it came to pass that well-nigh all of the sort left their priests. Moreover, a certain noble woman full oft dealt with the priest in a manor which she held and insisted that he leave his concubine. He said her nay and made answer: 'What are the priests to you?' She answered: 'Against you I cannot do judgment. Nevertheless, all upon this manor who are not clerks come under my sway.' Then she did give order that the priest's concubine be brought to her, and she made for her a large corona, saying: 'Because thou wilt not leave the priest I do wish to ordain thee into the priesthood.' But the bishop commanded the priest that he should leave this concubine or else his parish. But he, groaning and weeping, said that he would rather give up his parish than the woman. But she, seeing that he was made poor when the church was given up, held him in contempt and withdrew herself from him. And so the poor priest lost both church and concubine.

And, moreover, well-nigh all the women of the town, in whatsoever places the champion of God did visit, left their sinful homes and flocked about him. A great part of them he gave in marriage; and others he put in religious houses that they might live according to rule. Wherefore hard by the city of Paris, but beyond it, was founded the monastery of Saint Antony of the Cistercians, so that women of this ilk might be received there. But in other places and cities where the man of God blessed springs or wells, because a great multitude of sick gathered together, chapels were built and hospitals thereto.

And the Lord gave such authority and grace to his words that the masters and scholars of Paris came to hear him and brought their tablets to him and, writing on the reverse side, gathered words from his lips. And into every Christian land went forth the sound of his preaching, and the fame of his sanctity was everywhere spread abroad, and the disciples whom he did send forth to preach were received by all with exceeding great honour and reverence. But a certain one of them who was distinguished among them, called Master Peter of Rusia, put a blot on his glory. For he who sought the way of perfection and preached poverty was by his preaching filled full with riches and was made canon and chancellor of the church, and he who out of smoke ought to have brought forth light produced smoke from light. And thereby he not only made his own doctrine contemptible, but in this wise cast much reproach on the other disciples of Fulco.

When the man of God had saved every day many souls to the Lord, the sign of the cross was fixed upon his shoulder and he began by word and example to invite and urge and admonish princes and soldiers and men of every condition whatsoever to betake themselves to the Holy Land. And, moreover, he did begin to amass from the alms of the faithful an exceeding great sum of money, and this he did propose to give to poor men signed with the cross, soldiers and others. But by reason of covetousness or some other evil intent, he could not make these moneys to be collected; wherefore, according to the mysterious judgment of God, from that time his authority and the power of his preaching began to grow less among men. As the money increased, the fear and reverence decreased. But he himself not long thereafter was seized with fever and went the way of all flesh in the town which is called Neuilly, and there in the parish church he had served, he was buried, and because many came from far and near to his burial, the work upon the church which he had begun was altogether finished by the alms of the pilgrims who came thither. For he had at the beginning of his conversion, against the will of all the laity, torn down the old church and had promised his parishioners that he would finish the work, sumptuous though it was, without laying any burden on them.

NOTES

NOTES

1. So many ships came into the port of Marseilles in this century that the time of lading and of sailing was determined by lot. (*Stat. Mars., cl. De Sortibus navum.*) The traders left their cargoes in front of the three gates to the city, one after the other, each ship waiting in the small inlets of the islands for their turn. Sometimes they unloaded in these same inlets and the goods were ferried over. The most common merchant vessels of the Middle Ages were the *pamphiles*, strong, swift galleys; the *dromons*, next smaller; and the *galeides*, the smallest of all. There was also the *chalande*, a ship of great length and high speed, with two tiers of oars and a crew of one hundred men. After the tenth century the *dromons* had towers on deck as a protection against pirates. Usually these were halfway up the mainmast which rose from the centre of the vessel; others had towers fore and aft. In the smaller vessels, platforms surrounded by a crenellated parapet on a pillar took the place of towers; in the larger vessels the towers were several stories above poop and prow. They had all of the engines of destruction used in land sieges: heavy beams which worked horizontally like a battering ram; immense bulks of timber working vertically from the tip of the mast to shatter smaller craft; and around the masts, suspended chatelets or platforms in which were hidden slingers, archers, and stone-throwers. Under such conditions, sailors were of necessity as skilled in the use of arms as were the soldiers. While large fleets were never constructed nor maintained by the feudal governments, kings as well as republics had their own vessels and the Middle Ages did not lack large and handsome ships. Barons living near the sea usually had their own vessels for war and commerce, most of which were sailing ships, although those used for coastal trade were manned by oars. (*Pacta* in *Coll. des Doc. inéd.*, vol. I, p. 507.) Most of the vessels carried passengers, whose places were secured by a middleman, who leased the privilege and then found the passengers, most of whom were merchants bound with their wares to some foreign port. At first, merely to preserve the wood, the shipbuilders covered with pitch every part of the vessel exposed to air or to water. Then to relieve the sombreness, they were painted with brilliant colours prepared with wax — white, ultramarine, and vermilion. Pirates and men-of-war were camouflaged with green. The vessels of the wealthier towns were gilded and the sails were of cloth of gold or of purple, while coats-of-arms embroidered on taffeta or satin, images of saints, flags, and lighted beacons added to their gorgeousness.

2. Commerce between Marseilles and the Levant had existed since the foundation of the city, even during the Dark Ages. Under Chilperic a solitary of the place was fed during Lent by herbs a merchant brought him from Egypt. (*AA. SS.*, I, p. 145; Gregory of Tours, *Hist. Franc.*, lib. VI, p. 6.) In the Merovingian period all Orientals were called Syrians, whether Egyptian or Asiatic. Powerful communities of these and of Jews existed in Marseilles, Narbonne, and Bordeaux from the time of Charlemagne on. (Pigeonneau, vol. I, pp. 65–66, 72–73.) Sainte Geneviève is said to have communicated with Saint Simeon Stylites through Syrian merchants. After the conquest of Egypt and eastern Asia by the Moslems, traffic in Oriental wares fell into the hands of the Jews. In 418 A.D., when Honorius summoned an assembly of the Diocese of Gaul, he speaks of the 'opulent Orient, the perfumed Arabia, the honeyed Assyria, the fertile Africa, the valiant Gaul meeting to exchange goods.' (*Recueil des Historiens*, vol. I, p. 766.) During the first crusades, Marseilles established somewhat of a monopoly of eastern trade, carrying pilgrims and manufacturing arms, but by the thirteenth century such rival ports as Narbonne, Arles, and Montpellier were challenging her supremacy.

3. Blancard, *Documents inédits sur le Commerce de Marseilles au Moyen-âge*, vol. I, doc. 47. According to tradition these fairs of Champagne were held as early as the fifth century, but the first authentic mention of the one at Provins is in a document of Thibault III, dated 1137. It seems very evident that it existed prior to this time. In a list of fairs given in the Romance of Anseis, one of the Lorraine Cycle, the May Fair at Provins is mentioned among those founded in the ninth century. While similar concourses were found as early as the Roman days, they came into renewed prominence in the Middle Ages as pilgrims gathered at the shrine of some saint, and remaining there awaiting a miracle, had to be fed. Providing them with the essentials gave the opportunity of providing them also with the non-essentials, and it was not long before such gatherings proved so profitable that they were recognized, even instituted, by various monarchs, and awarded as marks of favour to monasteries and towns. It was to the advantage of all to have a known centre of supply in an age when travel was difficult and beasts of burden scarce, and more than one complaint exists of loss incurred when the fair was removed. The fairs of Champagne extended through the year with little intermission. January 1st the fair of Lagny was opened. (Pegolotti, *Practica della Mercatura*, in Pagnini, *Della Decima*, vol. III, p. 238, written 1335. Then came the fair of Bar, the Tuesday before Mi-Carême; that is, sometime between February 24th and March 30th. (D'Arbois de Jubainville, *Histoire de Bar-sur-Aube*, p. 37.) The May Fair of Provins was opened on the Feast of Saint Quiriace, the Tuesday before Ascension Day. The first fair of Troyes, called the Foire Chaude or the Fair of Saint-Jean, followed on

June 4th. These two were the most important of all. Then came the Fair of Saint-Ayoul held at Provins September 3d, and after this the Foire Froide of Troyes, also called the Foire de Saint-Remi, on the first of October. The normal length of these fairs was forty-six days. (Bib. Nat. fonds fr., no. 412; Bib. Pub. of Provins, *Cartulaire de Michel Caillot*, ff. 420–21; Bib. Nat. fonds fr., no. 1281, f. 312 (MS. of 1284); Bib. Nat. fonds fr., no. 25545, f. 17; Bib. Nat. ancien fonds fr., no. 5378.) Another fair, that of Saint-Martin, was held in Provins, but it never had the prestige of the other two and in the thirteenth century had begun to decline. The importance of the fairs of Provins lay in the accessibility of the town to all districts, north and south, and to the industries of its artisans. After Philippe le Bel tried to increase the revenue from them by raising the imposts, they declined. The war with Flanders in the fourteenth century led to their losing Flemish trade; then for some reason, the Lombards transferred to Germany and Bruges. Philip of Valois tried to revive them by removing the imposts, but was unsuccessful and the Hundred Years' War quite finished them.

4. This Jean de Manduel was later one of the most active leaders in the revolt of Marseilles against Charles of Anjou. In 1262, he was taken prisoner at Plaine-Saint-Miché, all of his goods were confiscated, and he was executed. The long list, still extant, of his possessions, though incomplete, gives an idea of what he must have owned. Among other things twelve houses and eight vineyards are mentioned, besides holdings in Majorca, Sicily, and Acre. (Archives des Bouches-du-Rhone, B 812, ff. 45–47.)

5. In the second half of the eleventh century, the silks of the East are frequently mentioned in the romances, especially brocades of gold and of silver from Bagdad and Persia, taffeta, *draps de Laret*, etc., from Cyprus. They also mention horses from Spain, oranges and wine from Sicily, sandalwood from Tripoli, coral from Acre, grain from Sardinia, articles which the few existing commercial documents also note; e.g., *Roman de Percival; Roman de Hervis*, etc.

6. The rivers were the best avenues of transportation when available, as one *bateau* could carry the load of five mules. On water as on land tolls were exacted by the *seigneurs* of the territory through which one passed; e.g., seventy-four were collected on the Loire between Roanne and Nantes. This money was supposed to go toward clearing the channel, constructing quays and towpaths, etc., but as a matter of fact very little of it seems to have been used in this way, and the merchants of the river towns, whose interest lay in the maintenance of navigation, coöperated to keep the channel clear, the towpaths in order, and to construct *magasins* and *quais*, often buying or farming the tolls. They came in time to regard as their property the part of the river which they managed and policed, exercising over it a species of

monopoly sanctioned by the *seigneurs*, who infeudated rivers and even the seas to merchants as they infeudated land to the barons; e.g., Henry II of England about 1150 gave to Rouen the commerce of Norway, England, and Ireland. At Paris only merchants of the city could bring goods to the port and no boat could navigate the Seine from Nantes to the *Grande Pont* unless conducted by a Hanse merchant or his representative. Any foreign merchant, who would sell goods in Paris and wished to debark at Pont de la Grève, must be accompanied by a merchant of the Hanse who shared his profits, as they only could sell merchandise from the vessels. (Felibien et Lobineau, pp. xcviii–xcix.) The merchants also had control of measures and collected taxes on loaded boats in order to construct new ports. Another source of income over which they exercised a monopoly was the transportation of pilgrims. (*Stat. de la ville de Marseilles*, livre IX, c. 28.)

7. However, Jean had had charge of certain expeditions to the Levant prior to that time, although it is not certain whether he went himself or sent agents. (Blancard, *l.c.*, doc. 24.)

8. The name of Stephen is replaced in the documents after 1230 by that of his son Bernard, who died in England in 1237; Jean then succeeded to the business.

9. His daughter's dowry is given as 6000*l.* in royal coronats, a goodly sum for those days. (Blancard, *l.c.*, docs. 141–42.)

10. Stephen was born in Mandolium, a small town east of Nîmes, and came to Marseilles prior to 1200. His father, Pierre Jean de Manduel, is mentioned as having directed the construction of the Pont de Crau at Arles in 1178. (Blancard, *l.c.*, p. xvi.)

11. Blancard, *l.c.*, doc. 1.

12. Blancard, *l.c.*, doc. 12.

13. Interesting descriptions of the Levantine towns have come down to us in the accounts of the merchants and travellers of the day. While no longer as strange to western eyes as they had been in the time of the first crusaders, owing to the interchange of customs which commercial influences had fostered, they were still quite characteristically Oriental. Most of the houses were two stories high and were built of stone with many more windows than were to be found in the west. In the centre was a court with a fountain and usually a garden. An outside staircase led to the richly decorated upper rooms whose walls were of coloured marble or frescoed after the Syro-Arabic manner. Great subterranean vaults connected the houses, and numerous gates across the narrow streets separated the various quarters. The public places were small, but ornate, with fountains and flowers. The great military orders had built towered castles like those in the fortified

cities in the home-land. Each quarter had its distinct shops and its own church. Among the natives the greatest luxury prevailed. Food was served on dishes of rare glass, of gold, silver, or porcelain. Spiced drinks, cooled by the snows of Lebanon were sipped from enamelled goblets: garments of silk and gold brocade were embroidered with pearls and other precious stones and were worn over the finest of linen tunics. In the towns of the interior, as well as in those on the coast, merchants had their own courts, commercial and maritime, and also their own warehouses. Caravans or ships bringing goods were examined by the *douane*, who spoke all languages fluently and 'who proceeded in his operations with sweetness, without violence or overcharge.' (Description given by Ibn Djobair, 1184, from Laurent, *Perig. medii ævi.*)

14. Blancard, *l.c.*, docs. 13–16, 25, 48.

15. This was not in the possession of the house of de Manduel until 1254. (See Blancard, *l.c.*, doc. 148.)

16. At this time Marseilles consisted of the upper or episcopal city and the lower or industrial *ville* situated on the port. The former section had its own small windswept beach which it glorified by the name of 'Porte-galle.' As it was beyond the rocky capes which bounded the harbour proper, it was so exposed to attack as to be practically useless. An accord made between the inhabitants of the two sections in 1219, and renewed in 1229, gave the upper city privileges on the port, in return for which they were to bear part of the expenses of its upkeep and maintenance. Fishing rights were open to all save in that portion south of the Lacydon which was under the jurisdiction of Saint-Victor and was never considered as part of the port proper. Here all fishing was subject to the consent of the abbot. The lower town was a commune in the twelfth century and became a republic in the early thirteenth by the privileges it bought of the vicomtes. Its history in the eleventh and twelfth centuries is dominated by struggles with Saint-Victor, with the vicomtes, the bishop, and the emperor as well as with the Counts of Provence, all of which did the city little good. In the thirteenth century, Marseilles began to recover its commercial prestige which had not flourished during the period of strife. The port was enlarged and a wall was built close to the encircling hills where the Boulevard Belzunce now runs. The houses were for the most part tall and narrow and backed on the harbour, protected by a wall. (*Recueil*, vol. XVIII, pp. 751–55.)

17. Marseilles had grown prosperous in the time of the early crusades by furnishing munitions and arms as well as by transferring crusaders and pilgrims. She carried 10,000 men for Richard I, and constructed the arms and fleet of Louis IX, somewhat later than this period. Her statutes, framed in the twelfth and thirteenth centuries, are most valuable for the study of mediæval commercial law. The commune was

organized industrially into corporations. A body of one hundred *chefs des métiers* represented the commercial interests; the merchants were held in great honour.

18. Marseilles was one of the cities where the corporation had developed into municipal government.

19. It was the duty of the consuls to inspect everything connected with the affairs of their city; to settle difficulties involving its citizens; to make requitals if their city had injured the rectors, consuls, lords, or inhabitants of any other place. If their own city were injured, they must claim damages; if these were denied, the offenders were refused entrance to Marseilles and any citizen of an unfriendly state was expelled and refused safe-conduct. The right to maintain a consul in any important city was highly prized and those appointed to hold this office from Marseilles were considered to be the most honoured of her citizens and were always men of ability.

20. The Porte Annonaria led to Arles. Tradition said it was built by the Romans.

21. Almaric, in vol. II of Blancard, docs. 376, 378, 585, 642, 681, 788, 791, 801, etc.

22. As the King of France forced the barons to indemnify the victims of robberies, it was less costly to suppress lawlessness than to pay for the damages inflicted. The Counts of Boulogne and the Dukes of Burgundy engaged after the first half of the thirteenth century to protect merchants going or coming, and to make good the damages which befell them in their lands. (Lefèvre, *Traité de l'origine des fiefs*, *Preuves*, 216; Chantereau-Lefébre Act of 1232.) Also the Parlement of Paris gave judgments ordering the lords to make good property stolen on their roads. (*Olim du Parl.*, vol. I, pp. 279, 328, 914.) In 1148 Garin, son of Salon, Vicomte of Sens, had held up and robbed near that town some *changeurs* of Vézelay on the Chemin du Roi. Thibault wrote Suger, then charged with the administration of France, demanding justice, as such an act was an injury and insult to the king. (*Recueil*, vol. XV, p. 5103.) Count Thibault of Champagne in 1243 gave to the merchants — Roman, Tuscan, Lombard, Provençal — who wanted to live in Provins, all liberty and exemptions from any duties outside their own houses and allowed them the right to their own justice, the right to weigh merchandise in their own houses, etc.

23. Pilgrims and clergy, as well as their goods, were exempt from tolls. (*Conc. Lat.*, 1123, c. XVI.) The chief tolls levied were *pontage*, for bridge and river; *caucaige*, for roads; *rouage*, for carriage; *pulverage*, for flocks; *rivage*, for embarking and debarking; *portage*, for entrance to a city gate; *conduit*, for right of transit; *guiage*, for escort where an armed attack was probable. This last was often demanded where there

was no apparent danger. If tolls and *octroi* levied were too exorbitant, the merchants chose a more advantageous road. (*Quer. Norm.*, nos. 124, 160.)

24. The merchants of Languedoc and Provence were grouped into a '*Societas et communitas mercatorum de France.*' (Levasseur, vol. I, pp. 83–85.) The merchants of Lombardy and of Tuscany were similarly organized. (*Le dit des marchéans*, in *Proverbes et dictons*, Crapelet, p. 157.)

25. Montpellier had a predominant influence among the Provençal cities and held special privileges in the Fair towns, especially those of Champagne.

26. The captain not only secured special protection for them, but assured the regularity of payments, and a uniform action concerning debts, etc. '*Capitanens mercatorum et universitas mercatorum de provincia et de lingua de hoc mundinas campaine frequentantium.*' (Germain, vol. II, pp. 43–44.) *Coutumes stille et usage de la court et chancellerye des Foires de Champagne et Brye.* (MS. Caillot, f. 446.)

27. Not even those over which safe-conduct extended, neither the *viæ regiæ* nor the road of the *seigneur.* However, as the latter came to understand the advantages good roads were to them, they made an effort to keep them in better repair. In 1203, Blanche of Navarre established a paved road and two bridges between Troyes and Meaux and made a contract with three *entrepreneurs* for seven years that tolls be paid by pilgrims, horses, and carriages for their maintenance. Bridges were often built by the 'Frères Pontifes.' In 1190, when a wooden bridge at Lyons crumpled after the passage of crusaders under Philip Augustus and Richard I, tolls were levied all over France to build stone ones; companies were formed, each pledging to build an arch. The Bishop of Soissons allotted, for building a bridge, one half the alms offered by pilgrims coming to venerate a relic at Châlons, the remainder of the sum being given by the cathedral (1205). (*Gall. Christ.*, vol. X, p. 129.) The old Roman roads in Gaul were still traceable; though sadly out of repair, they were the best to be found. Where they failed, rivers were used. The building of a road or bridge was often imposed as an act of penance in the eleventh century, as it was considered a meritorious act.

28. In 1190, the Archbishop of Arles held a synod to consider measures against brigands, and the Templars were charged to see to the safety of the more important roads and bridges. In the same century a bridge was built in Avignon under the enthusiastic leadership of a shepherd who was later canonised. The Frères Pontifes, whose mission was to guard travellers, originated in Florence and came to southern France in the twelfth century. They were prosperous for a time, but by the thirteenth century had quite disappeared. The Petit Pont at Paris is

attributed to them. They undertook to build a bridge at Lyons, a feat they were unable to accomplish because of the current.

29. The cross on roads and bridges was originally, perhaps, not of religious significance, but seems to have had some connection with the branch of a tree on which a flag was fastened to prevent or halt warfare. It was early used at fairs and was taken down when the merchants left. Later, it had a religious significance as well as being the sign of peace, and the peace of the market became the peace of the *ville*. The cross then was a permanent sign, and its peace extended about a league around the *ville*. Sometimes the cross marked the centre of the *ville;* sometimes, in the case of old towns, it was erected outside the walls in new quarters of merchants. Inns were erected, then houses for *comptoirs*, and then houses for those who came to live there the year round, and the peace of the market extended to all surrounding buildings.

30. They were often the subject of satire by the poets of the Middle Ages.

31. See Albericus, *Chron.*, for an extract of a lost work by Guy de Bazoches, describing the journey of crusaders from Champagne to Marseilles. (*M.G.H. SS.*, vol. XXIII, pp. 751–55.)

32. Provins was at this time one of the most interesting and prosperous of French towns. Her population, crowded within the walls and overflowing to the outlying *faubourgs*, numbered 80,000, ten times what it is to-day, as the pestilence of 1383 destroyed what the English wars spared, and the wars of religion finished the process. Like many mediæval cities it consisted of an upper, ecclesiastical, military *ville*, and a lower one, commercial and manufacturing. The former was encircled by a twelfth-century wall pierced by strongly fortified gates, the most notable of which was the Porte de Jouy, a masterpiece of military architecture. Other fortifications were the machicolated citadel, the Tour-aux-Pourceaux, the Tour de Gannes, the Tour-le-Roi, and the Grosse Tour. The long, gloomy palace of the counts was already built at this time; the twelfth century had seen the erection of a number of fortified dwellings such as the Hôtel Brabans. Of the churches, Saint-Quiriace, Saint-Thibault (now in ruins), Saint-Laurent (1157), Notre-Dame-du Châtel, Saint-Jean, were all built. So was the rich and powerful abbey of Saint-Jacques (1050), the Hôpital du Saint-Esprit for the aged, the poor, and the orphans, the Cistercian Hôtel Vanluisant, the Hôtel Dieu (1050), a leprosie, and the Hôtel Saint-Jacques for pilgrims. Scattered through the *ville* were vast *halles* rented by the *bourgeois* to foreign merchants at fair time. The lower town, called 'Anatilorum' (Canard-Cuir), was no less interesting. It was also strongly fortified and it had notable buildings: the churches of Saint-Ayoul (reconstructed 1196), Sainte-Croix (called Saint-Laurent until it became the possessor of a fragment of the True Cross), Notre-Dame-du-Val (later turned into a *sal-de-bal*),

the hall of the Templars, the Hôtel de Ville, the *halle* for fairs, the large *maisons* where merchants were lodged — all these belonged to the twelfth-century town. The streets were named for the artisans and their wares; there were markets for horses, for butter, for fish, and for cloth; and there were numerous mills on the banks of the river as well as dyeworks and tanneries. Jews existed in great numbers in Provins: in the upper town they congregated in the rue de Vieille Juiverie, near the Châtel; in the lower, in the rue aux Juifs, where they had a synagogue and a cemetery. Provins was noted for the many caves, which, in the upper town, formed a subterranean *ville*, and which were used for storehouses and granaries. It was noted also for its red roses brought by the crusaders from the Holy Land and erroneously called 'Red Roses of Provence.'

33. Saint-Ayoul was built in the eleventh century, but suffered from fires and wars. It is now partly desecrated, but a fine old twelfth-century portal, a reredos, and some good carvings remain as witnesses of its earlier beauty. In 1122, Abælard sought refuge in the priory of which the church is a dependency.

34. Destroyed by the English in 1358.

35. Completed in the early thirteenth century.

36. The first days of entry were devoted to the arrival, the establishment of their wares, etc.; then came ten days of sale of cloth; eleven of leather and furs; then sale of things by weight; and then days of payment. The fair must be closed six weeks after the opening, and then four days were allowed for payments during which time no goods could be sold. In these days the *lettres de foires* were taken. (*Cart. Caillot*, f. 420.)

37. The Grosse Tour was used at this time as a bell-tower for Saint-Quiriace. It was also called the 'Tour de César.'

38. The tanners were in front of Saint-Laurent; the jewellers from Paris were next them; the linen stalls were in front of the Bourg Neuf, and sheep were in pens down the side streets. (Bib. Nat., MS. 5992, f. 354 [1233].)

39. In the upper town the Spaniards, the merchants of Cambrai, of Lucca, of Troyes, of Lombardy, and of Brabant and *halles;* in the lower, those from Douai, Châlons, Lyons, Malines, Ypres, and Saint-Omer had similar quarters. There were also *hôtels* for those who came to make their fortunes or to seek pleasure at the fairs, such as the Hôtel des Allemands, the Hôtel d'Aurillac, etc. The *Vicus Angliæ* suggests an English quarter, though it may not have been connected with the fair.

40. The consuls of Toulouse thanked the dean and canons of Saint-Quiriace for ceding to them, '*pour y débiter leurs marchandises*' at the

fairs of Saint-Ayoul and of May, the great vault of the chapter with the '*pour pris*' and the house called Forcadas, March, 1222. (*Mémoires de la Société des antiquaires de France,* vol. VIII, new ser., p. 3151; *Cart. Caillot,* f. 257.)

41. It is now a *musée lapidaire.*

42. A fine light-weight wool, used for underwear.

43. Provins was famed for cutlery and for couvertures. (*Practica della Mercatura.*)

44. Such as butter and fish from Norway, herring and bacon from Denmark, Rhenish wine, rice from Aragon, grain from Castile, figs and raisins from Andalusia, and honey from Portugal.

45. Animals and agricultural products played an important part in these fairs. Languedoc sent wool to Italy; Normandy sent cattle to England and grain to Flanders, Sweden, Norway, and Navarre. Louis IX forbade *baillies* to prevent the circulation of grain, wine, and merchandise except in time of famine and war. (*Ord. des Rois de France,* vol. I, p. 74.)

46. Bourquelot, *Provins,* vol. I, p. 256.

47. The cry '*Are!*' or '*Hare!*' by a sergeant of the fair proclaimed its formal opening. It may have come from '*Haro,*' a Norman war-cry.

48. The loggia of the *changeurs* was a combination of exchange bureau and bank; money of all countries was received and exchanged. This loggia was the administrative centre of the fair.

49. The measure of cloth, varying in almost every town, certainly in every country, it was necessary to reduce them to a common standard. Here, for this purpose, the weights and measures of Provins were used; the town having its own. The standard of measure was the *aune,* and an iron rule about two metres long, now in the Bibliothèque Publique, dates from this period. Among the rules read was one forbidding them to sell water for wine, marten for sable, common wood for *mazelin* (that used for carving), and selling at too high a price.

50. The money of Provins was standard here. It was used all over Europe and was received where that of the Counts of Champagne and Brie was refused. In 1208, Countess Blanche made a contract with the Bishop of Meaux to coin the money of Troyes, Meaux, and Provins; two thirds of the profit was to go to her and the rest to the bishop. (*Cart. Comit. Campan,* f. 64 t.; Bib. Nat., MS. 3992.) Provins had had its own money since the time of Charlemagne. In 1230, the Emperor Frederick II paid for his absolution thirty-two thousand livres *Provisinorum.* The business of the fairs was often conducted by *lettres de change.* (Blancard, vol. I, docs. 1, 2, 484, 550, 554, etc.)

51. The chief officers of the fair were the two masters or guards who saw that the debts were collected. On one occasion they wrote the Mayor of London asking him to seize two Florentines who had fled thither leaving unpaid accounts at the fair. The chancellor of the fair had charge of the seal. (A reproduction of this is in Bourquelot, *Provins*, vol. I, p. 128.) Then there were lieutenants, clerks, notaries, and sergeants; the latter guarded the road as far as Dijon. At times there were three hundred of these.

52. At the May Fair, certain towns were always represented: Châlons, Rheims, Saint-Quentin, Cambrai, Lille, Ypres, Douai, Arras, Tournay, Péronne, Huy, Valenciennes, Gand, Bruges, Saint-Omer, Monstrelet, Abbéville, Amiens, Beauvais, Bailleul. The following provinces were also there: Picardie, Artois, Normandie, Île de France, Lorraine, Bourgogne, Franche-Comté, Lyonnais, Provence, Languedoc. The Italians were usually there with silks and glass; the Scots with wool; the Hungarians with wax and silver; the Germans with iron and steel; the Poles with gold, silver, and wax. In 1243, Henry III sent agents to Provins to buy silks and other objects '*nécessaires à notre personne.*' However, he did not include money for payment, as the roads were not safe, but asked the Count of Champagne to stand security for him, to the extent of two hundred livres.

53. The master of the trained monkeys paid entrance at the Porte du Petit-Châtel at Paris, but this was remitted if he gave a performance there. (*Livre des Métiers.*)

54. The *Coutoumme de Troyes* allowed nobles to engage in trade.

55. Roman de Hervis. (*Cart. de la ville de Provins*, in Bib. Provins, f. 166 t.)

56. See the Bull of Pope Gregory IX, dated 1227, to whom they carried their complaints.

57. Felibien et Lobineau, vol. I, p. xcv.

58. *Ibid.*, p. xcviii.

59. The Abbot Suger places the foundation of the fair in 1109, when the Bishop of Paris exhibited there a piece of the True Cross.

60. Charter of 1192, given by Felibien et Lobineau, *l.c.*

61. Charter of Philip Augustus of 1187, given in Felibien et Lobineau, *l.c.*

62. Charter of Louis le Jeune, 1170.

63. *L.c.*, c. 13.

64. *De Idol.*, c. xi, Migne, *Pat. Lat.*, vol. I, col. 675.

65. *De Regimine Principum*, lib. ii, c. 3, p. 545, in vol. XIX of *Opera*, ed. Ven., 1754.

66. *Gesta Gaufridi Constantiensis Episcopi, Recueil,* vol. XIV, p. 78.

67. *Statuts d'Arles,* Pardessus, vol. IV, *Lois Maritimes.*

68. E.g., Guy de Joinville, Bishop of Châlons, regulated the order of metal workers, obliging them to repair the bishop's palace free of charge and furnish all needed materials.

69. 'Quars leurs mestier n'apartient a nule âme forsque a saintes Iglise et aus barons et aus riches homes et nobles.'

70. Borrelli de Serres, pp. 40–41.

71. In 1313 thirty-two persons were killed by wolves in the suburbs of Milan.

72. *Recueil,* vol. XXI, p. 226.

73. Thomassin, *Anciennes et nouvelle discipline de l'Église,* vol. VI, p. 604.

74. Mansi, vol. XXII, col. 846, Concil. de Paris.

75. Martène et Durand, *Thes. Nov.,* vol. IV, col. 477.

76. Mansi, vol. XXIV, col. 1185.

77. *Regestrum Visitationum* of Eude Rigaud, p. 188.

78. Aubry, *Musique,* p. 10; Eude Rigaud, pp. 322, 390, 618.

79. Eude Rigaud, pp. 42, 240; Aubry, p. 52; Aubry, *Motet,* vol. III, p. 78, for some of the chants and songs.

80. Eude Rigaud, p. 105; Aubry, *Musique,* p. 20.

81. Mansi, vol. XXIII, cols. 676, 809.

82. Eude Rigaud, pp. 110, 351, 159, 332, 395.

83. *Ibid.,* pp. 237, 159, 369.

84. *Quer. Norm.,* nos. 45, 68, 76; *Romans de Hervis de Metz;* Miniature in MS. fonds fr. Bib. Nat., no. 146 (end of MS.); MS. Bod. Oxford, 264. See letter of Charles VII written April 17, 1445 (Martène et Durand, *Thes. Nov.,* vol. I, col. 1804), in which he says: '*Au tres grand vitupere et diffame de tout l'estat ecclesiastique, faisoint toutes eglises et lieux saints, comme dehors et mesmement durant le divin office plusieurs grandes insolences, dérisions, mocqueries, spectacles, publics, de leurs corps déguisements en usant d'habits indecents et non appartenants à leur estat et profession, comme d'habits et vestements de fols, de gens d'armes et autres habits seculiers et les aucuns usants d'habits et vestements de femmes, aucuns de faux visages ou autres telles illicites manierres de vestement et apostatant de leur estat et profession.*'

BIBLIOGRAPHY

BIBLIOGRAPHICAL NOTE

WHILE the almost continuous existence throughout the Middle Ages of groups of men and women in all parts of western Europe who were seeking salvation by the practice of evangelical poverty is beyond question, the material for their history is sparse and widely scattered. Only when their efforts found expression in the establishment of monastic orders, or when, by joining the ranks of heretics, they came into conflict with the ecclesiastical authorities, is any record of them found and such seldom includes statements as to their doctrines on poverty. Rather, since it is concerned with their departures from the accepted doctrines of the Church and since the practice of evangelical poverty was not inherently heretical, this is almost never mentioned. Consequently, it has been necessary to rely on a great body of indirect evidence found not only in material primarily theological, but in all that related to the life of the times, literary as well as historical. Even when the records are fullest, in the period just preceding the coming of the friars, there is little that relates to dogma or ceremonial. Moreover, since all information comes from the records of those who were being attacked for corrupt and unapostolic lives, it is of necessity inaccurate in certain respects.

The Waldensian records are most complete of any of these evangelical groups, but the earliest of these date from the fourteenth and fifteenth centuries, and are thus much later than the records of the Inquisition. Neither Cathari nor the sects allied to them left any information as to their origin or their peculiar doctrines. Of Arnold of Brescia, the most diligent research has revealed nothing that will throw any light on his position on the subject of evangelical poverty. The Poor Catholics disappeared during the Albigensian Crusade, leaving scarcely a trace of themselves. While the story of the monastic orders is more complete, their influence on the Franciscans is less direct, and their expression of the popular mind of the day, less positive.

Any study of the forerunners of Saint Francis, therefore, must of necessity include a wide range of contemporary literature which yields but meagre information. Miss Davison had made a careful survey of the more important printed sources. This expansion of her work includes an investigation of the manuscript material in the archives of southern France and of Italy which has confirmed the results of her researches without altering them appreciably.

The archives of Narbonne, Carcassonne, Avignon, and Arles are especially rich in records of the Inquisition, as are the Vatican and

Casanatense libraries in Rome. Milan has practically all that exists on the early Humiliati, although in the neighbouring cities, such as Cremona, Como, Verona, etc., are to be found later records bearing chiefly on their economic relations with the municipal authorities. Scattered codices in Vienna, Munich, Cambridge, Dublin, Geneva, and Paris, throw some light on the early Waldensians. Their own archives at Torre Pellice, near Turin, do not antedate the sixteenth century and relate chiefly to the later persecutions they endured and to their connections with the Lutheran and Calvinistic movements.

PART ONE

(a) Manuscript Sources

Austria.

Vienna, Imperial Library.

Cod. Klosterneuberg, *Johannes Leser.*

Cod. Vindobon. 3721, *Rescriptum hæresiarcharum* (14th cent.).

England.

Cambridge, Morland MSS. A–X. (On the Waldensians.)

Oxford, Codex Rawlinsonianus 239, *Notæ brevis de Waldensib.*

France.

Angers,

Cod. 410, *Statuts et Privilèges de l'Ordre de Grandemont.*

Dijon, Archives de la Côte d'Or, Cod. 156.

Grenoble,

Cod. 18, *Les premières chartres de la Grande Chartreuse* (1084).

596, *Recueil des décisions des chapitres généraux* (1298).

598, *Statuts de l'Ordre des Chartreuse* (14th cent.).

604, *Combinaison des anciens statuts.*

605, *Compilation des statuts anciens et nouveaux de l'Ordre de Chartreuse.*

43, *Bible dite Vaudoise.*

989, *Recueil des variantes de la traduction de la Bible en langue volgaire dite Vaudoise.*

Laon, Cod. 219, 225, *Res Præmonstratenses.*

Paris,

Bibliothèque de l'Arsenal, Cod. 2085, *Waldensian Gospels,* etc.

Bibliothèque Nationale,

Cod. fonds Lat. 10947. *Cartulaire de Clairvaux.*

nouv. acq. lat. 1250. *Ibid.*

Cod. fonds fr. 2425, 6447.

fonds fr. anc. 8086.

fonds Lat. 1315, 11847.

Bib. Reg. 4236, 4269.
Bib. Imp. 9752, 10448, 10891, 11847, 11848, 11886.
Reg. Lat. 734, 2001.
fonds fr. 1244.
Coll. Moreau, 1274.
Coll. Occitan., vol. vii.
Coll. Doat. *Documents relatifs à l'inquisition.*

Tours, Cod. 1000. *Documents relatifs à l'Ordre de Grandemont.*
1228. *Ibid.*

Troyes, Cod. 703, *Cartulaire de Clairvaux*, vol. I.

GERMANY.

Munich,
Cod. Windberg., *Articulos notabiliores sectæ Waldens.*
Cod. monac. lat. 544, *Summa contra hæreticos.*
Cod. lat. Bav. 311, *Rescriptum hæresiarcharum.*
Cod. Alderspac, 184, *Ibid.*

IRELAND.

Dublin, Trinity College Library.
Cod. ex Bibl. Usser., nos. 259–67, *Waldensian MSS.*

ITALY.

Assisi, Archivio del Sacro Convento.
Cod. 265, 330, 334, 338, 344, 349–50, 418, 686, all relating to the early Franciscans.

Brescia
Libreria dei Padri dell' Oratorio di S. Filippo Neri, Faiono *Brescia illustre nelle principale dignitá ecclesiastiche.*

Florence, Biblioteca Laurenziana,
Cod. Bib. Mugell. 13, *Salvi Burce Placent.*

Milan
Archivio Curia Archiv., Gregorius IX, *Bull*, *Cum felicis memorie* (contains the Rule of the First and Second Orders of the Humiliati).
Archivio Braidense.
Cod. AF IX, ii, no. 1.
AD XVI, i A, B.
AG XI, 3.
AD XV, 9, 22.
AE XV, 32, 28, 25, 26.
Archivio di Santa Maria della Grazie,
Cartelli, A, B, C, D, E, F, H, I, L, M, N.
Archivio Stato
F. R. Perg., S. Ambrogio, 110–14.
Sta. Maria sopra Varese, 213.
S. Marcellino.

S. Eustorgio, MS. Bregatti.
Sta. Maria di Brera.
Chiaravalle.
S. Leonardo di Bergamo.
Sta. Maria di Bergamo.
SS. Cosmo e Damiano di Bres.
S. Fedele di Como.
S. Benedetto di Cremona.
Bolle e brevi: *Ep. ad exterpandum*, 1259.
Cathologus cronologicus fidei quæsitarum Mediolani.
Miscellanea in *Sezione Storica*, busta 5, fasc. II.
Archivio Spedale Maggiore,
Perg., *Archivi speciali, Enti civili e religiosi.*
Biblioteca Ambrosiana, *Carte pagensi.*
A 233, Inf., Tristani Calchi Med., *Hist. Patriæ Præfatio.*
DS IV Raccolta della Croce 11, 14, 18.
G 301, Inf., G 302, Inf., Joannis Braidensis *Chronica.* 1421.
C 74, 103, Inf., *ibid.*
BS I, 19, *Chronica* (1419).
V 9, Sup., *ibid.*
T 258, Inf., *ibid.*
BS I, 19, Fratris Marci Bosii *Chronicon.*
S 89, Sup., *In historiam ac res ordinem Humiliatores pertinentes.*
D 273, Inf. (Rule of St. Benedict adapted to the Humiliati).
D 56, Inf., *ibid.*
F 82, Sup. (Constitution of the Humiliati).
H 210, Inf. (Another constitution).
H 267, Inf., *Breviario.*
I 197, Inf., *Brevario.*
Z 101, Sup., *Ordo ad recipiendas mulieres.*
D 58, Inf., *Omnis boni Principium.* (Rule of the Order.)
D 42, Inf., *Mediolani consuetudines*, 1216.
I 175, Inf., *Decreta varia Ducum Med.*
Y 55, Sup., *Cronaca.* 1162–1378.
S 119, Sup., *Cronache varie del sec.* XIII.
H 3, Inf., *Chronica Vicentiæ*, 1200–1311.
G 3, Inf., *Chronica Patav.* 1207–1260.
Pinerola, Biblioteca Communale.
Cod. I, N, 60–62, Garolla, *Dei Valdesi.*
Rome.
R. Archivio di Stato.
Tabularium S. Praxedis.
" *Sta. Maria in Via Lata.*
Biblioteca Apostolica Vaticana, Archivio segreto.
Cod. H 3, x; N 3, i; I 3, ix, 18, 19; I 6, vi; GG, x, 352; GG, iii, 46; GG ix, 76: I 3, i; A 6, 149; I 4, iv; SQ 46; SQ; iv, 207.

Biblioteca Apostolica Vaticana.
Cod. Arch di S. Pietro 381.
Vat. Lat. 300, 512, 677, 934, 2043, 2103–04, 2417, 2656, 3217, 3830, 3833, 4010, 4030, 4031, 4032, 4236, 4255, 4260, 4336, 4898, 5083, 5422, 5712, 5776, 6224, 6367, 7026, 7143, 7207, 7651, 7702, 7796.
Barb. Lat. 136, 538, 733, 1199, 1459, 2675, 3926, 4065, 9096. Ottob. 136, 1119, 1463, 2441.
Biblioteca Casanatense.
Cod. A IV, 7; A III, 10; A IV, 22; B III, 25; D III, 18; X VI, 42; A IV, 49.
Turin, Biblioteca Regis Victor Emmanuel.
Cod. J, vi, 33, Bernard de Besse, *De Laudibus.*
169, *Histoire véritable des Vaudois.*
13489, Boyer, *L'Histoire des Vaudois.*
Charvaz, *Delle vicende . . . dei Valdesi.*

SWITZERLAND.
Geneva.
Bibliothèque de la Ville, Cod. 205–09 (Waldensian documents).

(b) Collections of Sources

Acta Capitulorum Provincialium O.F.P. 1239–1302. ed. Douais, Toulouse, 1894.
Acta Pontificum Romanorum inedita, ed. Pflug-Harttung, Tübingen, 1881.
Acta Sanctorum Boll., Antwerp, 1643–1910.
Acta Sanctorum Ordinis S. Benedict., ed. Mabillon et d'Achéry, 1733.
Analecta ad Fratrum Minorum, ed. Evers, Leipzig, 1882.
Analecta Franciscana, Quaracchi, 1885–1917.
Analecta Sacra Ordinis Fratrum Prædicatorum, ed. Frühwirth, Rome, 1893, etc.
Annales Camaldulenses, ed. Mittarelli, Venice, 1735–73.
Annales Ecclesiastici, ed. Baronius et Spondanus, Lucca, 1738–56.
Annales Minorum, ed. Wadding, Lyons, 1635.
Annales Ordinis S. Benedict., ed. Mabillon, Lucca, 1739–45.
Annales Ordinis Cartusiensis, ed. Le Couteulx, 1887–91.
Annali d'Italia, ed. Muratori, Milan, 1773.
Antiquitates italicæ medii ævi, ed. Muratori, Milan, 1738–42.
Archiv für Litteratur und Kirchengeschichte des Mittelalters, Berlin, 1835.

Beiträge zur Sektengeschichte, ed. Preger, *Königliche Bayerische Akademie der Wissenschaften Philologische-historische classe*, vols. XIII, XIV.
Beiträge zur Sektengeschichte des Mittelalters, ed. Döllinger, Munich, 1890.

Bibliotheca ecclesiastica Mabillonica, n.p. (16–?)

Bibliotheca historica medii œvi, ed. Potthast, Berlin, 1862–68.

Bibliotheca Rerum Germanicarum, ed. Jaffé, Berlin, 1865.

Bibliothèque des Auteurs Ecclésiastiques, ed. Dupin, Paris, 1657–1719.

Bullarium Franciscanum Romanorum, Paris, 1759–1904; Quaracchi, 1908.

Canones Sanctorum Apostolorum, ed. Balsamon, Paris, 1561.

Capitularia Regum Francorum, ed. Baluze, Paris, 1780.

Cartulaire . . . de S. Dominique, Paris, 1893–1901.

Catalogus Testium Veritatis, ed. Flacius, Basle, 1556.

Chartulariium Universitatis parisiensis, ed. Denifle et Chatelain, Paris, 1889.

Collectio Judiciorum, ed. d'Argentré, Paris, 1728.

Collection des cartulaires de France in *Coll. de Doc. inéd. sur l'hist. de la France.*

Vols. I–II, *Cartulaire de l'abbaye de Saint-Père de Chartres*, Paris, 1840.

III–IV, *Cartulaire de l'église Notre-Dame de Paris*, Paris, 1850.

VIII–IX, *Cartulaire de l'abbaye de Saint Victor de Marseilles*, Paris, 1857.

Collection des documents pour l'histoire religeuse et littéraire du moyen-âge, ed. Sabatier, Paris, 1898.

Collection des textes pour servir à l'étude de l'histoire de la France, ed. Molinier.

Constitutiones Apostolicœ, ed. Ültzen, Rostock, 1853.

Constitutiones et Acta Publica Imperatorum et Regum, in *Monumenta Germaniœ Imperatorum et Regum*, Hanover, 1893–1904.

Corpus Documentorum Inquisitionis Hœreticœ Pravitatis Neerlandicœ, ed. Fredericq, Ghent, 1889–1906.

Corpus historicum medii œvi, ed. Eckhart, Leipzig, 1723.

Corpus Juris canonici, Lyons, 1614.

Documenti inediti sulla storia di Torino, ed. Cognasso, Pinerola, 1914.

Documents inédits pour servir à l'histoire littéraire de l'Italie, depuis le viiime *siècle jusqu'au xiii*^me^ *siècle*, ed. Ozanam, Paris, 1850.

Documents pour servir à l'histoire de l'Inquisition dans le Languedoc au xiiime *siècle*, ed. Douais, Paris, 1900.

Epistolœ cardinalium Romanorum (1153–59), in *Neues Archiv der Gesellschaft für ältere deutsche Geschichte*, vol. II.

Epistolœ pontificum romanorum ineditœ, ed. Löwenfeld, Leipzig, 1885.

Fermanentum trium ordinum beatissimo Patris nostri Francesci, Paris, 1512. (A collection of constitutions of the Order made by authority of Bonaventura.)

Fœdera, ed. Rymer, London, 1726–35.
Fontes juris canonici, ed. Galante, 1906.
Fonti per la storia d'Italia, Rome, 1898, etc.

Gallia christiana, Montbéliard, 1870.
Gesta Dei per Francos, Hanover, 1611.
Les Grandes chroniques de France, ed. P. Paris, Paris, 1836–38.
Gretser, Jacob, *Opera omnia*, Ratisbon, 1734–41.

Historiæ Francorum Scriptores, ed. Duchesne, Paris, 1636–49.

Italia Sacra, ed. Ughelli-Coletti, Rome, 1643.
Iter Italicum, ed. Pflugk-Harttung, Stuttgart, 1883.

Jus Municipale Vicentinum, Venice, 1567.

Layettes du Trésor des Chartes, Paris, 1863.
Liber Statutorum Franchiscarum ac immunitatum civitatis Pinerolii, Turin, 1602.
Limborch, Philipp von, *Liber Sententiarum Inquisitionis Tholosanæ*, Amsterdam, 1692.

Magnum Bullarium Romanum, ed. Cherubini, 1655.
Maxima Bibliotheca Veterum Patrum, Cologne, Lyons, Venice, 1618–1773.
Miscellanea, ed. Baluze, Lucca, 1677.
Monumenta Franciscana, ed. Brewer and Howlett, London, 1858.
Monumenta Germaniæ Historica, Berlin, 1879–1919.
Diplomatum regum et imperatorum Germaniæ.
Epistolæ sæculi xiii e regestis pontificum Romanorum selectæ.
Gestorum pontificum Romanorum.
Legum.
Poetarum latinorum medii ævi.
Scriptores.
Les Monuments primitifs de la Règle Cistercienne, Dijon, 1878.
Museum Italicum, ed. Mabillon, Paris, 1687–89.

Notizie e Documenti della Chiesa Pinerolese, ed. Caffaro, Pinerola, 1893–1903.
Nova Bibliotheca, ed. Labbé, Paris, 1657.
Nuovi documenti sui moti ereticali, ed. Tocco, in *Arch. Stor. Ital.*, 1901.

Patrologiæ Græcæ, ed. Migne, Paris, 1859, etc.
Patrologiæ Latinæ, cursus completus, ed. Migne, Paris, 1844–64.
Les poémes vaudois d'apres le MSS. inédit de Dublin, in Boll. Soc. Hist. Vaud., vol. XXIII, 1906.

Pontificum Romanarum vitæ, ed. Watterich, Leipzig, 1862.

Raccolta di Statuti municipali italiani, ed. Todaro della Galia, Palermo, 1887.

Recueil des chartes de l'abbaye de Cluny, Paris, 1876.

Recueil des Historiens des Gaules et de la France, Paris, 1869, etc.

Recueil général des anciennes lois françaises, ed. Isambert.

Regesta imperii, ed. Böhmer, Stuttgart, 1849.

Regesta pontificum romanorum, ed. Potthast, Berlin, 1874–75.

Regesta pontificum romanorum, ed. Jaffé, Leipzig, 1885–88.

Rerum Anglicarum Scriptorum Veterum, Oxford, 1684–91.

Rerum Bohemicarum antiqui scriptores, ed. Freher.

Rerum Britannicarum medii œvi scriptores, ed. Stubbs (Rolls Series).

Sacræ Annales, (Ord. Præmonstrat.), ed. Hugo, 1725.

Sacrorum Conciliorum nova et amplissima coll., ed. Mansi, Florence, 1759–98.

Sanctæ Ecclesiæ Florentinæ memorabilia, ed. Lamius (Lami), Florence, 1758.

Scriptores Ord. Præd., ed. Quétif et Echard, Paris, 1719–21.

Spicilegium . . . collectio veterum, ed. d'Achéry, Paris, 1860.

Statuta Mediolanensium, ed. Rubeus, Milan, 1598.

Statuti dei Mercanti di Roma, ed. Gatti, Rome, 1885 (thirteenth to seventeenth centuries).

Thesaurus Novus Anecdotorum, ed. Martène et Durand, Paris, 1717.

Thesaurus Veterum Inscriptionum, Milan, 1739–42.

Vetera Analecta, ed. Mabillon, Paris, 1723.

Vetera Humiliatorum Monumenta, Tiraboschi, Girolamo, Milan, 1766.

Veterum Scriptorum Amplissima Collectio, ed. Martène et Durand, Paris, 1724–33.

Wattenbach, *Deutschland Geschichtsquellen*, 1893.

Wegweiser zur Quellen und Litteraturkunde der Kirchengeschichte, Gotha, 1890.

(c) Primary Sources

Abælardus, Petrus, *Opera Omnia*, ed. Cousin, Paris, 1889.

Ademarus Cabannenses (†1034). *Historiarum*, in *M.G.H. SS.*, vol. IV, vol. X (for the Apostolics).

Alanus de Insulis (†1202). *Adversus Hæreticos*, in Migne, *Pat. Lat.*, vol. CCX. (A monk under Bernard at Clairvaux and later Bishop of Auxerre.)

Albericus monachus Trium Fontium (†after 1252). *Chronica*, in *M.G.H. SS.*, XXIII.

Andrea (Abbot of San Fidele, Strumi, Italy, †1097). *Sancti Arialdi Vita*, in *AA. SS.*, 27 Jun. (An eye-witness of the events he describes.)

Annales Brixienses (1152–73), in *M.G.H. SS.*, vol. XVIII.

Annales Colonienses Maxima, in *M.G.H. SS.*, vol. XVII.

Annales Trevirenses. Liège, 1670.

Anonymus Passaviensis (1260), in Gretser, *Opera Omnia*, vol. XII, pt. 1.

Le antiche cronache di Orvieto, ed. Gamurrini, in *Arch. Stor. Ital.*, 1889.

S. Antoninus. *Chronicon*, Nüremburg, 1484.

Arnulfus. *Gesta Archiepiscoporum Mediolanensium*, 925–1077, in *R.I.S.*, vol. IV.

S. Augustinus. *De Civitate Dei*, in Migne, *Pat. Lat.*, vol. XLI.

S. Bartolommeo degli Albizzi da Pisa. *Liber Conformitatum vitæ patris Francisci*, Bologna, 1590. (A work compiled in the fourteenth century from sources of the twelfth and thirteenth, and aiming to show how the life of Saint Francis conformed to that of Christ.)

Benedictus Cassinensis. *Regula Monachorum*, ed. Woelfflin, Leipzig, 1895.

Benedictus, abbatis Petriburgensis. *Gesta Henrici II*, ed. Stubbs, London, 1867.

Benzonis episcopi Albensis *Ad. Heinricum IV*, in *M.G.H. SS.*, vol. XI.

S. Bernardus, Abbas Claræ-vallensis. *Opera Omnia*, ed. Mabillon, in Migne, *Pat. Lat.*, vols. CLXXXII–CLXXXV.

Bernadus abbas Fontis Calidi (†1190). *Adversus Waldensium sectam liber*, in *Bib. Max. Vet. Pat.*, vol. XXIV.

Bernardus Guidonis (†1321). *De ordinibus Grandimontensi*, in Labbé, *Nova Bibl.*, vol. II.

—— *Practica Inquisitionis Hæreticæ*, ed. Douais, Paris, 1885.

Berthold von Regensburg (1220–72). *Predigten*, ed. Pfeiffer-Strohl, Vienna, 1862–80.

Bonacursus. *Vita Hæreticorum* in d'Achéry, *Spicilegium*, vol. I.

S. Bonaventura. *Opera Omnia*, Lyons, 1668.

Bonizo episc. Sutriensis tam Placentinus. *Chronicon Romanorum Pontificum*, in Migne, *Pat. Lat.*, vol. CL.

—— *Liber ad Amicum*, in Migne, *l.c.*

Burchardus. *Decreti*, in Migne, *Pat. Lat.*, vol. CXIV.

Burchardus et Cuonradus Urspergensium. *Chronicon*, in *M.G.H. SS.*, vol. XXIII.

Cæsarius Heisterbacensis (1180–1240). *Dialogus Miraculorum*, ed. Strange, Cologne, 1851.

Carmina Burana, ed. Schmeller, Breslau, 1883.

Cassianus, Johannes. *Opera Omnia*, in *Bib. Max. Pat. Lugd.*, vol. VII.

Cavitelli, Ludovico. *Annales*, Cremona, 1588.

Chronica de Mailros, in *Rerum Anglicarum Scriptorum Veterum*, Oxford, 1684–91.

Chronica Fratris Jordani, in *Coll. Doc. du moyen-âge*, Paris, 1908.

Chronica monasterii Casinensis, in *R.I.S.*, vols. IV, V.

Chronico Anonymi Laudunensis, in *M.G.H. SS.*, vol. XXVI.

Chronicon Turonensi auctore anonymo S. Martini Turon. canonico, in *Recueil des Historiens*, vol. XVIII.

Codex diplomaticus Ord. S. Augustini, ed. Maiocchi e Casacco, Pavia, 1905–13.

Codex Theodosianus, ed. Hænel, Bonn, 1842.

Conrad von Lichtenau. *Chronicon* (for Waldo at Rome; a confused account), Strassburg, 1609.

Corio, B. *L'istoria di Milano*, Venice, 1544.

Cornerus, Hermannus, O. Præm. *Chronica ad 1435*, in Eckhart, *Corpus*.

Cyprianus. *Opera*, Cologne, 1521.

Davide de Augusta. *Tractatus*, in Preger, *Beiträge*.

De Dedalo et Icaro (12th-century poem), in Ozanam, *Documents*.

Desiderius Abbatis Casinensi. *Dialogus de Miraculis a Sancto Benedicto*, in Migne, *Pat. Lat.*, vol. CXLIX.

The Didache, ed. Hitchcock and Brown, New York, 1884.

Disputatio inter Catholicum et Paterinum, in Martène et Durand, *Thes. Nov.*, vol. V.

Durandus von Mende. *Rationale Divinorum Officiorum*, Mainz, 1459.

Ebrardus Bethuniensis (c. 1200). *Liber Anti-hæresis*, in Gretser, *Opera*, vol. XII, pt. 2.

Edictum Alphonsi Regis Aragonum Contra Hæreticos, in *Bib. Max. Vet. Pat.*, vol. XXV.

Epistola ecclesiæ Leodienses ad Lucium papam II, in Martène et Durand, *Ampliss. Collect.*, vol. II.

Epistola Traject. Eccles. ad Archiepiscopum Coloniensem 1112, in d'Argentré, *Collectio Judiciorum*, vol. I.

Epistolæ cujusdam senatus fidelis Wezeli, in *Epistolæ Wibaldi*, in Jaffé, *Bibliotheca Rerum Germanicarum*, vol. I.

Ermengardus. *Opusculum Contra Hæreticos*, in Gretser, *Opera*, vol. XII, pt. 2.

Eusebius. *Historia Ecclesiastica*, in Migne, *Pat. Græc.*, vol. XX.

Franciscus Assisiatis, Opera Omnia, Paris, 1880.

Galvinus Flaminus. *Manipulus Florum*, in *R.I.S.*, vol. XI.

Gerohus Reicherspergensis Præpositus. *De Investigatione Antichristi*, ed. Scheibelberger.

Girardus (seventh prior of Grammont). *Vita S. Stephani*, in Martène et Durand, *Ampl. Coll.*, vol. VI.

Girardus de Fracheto. *Vitæ Fratrum Ordinis Prædicatorum,* 1203–54, in *Monumenta Ordinis Fratrum Prædicatorum,* vol. II, Louvain, 1893.

Godefridus Viterbensis. *Memoria Seculorum,* in *R.I.S.*, vol. VII.

Gregorius VII Papa. *Opera,* in Migne, vol. CXLVIII.

Gregorius Catinensis. *Regesta . . . Ecclesiæ Farfensis,* Rome, 1879.

Gregorius Episcopus Turonensis. *Historia Ecclesiasticæ Francorum,* ed. Gaudet et Taranne, Paris, 1836.

Guibertus Novigenti. *Opera,* ed. d'Achéry, Paris, 1651.

Guilelmus de Podio Laurentii. *Historia Albigensium,* in *Recueil des Historiens,* vol. XI.

Guilelmus Neubrigensis. *Historia Rerum Anglicarum,* London, 1856.

Guillaume de Tudela. *Ex Carmine de Bello Albigensium* (not certainly his), Paris, 1875.

Guntherus. *Ligurinus, sive de rebus gestis Friderici Ænobardi,* in *Veterum Scriptorum . . . ex Bibliotheca Justi Reuberi,* Frankfurt, 1584.

Hilarius. *Elegia de recessiu Petri Abælardo,* in Migne, *Pat. Lat.*, vol. CLXXVIII.

Historia Pontificalis, in *M.G.H. SS.*, vol. XX.

Honorius Augustodensis (c. 1112). *Summa Totius et Imago Mundi* (for Norbert), in *M.G.H. SS.*, vol. X.

Hugo Metellus. *Epistola ad Henrico Leuchorum episcopo,* in *Sacræ Antiquitatis Monumenta Historia,* vol. II, 1731.

Hugo Rothomagensis (1164). *De Ecclesia,* in *Bib. Max. Vet. Pat.*, vol. XII.

—— *Dogmatum Christianæ Fidei contra Hæreticos sui Tempori,* in Guibertus Novigenti, *Opera,* ed. d'Achéry, 1651. Appendix.

Hugonis de Lacerta. *Vita S. Stephani Ord. Grand. Institut. Discipuli,* in Migne, vol. CCIV.

Hugonis Farfensis. *Opuscula,* in *M.G.H. SS.*, vol. XI.

Humbertus de Romans. *Vitæ Fratrum Ord. Præd.*, Marseilles, 1875.

—— *Chronicon,* in Quétif et Echard, vol. I.

—— *Sermones,* Venice, 1603.

Ignatius of Antioch. *Epistolæ,* in *Bib. Max. Vet. Pat. Lugd.*, vol. II.

Index Errorum quibus Waldenses infecti sunt, in Gretser, *Opera,* vol. XII, pt. 2.

Innocentius III. *Opera Omnia,* in Migne, *Pat. Lat.*, vols. CCXIV–CCXVII.

Jacobus de Vitriaco. *Libri duo quorum prior Orientalis sive Hierosclymitanæ alter Occidentalis Historiæ nomine inscribitur,* Douai, 1597.

—— *Epistolæ Quattuor,* in Martène, *Thes.*, Nov., vol. III.

Saint Jerome. *Opera Omnia,* in Migne, *Pat. Lat.*, vol. XXII–XXX.

John of Salisbury. *Polycraticus*, in Migne, *Pat. Lat.*, vol. CXCIX.
Jonæ Aureliens. *De Culto Imaginum*, in Migne, *Pat. Lat.*, vol. CVI.

Lactantius. *De Mortibus Persecutorum*, in Migne, *Pat. Lat.*, vol. VII.
Landulfus Junioris. *Historia Mediolanensis*, in *R.I.S.*, vol. V.
Landulfus Senioris. *Historia Mediolanensis*, in *M.G.H. SS.*, vol. VIII.
La Nobla Leyczon, ed. Montet, Paris, 1888.
Legenda Trium Sociorum, Rome, 1899.
Leo of Assisi. *Speculum perfectionis*, in *Coll. de Documents pour . . . le moyen âge*, Paris, 1908.
Liber Potheris Communis Civitatis Brixiæ, ed. Cozzago e d'Ostiani, in *Historia Patriæ Monumenta*, vol. XIX, Turin, 1857.
Lucas Tudensis. *De Altera Vita Fideique*, in *Bib. Max. Vet. Pat.*, vol. XXV.

Map, Walter. *De Nugis Curialium*, ed. Wright, London, 1850.
Matthæus Parisiensis. *Historia major*, London, 1640.
Moneta Cremonensis. *Adversus Catharos et Waldenses*, Rome, 1753.

Narratio de Electione Lotharii, in *Forschungen zur Geschichte*, vol. VII, Göttingen, 1868.
Norbert. *Sermo ad Fratres*, in *Bib. Max. Pat. Lugd.*, vol. XXI.
Novaria Sacra seu de Ecclesia Novariensi, Novara, 1612.

Ottonis Frisingensis. *De Gesta Friderici I Imperatoris*, in *M.G.H. SS.*, vol. XX.
—— *Chronicon* in *ibid.*

Petrus Blesensis. *Tractatus, Quales sunt*, in Migne, *Pat. Lat.*, vol. CCXVII.
Petrus Cantor. *Verbum Abbreviatum*, in Migne, *Pat. Lat.*, vol. CCV.
S. Petrus Damianus. *Opera omnia*, in Migne, *Pat. Lat.*, vols. CXLIV, CXLV.
Petrus Grandimontensis prior quintus. *Epistolæ*, in Martène, *Thes. Nov.*, vol. I.
Petrus Pilichdorffius. *Contra Sextam Waldensium*, in *Max. Bib. Pat. Lugd.*, vol. XXV.
Petrus Vallium Cernaii. *Historia Albigensium*, in *Recueil des Historiens*, vol. XIX.
Petrus Venerabilis abbatis Cluniacensis IX. *Epistola sive Tractatus adversus Petrobrusianos Hæreticos*, in Migne, *Pat. Lat.*, vol. CLXXXIX.
Pipinus, F. *Chronicon*, in *R.I.S.*, vol. IX.
Potho of Prüm. *De Statu Domus Dei*, in *Bib. Max. Patr. Lugd.*, vol. XXI.
Procopius. *De Bello Gallico*, in *R.I.S.*, vol. I.

Radulphus de Coggeshall. *Chronicon Anglicanum* (1066–1223), in *Recueil des Historiens*, vol. XXIII.

Radulphus Glabrus. *Francorum historiæ*, libri V, in *Recueil des Historiens*, vol. X.

Refutatio errorum quibus Wald., incerto autore, in Gretser, *Opera*, vol. XII, pt. 2.

Regula ordinis Grandimontensis, in Migne, *Pat. Lat.*, vol. CCIV.

Reinerius Sacchonius. *Summa de Catharis et Leonistas*, in Martène et Durand, *Thes. Nov.*, vol. V.

Richard of Cluny. *Chronicon*, in Muratori, *Antiquitates Ital.*, vol. XII.

Rituel Cathare, ed. Clédat, Paris, 1887.

Romualdus Salernitanus. *Chronicon*, in *R.I.S.*, vol. VII.

Sacrum Commercium beati Francis cicum Domina Paupertate, ed. Minocchi, Florence, 1901.

Fra Salimbene Parmensis Ordinis Minorum. *Cronica*, Parma, 1857.

Seherus, abbas Calmosiacensis. *Primordia Calmosiacensia*, in *M.G.H. SS.*, vol. XII.

Stephanus de Borbone. *Tractatus*, ed. Lecoy de la Marche, Paris, 1877.

Stephanus Tornacensis. *Epistolæ*, in Migne, vol. CCXI.

Strassburg Manuscript, ed. Schmidt, in *Zeitschrift für Deutschen Historische Theologie*, Hamburg, 1852.

Sugerus. *Gesta Ludovici regis cognomento grossi*, in *Coll. des Textes de l'Hist. de la France.*

Tertullianus. *De Monogamia*, in Migne, *Pat. Lat.*, vol. II.

Theodorus de Apolda O. F. P. *Vita S. Dominici* (the best of the early biographies), in Quétif et Echard, vol. I.

Thoma de Celano. *Seraphici Viri S. Francisci Assisiatis vitæ*, Rome, 1806.

S. Thomas Aquinas. *Opera Omnia*, Rome, 1899.

Thomas de Eccleston. *De Adventu Minorum in Angliam*, in *Monumenta Franciscana*, ed. Brewer, vol. I.

Tolommeo dei Fradoni di Lucca. *Historia Ecclesia*, in *R.I.S.*, vol. XI.

Trithemius, J. *Annalium Hirsaugiensium*, 830–1513, St. Gall, 1690.

Udalricus Babenbergense. *Codex Epistolaris*, in Eccardus, *Corpus Historicum*, vol. II.

La Vie de St. Alexis, Poème de XIe Siècle, publiée par Gaston Paris, Paris, 1887.

Vita Antiquior
Vita Altera } S. Brunonis, in *AA. SS.*, III Oct.
Vita Tertia

(For a comment on the authenticity of these lives see *Hist. Litt. de la France*, vol. IX.)

Vita S. Petri Damiani, in Migne, *Pat. Lat.*, vol. CXLIV.

William of Malmesbury. *De Gestis Regum Anglorum*, in *Rerum Anglicarum Scriptores*, Oxford, 1696.

(d) Retrospective Sources

d'Alençon, Ubald. *De l'Origine Française de St. François d'Assise.*
—— *Les idées de St. François sur le Pauvreté.*
—— *Leçons d'histoire Franciscaine*, Paris, 1918.
Alessandro, Carlo. *Istoria della cittá di Verona*, Verona, 1796.
Allard, Paul. *Le Christianisme et l'empire Romain*, Paris, 1897.
Allen, A. V. G. *Christian Institutions*, New York, 1897.
Alphandéry, P. *Les idées morales chez les hétérodoxes latins au début du XIIIme siècle*, Paris, 1903.
d'Arbois de Jubainville, H. *Études sur l'état interieur des Abbayes cisterciennes* (12th–13th centuries).
Arnaud, E. *Essai historique et critique sur l'origine des Vaudois*, in *Bull. des Hautes-Alpes*, 1895.
—— *Histoire des persécutions endurées par les Vaudois du Dauphiné au XIIIme et XVme siècles*, 1896.
—— *Les mœurs des Vaudois . . . d'autrefois et d'aujourdhui*, 1896.

Benoist, Réné. *Histoire des Albigenses et des Vaudois*, 1691.
Bérard, Alexander. *Les Vaudois . . . du IXme au XVIIme siècle*, Lyons, 1894.
Berger, Samuel. *La Bible française au Moyen-âge*, Paris, 1884.
Bernardi, J. *Degli statuti di Pinerola*, in *Rivista dei communi italiani*, Florence, 1816.
Bernhardi, Wilhelm. *Lothar von Supplinburg*, Leipzig, 1879.
Bianchi, Giovanni Antonio, O. F. M. *Della potestá e della politia della chiesa*, Rome, 1745–51.
Biancolini, G. *Notizie storiche delle chiese di Verona*, Verona, 1750.
Boffito, P. Giuseppe Barnabito. *Gli Eretici in Piemonte al tempo del gran scismo*, 1375–1417, Rome, 1897.
Bonet-Maury, Gaston. *Les Précurseurs de la Réforme et de la Liberté de Conscience dans les Pays Latins du XIIme au XVme siècles*, Paris, 1904.
Bonghi, Ruggiero. *Arnaldo da Brescia*, Cittá di Castello, 1885.
—— *Vita di S. Francesco*, Cittá di Castello, 1884.
Boüard de Forest, Alain de. *Le Régime Politique et les Institutions de Rome au Moyen-âge*, Paris, 1920.
du Boulay, César Égasse. *Historia Universitas Parisienses*, Paris, 1665–73.
Boyd, William K. *Ecclesiastical Edicts of the Theodosian Code*, New York, 1905.
Breyer, Robert. *Arnold von Brescia*, in *Historisches Taschenbuch*, 1889.
—— *Die Arnoldisten*, in *Zeitschrift für Kirchengeschichte*, vol. XII.

Caffaro, A *L'Arte del Lanifico*, in *Pinerola e gli Statuti di essa*, Pinerola, 1893.
Campi, Pietro Maria. *Dell' istoria Ecclesiastica di Piacenza*, Piacenza, 1651.
Camus. *L'homme Apostolique en la vie de S. Norbert*, Caen, 1640.
Cantú, Cesare. *Gli Eretici d'Italia*, Turin, 1865–66.
Cardilla, Lorenzo. *Memorie Storiche dei Cardinale della Santa Romana Chiesa*, Rome, 1792–97.
Carutti, Domenico. *Storia della cittá di Pinerola*, Pinerola, 1893.
—— *La Crociata Valdese del 1488*, Pinerola, 1894.
de Castro, A. *Arnaldo da Brescia*, Leghorn, 1875.
de Cauzons, T. *Les Vaudois et l'Inquisition*, Paris, 1908.
Cipolla, Carlo. *Il Patarenismo a Verona nel secolo XIII*, in *Arch. Ven.*, N.S., vol. XXV.
—— *Un Amico di Can Grande*, in *Mem. R. Accad. delle Scienze di Torino*, 1902.
Clavel, Victor. *Arnauld de Brescia et les Romains*, Paris, 1868.
Comba, Emilio. *Histoire des Vaudois*, Paris, 1901.
—— *Cenno Sulle Fonti della Storia dei Valdese*, in *Arch. Stor. Ital.*, 1893.

Dalla Corto, Girolamo. *Dell' I storie della Cittá di Verona*, Venice, 1744.
Delarc, Odon. *S. Gregoire VII et la Réforme de l'Église*, Paris, 1889.
Delisle, Leopold Victor. *Mémoire sur les Actes d'Innocent III*, Paris, 1857.
Deutsch, S. M., *Peter Abälard*, Leipzig, 1883.
—— *Die Synode von Sens*, Berlin, 1880.
De Wette, W. M. L., *Geschichte der Christlichen Sittenlehre*, Berlin, 1823–24.
Dieckhoff, O. *Die Waldenser im Mittel-alter*, Göttingen, 1857.
Dmitrevaki, Michael von. *Die Christliche Freiwillige Armut bis zum XII^{ten} Jahrhundert*, 1913.
Douais, Mgr. Celestin. *Les Albigeois*, Paris, 1880.
Dresdner, A. *Kultur-und-Sittengeschichte der Italienischen Geistlichkeit in X^{ten} u. XI^{ten} Jahrhunderts*, Breslau, 1890.
Du Pré, Maurice. *Vie de S. Norbert*, Paris, 1627.
Du Pré, M. *Annales Ord. Præmonstratensis*, Namur, 1886.

Esame intorno alla confessione di Fede della Chiesa Riformata di Piemonte, Turin, 1658.

Fantuzzi, G. *Notizie degli Scrittori Bolognese*, Bologna, 1781–94.
Florival, Adrien de. *Étude historique sur le XIIme siècle; Barthélmy de Vir évêque de Laon*, Paris, 1877.
Francke, Heinrich. *Arnold von Brescia und seine Zeit* (a fanciful picture, E S. D.), 1825.
Friedberg, Emil. *Kirchenrecht*, 1895.

Fumagalli, I. *Delle Antichitá Longobardico-milanesi*, Milan, 1792.
Fumi, Luigi. *I Patarini in Orvieto*, in *Arch. Stor. Ital.*, 1875.

Galleus, Thaddeus. *Vita S. Norberti*, Antwerp, 1623.
Gasquet, Francis Aidan, Cardinal. *The English Præmonstratensians*, in Royal Hist. Soc. *Trans.*, London, 1903.
—— *The Old English Bible*, London, 1897.
Geudens, M. *St. Norbert*, London, 1886.
Gförer, August Friedrich. *Pabst Gregorius VII und sein Zeitalter*, Schaffhausen, 1859–61.
Giesebrecht, W. *Arnold von Brescia*, in *Sitzungs-berichte der königliche Baier-Akad. der Wissenschaft. Phil-hist. Classe*, 1873.
—— *Geschichte der Deutschen Kaiserzeit*, Leipzig, 1874–95.
Gilles, P. *Histoire ecclésiastique des églises vaudoises*, 1160–1643, Pinerola, 1881.
Gilly, W. S. *Introduction to Waldensian Researches*, London, 1831.
—— *Narrative of an Excursion to the Mountains of Piedmont*, London, 1825.
Giulini, G. *Memorie spettanti alla storia ... della città e della campagna di Milan*, Milan, 1760–71.
Gosselin, J. E. A. *Il Pouvoir du Pape au Moyen-âge*, Louvain, 1845.
Gregorovius, F. *Geschichte der Stadt Rom im Mittelalter*, Stuttgart, 1890.
Guerzoni, G. *Arnaldo da Brescia*, Florence, 1882.
Guibal, G. *Arnaud de Brescia et les Hohenstauffen*, Paris, 1868.
Guirand, Jean. *Le Consolamentum Cathari*, in *Revue des Questions Historiques*, 1904.

Halphen, L. *Études sur l'Administration de Rom au Moyen-âge*, in *Bibliothèque de l'École des Hautes Études*, 1907.
Hanegravius, Cornelius. *Compendia della vita ... di S. Norberto*, Rome, 1632.
Haupt, H. *Waldenserthum und Inquisition im Sudöstlichen Deutschland bis zur mitte des 14ten Jahrhundert*, in *Zeitschrift für Geschichtswissenschaft*, vol. I, 1885.
—— *Die Deutsche Bibel übersetzung der Mittelalterichen Waldenser*, Würzburg, 1885.
Hausrath, Adolf. *Arnold von Brescia*, Leipzig, 1895.
—— *Die Arnaldisten*, Leipzig, 1895.
—— *Petrus Abälard*, Leipzig, 1893.
Havet, Julien. *L'hérésie et le Bras Seculier au Moyen-âge*, in *Bibl. de l'École des Chartes*, vol. XLI.
Hefele, Carl Joseph von. *Concilien-geschichte*, 1873.
Helyot, Fontana. *Storia degli Ordini Monastici Religiosi e Militari*, Lucca, 1732.
Hertel, G. *Leben des Heiligen Norbertus*, Leipzig, 1883.

—— *Die Wahl Norberts zum Erzbischof von Magdeburg*, in *Geschichtsblätter für Stadt und Land*, Magdeburg, 1875.

Herzog, J. J. *Real-Encyclopädie für Protestantische Theologie und Kirche*, Hamburg, 1854–68.

Hinschius, Paul. *Das Kirchenrecht der Katholischen und Protestanten*, Berlin, 1869.

Histoire Littéraire de la France, Paris, 1733–1921.

Hugo, Charles Louis. *Annales Ord. Præm.*, Luxembourg, 1738.

—— *Vie de St. Norbert*, Luxembourg, 1704.

Jalla, Jean. *Histoire des Vaudois des Alpes et de leurs Colonies*, Pinerola, 1904.

Jostes, J. *Die Waldenser und die vorluthersche deutsche Bibel übersetzung*, Münster, 1885.

Jostes, J., und Haupt, Hermann. *Die Waldensische Urspring des Codex Teplenses*, Würzburg, 1886.

Jovius, Benedictus. *Historia patriæ*, Venice, 1629.

Keller, Ludwig. *Die Anfang der Reformation und die Ketzerschulen*, Berlin, 1897.

Krone, Julius. *Fra Dolcino und die Patariner* (for the *Regulæ Waldensium*), Leipzig, 1844.

Lami, Giovanni. *Antichitá Toscane*, Florence, 1766.

Lane-Poole, Reginald. *Illustrations of the History of Mediæval Thought and Learning*, London, 1920.

Lannes, Jean de. *Histoire du Pontificat du Pope Innocent II*, Paris, 1741.

Lattes, A. *Il Diritto Consuetudinario delle Cittá Lombarde*, Milan, 1899.

Lavisse, Ernest, ed. *Histoire de France*, Paris, 1902.

Lavisse et Rambaud. *Histoire Générale*, Paris, 1893–1901.

Lea, H. C. *A History of the Inquisition in the Middle Ages*, Philadelphia, 1888.

Le Paige. *Vita S. Norberti*, in *Bibliotheca Ord. Præmonstratensis*, Paris, 1633.

Lecoy de la Marche, Albert. *La Chaire française au Moyen-âge*, Paris, 1868.

Lefèvre, G., *S. Brunon et l'Ordre des Chartreuse.*

—— *De Anselmo Laudunensi Scholastico*, 1050–1117, Milan, 1895.

Leger, Jean (pastor of the Waldensian Church in Piedmont). *Histoire générale des églises évangéliques des vallées de Piémont*, Leyden, 1669.

Löbbel, Hermann. *Der Stifter des Carthäuser Ordens der heilige Bruno aus Köln*, Münster, 1899.

Luchaire, Achille. *Innocent III*, Paris, 1904–11.

—— *Le Culte des reliques*, in *Révue de Paris*, 1900.

Luscia, S. *Arnaldo da Brescia*, Maglie Capice, 1891.

Madelaine, G. *Histoire de S. Norbert*, Lille, 1886.

Maffejus, Raphael Volaterranus. *Opera omnia*, 1540.

Maitland, S. R. *Facts and Documents of the Waldensians*, London, 1862.

Mandonnet, P., *La Crise scolaire au début du XIIme siècle et la Fondation de l'Ordre des Frères Prêcheurs*, in *Revue d'histoire ecclésiastique*, 1914.

Mann, Horace K. *The Lives of the Popes*, London, 1902–10.

Marini, Gaetano Luigi. *I Papiri diplomatici*, Rome, 1805.

Marlot, G. *Histoire de Reims*, Reims, 1843–46.

McCabe, Joseph. *Peter Abelard*, London, 1901.

Melia, P. *The Origin, Persecution and Doctrines of the Waldensians*, London, 1870.

Milman, H. H. *A History of Latin Christianity*, London, 1854.

Molinier, Ch. *L'Inquisition dans le Midi de la France au XIIIme et au XIVme siècles*, Paris, 1881.

Monastier, A. *Histoire de l'Église Vaudoise*, Lausanne, 1847.

Montalembert, Charles, Comte de. *The Monks of the West*, London, 1861–79.

Montet, E. *Histoire littéraire des Vaudois*, Paris, 1885.

Morland, S. *A History of the Evangelical Churches in the Valley of Piedmont*, London, 1658.

Mosheim, J. L. von. *De Beghardis et Beguinabus*, Leipzig, 1790.

Mühlbacher, E. *Die Streitige Papstwahl des Jahres* 1130, Innsbruck, 1876.

Müller, Karl. *Kirchengeschichte*, Freiburg-im-Breisgau, 1892–1919.

—— *Die Waldenser und ihre einzelnen gruppen bis zum anfang des 14ten Jahrh.*, Gotha, 1886.

—— *Die Anfang des Minoriten Orden*, Freiburg-im-Breisgau, 1885.

Mussoni, S. *I Patarini in Rimini, La Romagna*, 1905.

Muston, Alexis. *Histoire des Vaudois*, Paris, 1850.

—— *L'Israël des Alpes*, Paris, 1851.

Nihusius. *Irnerius*, Cologne, 1642.

Odorici, Federico. *Arnaldo da Brescia*, Brescia, 1861.

—— *Storie Bresciane dai primi tempi*, Brescia, 1853–65.

Päch, Hugo. *Die Pataria in Mailand, 1056–77*, Milan, 1872.

Papencordt, F. *Geschichte der Stadt Rom im Mittelalter*, Paderborn, 1857.

Pelligrini, Carlo. *I Santi Arialdo et Erlembaldo*, Milan, 1897.

Perrin, Jean Paul. *Histoire des Vaudois*, Geneva, 1619.

Piancini, G. B. *L'Idea di Arnaldo da Brescia nella riforma di Roma*, in *Riv. Stor. Ital.*, 1887.

Pirenne, H. *Histoire de Belgique*, Brussels, 1903.

Prévost, Gustave. *Les Églises et les Campagnes au Moyen-âge*, Paris, 1892.

Prudenzano, F. *S. Francisco d'Assisi nella societá civile*, Naples, 1897.

Puccinelli, P. *Chronicon insegnis Abbatiæ SS. Petri et Pauli de Glaxiate Mediolani*, Milan, 1565.

de Rémusat, Charles François Marie, comte de. *Abélard*, Paris, 1855.

Reuter, H. F. *Geschichte Alexanders des dritten*, Leipzig, 1860–64.

Ristori, G. *I Patarini in Firenze nella prima metá del secolo xiii*, in *Riv. stor. crit. delle Scienze Teol.*, 1906.

Robolini, G. *Notizie storiche di Pavia*, Pavia, 1823.

Rocquain, Félix. *Des premiers abus du pouvoir théocratique et la Naissance de la Curie romaine* (1085–1136), Paris, 1882.

Rodocanachi, Emmanuel Pierre. *Les Institutions communales de Rome*, Paris, 1901.

Röhrich, R. *Die Gottesfreunde und die Winkeler am oberrhein*, in Illgen: *Zeitschrift für die historische theologie*, vol. X, 1840.

Ronchetti, Giuseppe. *Memorie Istoriche della cittá e chiesa di Bergamo*, Bergamo, 1807.

Rorengo, M. A. *Memorie Historiche dell' introduzione dell' Eresie nelle Valli di Lucerna*, Turin, 1649.

Rosenmund, S. *Die ältesten Biographien des heiligen Norbertus*, Berlin, 1874.

Rotondi, P. *La Pataria di Milano*, in *Arch. Stor. Ital.*, 1867.

Sabatier, Paul. *Life of Saint Francis of Assisi*, New York, 1914.

—— *Opuscules critiques*, Paris, 1901.

Sagittarius, Gaspare. *Historia critica S. Norberti*, Jena, 1683.

Saint Norbert et Tauchelm, in *Analecta Bollandiana*, vol. XII, Brussels, 1893.

Salvioli, G. *Trattato di storia del Diritto Italiano*, Turin, 1908.

Savigny, Friedrich Carl von. *Geschichte des römischen Rechts im Mittelalter*, Heidelberg, 1834–51.

Schmidt, C. *Histoire des Cathares*, Geneva, 1849.

Schnitzer, Joseph. *Berengar von Tours*, Stuttgart, 1892.

—— *Die Gesta Romanæ Ecclesia des Kardinals wider Gregor VII*, Bamberg, 1892.

Sigonius, Carolus. *Historiarum de regno italiæ*, Basle, 1575. (Shows the connection between the Dominicans and the Poor Catholics.)

Sommerlad, T. *Die Wirtschaftliche Thätigkeit der Kirche in Mittelalter*, Leipzig, 1900–02.

Sormani, N. *Breve storia degli Umiliati*, Milan, 1739.

de Stefano, A. *Le Origini dell' ordine degli Umiliati*, in *Riv. stor. crit. delle Scienze Teolog.*, 1906.

—— *L'attivitá litteraria di Valdesi primitivi*, Rome, 1916.

Stutz, Ulrich. *Geschichte des Kirchenlichen Benefizialwesens*, Berlin, 1895.

Tamassia, Nino. *L'affratellmento*, Turin, 1886.
Taylor, H. O. *The Mediæval Mind*, London, 1914.
Thomassin, Louis de. *Vetus et Nova Ecclesiæ Disciplina*, Venice, 1730.
Tocco, Felice. *Eresia nel Medio Evo*, Florence, 1884.
Todd, James Henthorne. *The Waldensian MSS. in the Library of Trinity College, Dublin*, London, 1865.
Tschudi, Ægidius. *Chronicon Helveticum*, Basle, 1736.

Vacandard, Elphège. *Arnault de Brescia*, in *Revue des Questions Hist.*, 1884.
—— *Vie de S. Bernard*, Paris, 1895.
Van Spillbeeck, Ign. *Vie de Saint Norbert*, Brussels, 1898.
Vanden Elsen, G. *Het Leven den heiligen Norbertus*, Averbode, 1890.

Winter, F. *Die Prämonstratenser der XII^{ten} Jahrhundert*, Berlin, 1865.

Zanoni, L. *Gli Umiliati . . . nei secoli XII–XIII*, Milan, 1911.
—— *I Valdesi a Milano nel secolo XII*, in *Arch. Stor. Lomb.*, 1912.
—— *Il Comune Italico nel Medio-evo*, Milan, 1907.

PART TWO: REFUGEES OF ANOTHER DAY

(a) Manuscript Sources

France.
Paris, Bibliothèque Nationale, Cod. fonds fr. 6447; fonds lat. 5406.

(b) Collections of Sources

Cartulaire Marmoutier pour Le Perche, Mortagne, 1894.
Chartes et Documents Originaux relatifs à la Province du Perche, ed. de Romanet O., et Tournier, H., Mortagne, 1896.

Mémoires pour servir de preuves a l'Histoire ecclésiastique et civile de Bretagne, ed. Morice, Paris, 1742.

Recueil de l'Origine de la Langue et Poésie Française, ed. Fauchet, Paris, 1581.

(c) Primary Sources

Bulla de Canonisatione Sancti Ludovici, in *Recueil des Historiens*, vol. XXIII.

Chronica Normanniæ, in *Historiæ Normannorum Scriptores*, Paris, 1619.
Chronica S. Stephani Cadomensis, in *ibid.*, Paris, 1619.
Chronicon Andrensis Monasterii, in d'Achéry, *Spicilegium*, vol. IX.

Chronicon Girardi de Fracheto, O. F. P., in *Recueil des Historiens*, vol. XXII.

Chronicon Rotomagense, in Labbé, *Nova Bibliotheca*, vol. I.

Chronique Anonyme intitulée Anciennes Chroniques de Flandre, in *Recueil des Historiens*, vol. XXII.

Chronique de St. Magloire, in *ibid.*, vol. XXII.

Extraits de la Chronique attribuée à Baudoin d'Avesnes, fils de la Comtesse Marguerite de Flandre, in *ibid.*, vol. XXI.

Extraits de la Chroniques de Saint-Denis, in *ibid.*, vol. XXI.

Fragment d'une Chronique Anonyme dite Chronique de Reims, in *ibid.*, vol. XXII.

Gesta Sancti Ludovici Noni, auctore monacho Sancti Dionysii Anonymo, in *ibid.*, vol. XX.

Guiart, Guillaume. *La Branche des Royaux Lingnages*, in *ibid.*, vol. XXII.

Guillaume de Nangis. *Chronicon*, in d'Achéry, *Spicilegium*, vol. XI.

Guillaume de Nangis. *Vita Sancti Ludovici*, in *Recueil des Historiens*, vol. XX.

Johannus de Columna, O. F. P. *E Mari Historiarum*, in *ibid.*, vol. XXIII.

Joinville, Jean, Sire de. *Histoire de S. Louys IX du nom*, ed. DuCange, Paris, 1668.

Mousket, Philippe. *Fragment de la Chronique Rimée*, in *Recueil des Historiens*, vol. XXII.

Querimoniæ Normannorum anno 1247, in *ibid.*, vol. XXIV.

Récits d'un Ménestrel de Reims au Trezième Siècle, ed. de Wailly, Paris, 1876.

Rigordus. *Œuvres*, Paris, 1882–85.

Robert Sainceriax (Sancerre). *Sermon en Vers*, in *Recueil des Historiens*, vol. XXIII.

Roger of Wendover. *Flores Historiarum*, vol. II (Rolls Series), London, 1887.

Vie de Saint-Louis, par le Confesseur de la Reine Marguerite, in *Recueil des Historiens*, vol. XX.

Vincentius Bellovacensis. *E Speculo Historiali*, in *ibid.*, vol. XXI.

(*d*) Retrospective Sources

d'Arbois de Jubainville, Henri. *Histoire des Ducs et des Comtes de Champagne*, Longny, 1869.

Ardouin-Dumazet, Victor Eugene. *Voyage en France*, vol. I, Paris, 1898.

d'Argentré, Bertrand. *L'histoire de Bretagne*, Rennes, 1668.

Bart des Boulais, Léonard. *Recueil des Antiquités du Perche*, in *Documents sur la Province du Perche*, Première Série, vol. I, Mortagne, 1890.

Berger, Élie. *Histoire de Blanche de Castille*, in *Bibliothèque des Écoles Françaises d'Athènes et de Rome*, vol. 70, Paris, 1895.

Borreli de Serres, Leon Louis. *Recherches sur Divers Services Publiques*, vol. I, Paris, 1895.

Bry, Gilles. *Histoire des Pays et Comté du Perche et Duché d'Alençon*, Paris, 1680.

Chantereau-Lefèbre, Louis. *Traité des Fiefs*, Paris, 1662.

Courtin, René. *Histoire du Perche*, in *Documents sur la Province du Perche*, Mortagne, 1893.

DuCange, Charles Dufresne, sieur. *Observations sur l'Histoire de St. Louys par Joinville.*

Duchesne, André. *Histoire Généalogique de la Maison Royale de Dreux*, Paris, 1631.

Histoire Généalogique des Maisons de Guines, d'Ardres, de Gand et de Coucy, Paris, 1631.

Duplessis, Toussaint. *Histoire de la Ville et des Seigneurs de Coucy*, Paris, 1728.

Hoffmann, H. *Le Monnaies Royales de France*, Paris, 1875.

Hommey, L. *Histoire Général Ecclésiastique et Civile du Diocèse de Séez*, vol. I, Alençon, 1899.

Jousset de Bellême, F. *Le Vieux Bellême*, 1868.

La Borderie, Arthur Lemoyne de. *Histoire de Bretagne*, vol. III, Rennes, 1899.

Lecoy de la Marche, A. *La France sous St. Louis et sous Philippe le Hardi*, Paris, 1894.

Lefevre-Pontalis, Eugène. *Le Château de Coucy*, Paris, 1909.

Le Nain de Tillemont, L. S. *Vie de Saint-Louis*, vols. I and III. (Published by the Société de Histoire de France. Paris, 1847.)

L'Épinois, Ernest de Buchère. *Histoire de la Ville et des Sires de Coucy*, Paris, 1859.

Lobineau, Gui Alexis. *Histoire de Bretagne*, vol. I, Paris, 1707.

Longnon, Auguste. *De la Formation de l'Unité Française*, Paris, 1890.

Morice, Pierre Hyacinthe. *Histoire Ecclésiastique et Civile de Bretagne*, vol. I, Paris, 1750.

Note sur la Monnaie Tournois et la Monnaie Parisis de Saint-Louis, in *Recueil des Historiens*, vol. XXI.

Petit-Dutaillis, Ch. *Étude sur la vie et le Règne de Louis VIII* (1187–1226), in *Bibliothèque de l'École des Hautes Études*, Paris, 1894.

Philippe de Remi, Sire de Beaumanoir. *Coutumes de Beauvoisis*, Bourges, 1690.

Poisignon, Maurice. *Histoire Générale de la Champagne et de la Brie*, Châlons-sur-Marne, 1896.

de Romanet, O., Vicomte. *Géographie du Perche et Chronologie de ses Comtes*, Mortagne, 1890.

Simonde de Sismondi, J. C. L. *Histoire des Française*, vol. VII, Paris, 1826.

Viollet, Paul. *Histoire du Droit Civil Français*, Paris, 1893.

—— *Les Établissements de St. Louis*, Paris, 1881.

de Wailly, Joseph Noel (Natalis). *Mémoire sur la Date et la Lieu de Naissance de Saint-Louis*, Paris, 1866.

Wallon, H. *St. Louis et son Temps*, Paris, 1875.

PART THREE

(*a*) MANUSCRIPT SOURCES

ENGLAND.

London, British Museum Library, Cod. Egerton, 274.

FRANCE.

Archives des Bouches-du-Rhone, Cod. 812.

Statuts de la ville de Marseilles, livre IX, c. 28; livre XL, *de Sortibus Navis.*

Paris, Bibliothèque Nationale.

Fonds fr. Cod. 3992, *Cartulaire comit. Camp.*

25545, *Les foires de Champainne et de Brie.*

Anc. fr. Cod. 5378, *Recueil de pièces concernant la Champagne*, 1199–1540.

7019, *Indication des foires de Champagne.*

7225–6, *Chansons des Troubadours du XII*[me] *siècle et du XIII*[me].

Fonds lat. 16537,

fonds fr. 12581, '*Ci commenc la devisions des foires.*'

412,

2625,

Bibliothèque de l'Arsénal, Cod. 181. Hervis de Metz.

Provins, Bibliothèque de la ville.
Cod. 176, Censier de l'Hôtel Dieu.
158, *Foires de Champagne.*
81, *Cartulaire Caillot.*
127, *Cartulaire de la ville*, fonds Michelet.

(*b*) Collections of Sources

Anciens Poèmes Populaires Italiens, ed. Luchaire et Morpurgo.

Archives de l'Hôtel Dieu de Paris, 1157–1300, Paris, 1894.

Cartulaire de la ville de Blois, Paris, 1907.

Cartulaire du Chapitre de la Cathedrale d'Amiens, ed. Daire, Amiens, 1905.

Cartulaire du Diocèse de Troyes, ed. Lalore, Paris, 1875–90.

Cartulaire Générale de Paris, ed. Lastrie, vol. I, 528–1180, Paris, 1887.

Catalogue des Actes de Philippe-Auguste, ed. Delisle, Paris, 1856.

*Cent Motets du XIII*me *siècle*, ed. Aubry, Paris, 1908.

Chansons Nationales et Populaires de France, ed. Dumersan et Ségur, Paris, 1852.

Choix des Poésies Originales des Troubadours, ed. Raynouard, Paris, 1816–21.

Les Chroniques de Normandie, ed. Michel, Rouen, 1839.

Collection des Documents sur l'Histoire de France, ed. Michel, Paris, 1836, etc.

*Collection des Lois maritimes antérieures au XVIII*me *siècle*, ed. Pardessus, Paris, 1828–45.

Collection des ouvrages dramatiques le plus remarkable depuis les mystères jusqu'à Corneille, ed. Viollet-le-Duc, Paris, 1854–57.

Collection des poètes française du moyen-âge, ed. Hippeau, Paris, 1874.

Diplomata, chartæ, etc., ad res gallofrancicas spectantes, ed. Pardessus, Paris, 1843–49.

Documents Historiques inédits, ed. Figeac, Paris, 1841.

Documents inédits sur le commerce de Marseille au Moyen-âge, ed. Blancard, Marseilles, 1884.

*Documents inédits sur l'histoire politique de Marseilles au XIII*me *siècle*, ed. Blancard, in *Bibl. de l'École de Chartes*, vol. XXI.

Documents Parisiens sur l'Iconographie de St. Louis, ed. Longnon, Paris, 1882.

Documents pour servir a l'histoire de l'armement au moyen-âge, ed. Giraud, Lyons, 1895–99.

Documents relatifs à l'histoire de l'industrie et du commerce en France, ed. Fagniez, Paris, 1898–1900.

Documents relatifs au comté de Champagne et de Brie, 1172–1361, ed. Longnon, Paris, 1907.

Documents statistiques sur les routes et ponts, ed. Lucas, Paris, 1883.
Documents sur les relations de la royauté avec les villes, ed. Giry, Paris, 1885.

Les établissements de Rouen, ed. Giry, Paris, 1883.

Fabliaux ou contes du XIIme et XIIIme siècles, ed. Le Grande d'Aussy, Paris, 1779–81.
Fragments de comptes du XIIIme siècle, ed. Bourquelot, in *Bibliothèque de l'École des Chartes*, vol. XXIV.
Fragment d'un Anthologie Picarde (XIIIme siècle), ed. Boucherie, Paris, 1872.

Histoire de France par les écrivans contemporains, ed. Paris et Mennechet, Paris, 1836–39.

Lais inédits des XIIme et XIIIme siècles, ed. Michel, Paris, 1836.
Langlois, C. V. *La vie en France au Moyen-âge*, Paris, 1908.
Lateinische Hymnen des Mittelalters, ed. Mone, Freiburg-im-Breisgau, 1853–55.
Li livres de Jostice et de Plet, ed. Rapetti et Chabaille, Paris, 1850.

Ordonnances des Rois de France, ed. Pardessus, Paris, 1723–1847.

Peregrinatores Medii-œvi quattuor, ed. Laurent, Leipzig, 1864.
Poémes et legendes du moyen-âge, ed. G. Paris, Paris, 1900.
Poésies populaires latines du moyen-âge, ed. Du Meril, Paris, 1847.
Popular Treatises on Science written during the Middle Ages, ed. Wright, London, 1841.
Proverbes et dictons populaires aux XIIIme et XIVme siècles, ed. Crapelet, Paris, 1831.

Recueil d'anciens textes bas-Latins, Provençaux et Français, ed. Meyer, Paris, 1877.
Recueil des chansons populaires, ed. Roland, Paris, 1883–90.
Recueil de chants historiques français depuis le XIIme jusqu'au XVIIIme siècle, ed. Le Roux de Lincy et Tusseraud, Paris, 1867.
Recueil de motets français des XIIme et XIIIme siècle, ed. Raynaud, Paris, 1883.
Recueil de textes du XIIIme siècle, ed. Quantin, Auxerre, 1854.
Recueil général des fabliaux des XIIme et XIVme siècles, ed. Montaiglon, Paris, 1872–90.
Registres des métiers et marchandises de la ville de Paris, in *Bibl. de l'École des Chartes*, vol. XXXIV.
Registres judiciares de quelques établissements religieux du Paris au XIIIme et au XIVme siècles, ed. Viollet, in *ibid.*

Regestrum Visitationum Archiepiscopi Rothomagensis, 1248–1269, Rouen, 1852.

Réglemens sur les Arts et Métiers de Paris au XIIIme siècle, ed. Depping, Paris, 1837.

Repertorium Hymnologicum, ed. Chevalier, 1897–1912.

Trouvères Belges du XIIme au XIVme siècle, ed. Scheler, Brussels, 1876.

(c) PRIMARY SOURCES

Adenez le Roi. *Beuves de Commarchis*, Brussels, 1874.

Aucassin et Nicolette, ed. G. Paris, Paris, 1904.

Baldwin, I. *Le Livre de Baudoyn*, ed. Serrure et Voisin, Brussels, 1836.

Benoit. *Chronique des ducs de Normandie*, ed. Michel, Paris, 1826–44.

Bernardus Teutonicus. *Descriptio terræ sanctæ*, ed. Laurent, Leipzig, 1855.

La Bible au Seigneur de Birzi Barbazan, in Langlois, E., *Fabliaux et contes des XIme–XVme siècles*, Paris, 1808.

La Bible Guiot, ed. Langlois, Paris, 1908.

Chanson d'Anseis de Metz, Paris, 1904.

Chanson de la Mort de Beques de Balin, in LeGlay, *Fragments d'épopées romans du XIIme siècle*, Paris, 1838.

Coucy, Renaud, Chatelain de. *Chansons*, ed. Michel, 1837.

Chronique de l'Anonyme de Bethune, in *Recueil des Historiens*, vol. XXIV.

Guillelmus Britonis Armoricus. *Philippidos*, in *Recueil des Historiens*, vol. XVII.

Guillaume le clerc de Normandie. *Le Besant de Duc*, ed. Ernst Martin, Halle, 1869.

—— *Le Bestiare*, ed. Ernst Martin, Halle, 1872.

Guillot de Paris. *Le Dit des Rues de Paris* (1300), ed. Mareuse, Paris, 1875.

Itinera et Descriptiones Terræ Sanctæ, ed. Tobler, Leipzig, 1874.

Li Jeux de Adam de la Halle, ed. Michel, Paris, 1839.

Le Livre d'Or des métiers, ed. Michel, Paris, 1851.

Le VI Livre des Statuts de Marseilles, ed. Cremieux, Aix-en-Provence, 1917.

Marie de France. *Poésies*, ed. Roquefort, Paris, 1820.

Marino Sanuto, Sen. *Liber Secretorum fidelium crucis*, in Bongars, *Orientalis Historiæ*, Hanover, 1611.

Ordericus Vitalis. *Historiæ Ecclesiasticæ*, ed. Delisle, Paris, 1884–85.

Philippe de Remi, sire de Beaumanoir. *Œuvres poétiques*, Paris, 1884–85.

Richard le Pèlerin. *Chanson d'Antioch*, Paris, 1862.
La Roman de la Rose, ed. Michel, Paris, 1864.
La Roman de Renard, ed. Meon, Paris, 1826.
Le Roman de Fauvel, Paris, 1907.
Li Romans de Garin le Loherain, Paris, 1833–35.
Ruteboeuf. *Œuvres complètes*, ed. Jubinal, Paris, 1874.

Sarrazin. *Roman de Ham*, ed. Michel, Paris, 1840.

Theophilis presbyter. *Schedula Diversarum Artium*, Vienna, 1874.
Thibaut, IV, Roi de Navarre. *Poésies*, ed. Lévesque de la Ravallière, Paris, 1742.

Vita Udalrici Cellensis, in *M.G.H. SS.*, vol. XII.

Wilbrandt von Oldenberg. *Reise nach Palestine und Kleinasien*, ed. Laurent, Hamburg, 1859.

(*d*) Retrospective Sources

Alengry, Ch. *Les Foires de Champagne*, Paris, 1915.
d'Arbois de Jubainville. *Du Revenu des Comtes de Champagne au XIIIme siècle*, in *Bibl. de l'École de Chartes*, vol. XXVI.
——*Histoire de Bar-sur-Aube.*
Aubrey, P. *La musique et les musiciens de l'église en Normandie au XIIme siècle*, Paris, 1906.

de Beaucorps, A. *Maisons-Dieu au Moyen-âge*, Paris, 1866–67.
Beaurepaire, Ch. de. *La vicomté de l'eau de Rouen*, Rouen, 1866.
Bédier, C. M. J. *Les légendes épiques*, Paris, 1899.
——*Les plus anciennes danses Français*, in *Revue des Deux Mondes*, 1906.
Berty A. *Topographie historique du vieux Paris*, Paris, 1866.
Blancard, L. *Le Besant d'or sarrazinos pendant les croisades*, Marseilles, 1880.
—— *Note sur la lettre de change à Marseilles au XIIIme siècle*, in *Bibl. de l'École des Chartes*, vol. XXXIX.
Boüard de Forest, Alain de. *Études de diplomatique sur les actes des notaires du châtelet de Paris*, Paris, 1910.
—— *Le Régime Politique et les institutions de Rome au moyen-âge*, 1252–1347, Paris, 1920.
Bourquelot, Félix. *Études sur les foires de Champagne aux XIIme, XIIIme et XIVme siècles*, in *Mémoires Présentés par divers savants a l'Académie des Inscriptions et Belles-Lettres*, Paris, 1865.

—— *Histoire de Provins*, Paris, 1839.

Brémond, E. *Marseilles au XIIIme siècle*, Marseilles, 1905.

Brenet, M. (Bobillier, Marie). *Les Musiciens de la Sainte-Chapelle du palais*, Paris, 1910.

Carrière, V. *Histoire des Templiers de Provins*, Provins, 1919.

Catel, G. *Histoire des comtes de Toulouse*, Toulouse, 1623.

Champeaux, Alfred de. *Le Meuble*, Paris, 1885.

Championnière, P. L. *De la propriété des eaux courantes du droit des rivérains et de la valeur actuelle des concessions feodales*, Paris, 1848.

Cibrario, Luigi. *Della Economia Politica del medio evo*, Turin, 1861.

Conder, Claude Reignier. *The Latin Kingdom of Jerusalem, 1099–1291*, London, 1897.

Constans, Léopold. *Une rédaction provençale du Statut maritime de Marseilles*, in *Romanische Forschungen*, 1907.

Curschman, F. *Hungersnöte im Mittelalter*, Leipzig, 1900.

de la Paquerie, Ch. *La Vie féodal*, Tours, 1900.

Delisle, Léopold Victor. *Études sur la condition de la classe agricole et l'état de l'agriculture en Normandie au moyen-âge*, Évreaux, 1851.

—— *Littérature latine et histoire du moyen-âge*, Paris, 1890.

Depping, George Bernhard. *Histoire du commerce entre le Levant et l'Europe*, Paris, 1830.

Dobiache-Rojdestvensky. *La vie paroissiale en France au XIIIme siècle.*

Dodu, G. *Le royaume Latin de Jerusalem*, Paris, 1914.

Dulaure, Jacques Antoine. *Histoire de Paris*, Paris, 1825.

Eiglier, J. *Étude historique sur la droit de marque ou de représailles à Marseilles aux XIIIme, XIVme et XVme siècles*, Marseilles, 1888.

Fagniez, G. *Études sur l'industrie et la classe industrielle a Paris au XIIIme et au XIVme siècles*, Paris, 1877.

Faral, E. *Mimes français du XIIIme siècle*, Paris, 1910.

Felibien, M., et Lobineau, G. *Histoire de la ville de Paris*, Paris, 1725.

Finot, J. *Étude historique sur les relations commerciales entre la Flandre et la France au moyen-âge*, Paris, 1894.

Fournier, P. E. L. *Les officialitiés au Moyen-âge, 1180–1328*, Paris, 1880.

Franklin, A. *Les anciens plans de Paris*, Paris, 1878.

Gautier, Émile Théodore. *Histoire de la poésie liturgique au moyen-âge*, Paris, 1886.

Géraud, H. *Les routier au douzième siècle*, in *Bibl. de l'École des Chartes*, 1841–42.

—— *La Taille de Paris sur Philippe le Bel*, Paris, 1846.

Germain, Alexandre. *Histoire du Commerce de Montpellier*, Montpellier, 1861.

Gilles, J. *Les voies romaines dans le département des Bouches du Rhone*, Paris, 1884.

Haussmann. *Histoire générale de Paris*, Paris, 1881.

Heyd, W. *Histoire du commerce du Levant au moyen-âge*, Leipzig, 1885.

Huvelin, P. *Essai historique sur le droit des Marchés et des Foires*, Paris, 1897.

Imbert de la Tour. *La liberté commerciale en France aux XII*[me] *et XIII*[me] *siècles*, Paris, 1890.

Jal. Auguste. *Mémoire sur quelques documents génois relatifs aux deux croisades de Saint Louis*, Paris, 1842.

Jubinal, A. *Jongleurs et Trouvères*, Paris, 1835.

Julliany, Jules. *Essai sur le commerce de Marseilles*, Marseilles, 1842.

Lalanne, Ludovic. *Des pélérinages en Terre sainte avant les Croisades*, in *Bibl. de l'École des Chartes*, 1845–46.

Lambert, G. *Essai sur le régime municipal en Provence au moyen-âge*, Toulon, 1882.

Langlois, C. V. *La Société française au XIII*[me] *siècle d'apres dix romans d'aventure*, Paris, 1904.

—— *La connaissance de la nature et du monde au moyen-âge*, Paris, 1911.

Lattes, Alessandro. *Il diritto commerciale nella legislazione statutaria delle citta italiane*, Milan, 1864.

Legrand d'Aussy Pierre. *Mémoire sur l'état de Marine en France* (14th century), in *Mémoires de l'Institut Sciences morales et politiques*, vol. II.

—— *Histoire de la vie privée des Français*, Paris, 1782.

Lentheric, C. *La Grèce et l'Orient en Provence*, Paris, 1878.

Le Roux de Lincy, A. J. V. *Paris et ses historiens aux XIV*[me] *siècle*, Paris, 1867.

Levasseur, E. *Histoire des classes ouvrières et de l'industrie en France avant 1789*, Paris, 1900–01.

—— *Histoire du Commerce de la France*, Paris, 1911–12.

—— *Rôles des Fiefs du Comté de Champagne sous le regne de Thibaut le Chansonnier*, Paris, 1877.

Lucas, Felix. *Étude historique et statistique sur les voies de communications de la France*, Paris, 1873.

Luchaire, Achille. *Les communes française a l'époque des Capétiens directs*, Paris, 1890.

—— *Histoire des institutions monarchique . . . sous les premiers Capétiens, 987–1190*, Paris, 1883.

—— *Mélanges d'histoire du moyen-âge*, Paris, 1897–1908.

—— *La Société française au temps de Philippe-Auguste*, Paris, 1901.

Luquet, G. F. *Aristotle et l'Université de Paris pendant le XIIIme siècle*, Paris, 1904.

Malo, H. *Un grande feudataire, Renaud de Dammartin et la coalition de Bouvines*, Paris, 1898.

de Martonne, A. *La piété du moyen-âge*, Paris, 1855.

Mas Latrie, René. *Du droit de marque ou droit de représailles au moyen-âge*, Paris, 1875.

—— *Relations et commerce de l'Afrique septentrionale ... avec les nations chrétiennes au moyen-âge*, Paris, 1886.

—— *Traités de paix et de commerce concernant les relations des chrétiens avec les Arabes et de l'Afrique septentrionale au moyen-âge*, Paris, 1867.

Masson, P. *Marseilles et la colonisation française*, Marseilles, 1906.

Michel, F. *Le commerce, la fabrication, et l'usages des étoffes de soie, d'or, et d'argent pendant le moyen-âge*, Paris, 1852–54.

Miller, W. *The Latins in the Levant*, London, 1909.

Moreau, Jules. *Notice sur les Sires de Coucy*, Chauny, 1871.

Papon, Jean Pierre. *Histoire générale de Provence*, Paris, 1777–86.

Paris, Gaston. *Les Lapidaires Française au Moyen-âge*, Paris, 1882.

—— *La Littérature Française au Moyen-âge* (XIme–XIVme siècle), Paris, 1905.

Pardessus, J. M. *L'Origine du Droit Coutumier en France*, Paris, 1833.

—— *L'Organisation Judiciare et l'Administration de la Justice*, Paris, 1851.

Pigeonneau, H. *Histoire du commerce de la France*, Paris, 1885.

Pirenne, H. *Villes, marchès et marchands au moyen-âge*, in *Revue historique*, 1898.

Pitard, P. *Légendes et récits pécherons*, Alençon, 1875.

Portal, Félix. *La République Marseillaise du XIIIme siècle*, Marseilles, 1907.

Renon de Chauvigné, Jean-Baptiste. *Recherches Critiques sur la ville de Paris avec le plan de chaque quartier*, Paris, 1775.

Revelle, A. *Les paysans au moyen-âge*, Paris, 1896.

Rey, A. E. Guillaume. *Étude sur les monuments de l'architecture militaire des croisés en Syrie et dans l'île de Chypre*, Paris, 1871.

—— *Recherches géographiques et historiques sur la domination des Latins en Orient du XIIIme et XIVme siècles*, Paris, 1877.

Riboldi, Ezio. *I Contadi rurali del Milanese* (sec. IX–XII), in *Arch. Stor. Lomb.*, vol. XVI.

Roquefort, Jean. *De l'État de la Poésie Française dans les XIme et XIIme siècles*, Paris, 1815.

Saint-Pelaye, Jean Baptiste de la Curne de. *Mémoires sur l'ancienne chevalerie*, Paris, 1826.

Salvemeni, Gaetano. *Un comune rurale del secolo XIII*, Florence, 1898.

Salvioli, G. *Trattato di Storia del Diritto Italiano*, Turin, 1908.

See, H. *Les classes rurales du Moyen-âge*, Paris, 1901.

Speck, E. *Die Gegen den Handel der Lateiner mit den Saracenen Gerichteten kirchlichen und staatlichen Verbote*, Zittau, 1880.

Tardif, A. *Le droit privé au XIIIme siècle d'apres les coutumes de Toulouse et de Montpellier*, Paris, 1886.

—— *La procédure civile et criminelle aux XIIIme et XIVme siècles*, Paris, 1885.

Vaissette, Joseph, et Vie, Claude de, *Histoire général du Languedoc*, Paris, 1730–45.

Verdillon, A. *Dissertation sur l'ancienne topographie de Marseilles*, Marseilles, 1873.

Vignon, E. J. M. *Études Historiques sur l'administration des voies publiques en France*, Paris, 1862.

Viollet-le Duc, Eugène. *Dictionnaire raisonné du mobilier français de l'époque Carlovingienne à la renaissance*, Paris, 1871.

Walford, Cornelius. *Fairs Past and Present*, London, 1883.

Walker, W. *The Increase of Power under Philip Augustus*, Leipzig, 1888.

Wilmotte, M. *Une Nouvelle Théorie sur l'origine des Chansons de Gestes*, in *Revue historique*, vol. CXX.

INDEX